Commendations

This book is faith-filled, data-driven, and practical. It is an eye-opener that encourages every church leader to be creative, intentional, and diligent in passing on faith to the next generation. It's a must-read for any leader who is serious about discipling, not entertaining, the new generation.

Manuela Castellanos
Pastor and Speaker, G12, Colombia

As a worship leader and next-generation leader in Asia, I find *The New Generation and the Holy Spirit* to be an essential guide for equipping young leaders in Spirit-filled worship and mission. This book offers profound wisdom and practical strategies for raising a new generation of empowered believers.

Peter Sung Min Cho
Isaiah 6tyOne, Korea

This incredible book shares the powerful truth that there is no "Junior Holy Spirit." The same Spirit who works in adults empowers the next generations to live fully in God. It is a must-read for parents, teachers, and leaders who want to shape the future through a Spirit-filled generation.

Lucas Yutaka Hayashi
Pastor of Zion Church, São Paulo, Brazil

The New Generation and the Holy Spirit offers timely insights into equipping young leaders through Spirit-empowered discipleship. Addressing modern challenges, it provides theological reflections and practical strategies for fostering intergenerational dialogue, revival, and mission—empowering the Church to navigate today's rapidly changing world.

Rev. Stephen Yenusom Wengam
General Superintendent of the Assemblies of God, Ghana
Vice Chairman, Africa Assemblies of God Alliance

Foreword

I am a revivalist, and I come from a line of revivalists going back to my grandfather who was saved in the Welsh Revival. Our church, Planetshakers, was birthed in revival. The two things I believe God has given Planetshakers Church to champion are the presence of God and the emerging generation. In Acts 2, the first church began on the day of Pentecost in what was essentially a youth revival. God took a group of radical young people and encountered them with His presence and power! Those young people turned the world upside down in their generation. Every revival, just like that first one, occurs when a new generation encounters the power and love of God as the Holy Spirit is poured out afresh.

With that in mind, our world is broken, and all the signs point to the time being short. This is why we stand, in this present moment in history, in what is almost certainly our greatest need for fresh revival in the newer generations. I have a sense of excitement in my spirit that the winds of revival are beginning to blow once again. And I believe God has saved his best for last. I believe that we are on the brink of the greatest revival this planet has yet seen: a revival that will occur, and indeed has already begun to occur, in the emerging generations—a revival that will usher in the return of Jesus Christ.

And yet Christianity is only ever one generation old. This is why, even (and especially) in these last days, we need strong Spirit-empowered local churches that experience revival and carry the unchanging message of the gospel from generation to generation. And so it is with great enthusiasm that I commend to you this collection of studies. All of them have been authored by Spirit-empowered scholars who share the same passion to usher in a fresh move of God and to champion the new generation. I believe that this book will help strengthen the global church and prepare her for her greatest season. May God bless and inspire you as you read!

Russell Evans
Founder / Global Pastor, Planetshakers, Australia
Vice-Chair of the E21 Global Council

THE NEW GENERATION
&
THE HOLY SPIRIT

BUILDING
A SPIRIT-EMPOWERED
FUTURE

E21 GNSES Series

Empowered21 (E21) series titles are based on annual Scholars Consultations organized by E21's Global Network of Spirit-Empowered Scholars (GNSES). The Consultations bring Spirit-empowered scholars and practitioners from various parts of the world to connect around an issue that faces global Spirit-empowered Christianity. In support of the movement's vision for "EveryONE by 2033," each Scholar's Consultation explores a different theme in the role of Spirit-empowered communities presenting Christ's good news and nurturing the new generation.

Human Sexuality & The Holy Spirit: Spirit-Empowered Perspectives. Wonsuk Ma, Kathaleen Reid-Martinez, Annamarie Hamilton, editors.
   ISBN: 978-1-950971-00-8, softcover; ISBN: 918-1-95071-01-5, e-book.

Proclaiming Christ in the Power of the Holy Spirit: Opportunities & Challenges. Wonsuk Ma, Emmanuel Anim, Rebekah Bled, editors.
   ISBN: 978-1-950971-03-9, softcover; ISBN: 978-950971-05-3, e-book.

Good News to the Poor: Spirit-Empowered Responses to Poverty. Wonsuk Ma, Opoku Onyinah, Rebekah Bled, editors.
   ISBN: 978-1-950971-11-4, softcover; ISBN: 978-1-950971-12-1, e-book.

The Remaining Task of the Great Commission & The Spirit-Empowered Movement. Wonsuk Ma, Opoku Onyinah, Rebekah Bled, editors.
   ISBN: 978-1-950971-20-6, softcover; ISBN: 978-1-950971-21-3, e-book.

The Pandemic & the Holy Spirit: From Lament to Hope and Healing. Wonsuk Ma, Opoku Onyinah, Rebekah Bled, editors.
   ISBN: 978-1-950971-22-0, softcover; ISBN: 978-1-950971-23-7, e-book.

Explore These Other E21 GNSES Titles

Global Renewal Christianity: Spirit-Empowered Movements Past, Present, and Future. Vinson Synan, Amos Yong, editors.
   Volume 1: Asia and Oceania.
      ISBN: 978–1–62998–688–3
   Volume 2: Latin America with Miguel Álvarez, editor
      ISBN: 978–1–62998–767–5
   Volume 3: Africa, with J. Kwabena Asamoah-Gyadu, editor
      ISBN: 978–1–62998–768–2
   Volume 4: Europe and North America.
      ISBN: 978–1–62998–943–3

The Truth About Grace: Spirit-Empowered Perspectives. Vinson Synan, editor.
   ISBN: 978-1-62999-504-5, softcover; ISBN: 978-62998-505-2, e-book.

THE NEW GENERATION & THE HOLY SPIRIT

BUILDING A SPIRIT-EMPOWERED FUTURE

Edited by
Wonsuk Ma, Opoku Onyinah, Barry L. Saylor,
and **Rebekah Bled**

ORU PRESS
Tulsa, Oklahoma USA

The New Generation and The Holy Spirit: Building a Spirit-Empowered Future
Copyright ©2025 Oral Roberts University and Contributors

Published by ORU Press
7777 S. Lewis Ave., Tulsa, OK 74171 USA

https://orupress.org/

ORU Press is the book and journal publishing division of Oral Roberts University.

All rights reserved. No part of this publication may be reproduced, stored in a retrieval system, or transmitted in any form or by any means without the prior permission of the publisher. Brief quotation in book reviews and in scholarly publications is excepted.

Published in the United States of America with permission from Empowered21. https://empowered21.com.

Empowered21 aims to help shape the future of the global Spirit-empowered movement throughout the world. This kingdom initiative is served by Oral Roberts University in Tulsa, Oklahoma, www.oru.edu.

Cover design by Jiwon Kim
Editorial Assistant: Jaime L. Riddle
Interior Designer and Compositor: Sandra Kimbell

ISBN: 978-1-950971-25-1 *(softcover)*
ISBN: 978-1-950971-26-8 *(e-book)*

Printed in the United States of America

Contents

Commendations	i
Foreword	iii
Preface	xiii
Introduction	1
Opoku Onyinah, Wonsuk Ma, and Barry L. Saylor	

Part I: Laying the Foundation

1. The Next Generation and the Holy Spirit: Keynote Address — 11
   Randy Clark

2. An Admonition to the New Generation in Deuteronomy — 25
   Daniel D. Bunn, Jr.

3. Global Youth Culture: Exploring Trends and Imagining the Church's Response — 41
   Barry L. Saylor and Patricia Savage

4. Seven Elements of a Youth-Friendly Church: A Global Survey of the Best Practices of Churches that are Remarkable at Reaching and Discipling the Young Generation — 59
   Ron Luce

5. Children's Stories in the Gospel of Mark: A Sermon — 77
   Douglas Petersen

Part II: Preserving and Reaching the New Generation

6. Born-Frees to Born-Again: A Look at the History of the Spirit-Empowered Movement in Namibia and its Appeal to the Post-Independent Generation — 87
   Caroline Polly Tjihenuna

7. Reaching Burmese Americans: A Reflection on the Myanmar World Cup USA — 103
   Kham Khai and Samuel Khai

8. Children's Ministry from a Missional Perspective
 and a Mission Strategy to Help Teachers for Children's
 Ministry through an Online Platform: A Case Study
 Jane C. Kim 121

9. Individualized Faith or What? A Reflection on the
 Pressure of Shaping Christian Faith in the Swedish Context
 Ulrik Josefsson and Fredrik Wenell 141

Part III: Forming and Empowering the New Generation

10. Global Christianity and Gen Z:
 What is the Hope for the Future of Faith?
 Antipas L. Harris 161

11. A New Wave of the Spirit: Second Generation African
 Pentecostals in the West and their Contribution
 to Pentecostalism
 Caleb Nyanni 185

12. Rejuvenation of a Denomination: The Experience
 of the Church of Pentecost, Ghana
 Charles Prempeh 201

13. *Hikikomori* Ministry: The Possibilities of Empowering
 Japanese Young Adults
 Chaa Chaa Ogino and Michio Ogino 219

14. How to Grow a Church Younger: Five Universal Strategies
 Tan Seow How and Cecilia Chan 235

15. Planetboom: A Case Study in the Effects of
 Youth-Led Revival in Australia
 Clayton Coombs, Andrew Harrison, and Susannah Harrison ... 253

16. *Kata Pneuma*: European International Churches
 and Next Gen Immigrant Youth
 Anthony J. Gryskiewicz 269

17. Reimagining the Holy Spirit as Life-Giving
 Spirit for the Next Generation
 Alexander Stavnichuk and Jean-Daniel Plüss 285

18. The Role of Pastors' Children and Young Leaders
 in Preserving an Awakening in their Generation
 Juan Sebastian Rodriguez 305

19. Using the Volunteer Function Inventory to Activate Aging Adults as Spirit-Empowered Disciple-Makers for the Next Generation *Kerry Loescher*	317
20. Preparing and Sending Gen Z into Every Person's World: Encounter and Equipping through Chapel at Oral Roberts University *Allie Mendoza and Kimmie Simon*	337
21. Parental Covering and Resourcing: Preserving the Future of the Church by Setting the Next Generation up for Success *Jamie Austin*	353
Postscript: The God of Hope, Across Generations *Jaime L. Riddle*	371
Contributors	387
Select Bibliography	393
Name and Subject Index	399

Preface

This book began its journey from the 2022 annual Scholars Consultation of Empowered21. This meeting broke new ground as a joint gathering with the World Alliance for Pentecostal Theological Education (WAPTE) of the Pentecostal World Fellowship (PWF). (See more in Introduction). The plan was even more ambitious for attempting to add a third partner—the International Theological Institute of Yoido Full Gospel Church, Seoul, Korea, the host church of the triennial Pentecostal World Conference. The implications of this joint effort went beyond more hands in planning and managing the academic conference; it symbolized the coming together of two global networks of Pentecostal-Charismatic churches and ministries. And this pattern is expected to repeat every three years when the Pentecostal World Conference is held.

This collaboration has broadened and enriched the Spirit-empowered voices in our consultations as seen in this book. The three organizers of the 2022 Consultation, therefore, want to express their deep gratitude to the leadership of both PWF and Empowered21.

This volume also sees a new hand in the editorial team. Rebekah Bled, who has served the editorial team, concludes her service with this volume, and we all want to thank her for her exceptional contribution to five titles in the series. We are also pleased to welcome Jaime Riddle as the editorial assistant. The two ladies partnered to produce this volume together, and Jaime is expected to manage the editorial process from this title on.

This title also introduces the new series name: The GNSES Series. The Global Network of Spirit-Empowered Scholars (GNSES) was organized in 2023 as a working group of Empowered21. Thus, the new series name reflects this. We will have more about GNSES in the next title, which comes from the 2023 Amsterdam Consultation.

Finally, the editorial team wishes to express its gratitude to: the leadership of Empowered21 for their continuing support of GNSES's academic activities; Professor Jiwon Kim for his continuing work on the book covers; the ORU Press team for its deep commitment to the publication of this series; and, above all, the contributors for their valuable contributions to bless Spirit-empowered believers and communities worldwide, and their healthy future.

We all bring this book to the Lord as our "living sacrifices."

Editors
Fall, 2024

Introduction

Opoku Onyinah, Wonsuk Ma, and Barry L. Saylor

There is hardly any equivocating that the social and political contours of the modern world have significantly changed. The socio-political transformation of the world has increased exponentially since the mid-twentieth century, when the Western world secularized its culture and allowed for its values and norms to be subjectively defined.[1] Perhaps what has been more ambiguous is how young people, whom we may call the new generation, are appropriating the liberties that the modern world is offering them. We cannot make sense of how they are navigating the modern world without coming to terms with what is driving the socio-political changes in our world.

In responding to the above issue, it is important to mention that the idea of "modern" is not neatly conceptualized; to say the least, it is highly subjective. We cannot assume that the world in terms of its governance and how young people respond to it is stable or ossified. Thus, much as the term or concept "modern" may be a subject of contention, the point is also true that the way the new generation appreciates life, and how they engage the opportunities and challenges life throws at them, are hardly comparable to older generations.

Concurrently, whereas Max Weber considered formalization and institutionalization as critical in marking the Western world's ruptures with its past—leading to his notion of modernity—modernity is also about what formalization entails.[2] In this sense, we posit that the formalization of society has been enabled by several things, including the recession of institutional religion in the Western world, the re-democratization of religious space in the developing world, and the increasing rise in radical atheistic scholarship.

These indices have enabled modernity, but they have also been connected and aided by the online revolution. Since the 1970s, the internet has been unprecedented in redefining the tapestries of knowledge and power, and reconfiguring power relations.[3] Generally, the older generations in many cultures are respected for several reasons, including the knowledge they have about the past, and the resources they possessed which younger people did not have. However, the internet revolution has progressively deconstructed the epistemic monopoly that older generations have enjoyed. Now that the world is subsumed in the "Information Age," knowledge is contestably democratized, making it possible for young people to make decisions and act upon them with minimal or no consultation with the older generations. Additionally, the digital revolution which has enabled the social media phenomenon in so many parts of the world, has significantly redefined social relations. The social media world has permitted those with savvy in internet technologies to form part of the virtual world or cyborg.

The same space and means have also redefined the economic relationship between the older and younger generations. For example, before the world was held captive in the coronavirus pandemic in March 2020, businesses were slowly migrating online in what is known as the digitalization of businesses, the force of which was universally felt. All the same, the end of the pandemic completely redefined the nature of work, encouraging businesses that were already online to keep the digital domain as their primary world. With young people seeking economic empowerment online, they are increasingly becoming financially independent from the older generation and doing so through impersonal economic transactions.

In addition to the social and economic independence that the younger generation is achieving, there is another concern in the rise of Artificial Intelligence (AI). The AI revolution has notably concerned religious conservatives, however it is not only the conservative religious constituency that is concerned about how AI is reshaping our world and relations. Educationists and academics are also concerned with AI and engines like ChatGPT, which have stimulated discussions about the future of human cognitive capacities and academic integrity.[4]

Bringing the above together on the theme of our presentation and book, the orienting questions are: What is the Holy Spirit's role in this modern landscape? Is it possible for the church to revisit the centrality of the Holy Spirit in reshaping the world? We ask these questions because, as much as modern technology has advanced, the moral and social challenges that require the presence and enablement of the Holy Spirit are also with us. For example, when concerns are raised about the future of work and human relations, the answer often given is the restoration of humanly-shared social values. But these social values (much of which is about love in a world of difference) cannot be ensured by science and technology. The mobile telephone, for example, may help one to talk, but not to talk with love or compassion. Meanwhile, love and compassion, which are the fruits of the Holy Spirit, are universally needed to help the new generation answer the present existential question: How do I live my faith in a world of increasing pluralities?

Joint Consultation in Seoul, Korea

At the Pentecostal World Conference and Empowered21 gathering in 2022, the Scholars Consultation invited the World Alliance for Pentecostal Theological Education (WAPTE) of the Pentecostal World Fellowship and the International Theological Institute of Yoido Full Gospel Church for a joint consultation in Seoul, Korea.[5] The Consultation was held physically and virtually at Yoido Full Gospel Church. It sought to reflect on how the global Spirit-empowered church might best facilitate a sense of the Holy Spirit and revival in the emerging generation across the globe.

Theme Description

The organizers, Wonsuk Ma and Opoku Onyinah of Empowered21, Barry Saylor of the WAPTE, and Hosung Kim of Yoido Full Gospel Church developed the following theme description to elaborate on the subject:

> The Consultation theme aligns closely with the intergenerational purpose of the three partners and shares their hope to strengthen the global church in reaching and empowering the next generation. The organizers are mindful of hearing and learning from younger voices to recognize and appreciate the calling that leaders of the emerging generation have received and owned to reach their own generation and beyond. The Scholars Consultation (and the Empowered21 movement) focuses on the new generation and its emerging leaders, churches, and initiatives within Spirit-empowered traditions. The organizers are also convinced that the existing generations and church leaders have a distinct role in facilitating, training, assisting, and empowering new leaders and their ministries. Thus, each Consultation plans to bring the current and younger generations together to share their understanding of God's mandate to reach the nations with the gospel, to explore ways to prepare the future of the church and its mission, and to pray together for the Spirit's empowerment upon each generation.

Consultations explore both conceptual and contextual studies. The former may include biblical, historical, and theological studies, while the latter brings practical concerns and successful ministry cases in reaching out to, nurturing, and empowering the next generation for the expansion of God's kingdom. The following sample questions guided the studies presented; and, as expected, presentations often covered multiple questions from the list or outside of it:

1. Understanding Millennials and Gen Z:
   - What are the characteristics of these generations to be considered for evangelism?
   - How are new Spirit-empowered leaders shaped?
   - What is the attitude of the younger generation towards Spirit-empowered beliefs and practices?
   - How does the younger generation define themselves and their call as Christians?

2. Ministries:
   - How do revivals occur among the new generation, and what are their distinct characteristics?
   - How are new Spirit-empowered churches established, and how are they different from existing ones?
   - What are Spirit-empowered approaches of younger communities that reach their own and younger generations?
   - What is the role of the Holy Spirit for a young dynamic church to sustain its vibrancy within a changing world?
   - How do healthy multi-generational churches have different roles for various generations?

3. Formation and Discipleship
   - What are examples of intentional Spirit-empowered discipleship that prepares and empowers the younger generation to reach their own and next generations?
   - How can the existing generation serve and empower leaders and churches of the next generation?
   - What are theological and practical challenges that new leaders and churches face and need to overcome?
   - How does one generation effectively hand the baton to the next?
   - What is the role of theological education in equipping Spirit-empowered leadership in the new generation?

The Scholars Consultation

There were ten full-length presentations and six summary forms. Out of the sixteen, four presented virtually. Among the ten full-length presentations, seven were regionally-based studies on youth and cultural factors influencing their faith and relationship with the Holy Spirit. Two studies addressed global samples of data examined youth culture and the response of the Spirit-empowered church. Many studies were jointly authored, increasing the number of contributors.

Additionally, the joint effort yielded a good number of scholars who were new to Scholars Consultations. Studies included sociological, ecclesiological, contextual/experiential, and historical approaches. The presentations cut across various regions: Europe, Africa, North America, Asia, and global. The ten full-length presentations are listed below:

- Randy Clark, "The New Generation and the Holy Spirit" (Keynote address)
- Barry L. Saylor and Patricia Savage, "Trends of Global Youth Culture and the Church's Response: Through the Lens of OneHope"
- Caroline Polly Tjihenuna, "Born-Free's to Born-Again: The Engagement of the Spirit-Empowered Movement with the Post-Independent Youth of Namibia."
- Caleb Nyanni, "A New Wave of the Spirit: The Next Chapter of the Spirit Among Afro-Westernized Churches"
- Kham Khai and Samuel Khai, "Reaching Burmese Americans: A Reflection on the Myanmar Cup USA"
- Ulrik Josefsson and Fredrick Wenell, "Individualized Faith or What? A Reflection on the Pressure of Shaping Christian Faith in the Swedish Context"
- Ron Luce, "Ten Elements of a Youth-Friendly Church"
- Chaa Chaa and Michio Ogino, "How *Hikikomori* (Acute Social Withdrawal) can be Ministered to: The Possibilities of Empowering Japanese Young Adults"
- Charles Prempeh, "Rejuvenation of a Denomination: The Experience of the Church of Pentecost, Ghana"
- Antonio Gryskiewicz, "*Kata Pneuma*: European International Churches and Next Gen Immigrant Youth"

Also, the following participants shared the outlines of their studies to be included in this book or the next: Jun Kim, Joshua Banda, Mutale Kaunda,

Clayton Coombs, and the Jean-Daniel Plüss–Alexander Stavnichuk team. Kathaleen Reid-Martinez, the provost of Oral Roberts University, brought a biblical reflection on the second day. At the conclusion of the Scholars Consultation, Victor Lee, the president of the Asian Pentecostal Society, graciously invited the participants to its relaunch program. The host church provided warm hospitality, including meals.

This Present Volume

Editors began to work with the presenters to revise their original presentations and work with less-developed studies, whose abstracts were shared in the Consultation. Not everyone was able to fully develop the studies, but three completed for this volume include:

- Jane C. Kim took over the study plan presented by Jun Kim, "Biblical Foundation of Children's Ministry from a Missional Perspective and a Mission Strategy to Help Teachers for Children's Ministry through an Online Platform: A Case Study."
- Clayton Coombs teamed up with Andrew and Susannah Harrison to complete "Planetboom: A Case Study in the Effects of Youth-Led Revival in Australia."
- The Stavnichuk-Plüss team produced "Reimagining the Holy Spirit as Life-Giving Spirit for the Next Generation."

The editors also recruited additional studies to strengthen the collection:

- Juan Sebastian Rodriguez kindly revised his presentation to the Pentecostal World Conference, "The Role of Children of Pastors and Young Leaders in Preserving an Awakening in Their Generation." We welcome this Latin American perspective.
- Daniel D. Bunn, Jr. of Oral Roberts University adds an Old Testament study, "An Admonition to the New Generation in Deuteronomy."
- Douglas Petersen's powerful preaching on children, delivered in 2023 in Singapore, brings a pulpit presentation to the book, "Children's Stories in the Gospel of Mark: A Sermon."
- Antipas Harris' conference presentation is also added to this book, "Global Christianity and Gen Z: What is the Hope for the Future of Faith?"
- Tan Seow How and Cecilia Chan of Singapore share their extraordinary journey in planting a next generation church in Singapore, in "How to Grow a Church Younger: Five Universal Strategies."

- Kerry Loescher of Oral Roberts University contributes "Using the Volunteer Function Inventory to Activate Aging Adults as Spirit-Empowered Disciple-Makers for the Next Generation."
- Allie Mendoza and Kimmie Simon of the same university showcase a campus chapel program as a ground for nurturing next generation leaders, in "Preparing and Sending Generation Z into Every Person's World: Encounter and Equipping through Chapel at Oral Roberts University."
- Jamie Austin shares his experience rejuvenating a local congregation in "Parental Covering and Resourcing: Preserving the Future of the Church by Setting the Next Generation Up for Success."
- The book is closed with a comprehensive postscript prepared by Jaime L. Riddle.

The organizers and editors have been careful not to pretend that the present generation can shape the next one—the agent will ultimately have to be the Holy Spirit. One area where the planners have worked hard is planning the Consultation and editing of the book to promote the new generation's voice. The editors feel reasonably successful in doing so and have organized the above contents into three sections: "Laying the Foundation," "Preserving and Reaching the New Generation," and "Forming and Empowering the New Generation."

Notes

1 See Steve Bruce, *Religion and Modernization: Sociologists and Historians Debate the Secularization Thesis* (Oxford, U.K.: Clarendon, 1992).

2 This is a major point in his book, Max Weber, *Bureaucracy* (London: Routledge, 1948).

3 See, for example, Craig Gauld, "Democratising or Privileging: The Democratisation of Knowledge and the Role of the Archivist," *Archival Science* 17 (2017), 227–245.

4 See Debby R. E. Cotton, Peter A. Cotton, and J. Reuben Shipway, "Chatting and Cheating: Ensuring Academic Integrity in the Era of ChatGPT," *Innovations in Education and Teaching International* (2023), 1–12.

5 Yoido Full Gospel Church was the host of the 26th Pentecostal World Conference.

Part I
Laying the Foundation

1 The New Generation and the Holy Spirit: Keynote Address

Randy Clark

Introduction

Several years ago, I was praying and asking God to give me an opportunity to speak to young people in higher education. I prayed, "Would you open up the door to colleges, universities, and training schools?" I had been asking this for some time and someone found out about it: I was located near Regent Divinity School and was suddenly invited to speak to two classes. I rushed to the school, they took me to one of the rooms, and I did not even know what the class was about, but found out it was a leadership class.

Having never taught a leadership class, I walked in, and God dropped what I was supposed to teach on, which was three characteristics of a history maker in the world through the church. At that time there was a song by the band *Delirious?* called "History Maker."[1] I wrote on the board the first qualification for leadership: that the person who is a history maker usually has a very powerful experience of being baptized in the Holy Spirit or filled with the Holy Spirit. Secondly, they have an understanding of what Spirit-baptism is for, which is usually communicated to them through a prophetic word or the Lord himself revealing it to them. Thirdly, that Spirit-baptism and consequent understanding of their destiny creates a very strong faith that causes a person to persevere in the midst of very special circumstances.

I believe that as we look at the next generation and the Holy Spirit, what is important is what God wants to do in the upcoming years, and what the key leaders of this generation will experience. In other words, this next generation will have its history makers. I believe this is true because Jesus said, "I will build my church and the gates of hell shall not prevail against it" (Matt 16:18).[2] No matter how bad things look, even if culture becomes more anti-Christian, God can cause a great revival to come, roll back the tide, and cause things to change. And this may very well be in the hands of young people all over the globe right now.

Biblical Examples

There is a biblical paradigm in both the Old and New Testaments for God calling young adults into ministry. For example, Joseph was 17 when he was sold into slavery (Gen 37:2). According to Genesis 41:46, he was only 30 years old when he became vice-regent next to Pharaoh, over all the land. King David is traditionally said to be 13 to 15 years old—having just attained the age of Hebrew manhood—when he killed Goliath. Jeremiah may have been between 13 and 16 years old when he began his prophetic ministry, having been called to this even before birth (Jer 1:5). The historian Josephus says Samuel was 12 years old when the Lord spoke to him and gave him a prophecy for Eli.[3]

When we look to the New Testament, we see that all of the disciples of Jesus except Peter were probably under 20 years old when he called them. One of the reasons we say "except Peter" is because he was married and had to be over 20 to pay the temple tax (Matt 17:24–27).[4] The other disciples were with Peter and Jesus, but no indication that they paid the tax. Yet even Peter could have been as young as 18 or 19 when he was first called by Jesus. We also know from studying the history of that time, that rabbinic disciples were almost always between 13 and 30 years old, and the most common age that someone was called to be a student was between 15–20, the ages typical of entering a rabbinical school and the age typical for marriage, respectively.[5] Additionally, according to Exodus 30:14, twenty was the age that one was counted for the census and therefore had to give an offering.

Timothy, another New Testament example, was only a "youth" when the Lord called him through Paul (1 Tim 4:12). Fourteen years later, Paul writes his first letter to Timothy, which encourages him that he was doing a great job. Paul, the elder, is concerned about the issue of Timothy's youth discrediting his calling (e.g. 2 Tim 3:14–15). At that point, Timothy could have been around 30 years old, but whatever age he was, it is clear that a lot of other church leaders were older than him; to them, he was still perceived as young for the responsibilities he had in that culture. Thus, there are boundless examples, in the Old and New Testaments, of God calling teenagers and sometimes even children to be history makers.

Historical Examples

Besides looking at the Bible, when we look at historical revivals and moves of God, when God began to push back the enemy and establish his kingdom in greater measure, he often used younger people. George Whitefield (1714–1770), was one of the most famous figures of the Great Evangelical Revival in England, led by him and John Wesley, who was in his early thirties. Whitefield was only 21 years old and the more famous of the two, as far as being a great preacher. In fact, he was one of the greatest preachers and evangelists in English-speaking history. To reach this height, he would have had to begin ministry school and preparations when he was younger than 21, still a teen.[6]

Another famous Englishman, Charles Haddon Spurgeon (1834–1892), was one of the greatest Baptist preachers of all time. What I didn't know was that he started preaching at age 16, started pastoring at age 17.[7] An older leader in his church who saw potential in him encouraged him to take their church, a small church of forty people, when he was only 17. He did, and the church quickly grew to 400 people. By the time Spurgeon was 20 years old, he had already preached 600 different sermons. By age 21, he became the pastor of one of the largest Baptist churches in London.

For our purposes, what is interesting is that he was told by an older leader in the church, Richard Knill, when he was only a 10-year-old boy that one day he would preach to thousands. I doubt whether that leader specifically said to Charles, "I have a prophetic word for you." I doubt if Knill even thought he was speaking prophetically—but we realize that was a prophetic word. Sometimes people move in the gifts of the Spirit when they do not understand the gifts of the Spirit.

Also, some people do not have language for gifts of the Spirit but have experiences in gifts of the Spirit. I have a set of Spurgeon's sermons, and one time I came across one with a word of knowledge he gave out—and the person repented right there. Spurgeon got words of knowledge and prophetic words. He didn't call them that, but he said what God was showing him, which brought power to his ministry. Spurgeon was also noted for having a powerful ministry of healing. He visited sick people of his church and prayed for them in their homes. He had an incomplete education, but he was extremely well read with a library of 12,000 volumes. He was an amazing preacher. So, we see at 10 years old he was prophesied to by Knill, then at 16, God called him. By 21 years old, he had a large church and became a history maker in his time.

Another man, the Welshman Evan Roberts (1878–1951), was a very young history maker. When he was 26 years old, he led the Great Welsh Revivals for two years.[8] At 10 years old, he began memorizing scripture, going to church, and praying every day. He prayed for revival as a teenager and studied for the ministry in his early twenties. He received a baptism in the Spirit, and almost immediately revival broke out and formal study ended. He formed a team at age 26, and everyone was a teenager on his team! He had a vision that 100,000 young people would be saved in Wales, and it happened in one year.

Sadly, his story doesn't end well. Due to the stress of the revival and the emotional drain on him, his health broke like many other evangelists that I know of in the twentieth century, from preaching night after night. Sometimes revivals end because of the breaking of the physical or emotional health of the one leading it. Evan Roberts was also affected by an elder who, in my opinion, negatively impacted him by bringing confusion and doubt to some of the things he had taught and experienced when he was younger. As a young revivalist, he might have needed more support and encouragement than he received.

Contemporary Examples

Young people have been used not only in biblical and historical revivals, but in current revivals. Ed Silvoso, who was raised in Argentina but later came to the USA, has had a huge impact on the church in Latin America. He served as an evangelist and a national youth leader from 13–23 years old. All members of his first evangelistic team were teenagers. God anoints you and can use you even though you are young.

The seminary I went to, Southern Baptist Theological Seminary, had a Billy Graham room that contained diverse Billy Graham memorabilia. Under the glass was his high school yearbook, turned to his photo page. It had a caption under it which read, "life's goal—to be an evangelist." He would have been around 18 years old when that picture was taken. Coincidentally, he preached his first sermon at age 19.[9] Graham was one of the greatest preachers of all time, and one of the greatest evangelists of the twentieth century, preaching to over one million at a time.[10] He preached his last crusade at 86 years old. He continued to serve the Lord until the last days of his life in 2018.[11]

Years ago, I met a great leader in Cambodia, SoPhal Ung.[12] He was raised a Buddhist and was saved after being healed from being in a coma for three months. Being healed brought about a sense of God's call to ministry in his early twenties. He entered Bible school and started seven house churches. But he wanted to preach and had been cleaning floors when, one day, a church leader shocked him saying he wanted him to preach that very night. He didn't have a message, so he asked God to give him something and preached on John 3:16. In the middle of his preaching, he got a word of knowledge: Ung felt like God told him there was an 81-year-old woman who was blind and had been blind for 18 years. He looked out at the small crowd and didn't see an old woman, so he struggled with giving the word of knowledge. What he didn't know was, that outside there were people who could not get in, and right outside the door was a woman who was 81 and been blind for 18 years. She came in and got healed of her blindness.

SoPhal Ung became an apostolic leader in Cambodia. He has led thousands to the Lord and started many churches and orphanages. He is also one among seven church leaders, out of 17,000, who has been captured and put in a torture prison. He has experienced apostolic suffering and angelic visitations, but God has used him mightily. He began this road in his early twenties, and many of those following him have been teenagers. SoPhal's daughter told me that, for her dad, hearing the word of God was literally a matter of life and death. She testifies that there was a time when the Lord warned him that fifty people walking home from church should turn around because they would be ambushed at the Thailand border. The ones who didn't believe SoPhal really heard God walked across the border and were killed. The others turned back and lived.

Randy's Story

Now I want to tell you about one other person who is not famous—not a great apostle in the world but an important person in my life. Joe Hordon was called to preach when he was 9 years old. Someone went to his farm, pulled in the driveway, and heard yelling in the background. Joe's father came out and told him that was little Joey; he's practicing preaching to

16 The New Generation & The Holy Spirit

the cows in the pasture. Joe loved God and gave himself to God entirely. My mom told me that when she was younger that she remembered another preacher would take Joey to Baptist churches in the country. He would put a wooden box right behind the pulpit, and Joey would stand on it to preach.

God used that man in his early thirties, in 1970, in my church that I was a member of at age 18. Joe came a week different than planned because God initiated revival through the Jesus Movement. When Joe came, over two hundred people got saved in my church and eleven young men were called into ministry; I was the second of the eleven. Now Joe worked a 40-hour work week at a blue-collar factory job, but then would get off work, get in his car, and drive sometimes an hour or more to preach before driving home to go to work the next day. He did this for three years. He is not famous, but God used him to reach a lot of people, including me. Under his ministry, I was called to preach.

This testimony reminds me of an evangelist named Mordecai Ham (1877–1961). He was preaching in North Carolina and wrote one night in his diary, "Not a very good night. Only two teenagers accepted the Lord." Later, he should have put an addition because one of those teenagers was Billy Graham.[13]

Sometimes God uses you to touch somebody else. Brother Bradshaw helped little Joey Hordon. Richard Knill prophesied to the 10-year-old Charles Spurgeon. Mordecai Ham reached the teenage heart of Billy Graham. And Jack Taylor encouraged me. Jack Taylor (1933–2021) was saved at 10 years old. He preached his first sermon at 14 years old. He took over a Baptist church at 26 and grew it to 3,000 members. His church broke out in revival, and he saw God save 2,000 people in six months. At 36 years old, he was baptized in the Holy Spirit. He then wrote a book about a victorious life[14] and walked away from a church of 8,000 congregants to become an itinerant minister. He was one of my spiritual fathers who spoke into my life. He preached until he died just recently at 88 years old. I thank God for Jack and the role he played in encouraging me. You can see in many of the stories I've told that there is an important role that older Christians play in helping young Christians to be encouraged. Often, it is the deciding factor.

As mentioned, I was called to preach at 18. I had been saved at age 16. My grandma heard the voice of God speak to her and say he was going to call me into ministry. She did not tell me, however, until I announced my call to go into ministry. I experienced three very powerful physical healings which got me out of the hospital in twenty days instead of the seven to eleven weeks my prognosis dictated. On my first day of college, I heard God say, "The issue of your life is going to be the Holy Spirit." So all the way through college and seminary, I tried to focus any way I could to take classes that dealt with the Holy Spirit.

I read about Charles Finney being baptized in the Spirit and him feeling like he would die from the power, electricity, and love going through him. Dwight L. Moody testified of the same thing. At 19 years old, I cried out that I wanted God to fill me with the Spirit so strongly that I would fear I would die. I had been pursuing God and the Holy Spirit, but it was when I was 32 years old, that God filled me with the Spirit. And it was age 37 when I was filled so powerfully that I was afraid I would die from the power. Ironically, at age 41, I had another experience, and it was peaceful. As a result of that, all heaven broken loose in my life and my church, which set things up for me to go and be used in the revival that started in Toronto, Canada.

Leaders Influenced by Randy's Ministry

From the revival in Toronto, I think of the Bakers, Heidi and Rolland. We are very good friends, and I know their story well. Heidi was 16 years old when God saved her, filled her with the Holy Spirit, took her into visions and showed her the three continents she would spend her life in. Rolland was 18 when God called him to preach. They are two great missionaries; thousands of churches have been started because of them, and over one million people have come to the Lord. Additionally, the unreached Makhuwa tribe of four million people has been penetrated by the gospel with dead raisings, the blind seeing, and the lame walking.[15]

They express that what encouraged them were the words and the baptisms in the Holy Spirit. Heidi had several of them. One happened in Toronto while I was there, and God used me to give her a prophecy. When I went to Mozambique, God spoke to her again that thousands of churches were to be started through their ministry and millions would come to Jesus. But these history makers started out at 16 and 18 years old.

I asked one of my best friends, Bill Johnson, who said age 21 was his year. After he served his dad as an assistant for two years, starting at age 19, he realized the call on his life. He is one of the greatest preachers and church leaders, operating out of Bethel Church in Redding, California. So many churches and pastors around the world have been influenced by him, and it all started when he was a young man. Music from his church continues to influence young people around the world, and is a beautiful picture of older and younger generations lending their gifts to each other.

I think of Henry Madava, a leader in Ukraine, as another historical revivalist in this day. He was called in his mid-twenties to preach. He was a youth leader, and one day the senior preacher didn't show up. He preached for a few minutes, and then closed his eyes to pray. He was in an Evangelical church. But he heard smacking sounds: people were falling to the ground. He didn't know what to do! It was amazing what God was doing. From there, he went to Ukraine from a southern African country to study engineering. When he graduated, he had already reached so many people that he now has one of the largest churches in Ukraine. There are thousands in it, and he has seen people raised from the dead. He is an amazing man of God who is being used to affect the world.

Revivalists Who Did Not Know God

Not everyone has the same history. Sometimes God takes people who are in rebellion, who do not even know him, but he calls them to serve. I can think of three people like that: Che Ahn, Randy McMillan, and Cesar Castellano. Randy McMillan is American but spent his life in Cali, Colombia. Cesar Castellano is from Colombia. Che Ahn's apprehension by God happened on the East Coast, but he pastors in California.

Che was saved at a *Deep People* rock concert. He was on drugs when he was touched. The Lord called him, this rebellious 18-year-old, while he was in the hippie lifestyle. A radical love for Jesus overwhelmed him. Then he became an apostle used around the world, particularly in Asia. His church in Pasadena, California has several thousand today, and he is the chancellor of the Wagner Leadership Institute.

Cesar Castellano, in Bogotá, was called when he was a nominal Roman Catholic and was high on drugs. The Lord spoke to him audibly, which scared him. He told God, if this is you, I don't want to meet you in this state I am in. Come back at 9:00 p.m. tomorrow, and I'll be waiting on you. He did not realize it was inappropriate to give God conditions—he meant it from a pure heart. At 9:00 p.m. the next night, God's voice and presence came. Cesar had a sovereign salvation. He was in his late teens or early twenties, and started leading people to the Lord. Many got saved then, and now he and his wife started the fastest-growing church in Colombia. They also started a movement of churches, powerfully impacted by a prophetic word given by Randy McMillan about "twelve." From this, Cesar started the G12 movement which has impacted and transformed churches all around the world.[16] But this all started when he was young.

Later in life, a hitman went by the Castellanos' SUV while their children were in the car with them. They sprayed the car with bullets. It was an assassination attempt against his wife who was a senator at the time. Cesar got shot in three places and still has one bullet in his neck. His wife was also wounded, and they went to the U.S. to recuperate. Their church in Bogotá grew by the thousands, however, while they rested.

Randy McMillan's story is one of the craziest I have ever heard. When he was about 20 years old, he was backslidden. He had not been going to church but was partying instead. He was getting ready to go to the New York area from Jacksonville, Florida when he went to his dorm room to pack, locked the door, turned around, and experienced a visitation of Jesus. Whether it was only a vision, he couldn't really tell; he thought it was Jesus. He began to wail because he was instantly aware of his sinfulness—the holiness of Jesus came on him. People heard him wailing from outside and started beating on the door. But as he has this experience, Jesus tells Randy that he has been called to be a missionary and will spend most of his life in a country that does not speak English. Randy was so impacted that his father, a very famous attorney, thought he was having a mental breakdown. At one point his mother asked her husband, "What if this really was God who spoke to our son?"

It was God. Randy married Marcy while at college in Jacksonville. They led Bible studies together. Then they went to spend their lives in Cali, Colombia. There, Randy was confronted by demonic presences. One time the enemy appeared to him, and he felt cold and sick all of a sudden. A demon spoke to him and said, "We'll kill you if you don't get out of Cali." Randy testifies that it took him six months to recover. But he knew God had destined him for Cali. Just because you have opposition doesn't mean you are outside the will of God. In fact, Randy had an apostolic anointing. He had a vision of calling for stadium crusades. He brought people out to worship and pray all night long. Right after that, the drug cartels were busted. At 59, Randy died of heart disease, but how God used him—and it started when he was young.

Recently, I read about a young Bolivian, Julio Cesar Ruibal (1953–1995) who also had influence in Cali, Colombia and led stadium crusades.[17] He was saved at a Kathryn Kuhlman crusade in his late teens and filled with the Holy Spirit shortly after. God used him to ignite a revival when he went back to the U.S. from Bolivia. He started Bible studies and over 5,000 in a short period of time came to the Lord. He also saw healings. The president was so affected by it that he allowed Julio to use his own airplane to fly. The president would call the mayors of the cities where Julio did crusades and tell them to allow a holiday so they could fill the stadiums. Between 30,000 to 60,000 came. Revival took over the nation and spread throughout Latin America. Many around him were young adults. Later, Julio went to Cali and started a church that grew to thousands, but in 1996, he was shot by hitmen, martyred for his faith.[18]

Conclusion

What do we learn from these people's lives? God still calls young people to be history makers and revive his church. Even today, many of my interns, like Will Hart at age 18, have gone on to do great things. Some students in my seminary are older, in their thirties, but when I talk to them about how old they were when they got passionate about the Lord it was when they were teenagers. Many people I am aware of, who are really being used by God right now powerfully, came to God and began serving God while still teenagers.

This is why a ministerial focus on the next generation is always warranted. It never wanes. Many young people have an interest in spiritual things like Heidi Baker did; even as a child, she had a deep spiritual interest. She was called from the mother's womb. I believe the same thing about myself.

We also learn that Spirit-baptism is integral. These history makers experienced mighty baptisms in the Spirit. Their experiences in the Spirit created faith that allowed them to endure torture, persecution, and prison. God imparted great faith to persevere in light of opposition, and by showing them his faithfulness throughout their lives. Some were even sovereignly chosen in a state of being backslidden. God sought them, he called them, and filled them with his Spirit just like he has done since biblical times.

Some of the greatest leaders of our time—and something about God's choices—are those where he reaches down and takes people who may not look like a Rolland Baker (who sat on his grandfather's lap hearing stories of great revival). He chooses some who did not have that influence and says anyway: I need you.

This is why we should never stop talking about the importance of the baptism of the Holy Spirit. We can never lessen the importance of focusing on being filled with the Holy Spirit and trusting God to raise up leaders for the next generation to do what he has called them to do. So when we think about the Holy Spirit and this upcoming generation, I'm not worried. In Matthew 16:18, Jesus assured us that he would build his church and the gates of hell would not prevail against it. Jesus has a history of calling young people into his mission. He is not going to let any generation go without an opportunity with the church existing. Wherever there is a church, Jesus will call people, while young, to serve him. And they will do so faithfully, as they are empowered by his Spirit.

Notes

1 Martin Smith, "History Maker," 1997, YouTube, https://www.youtube.com/watch?v=jM8M_xgKbrc/, accessed June 12, 2022.

2 Scripture quotations are from the English Standard Version.

3 Josephus, *A.J. 5.10*, Internet Sacred Text Archive, https://www.sacred-texts.com/jud/josephus/ant-5.htm/, accessed June 12, 2022.

4 Sebastian Selvén, "In or Out–the Privilege of Taxation: The Half-shekel and the Temple Tax in the Talmud Yerushalmi," 2014, 72, *SVENSK EXEGETISK ÅRSBOK* (81), https://www.divaportal.org/smash/get/diva2:1067961/FULLTEXT01.pdf/, accessed June 12, 2022.

5 Lois Tverberg, "The Reality of Disciples and Rabbis," September 16, 2013, Our Rabbi Jesus: His Jewish Life and Teaching, https://ourrabbijesus.com/a-question-about-disciples-rabbis/, accessed May 15, 2024.

6 For more, see Arnold A. Dallimore, *George Whitefield: God's Anointed Servant in the Great Revival of the Eighteenth Century* (Wheaton: Crossway, 2010).

7 For more, see Charles Haddon Spurgeon, Susannah Spurgeon, and Joseph Harrald, eds., *C. H. Spurgeon's Autobiography, 1834–1854* (Madison: University of Wisconsin, 1899),

GoogleBooks, https://www.google.com/books/edition/ C_H_ Spurgeon_s_Autobiography_1834_1854 /BKxZAAAAMAAJ?hl= en&gbpv=1&dq=richard+knill+charles+spurgeon&pg= PA35&printsec=frontcover/, accessed June 12, 2024.

8   For more on Evan Roberts, see Gomer Morgan Roberts, "Roberts, Evan John (1878–1951), *'Y Diwygiwr'* [the Revivalist] revivalist preacher," *Dictionary of Welsh Biography*, https://biography.wales/article/s2-ROBE-JOH-1878/, accessed June 11, 2024; also "Keys for Revival: Evan Roberts," The Revival Library, https://revival-library.org/revival-resources/for-revival-seekers/revival-tips-from-history/evan-roberts-keys-of-revival/, accessed June 11, 2024.

9   "Where was the Rev. Billy Graham's First Sermon?" February 21, 2018, WSOCTV, https://www.wsoctv.com/news/local/where-was-the-rev-billy-grahams-first-sermon/704710172/#:~:text=Graham%20was%2019%20years%20old,preached%20there%20for%2015%20years/, accessed June 12, 2022.

10 "Billy Graham Preaches to 1.1 Million in Korea," June 3, 2013, The Billy Graham Library, https://billygrahamlibrary.org/june-3-1973-billy-graham-preaches-to-1-1-million-in-korea/, accessed June 11, 2024.

11 For more, see Billy Graham, *Just As I Am: The Autobiography of Billy Graham* (New York: Harper Collins, 1997).

12 The following testimonies are documented in full in Randy Clark, *Almighty Is His Name: The Riveting Story of SoPhal Ung* (Lake Mary, FL: Charisma House, 2016).

13 Edward E. Ham, "The Day Billy Graham found Christ," October 28, 2009, Billy Graham Evangelical Association, https://billygraham.org/story/the-day-billy-graham-found-christ/, accessed June 11, 2024. Graham's testimony of that night can be found at "Billy Graham's Decision for Christ," August 16, 2023, The Billy Graham Library, https://billygrahamlibrary.org/blog-from-the-archive-billy-grahams-decision-for-christ/, accessed June 12, 2022.

14 Jack R. Taylor, *The Key to Triumphant Living* (Nashville: Baptist Sunday School Board, 1971).

15 For more, see autobiography and works at "Heidi Baker, Ph.D.," 2024, https://rollandheidibaker.org/heidi-baker#:~:text=Heidi%20Baker%2C%20PhD&text=We%20met%20at%20a%20small,began%20ministeringp%20together%20in%20Asia/, accessed June 12, 2024. Also Randy Clark, *There Is More: Reclaiming the Power of Impartation* (Mechanicsburg, PA: Global Awakening, 2010), GoogleBooks, https://books.google.com/

books?id=wqW_bKU6vOYC&pg=PA54&lpg=PA54&dq=rolland+and+heidi+baker+story+millions+coming+to+the+Lord&source=bl&ots=b2jbYG8jCy&sig=ACfU3U2DqDrOAHrYg-NB79wek4U_OJ4EiQ&hl=en&sa=X&ved=2ahUKEwibn6XW_tP8AhXYnGoFHQEHDjQQ6AF6BAglEAM#v=onepage&q=rolland%20and%20heidi%20baker%20story%20millions%20coming%20to%20the%20Lord&f=false/, accessed June 11, 2022.

16 See "Pastors Cesar and Claudia Castellanos," G12 Pasión por Dios, https://g12.co/en/cesar-and-claudia/, accessed June 12, 2024.

17 For more on Julio Cesar Ruibal, see J. Lee Grady, "The Marks of Genuine Revival," December 10, 2022, CBN.com, https://www2.cbn.com/article/not-selected/marks-genuine-revival/, accessed June 11, 2024; also "Day 32: Bolivia's Apostle to the Andes," September 16, 2020, The Jesus Fast, https://thejesusfast.global/day-32-bolivias-apostle-of-the-andes/, accessed June 11, 2024.

18 "Prominent Bolivian Evangelist Murdered," February 5, 1996, *Christianity Today*, https://www.christianitytoday.com/ct/1996/february5/6t2099.html/, accessed June 12, 2024.

2 An Admonition to the New Generation in Deuteronomy

Daniel D. Bunn, Jr.

Abstract

In Deuteronomy, Moses exhorts the people on multiple occasions to respond to the LORD "today." What is intriguing is that he speaks to the new generation, not the old one, about what God has done for them. Thus it might seem, on the surface, that Moses has gotten confused about his audience! This chapter will explore the agenda of Deuteronomy concerning the formation of the theological identity of the audience. Though the audience is one that is separated *chronologically* from the original audience, Moses bridges the gaps between the two through their *theological* unity as the one people of God. Accordingly, Moses' use of the word "today" points not to a chronological moment, but rather a theological one: having heard the address of the LORD to the one people of God across time and space, the new generation must determine whether they will trust and obey. This challenge extends even to newer generations. Will the next generation of the Spirit-empowered movement hear the address of the LORD and obey?

Introduction

Readers of Deuteronomy have long observed that the book stands at a crucial juncture historically, geographically, and theologically in the Old Testament. The wilderness wandering has come to an end. The people will now enter the land of promise, which will be the primary setting for the narrative that will stretch to 2 Kings. In many ways, it wraps up, albeit loosely, the narrative thus far. At the same time, it provides important thematic threads that will run through what follows. Historical-critical scholars have debated whether the book was written as the conclusion to what precedes, or as the introduction to what follows. Perhaps the book has been placed intentionally as a hinge in the story.

Theologically, the text presents Israel at a crisis moment. In Exodus, God delivered them mightily out of Egypt in commitment to the promises he had made to Abraham and out of his love for the people. The LORD did this in order that he might be their God and they might be his people. Exodus 19:4–5 summarizes well the journey out of Egypt and the impending journey to the land of promise: the LORD says, "You yourselves saw what I did to the Egyptians and how I lifted you up on eagles' wings and brought you out to me. So now, if you faithfully listen to my voice and keep my covenant, then you will be for me more treasured than all the peoples of the earth."[1] Out of his love for them, God has delivered Israel and made them his special people. However, their vocation as God's people will be fulfilled as they obey him. In light of their chosen status, God makes Israel a "light to the nations" such that in their obedience to God and worship of him, they will draw other nations to God.

They will soon cross into the long-promised land and the older generation will all pass away; Moses will be gone by the end of the book. Moses therefore prepares the new generation for their journey into the Promised Land by looking again at the promises that God made to the older generation. In this way, Moses ensures that they know the promises of God and the obedience that he desires. The narrative therefore invites readers to wonder whether the people will remain faithful to the LORD once they come into the land. Deuteronomy is devoted to preparing the new generation for this transition. What will guide them successfully into the emerging future?

In this study, I look closely at the strategy that Deuteronomy implements for preparing a new generation for living faithfully before God in the Promised Land. I center especially on the word "today," which occurs regularly throughout the book. I will urge that Moses' use of this word in his speeches to the people is not primarily chronological, but theological: it is the crisis point, the moment of decision. As Deuteronomy uses it, the word achieves the theological collapse of time into this one crisis moment. The implication is that "today" is an ever-present moment for the people of God to choose obedience. I will examine three chapters—Deuteronomy 5, 8, and 30—as representative of the overall theological agenda that the book aims to achieve. I will argue in turn that the LORD has spoken to the one people of Israel, across time and space, and expects and hopes for their obedience. The new generation must then, as it also must now, embrace their identity, heed the word of the LORD, and trust in him.

Deuteronomy 5

Deuteronomy 5 provides intriguing space for reflecting on some of these matters. Moses speaks of the covenant that the LORD made with the people of Israel. He recalls the well-known episode from Exodus 20, the giving of the Ten Commandments. He repeats these words, with slight modification. In essence, though, the passage echoes that previous event.

The passage opens in verse 1 with Moses gathering the people and exhorting them to heed the instruction that he will provide them: "Hear, Israel, the statutes and the judgments that I am speaking in your ears today; you will learn them and guard them to do them." Then, before recounting the statutes and ordinances, Moses characterizes his audience: "The LORD our God made a covenant with *us* on Horeb. Not with our *ancestors* did the LORD make this covenant, but with *us, we, these* who are here today, all of us who are alive" (5:2–3, emphasis added). Moses draws a distinction between the current generation and the previous generation. However, what he says about the covenant appears to stand in tension with the wider Pentateuchal narrative itself. It was, in fact, the previous generation with whom the LORD established a covenant. Why, then, does Moses characterize the present community as well as the past one in this way?

It appears that Moses is making a theological claim that supersedes chronological realities. According to Nelson, "Horeb and Moab involve the very same audience in a literary and ideological sense that transcends the actual chronology set forth in Deuteronomy."[2] By speaking of the present generation as those with whom the LORD has made the covenant, he is inviting them to conceive of themselves as belonging to the community that stood at Horeb. As Woods puts it, they "were called to identify fully with the Horeb covenant, as though they were present at its original making."[3] By exhorting the present generation in this way, Moses moves the audience, hermeneutically, beyond a schema in which they would determine what the covenant "meant" for the past generation and then what it might "mean" for the present. He goes further: by having the current audience declare that the covenant was directed at them originally, it is that same Sinaitic covenant that is binding for them.[4] As

Weinfeld poignantly states the matter, "Israel throughout its generations is thus presented in Deuteronomy as one body, a corporate personality."[5]

If Moses thus identifies the new generation with the old generation, as members of the same body of Israel that received the covenant, then what he means by "today" in verse 1 merits further reflection. Moses exhorts the people to obey the statutes and ordinances that he commands them "today." This word certainly refers to the moment at which he relays the words to the people at the edge of the Promised Land. Yet this might not be all that it signifies. This statement immediately precedes his collapse of the chronological distinction between this generation and the community at Sinai in favor of theological unity as the one body of Israel. Further, the statutes and ordinances that he has in mind are the same ones that were spoken in Exodus 20.

I suggest that the word "today," therefore, refers not only to a *chronological* moment in time, but to a *theological* moment of decision. The statutes and ordinances spoken to the earlier generation are now spoken to the new generation. The theological drama centers on the latter's response. To this new generation, as well as to the older one, the invitation is open to heed the command of the LORD today—that is, in this moment, *now*. By embracing their theological identification as the same community of Israel that stood at Sinai, the new generation must also embrace the exhortation to heed the same command of the LORD now.

The chapter ends with Moses further sketching the nature of the response that the LORD desires from the people. Recalling the giving of the Ten Commandments in Exodus 20, Moses reminds the present audience of the initial response of Israel to their awesome experience of the LORD's presence: "if we were to hear the voice of the LORD our God again, then we will die" (v. 25). The LORD accommodates their request but expresses anguish: "If only their hearts were like this: to fear me and to keep all of my commandments every day so that it would go well for them and their children forever" (v. 29). The language used here expresses a wish. Craigie suggests that the response of the people was genuine and proper, but "it was nevertheless regrettable that the people could not show the same reverence in the more mundane affairs of life."[6] Thus, the orientation of their hearts and minds toward the LORD, not only active response to specific instructions, was always primary.

The theological identity of the people of Israel as Moses is attempting to sculpt it therefore extends across time and space. It takes up chronologically disparate people groups—the old generation and the new generation—and unites them as the one body of Israel to whom the LORD speaks. As one body, then, this unified people group faces the one exhortation that always follows the hearing of the word of the LORD: they are to obey what the LORD says "today." This logically extends not only backward in time, but also forward: subsequent generations will be invited to re-conceptualize their share in the identity of the people of Israel by hearing the word declared and by responding "today." And their obedience always should flow out of their fear of the LORD. It is as they grow more deeply in their trust in the LORD that things will go well for them.

Deuteronomy 8

Deuteronomy 8 falls within the subsequent chapters that lay out the details of the covenant relationship between the LORD and Israel. This chapter aims to frame theologically Israel's life with God—past, present, and future. The goal is to prepare the new generation to live faithfully now in the land to which they are going. The chapter gives a template, in a sense, for what faithful living looks like.[7]

The chapter begins by looking backward. In 8:2–5, Moses exhorts Israel to remember. They are to remember "all of the road on which the LORD led you this forty years in the desert" (v. 2). Obedience to the LORD is regularly cast in Deuteronomy and other parts of the Old Testament alongside the metaphor of journeying on a road. The road was one aimed at humbling the people through testing them. The LORD tested them "to know that which was in your heart: would you keep his commandment or not?" (v. 3). Moses here provides explicit hermeneutical interpretation of the entire wilderness journey. The LORD was trying to determine whether the people would obey him.

The language of "test" recurs throughout the Old Testament. Most poignant for the current discussion are two occurrences: Genesis 22:1 and Exodus 20:20. In both occurrences, the word "test" is associated with the "fear of God." In Genesis 22, after Abraham has arrived at the point at which he was willing to sacrifice his son, the angel of the LORD intervenes, proclaiming, "For now I know that you fear God since you did not withhold your son, your only son, from me" (v. 22). The purpose of the test was to demonstrate whether Abraham was one who had the fear of God. Likewise, in Exodus 20, after the giving of the Ten Commandments, Moses tells the people of Israel, "Do not be afraid, because God has come for the purpose of testing you and in order that his fear will be on you, so that you do not sin" (v. 20). Testing reveals and produces the fear of God, which in turn prevents people from sinning.

These earlier texts from the Pentateuch inform subsequent occurrences of testing. Readers who have been trained by those earlier passages might see a more expansive portrait being painted in Deuteronomy 8, then. The purpose of the LORD in the wilderness was, as verse 3 indicated, to test the people, to see whether they would obey. But obedience itself flows out of a still deeper reality: the fear of God.[8] The fear of God, as it is informed especially by Genesis 22, does not refer to a response of terror to the LORD. In fact, Exodus 20:20 distinguishes between being "afraid of God" and having the "fear of God" by using both meanings of the same verbal root in the same sentence. The fear of God reflects a deep commitment to the LORD that is borne out of an experience with him and knowledge of his character. Encountering the LORD and knowing the LORD produces trust in the LORD, which in turn results in obedience to the LORD. Therefore, working backward, obedience to the LORD reveals that one knows the LORD; disobedience, however, reveals that one does not. The people in the wilderness, in their disobedience, show that they do not know and trust in the LORD.

As the new generation prepares to enter the Promised Land, Moses invites them to look backward at the experience of the previous generation. This was marked by disobedience that resulted from not knowing the LORD amid their testing. The specific arena for testing that is mentioned was the lack of sustenance. As is well known, the LORD provided water and manna to the Israelites, but he provided it only once they were thirsty and hungry (Exod 15–16). Further, the food was one with which they were not familiar. The LORD did not provide them an abundance of food; he provided only what was necessary for each day. The goal of the specific test was that, in their hunger, the people would "know that one does not live by bread alone, but by everything that comes from the mouth of the LORD" (v. 3).[9] Would the people trust the LORD when he said that he would bring them to the land of promise? The present generation is challenged by Moses to remember the LORD. Knowing the LORD, fearing the LORD, and obeying the LORD—these are the ingredients for success in the land.[10]

Moses' appeal to the new generation gains additional significance as Moses contrasts the land of scarcity with the land of plenty to which they are going (8:7–10). Though the new generation has previously been invited to see the theological collapse of time and identity in the one people of Israel, their experience will be different than that of the previous generation. Whereas the older generation had little bread, the new one will experience abundance of bread. Water and natural resources will also be copious. In many ways, then, their experience will be different—so different indeed, that they may be inclined to think that they have moved beyond the time of testing.

In verses 11–20, however, Moses casts the new generation's imminent success as both a blessing and an additional test.[11] He says in verse 11, "Watch yourself, lest you forget the LORD your God by not keeping his commandments, his judgments, and his statutes that I am commanding to you today." Here again the word "today" occurs. As discussed above, in Deuteronomy 5:1, "today" is associated with hearing and doing the word of the LORD that was spoken from Sinai. I argued above that Moses collapsed the theological distinction between the people in Moab and the people at Sinai. Further, I suggested that the word "today" is the ever-present theological moment of decision for the audience: will they respond *now* to the word of the LORD? Now, in Deuteronomy 8:11, Moses extends the implications of that theological collapse into the yet-to-be-determined future. The command of the LORD is not only spoken today, but it will continue to be spoken once the people have possessed the land. When they live with plenty, will they still heed the commands of the LORD?[12]

Indeed, Moses speaks of the future as if it is a certain present: "*when* you have eaten your fill..." Again, he collapses time, but here it is the future that collapses into the present. The threat that will arise in the land is the threat of self-sufficiency: "...then do not exalt yourself, forgetting the LORD your God..." (v. 14). In times of plenty, the people might forget that it is the LORD is the source of blessing.[13] The same LORD who provided basic sustenance in the wilderness is the source of exuberance in the Promised Land.[14] In both cases, the people will be tested to see whether they will rely on the LORD as the source.

Moses continues to sculpt the identity of the people of God in Deuteronomy 8. He looks backward and forward to pose the life of the people as one marked by ongoing tests. The type of test might vary—previously, it was in scarcity; in the future, it will be in plenty—but the presence of testing remains. The testing has as its aim the revelation of the people's level of trust in God and the greater formation of that trust. Trust reveals itself in remembering and obeying the word of the LORD. Each moment, "today," is an opportunity to choose trust and obedience. Moses challenges the new generation to remember what God has done in order to know who God is. Their success in the land of plenty hinges on their ability to properly remember their dependence on God, their source of provision.

Deuteronomy 30

Much later in Deuteronomy, Moses looks even further ahead: he considers a time after the people have lived in the land, namely, the time of exile. In verses 1–5, he speaks of a time at which the blessings and curses he has outlined in previous chapters have come upon the people. Considering what has been seen so far in Deuteronomy 5 and 8, readers can imagine that the scenario that Moses considers must follow after the people have disobeyed and forgotten the LORD. This note tampers the hopefulness readers might have had when they read Deuteronomy 8. However, the words spoken here are still words of hope: even when the people find themselves in a strange land as foreigners, still there the LORD can gather them and establish them again in their land.

Moses indicates what must happen for the people to be restored: they must "cause [the words of the instruction] to return to your heart," "return to the LORD your God," and "obey his voice according to all that I am commanding you today" (vv. 1–3). In other words, the key to living again in God's favor is again to remember, obey, and trust the same word of the LORD spoken by Moses. They must embrace the collapse of time and identity, seeing themselves as the same Israel that stood at Sinai and Moab, hearing the one word of the LORD that has been proclaimed, and responding appropriately "today."

The next section (vv. 6–10) speaks of the opulence that God will bring upon the people if they do return to him. The LORD will work against the enemies of Israel (v. 7); the people will experience fruitful children, livestock, and vegetation (v. 9); the LORD will delight in prospering them as he delighted before. The action of returning to the LORD is explored in more depth here, too. In verse 6, Moses says that the LORD will "circumcise your heart...so that you will love the LORD your God with all your heart and with all your soul, so that you will live." Scholars debate the details and implications of the circumcision mentioned. Woods identifies three modern approaches. One approach sees the LORD's circumcision as a precondition for Israel's appropriate response. A second approach regards Israel's repentance and obedience as a precondition for the LORD's acts. A third approach, a middle way, identifies the balance between Israel's repentance and the LORD's grace.[15] Though the discussion is important and merits further investigation, the third option seems to hold up the dynamics that have been central in the rest of the chapter: the LORD will continue to extend grace to the people even in exile, but the people must respond appropriately.

The language of this section echoes Deuteronomy 6. The exhortation to love the LORD "with all your heart and with all your soul," which occurs in 30:6 and 30:10, echoes Deuteronomy 6:5. In both chapters, it is intricately connected to "keeping his commandments" (30:8, 10; cf. 6:5–9). Both chapters offer thorough, nuanced portrayals of life with God. Turning to God, loving God with one's whole being, and obeying God are parts of one, indivisible response to God's goodness. That is, the people must commit themselves fully to the LORD. They do this by putting the LORD and his command always before them and obeying him. The same manner of living faithfully before God is put before the people toward the beginning and the end of Moses' words to the people.

What significance might this connection between Deuteronomy 6 and 30 have? First, it reveals that the will of God and the word of God remain steady across time. When Israel finds itself wandering in the wilderness, the LORD desires that they would love him with their whole being and keep his command. When Israel finds itself living prosperously in the land, the LORD desires that they would love him with their whole being and keep his command. When Israel finds itself exiled for its unfaithfulness, the LORD desires that they would love him with their whole being and keep his command. The collapse of time and identity in the one people of Israel puts before them a singular vocation: love the LORD with their whole being and keep his command. This is something the older and newer generations today can keep in mind.

Second, together, these bookend chapters provide a sort of "hermeneutical key" for Moses' speech to the people that comes between them. Much of the book of Deuteronomy is a retelling of the content from Exodus through Numbers—specifically, the instruction on life before God and with one another. This content is notoriously complex. Apart from what to make of any particular instruction, Deuteronomy 6 and 30 speak to the collection as a whole. Here, they show that the specific instructions intend overall to form wise people. The people would be mistaken if they were to treat the specific instructions as an exhaustive, objective code. The instructions are always set within a relational context. Further, within the context of wilderness testing, they represent opportunities for the Israelites to demonstrate their willingness to listen to the voice of the LORD. In other words, rote obedience to a preexisting set of laws was never the goal. Rather, the instruction given is a means of forming trust in the LORD and wisdom in how to live that out—in the present and in the future. For the new generation that is entering into the land, relying on the instruction of Moses is not enough to ensure faithfulness. They must continually demonstrate, in their obedience to that instruction, that they trust in the voice that spoke the words. This is also relevant to the Spirit-empowered movement of today.

In the rest of the chapter, Moses speaks more generally about obedience to divine instruction. In verses 11–14, he speaks to the possibility of obeying the instruction. He begins by saying that the command is not too wonderful or far off for the people (v. 11). It is not up in heaven (v. 12) or across the sea (v. 13), so that someone must go retrieve it. Rather, "It is very near to you; it is on your mouth and in your heart for you to keep" (v. 14). Moses' words here avert any excuse that the people might devise about the impossibility of obedience. Thus, the LORD has done all that is necessary to ensure success; the LORD thinks that it is possible that they can obey and expects them to do it. Any failure rests solely on their decision not to trust the LORD.

Having established that the people have a genuine decision to make and can choose appropriately, the final section (vv. 15–20) characterizes the choice that is before the people. Moses identifies two options: (a) life and good, (b) death and evil (v. 15). Though in the detail of the instructions the people may wish to characterize their life before God in more complicated ways, Moses here indicates that the matter is relatively black-and-white. Every decision they make is either leading them on the path of life or on the path of death. He then explicates the details of each path. The path of life is "loving the LORD your God, walking in his ways, and observing his commandments, his statutes, and his judgments" (v. 16). The way of death is turning their hearts away from following the LORD, not hearing the LORD, and bowing down to other gods (v. 17). In other words, the people will serve and be led by a god; they must choose whether the LORD will be the one whom they serve. Choosing to serve the LORD leads to long life; choosing to serve other gods leads to quick death (vv. 18–20).

Verses 11–20 appear to follow the logic of Genesis 2–3. In both accounts, a few key factors are clear: God communicates clearly what his expectations are; God expects that the people can and should listen, for their own sake; the choice before them is between life and death. Deuteronomy 30:11–20 thus seems to attach itself to a broader canvas that extends across the Bible. One important question that has guided much of the Pentateuch up to this point has been: God speaks; will people listen? The pattern has involved primary characters such as Adam and Eve, Noah, Abram/Abraham, Moses. It has been implicit with other characters—Hagar, Joseph, the midwives in Egypt. Some have responded positively; others, negatively; still others, in a mixed fashion. With each subsequent encounter, readers are invited to ask again: will God's people obey? Therefore, with this part of his speech, Moses grafts the people of Israel into this longstanding theological pattern.

As a whole, then, Deuteronomy 30 works to expand the horizon of the theological framework that has been sketched in the book up to this point. First, it looks way ahead—to a time beyond the wilderness, beyond entrance into the Promised Land, into exile—and shows the new generation that even then, they can still be the one people of God to whom God addresses the same word that he addressed to the people at Sinai. They face the same crisis moment: will they listen to the LORD, trust in the LORD, and obey the LORD? Second, though more subtly, it looks into the distant past, even perhaps back to the Garden of Eden, and shows that the people have always faced the same theological challenge: having heard the LORD, will they obey? Will they choose life? "Today" extends far off into the future, as well as back to the beginning, when the LORD first spoke to humans in the garden.

Summary and Implications

This study has investigated the theological agenda of Deuteronomy concerning the identity of the people of Israel and the "today" of which Moses speaks. I have argued that Moses, in his ongoing speech to Israel, works carefully to conjoin these two aspects theologically. Though the new generation is separated chronologically and geographically from the old generation, Moses bridges those gaps with the theological unity of the one people of Israel. It is the one people of God to whom the address of God comes. Thus, the people must decide to embrace their identity as the people of God. The use of "today" by Moses speaks not of a chronological moment, but a theological one—the moment of hearing and responding to the word of the LORD. Those who embrace their belonging to the one people of God must then determine to hear and to obey what God says in response.

Deuteronomy 5 laid the groundwork for this agenda. There, Moses articulated the connection of the current generation to the Sinai covenant. Further, he spoke of that moment at Sinai as well as the current moment at Moab as "today," thus collapsing those two moments theologically. The word of the LORD has been spoken; he has provided instruction. The word spoken and the obedience demanded remain consistent across time and space.

Deuteronomy 8 explored the dynamic of testing that marks life as the people of God. The ongoing insistence in Deuteronomy on the need for the people of God to respond today in obedience is fundamentally concerned with demonstrating current trust in the LORD as well as fostering future trust. In Deuteronomy 8, obedience is the outward display of the inner disposition of the fear of the LORD. This was true in the wilderness, but it will also be true for the people who come into the abundant land of promise.

Deuteronomy 30 took a wider angle, looking far ahead to a future exile as well as back to the past, even perhaps to the Garden of Eden. The force of this broad scope is to show that the same challenge has always been put before the one people of God: having heard the LORD speak, would they listen? Deuteronomy 30 somberly anticipates that the people will not live faithfully and will therefore experience exile. But at the same time, it looks hopefully forward: even in exile, if the people will determine to remember their identity as the one people of God and will obey the LORD today, then the LORD will bless them richly.

Readers of Deuteronomy know that the end of the book is not the end of the narrative. Thus, they might wonder how the agenda sketched above will play itself out, going forward. As Deuteronomy itself already anticipated, the people do go into exile. The narrative opened in the Pentateuch extends naturally to 2 Kings, which ends with the Babylonian captivity. Thus, the warning and hope built into Deuteronomy 30 become a relevant word. Subsequent books—Joshua, Judges, Samuel, Kings—provide readers with the concrete realization of the many of the words spoken in the chapters from Deuteronomy discussed above. The people come into the land, and the LORD is with them. When they trust in the LORD, they overcome; when they trust in themselves, they fail. When they experience prosperity, they regularly forget the LORD. The LORD then turns them over to their enemies, from where they cry out to the LORD. The LORD then delivers them and blesses them once again.

Along the way, certain individuals emerge as representatives of the sort of trust and obedience that the LORD seeks: Joshua, Deborah, Samuel, David, Hezekiah, Josiah—these figures stand out for their humble trust in the LORD as ones who are capable and willing to deliver them. Especially intriguing is the presence of certain figures, such as Rahab (Joshua 2), who stand outside the people of Israel, yet demonstrate a deeper awareness of the LORD than many inside do. Overall, though, the people of Israel do not fare well. The narrative ends with the fall of God's people and a fickle hope. However, as Deuteronomy 30 already indicated, impossibly hopeless future situations are not utterly hopeless with God. Readers who come to the end of 2 Kings might read the whole narrative up to that point as an indictment of their failure so far and as an exhortation to trust now in the LORD: perhaps he will restore them yet.

The way forward for each subsequent generation will be marked by a similar pattern. They must first look backward, learning from the past. They must embrace their identity as the one people of God across time and space. They must know the LORD, trust the LORD, and obey the LORD. They must do that now, "today." If they do, then things will go well for them. They will find themselves walking on the path that leads to life and prosperity.

As the Spirit-empowered movement continues to grow unabated, it finds itself perhaps in periods of change from one generation to the next. As the newer generation prepares to lead the movement into the future, it might find the book of Deuteronomy to be a formidable resource for reflecting on the way forward. A few observations suggest themselves. First, the way forward will include looking backward. This is so because it is the Spirit of God that has enlivened the movement up to this point, and the same Spirit must be the foundation of any further work. In order to grasp what the Spirit is now doing, the new generation must become acquainted with what the Spirit has been doing. Continuity is a characteristic of the Spirit's work. Second, the way forward will be centered on humble obedience to God's voice. At the heart of the Spirit-empowered movement is the desire to hear and obey the voice of God. Being attuned thus to the voice of God will ensure faithfulness. It will also be the way in which the new generation bears witness in their mission to the world around them. Third, the way forward will be marked by continuous renewal and reformation. Spirit-empowered Christians must exist paradoxically in the wilderness, awaiting the fullness of God's presence, as well as in the Promised Land, enjoying the peace of God granted so far. Each day—*today*—must become a moment of trust in God and obedience to his voice.

Notes

1 All translations are the author's, unless otherwise noted.

2 Richard D. Nelson, *Deuteronomy: A Commentary*, Old Testament Library (Louisville, KY: Westminster John Knox, 2004), 79.

3 Edward J. Woods, *Deuteronomy*, Tyndale Old Testament Commentaries (Nottingham, U.K.: InterVarsity Press, 2011), 120.

4 Moshe Weinfeld, *Deuteronomy 1–11: A New Translation with Introduction and Commentary* (New York: Doubleday, 1991), 238. Weinfeld offers a helpful perspective on Moses' language regarding the previous generation: what is said in vv. 2–3 is not meant to imply that God did not enter into a covenant relationship with that generation, but rather that his real intention was to conclude the covenant with the new generation, 239.

5 Weinfeld, *Deuteronomy 1–11*, 238.

6 Peter C. Craigie, *The Book of Deuteronomy*, New International Commentary on the Old Testament (Grand Rapids: Eerdmans, 1976), 161.

7 Woods, *Deuteronomy*, 150.

8 According to J. G. McConville, *Deuteronomy*, Apollos Old Testament Commentary (Downers Grove: InterVarsity Press, 2002), 169, "While Deuteronomy has in common with Exodus a concern with obedience to Yahweh's commands, it looks for a faithfulness that goes deeper than obedience in particular instances, or mere acquiescence in written documents... The faithfulness required by Yahweh is expressed in trust."

9 Woods, *Deuteronomy*, 153, calls attention to the emphasis in v. 3 of "the greater need to obey every life-giving word that comes from the mouth of God, of which the provision of manna in the wilderness may be seen as an encouraging beginning towards this end..." (emphasis original). McConville, *Deuteronomy*, 170, observes that the command speaks to humanity generally, not to Israel specifically. "Here Israel's experience is explicitly made a paradigm of human experience in general..."

10 As Nelson, *Deuteronomy*, 389, says, "Manna provided the central lesson: the 'necessities of life' are of only relative importance when compared to Yahweh's decrees." Weinfeld, *Deuteronomy*, 108, adds "God is able to guarantee the existence of man even when nature does not.... By causing deprivation and lack of food, God tests man to see whether he really puts his trust in him."

11 Nelson, *Deuteronomy*, 111, says of testing: "[It is] to bring someone into a critical situation in order to observe reaction and behavior. Testing provokes a decision that proves character and faith."

12 Woods, *Deuteronomy*, 155.

13 Nelson, *Deuteronomy*, 108, expresses the matter well: "The wilderness was a training ground and a paradigm of life with God. The land, by the very fact of its richness, is potentially a place of spiritual danger."

14 Nelson, *Deuteronomy*, 111.

15 Woods, *Deuteronomy*, 290–291.

3 Global Youth Culture: Exploring Trends and Imagining the Church's Response

Barry L. Saylor and Patricia Savage

Abstract

In the spring of 2020, OneHope, a global mission agency focused on reaching youth and children around the world, embarked on a research project examining the world's teenagers. At the time, all teens were among the nearly two billion young people commonly called Generation Z, a population that comprises approximately one-fourth of the world's population. These young people have a unique and diverse viewpoint as a result of their life experiences and the world they are growing up in. This research project reveals the habits, struggles, beliefs and influences of this global generation. The data also reveals their views of God, Jesus, the Bible, and the Christian church. At the time, OneHope's study was the most comprehensive of its kind in terms of taking a deep look at the faith of this generation globally, and it continues to influence many leading youth and children's ministry initiatives around the world.

Introduction

In Mark Noll's book, *The New Shape of World Christianity,* he describes a "Christian Rip Van Winkle" who wakes up in the twenty-first century after sleeping through the latter half of the twentieth. Noll describes what this fictional character might experience:

> As Rip Van Winkle wiped a half-century of sleep from his eyes and tried to locate his fellow Christian believers, he would find them in surprising places, expressing their faith in surprising ways, under surprising conditions, with surprising relationships to culture and politics, and raising surprising theological questions that would not have seemed possible when he fell asleep.[1]

Noll goes on to describe these differences, concluding that "the Christian church has experienced a larger geographical redistribution in the last fifty years than in any comparable period in its history, with the exception of the very earliest years of church history."[2] He argues that, while the average Christian of fifty years ago was a European male, today's would be a Latin American or African female.[3]

There has therefore been a concerted effort to shift the focus of ecclesial research toward the Global South, as the increasingly secular[4] West begins to recognize what it has to gain from the lessons of its southern neighbors. However, research into youth culture has lagged in ecclesial curiosity in comparison to that of the broader church. Rode Molla, an Ethiopian youth minister who came to the United States to study youth ministry, expressed this reality in his context when he identified his experience as "an Ethiopian ministry grounded in Western Evangelical sensibilities."[5] Molla's concern can be validated, as up to this point a predominance of research into youth culture has centered almost exclusively on American and European populations, even while most young people now live in the Global South.[6]

Molla describes this problem in relation to a common Western perspective on youth culture: "[the shallow, instrumental theology of] Moralistic therapeutic deism, which seems a pivotal concept for understanding the spiritual lives of youth in the U.S., makes little sense in an enchanted world where the gods are actively involved in the daily undertakings that make up a life. The idea of a youth group mimicking and competing with culture by creating a safe social club is impossible [in Ethiopia]."[7] It is imperative that the primarily Western perspective from which youth culture has traditionally been explored be expanded as the church considers its impact on the next global generation.

OneHope's Study: Background

It was in response to this research gap that OneHope's Global Youth Culture (GYC) study was born. OneHope's first venture into studying youth culture was represented in its Attitudes and Behaviors of Youth (ABY) study from 2007–2011.[8] Our ABY study sought to understand the spiritual state of youth and included data from more than 152,000 teenagers in 44 countries. The GYC study followed in the steps of ABY, transitioning from researching Millennials to the more recent generation of global young people, Generation Z (now referred to as Gen Z).[9]

In contrast to the predominantly Western perspective represented in most youth culture research, OneHope has sought to understand youth culture globally, both in global trends and in how it might differ across regions of the world. This was first evident in the ABY study and continues

Global Youth Culture 43

in GYC, a global study of digitally connected young people and their attitudes, behaviors, and beliefs.[10] For this study, OneHope identified the following research objectives:

- To provide actionable information on the state of Gen Z to the church.
- To provide advocacy pieces that can be used both by OneHope and its partners.
- To amplify the voice of Gen Z within the church community.
- To discover the extent to which there are homogenous values or beliefs across regions among this age group.
- To inform cultural topics in products and programs, ancillary resources, and strategy discussions.

The ensuing study surveyed 8,394 teens aged 13–19, across twenty countries, from various religious persuasions, who have regular access to the internet. Note that the results are not meant to reflect the viewpoint of all teens, but specifically those who are digitally connected. Data was collected between February 24 and March 27, 2020, before the effects of the coronavirus global pandemic were felt in a widespread way. As a result, this research reflects teens' beliefs and behaviors before national lockdowns and quarantine orders went into effect.

The data from this study reveals the habits, struggles, beliefs and influences of this global generation. The data also reveals their views of God, Jesus, the Bible, and the Christian church. The data points we collected from thousands of teens worldwide create a picture of this generation that includes some surprising discoveries and untold stories.

Religious Attitudes and Behaviors

A few key points stood out in the global sample. First, over half of teens globally say they never read their religion's scriptures on their own. This does not mean that teenagers do not see value in religion though, because the same percentage (52%) believe all religions teach equally valid truths. Christians are just as likely as non-Christians to say this. Muslim young people are the most disciplined of any religion when it comes to religious service attendance, scripture engagement, and prayer. Overall, two in three teens say their faith, beliefs, or spiritual journey are an important part of their identity. And teens who do not go to church largely report that they are open to attending if invited. Also, most say the Christians they know are kind and caring.

Globally, approximately two in five teens identified themselves as Christian, one in four as another religion, and one in three as atheist, agnostic, or having no religion. Of all the regions we studied, Africa had the highest percentage of Christians, while Asia had the lowest. In addition, there were some points that stood out among the 43 percent of teenagers in the study who self-identified as Christian. It is notable that 40 percent of these young people said they never read the Bible at all, and that only 7 percent display the beliefs and habits of a "Committed Christian."[11]

The Committed Few

Some of the most interesting faith-related findings surfaced when we narrowed our focus to Christian teens who are committed to traditional Christian beliefs and practices. We learned that what it means to call yourself a Christian can differ greatly depending on the person, their surroundings, and their cultural context. For purposes of this research, OneHope created a definition of the beliefs and behaviors that would indicate a respondent is a Committed Christian. The six traits of Committed Christian teens, as identified in our survey, are as follows:

- Belief that God exists and a person can have a personal relationship with him.
- Belief that Jesus is the Son of God.
- Belief that forgiveness of sins is only possible through faith in Jesus Christ.
- Belief that the Bible is the Word of God.
- Pray at least weekly.
- Read scripture on their own at least weekly.

Globally, approximately one in fourteen young people meet this definition of Committed Christians.[12] While 43 percent of our sample align themselves with Christianity as a religion, just 7 percent display the beliefs and behaviors that indicate they are committed to their Christian walk. Older teens are more likely to be Committed Christians than younger teens. But numbers are low for every age group. The remaining third (36%) of Christians who did not meet the definition for Committed are called "Nominal Christians" in this study. The research revealed a significant difference between the numbers of Nominal Christians and Committed Christians in every region across the world:

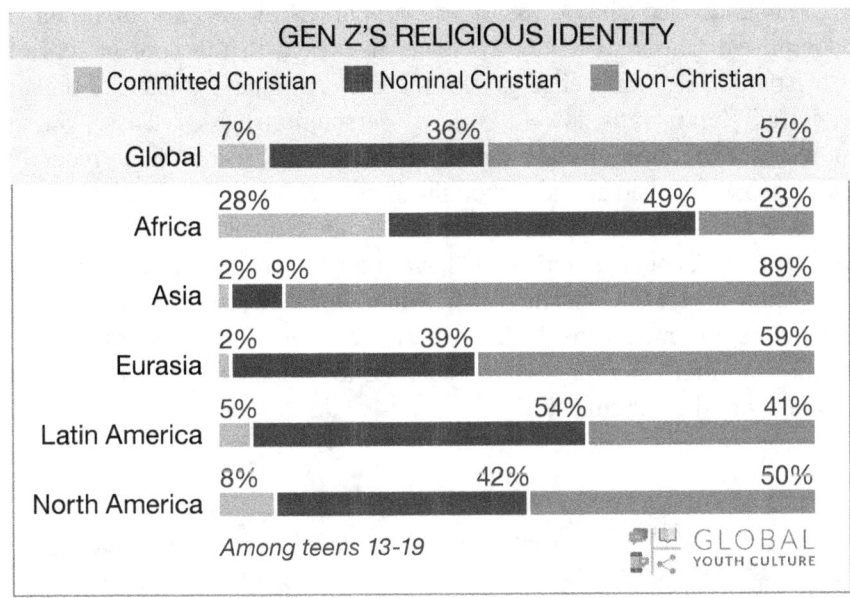

Figure 1: OneHope's Study on Nominal versus Committed Christians in Gen Z, by Global Region

Each region has interesting differences. Africa was the most Christian region in the study, and correspondingly had the highest percentage of Committed Christian young people. Asia demonstrated the lowest numbers of identifying Christians overall, while Eurasia tied for the lowest percentage of Committed Christians. Latin America showed the biggest gap between Committed and Nominal Christians. North America also reported a wide gap between Committed and Nominal numbers consistent with overall global totals.

The Benefits of Being Committed

Committed Christian young people display markedly different religious behaviors and convictions than other Christian teens. Committed Christians are more than three times as likely to attend church at least weekly, compared to Nominal Christians. They strongly believe they have a responsibility to share their faith with others and put that conviction into action by evangelizing. Committed Christians are nearly twice as likely as Nominal Christians to be engaging in spiritual conversations with non-believers.

The data also shows that there are practical benefits to being a Committed Christian. Globally, teens who hold to the core beliefs of Christianity, regularly engage with the Bible, and have a habit of prayer reported significantly lower levels of personal struggles. These young people are much less likely than other teens to say they have recently been depressed, had suicidal thoughts, or made a suicide attempt within the past three months. They are also less likely to report they are confused about their gender identity or have recently experienced same-sex attraction. Overall, Committed Christians reported lower rates of at-risk behaviors and mental health issues on nearly every item we measured, while Nominal Christians were observed to be very close to the global average of all teens surveyed.

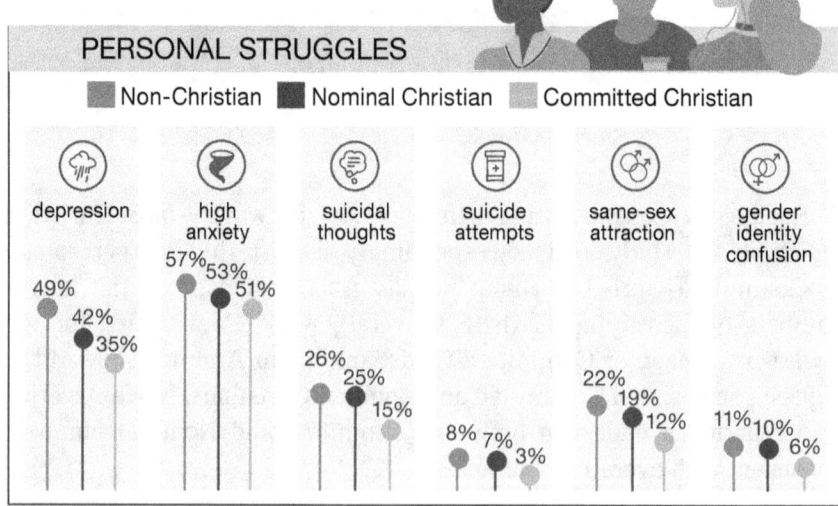

Figure 2: OneHope's Study on Personal Struggles, According to Self-Reports of Christian Commitment

Spirituality as an Identity

Teens across the globe are surprisingly open to the concept of being spiritual, regardless of their religious affiliation. Two in three teens globally say their faith beliefs or spiritual journey are an important part of their identity. Notably, nearly half (44%) of teens of no religion still say this. The data also revealed that teens have a positive perception of Christian believers in their lives: 71 percent of non-Christian teens said most Christians they know are kind and caring. However, in some Asian countries, a significant number of teens said they do not know any Christians at all.

When Everything is Truth

Today's teens are unwilling to say that truth can be found in only one religion. Over half of teens globally (52%) believe all religions teach equally valid truths. Among Christian teens, the rate of agreement is 53 percent. Teens of some religions such as Islam, Buddhism, and Hinduism are even more likely to believe this.

Perhaps this is a result of Gen Z's spiritually open attitude, as this mindset appears to be shared by young people across religions and regions. In fact, if faith is an important part of their identity, teens are much more likely—not less—to take this position (67%). This points towards an interesting paradox of today's generation: young people assert that a spiritual journey is an important part of their identity without an exclusive view of where truth can be found. Even Christian teens appear to be influenced by this thinking. A significant minority (30%) disagree with the statement that forgiveness of sins is only possible through faith in Jesus Christ.

Spiritual beliefs are seen as largely personal and not communal. Nearly half (46%) of teens say they never talk about religious or spiritual things with others who do not share their beliefs. Around 30 percent say they have these types of spiritual conversations monthly or more often, and Christian teens are not evangelizing much more than the average.

Implications

It is important to remember that this portrait of teens' religious attitudes and behaviors is just a snapshot. These habits are far from fixed in the lives of young people and may differ significantly as they age. Still for the moment, this research gives us valuable insight into teens and points toward some practical applications.

First, we must find ways to capitalize on this generation's spiritual openness. This generation displays an open-mindedness to the idea of being spiritual, and many non-believers say they are willing to visit a church. In addition, they already have a positive perception of Christians as kind and caring. Conversations that begin with the shared premise that humans are intended to be spiritual may open doors to a deeper exploration of faith.

Second, we must clarify that following Christ is both an identity and a discipline. Teens who hold to the core beliefs of Christianity and pair those with a habit of scripture engagement and prayer see many positive differences compared to the lived realities of Nominal Christians or other teens. Discipleship of this generation that focuses on these core beliefs and practices may bring many parts of their lives into order.

Third, we must communicate that some truths are meant to be exclusive. Christian teens in this study seem unwilling to commit to a singular view of truth or embrace a responsibility to share that truth with others. This prioritizes the spiritual journey over the goal of finding truth worthy to implement.

Personal Experiences and Struggles

This study revealed that a significant number of Gen Z teens are struggling with their mental health, reporting high anxiety, loneliness, depression, and suicidal ideation and attempts. One in four teens globally report having had suicidal thoughts within the last three months, and one in fourteen say they attempted to take their own life within the past three months. Girls are struggling more than boys when it comes to their mental health, and they are almost twice as likely to say they attempted suicide.

Sexuality also continues to be an issue of concern for teenagers. Three in ten teens globally report having been sexually active in the past three months, a rate even higher among Christians (33%). One in five teens reported feeling sexually attracted to someone of the same gender within the past three months.

Mental Health

Adolescence is a time of life that can be filled with difficulties on multiple levels. A lot is going on for young people, and teens in this study were upfront in telling us that they are dealing with some serious personal struggles. Nearly two out of three teens reported feelings of loneliness, more than half reported high anxiety, and nearly half reported depression.[13] Keep in mind that data for this study was collected pre-pandemic.

We also asked teens to self-report if they had, within the last three months, experienced suicidal thoughts or made a suicide attempt. One in four teens globally reported suicidal thoughts, with four nations reporting rates of one in three or greater. Suicidal ideation took a range of forms, from casual, largely isolated thoughts all the way to detailed, involved planning. Of course, not all suicidal ideation leads to actual attempts. However, 7 percent of teens (one in fourteen) globally did report an attempt within the past three months, with four nations reporting rates greater than one in ten.[14]

Correlating Factors

Research literature on this topic points to several factors that can correlate with a young person's risk for suicide, including LGBTQ+ issues, substance abuse, bullying, and symptoms of anxiety or depression.[15] Our research revealed similar connections. Teens struggling with gender identity or same-sex attraction have a much higher suicide risk, along with teens who report being victims of online bullying and those dealing with mental health issues. Alcohol and recreational drug usage were also observed to accompany higher rates of suicidal ideation and attempts.

Girls Struggle More

Teen girls are struggling much more than teen boys when it comes to their mental health outlook. This is true regarding loneliness, high anxiety, depression, suicidal thoughts, suicide attempts, same-sex attraction, and gender identity confusion. It is notable that being a Committed Christian does not change the story between girls and boys. Personal struggle rates were observed to be lower overall among Committed Christians, but the significant gender gap remained on each of the mental health items.

Teens and Sexuality

Globally, three in ten teens report being sexually active within the past three months. This may represent a broad spectrum of potential behaviors, but in responding to this question, teens defined for themselves what it meant to be sexually active. Any teens who reported being married were excluded to ensure this statistic represented only sex outside the context of marriage. African teens were the most likely to report extramarital sexual activity, and teens in Asia the least likely.

Notably, engaging in sexual activity appeared to be divorced from moral beliefs on the subject. Christians were more likely, on average, to report recent sexual activity than teens of other religions. Additionally, though they affirmed the biblical stance that sex should be reserved for marriage, Committed Christian teens were just as likely to be engaged in sexual activity as Nominal Christians.

Pornography is a Real Problem

Nearly half (48%) of teens admitted to looking at pornography. Boys were much more likely than girls to have looked at pornographic material within the last three months (56% vs. 40%). There is also a trend in the data by age, with older teens using pornography more than younger teens. But being young does not guarantee you are sheltered from this. Among 13 to 15-year-olds, 40 percent said they had viewed pornography recently.

Implications

The struggles Gen Z reports are deeply concerning. Every young person's situation is different, and there is no one answer to their challenges. Yet, the Spirit-empowered community and older generations must be aware of the nature and seriousness of the lived realities teens say they are experiencing. A few considerations became clear in our study, which may help move the church from empathy to action.

First, Christian teens need discipleship in the area of sexuality. Many of today's young people are separating sex from the sacred context of marriage and treating it merely as an act for individual pleasure. Committed Christians demonstrate an understanding that premarital sex is wrong, but their moral convictions are not keeping them from engaging in sexual activity. It is not enough to teach teens what the Bible says. The church must find a way to guide young people to a more biblical lifestyle that values and stewards the gift of sexuality.

Relatedly, pornography usage is a significant issue for this generation. The data shows that we cannot assume that age or religion protects a teen from viewing pornography. Even teens who hold Christian beliefs and engage in Christian disciplines struggle in this area.

Finally, girls may need additional support. The differences in personal struggle rates by gender are undeniable, and the high mental illness rates among girls cannot be ignored. Being a Committed Christian helps overall but does not close the gender gap. Spirit-empowered communities would do well to consider the unique struggles girls may be facing and how to encourage mature women of faith to disciple this next generation.

Gender Identity and Relationships

Around half of teens globally hold to a traditional view of gender, saying that it is primarily based on the sex a person is born with. But the other half of today's teens believe gender is a choice—something that can be self-determined according to personal feelings or a person's sexual attractions. Therefore, a large number of Gen Z believe gender is not an objective reality but a subjective one.

This generation's opinions about gender vary widely based on their global region. In Latin America, for example, GYC found that the number of teens who see gender as self-selected is close to twice that of teens who believe gender is assigned at birth. By contrast, most teens in Africa do not see gender as a choice. Our research found that nearly three out of four teens in African countries believe that gender is primarily based on a person's sex at birth.

Gender Identity and Change

While many teens agree with the concept that gender issues are subjective, our research showed that far fewer teens reported personally experiencing gender identity confusion or having a desire to change their gender. We found 10 percent of teens globally said they had experienced gender identity confusion within the past three months, and 15 percent expressed an affinity to be a different gender. Girls were slightly more likely than boys to say they were struggling with their gender identity (12% vs. 9%) and communicated a different perspective than boys on the topic overall. The majority of girls (59%) reported believing that gender is primarily based on a person's feelings or desires, compared with 42 percent of boys who said the same. Girls were much more likely than boys to say it is ok for someone to change their body to become a different gender (52% vs. 32%).

The Influence of Religion

A teen's religion was found to have a visible impact on their opinions about gender identity. Of all religions, Muslims adhere most strongly to the traditional view of gender: 62 percent of Muslim teens say gender is based on sex at birth, followed by 50 percent of Christians, and 41 percent of teens of other religions. Teens who say they have no religion lead the way in believing gender is self-determined based on how a person feels or their sexual attractions.

However, the viewpoint is much different among Committed Christian teens who hold to the core beliefs of their faith as well as say they have a habit of Bible reading and prayer. Seven in ten Committed Christian teens hold to a traditional view of gender, and only 10 percent believe that altering your body to change genders is acceptable.

Same-Sex Attraction

A significant proportion of Gen Z shares that same-sex attraction is something they have experienced. One in five teens globally report having felt sexually attracted to someone of the same gender within the past three months. Nominal Christians were more likely than Committed Christians to report this. In examining this topic alongside other variables in our study, several interesting connections were revealed. For example, girls were twice as likely to feel same-sex attracted than boys (28% vs. 13%). A young person's experience in their home also seems to play a role. Teens who said they had a poor family experience were more likely to report experiencing same-sex attraction than if they had a good family experience (30% vs. 18%). Religion likewise appears to be a mitigating factor. Teens who identify with any kind of religion are less likely to be same-sex attracted as compared to teens who report they have no religion (18% vs. 25%). Same-sex attraction is also much lower among Committed Christians (12%).

Finally, same-sex attraction appears to cluster with other behaviors. Of teens who reported a recent suicide attempt, nearly half (46%) also reported same-sex attraction. Teens are twice as likely to report same-sex attraction when other factors are present in their lives, such as recreational drug usage, depression, anxiety, or pornography. This data shows that same-sex attraction is not an isolated behavior, but that some teens are struggling deeply in multiple areas of their lives.

Implications

While these findings have many implications, young people are looking for help as they navigate the twenty-first century world of identity and relationships. A few practical responses for the church to consider include, first, that young people need to see the church as a place of belonging in the midst of their struggles. Churches in the twenty-first century are challenged to be places where young people can come with their questions and struggles, and find love alongside sound teaching and discipleship. Second, churches must become places where conversations about identity and relationships are natural. As the church recognizes the hunger for these resources, it is imperative that it steps forward with biblical answers and perspective. Lastly, church leaders must continue educating themselves to speak about these complex topics. They must be resourced with understanding from a Christian worldview, while communicating truth with empathy.

Influences and Guiding Voices

Teens have opinions on many things, but these viewpoints are rarely formed in isolation. We were curious about this generation's biggest influences and who they trust for guidance and advice regarding some of life's most important questions.

Teens Trust Family

Teens report turning to family for guidance on some of life's most important topics. Family members are the top influence when it comes to questions about the meaning of life (41%) or what is right and wrong (50%). Friends, peers, and social media round out teens' top influences, with teachers or counselors, religious leaders or texts, and offline media appearing much lower on their list.

When it comes to morality, Latin American teens lean more strongly on family than teens in any other region of the world. Three in five teens in Latin America say family is their go-to for information or guidance on what is right and wrong. However, family remained the most important guiding voice for morality and meaning in life, even in countries where young people report negative family experiences. For example, the U.S. was the lowest-ranking country in terms of teens' family satisfaction. However, U.S. teens are higher than average in saying they go to family most often for information or guidance about what is right and wrong (52%) or the meaning of life (42%). It would appear that despite negative experiences, parents and family members continue to be trusted influences in teens' lives.

A Different Conversation

Teens' reliance upon family was not reflected, however, in the topics of gender, sexuality, and sexual issues. This conversation looks very different with teens reporting the internet as the guiding voice here, with more than one-third of teens saying they turn to social media most often for input on these topics. Friends or peers claim the second most influential spot (23%), with family members rounding out the top three (20%). Notably, religious leaders or scriptures fall to the very bottom of this list (4%).

Even among Christian teens, online sources or social media displace family as the top influence on gender and sexuality. When it comes to these topics, the voice of culture appears to be drowning out other voices, such as family, scriptures, or the church. However, we do see significant differences among Committed Christians who hold to the core beliefs of Christianity and have a habit of Bible reading and prayer. Committed Christian teens are around four times more likely than Nominal Christians to say they go most often to religious leaders or texts for guidance on sexually related topics.

Implications

Committed young people are more open to conversations on gender and sexuality, but follow-up reveals few churches have much to say on the topics other than what not to do. The church needs a robust theology of human flourishing that captures these conversations and brings them into the light of scripture in winsome ways.

Conclusion

The purpose of this study has been to present a global perspective on youth culture and open the door to creativity in the global church's response. This paper should not be seen as an attempt to level global youth culture into one homogenous experience,[16] but to promote a nuanced approach that considers these transnational matters alongside local experience. These trends point to global themes evident in digitally connected youth, while continuing to recognize the necessity to examine and address these themes in context.

Our Global Youth Culture survey, therefore, serves as a call to action for the global church, but also as a call to wisdom. Craig Ott offers a helpful understanding in his handbook on cross-cultural teaching, warning that "While creeds or catechisms may indeed be equally *true* everywhere, they may not be equally *relevant* everywhere, and they are certainly not exhaustive—they don't say all that can or needs to be said."[17] In the same way, while data is equally true around the world, it must be weighed with wisdom about whether it says all that can or needs to be said in each culture.

Ministries who would seek to pass our Christian faith to the next generation are called to journey alongside developing young people. This is a commission that comes with a specific challenge. As Noll says, "The gospel comes to each person and to all peoples exactly where they are... Yet even as the gospel dignifies individual cultures, by entering into all of them so particularly, it also calls all believers together to a pilgrim journey, and that journey inevitably involves rejecting some aspects of the native culture."[18] Noll speaks of a global culture—which is certainly relevant to this study—but within that, he recognizes youth culture as a form of individual culture to which the gospel has been fashioned.

This study has sought to give voice to the issues that young people globally are facing in order to more strategically confront the narratives of culture with the better story of God and his kingdom. From these findings, the global church can recognize a few key conclusions:

First, scripture reading is foundational to strengthening the faith of young people. Since a majority admits they are not personally engaging scripture, the church must creatively invite Gen Z into a deeper understanding of the Word of God so that they can internalize its foundational truths and loving boundaries for their lives. Churches must show young people the beauty and wisdom of scripture.

Second, churches cannot assume their relationship with young people will last. We can see in the growing number of young people who have no faith or whose faith has become nominal that more must be done to create a sustained engagement with the church. Personally identifying as a Christian cannot be the final goal, but it is rather a journey alongside each young person to discover a flourishing life through Christ.

Lastly, the global church must recognize the complexity of this cultural moment. As young people face an unparalleled cultural milieu, they need loving adults who will come alongside them to guide them and encourage them along the way. As churches seek to journey alongside the next generation, let it be done in a way that honors their experience and struggles, while holding to the hope and truth of the gospel message.

Notes

1 Mark A. Noll, *The New Shape of World Christianity: How American Experience Reflects Global Faith* (Downers Grove: InterVarsity Press Academic, 2009), 19–20.

2 Noll, *The New Shape of World Christianity*, 21.

3 Noll, *The New Shape of World Christianity*, 21–22.

4 This philosophy is thoroughly addressed in Charles Taylor's work and is introduced first in Charles Taylor, *A Secular Age* (Cambridge, MA: Belknap Press, 2007), 3. Taylor defines "secular" as a ". . . focus on the conditions of belief. The shift to secularity in this sense consists, among other things, of a move from a society where belief in God is un-challenged and indeed, unproblematic, to one in which it is understood to be one option among others, and frequently not the easiest to embrace." This understanding of secularism aligns with the individuality of religious belief uncovered in numerous studies on youth culture, specifically the foundational National Study of Youth and Religion, conducted in the US.

5 Benjamin T. Conner and Rode Molla, "Beyond the Limitations of Applying Western Youth Ministry Thoughts to an Ethiopian Context—A Case Study," *Journal of Youth Ministry* 16:3 (Fall 2018), 48–65.

6 Joschka Philipps, "A Global Generation? Youth Studies in a Postcolonial World," Societies 8:1 (2018), https://doi.org/10.3390/soc8010014.

7 Conner and Molla, "Beyond the Limitations," 48–65.

8 *Attitudes & Behaviors of Youth: A Global Study* (Pompano Beach, FL: OneHope, 2012).

9 *Global Youth Culture: Global Report* (Pompano Beach, FL: OneHope, 2020), www.globalyouthculture.net/ accessed June 12, 2024.

10 "Digitally connected" refers to those who have regular access to the internet.

11 This term will be defined in more detail below.

12 Note that these teens self-identified as Christian, but not as Jehovah's Witnesses or Mormon. Committed Christians may be from a variety of Christian traditions as long as they display the six traits identified.

13 Note that these are not clinically defined levels of depression or anxiety. Teens interpreted for themselves the terms provided and self-reported these experiences.

14 This data is self reported by teens, not drawn from hospital records or country incident reporting, which in many cases forms the basis of other research studies on this topic.

15 CDC WONDER Online Database, "Underlying Cause of Death, Multiple Cause of Death Files 2015–2017," Center for Disease Control and Prevention, https://wonder.cdc.gov/, accessed March 1, 2020.

16 As addressed in Philipps, "A Global Generation?": "We must be wary of the notion of globalization as homogenization, the idea that increased intercultural contact will imply some sort of 'cultural levelling.' However much transnational dynamics may intertwine people and systems of meaning, and however much today's cultural resources are virtually shared across the globe, one must not forget that these resources are interpreted and put to use in radically different ways."

17 Craig Ott, *Teaching and Learning Across Cultures: A Guide to Theory and Practice* (Grand Rapids: Baker Academic, 2021), 17.

18 Noll, *The New Shape of World Christianity*, 190–191.

4 Seven Elements of a Youth-Friendly Church: A Global Survey of the Best Practices of Churches that are Remarkable at Reaching and Discipling the Young Generation

Ron Luce

Abstract

Academia is replete with studies that document evidence that in North America, and almost every Christianized part of the world, less of each generation is being reached for Christ. The problem statement this paper seeks to resolve is: given the eminent diminishing number of young Christians worldwide, what is the best possible actionable plan to change the trajectory of the global church? After studying churches that are remarkable at reaching and discipling the younger generations, and defying negative growth, the author has curated best practices that are actually working so that other church leaders can gain hope and be encouraged to take a fresh approach. Leaders will be empowered to claim this generation for Christ.

Introduction

Journals are replete with studies that demonstrate the worldwide waning of Christianity. In the United States, the average age of a megachurch attendee is 40 years old, while the average age of a church member with fewer than one hundred people is 53 years old.[1] While it is widely known that youth who attend church in North America stop going in their adult years,[2] Samuel Smith has recently found that the "nones" (those who identify with no faith at all) are more numerous than Evangelicals in America.[3]

Findings like these can be replicated all over the world. According to a Church of England report, the average age of a church attendee in Great Britain is 61 years old.[4] In Russia, after a resurgence of faith and attendance in the Russian Orthodox Church after the fall of the Iron Curtain, Russian Orthodox Metropolitan Hilarion Alfeyev (the level of Cardinal assisting the Patriarch of the Russian Orthodox Church) admits he is startled by the egregious absence of youth and troubled about what this means for their future.[5]

In Asia, South Korea shows how quickly a revival can come and go if it is not successfully passed to the next generation. Most Christian leaders have heard of the amazing Korean revivals of the 1970s and 1980s in this traditionally Buddhist land; Christianity grew from 2.0 percent in 1945[6] to 29.3 percent in 2010.[7] The tragic reality today, however, is that only 1.7 percent of Korean youth[8] identify as Christians; fewer than before the revival. As a result, in the past ten years, 10,000 churches have closed simply because their elderly passed away and no one was left to lead.[9] Christian leaders in other parts of Asia have taken note. Dr. Ronnie Mandang, the leader of the Indonesian Evangelical Alliance, lamented, "After the revival in Indonesia forty years ago that sparked all the megachurches we have today, really we are not reaching the next generation. If this could happen in South Korea, it could happen here too."[10]

While Christianity is predicted to keep growing until 2050 by 35 percent, this number means it will barely keep up with global birth rates—which are also 35 percent for the same period. Additionally, this percentage is misleading because the only reason it remains the same is due to revivals in sub-Saharan Africa in places that have been mostly Christianized. In reality, global Christianity is shrinking.[11]

Other research can be misleading as well. Islam is currently growing at 1.9 percent annually, mostly by birth rate, while Pentecostal Christianity is growing at 2.2 percent annually. Some have, therefore, hailed Pentecostalism as the "fastest-growing religion in the world."[12] Yet, a quick use of a calculator will show that the actual number of 1.9 percent of the annual growth of 1.6 billion Muslims is significantly more than the 2.2 percent growth of 600 million Pentecostals,[13] many of whom are converting from other forms of Christianity. At the present rate, Christianity will not continue to be the dominant belief system in the world. This is why we must rethink how we are impacting the next generation, which needs to know Christ.

In a dramatic depiction of the church's lack of impact on the next generation, the Pew Research Center reports that the "median age of Christians worldwide is 30, while the median age of Muslims is 23."[14] Moreover, in 2015, Pew Research came out with a shocking study that reported that Muslims were the only major religion predicted to increase faster than the global population as a whole. They stated:

Between 2015 and 2060, the world's population is expected to increase by 32% to 9.6 billion people. Over that same period, the number of Muslims—a major religious group with the youngest population and the highest fertility—is projected to increase by 70%. The number of Christians, by contrast, is projected to rise by 34%, slightly faster than the global population overall yet far slower than Muslims.[15]

Pew Research proceeded to demonstrate how Muslims are projected to rise from 23 percent of the world's population in 2010, to 30 percent by 2050. This significant proportion increase is largely due to the young age and high fertility rate of Muslims relative to other religious groups.[16] More concerning is that, between 2015 and 2020, Christians were projected to experience the largest losses: about five million people globally were expected to become Christians in this five-year period, while thirteen million were expected to leave Christianity, with most of these departures joining the ranks of the religiously unaffiliated.[17] If this current momentum continues, by 2050, Pew Research predicts that for the first time in history, Islam will be almost equal to all forms of Christianity combined (Catholic, Orthodox, and Protestant).[18]

After decades of churches in the United States closing and eclipsing those newly planted, in 2019 we celebrated approximately 4,000 birthed in the U.S.[19] However, post-pandemic, research shows that 84 percent of churches are declining or experiencing a growth rate below the population growth rate for their communities.[20] According to Linda K. Stroh, understanding the problem to be solved, along with carefully guided research, could lead to meaningful solutions.[21] I propose the following clear problem statement: Given the eminent diminishing number of young Christians worldwide, what is the best possible actionable plan to change the trajectory of the global church?

The Opportunity

With the problem clearly stated, I spent three years traveling the world studying churches to discover who was contradicting these trends, what their systems were, and what best practices ministry leaders might apply in their local contexts. From personal observation, the following seven best practices make churches remarkable at reaching and discipling the young generation. They are self-perpetuating, defy the aging-out trend, and create mature disciples while increasing church growth exponentially.

Process-Oriented versus Event-Oriented Churches

Youth-friendly churches demonstrate a system process captured in a Causal Loop Diagram (CLD), as illustrated below in Figure 1.[22] This takes away the mystery of the aging church and can help pastors plan for a brighter future. Although the graphic initially appears a tangled mess, this CLD illustrates an *event-oriented church*, which I argue is inadequate compared to a *process-oriented church*. Event-oriented churches grow linearly, based on how many people come to services or activities by invitation or advertisement. Even though most pastors and leaders would not call themselves event-driven, most leaders measure success on how many people attend each week, therefore leaning event-oriented.

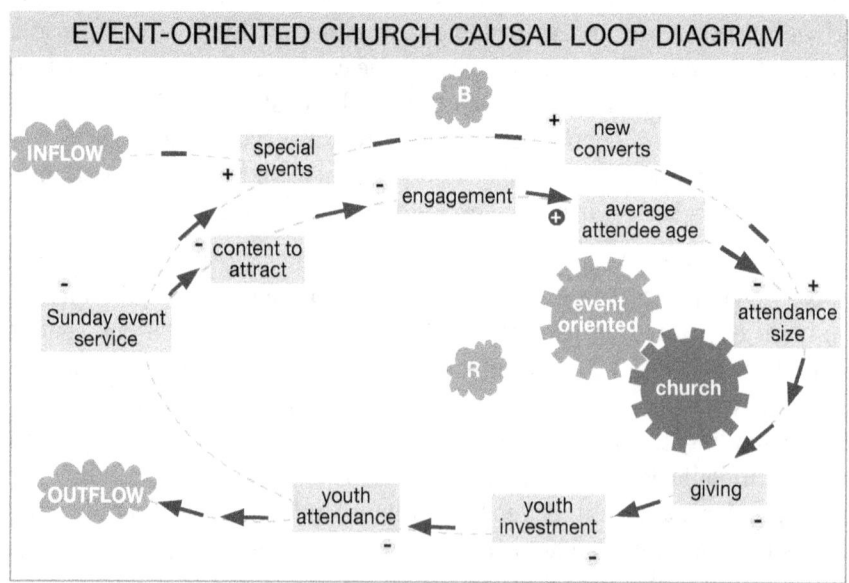

Figure 1: Luce, Ron., (2016). Growing Your Church Young; A new way of defining success in ministry. *Charisma Leader*

We will start our analysis from the middle of this picture. Current realities demonstrate the average age of attendees in churches continues to grow older and older (thus the plus sign indicating age is increasing, and a red dot denoting a negative trend). If you follow the arrow around to the right, as a result attendance grows smaller, which is linked to a smaller amount of giving. In most cases, less giving means less investment in youth, resulting in diminishing attendance as most churches have a tough time hanging onto parents who start going elsewhere in search of a youth program. In this event-driven system, the Sunday service gets smaller, which is the centerpiece of church life. The Sunday event-driven service leads to content that attracts people, which tends to lessen the engagement of those who are already Christians and want to grow deeper in their faith. Disengagement continues among those with smaller attention spans and higher thresholds of entertainment. As the latter group stops coming, the average age of church attendees increases.

In the event-oriented CLD, the outer loop builds on the philosophy of hosting *special events* (concerts, revivals, special speakers) which are designed to bring new visitors and provide input to the church. Following that outer circle around is where it gains most of its new converts that feed back into the size of attendance in the overall loop. This is a balancing loop, as it provides inflow to the church while others are leaving, keeping it about the same size.

However, the inner circle is a self-reinforcing cycle where—left to its natural tendencies—the church will get smaller and smaller. The outer loop provides a balance to keep the church from shrinking in size, but it is a deceptive measurement. The church does not get smaller because it keeps planning events to bring in more people. The insidious side of this is that it may appear as though everything is fine if a church does not shrink in size, but if the average age of attendees continues to rise, it dies slowly.

Alternatively, exponentially growing churches demonstrate that investing in youth is the key intervention in church decline. The *process-oriented church* CLD[23] in Figure 2 depicts an exponential church's approach to investing significantly, financially, and relationally into reaching, building, and training to lead the next generation. Based on this systemic approach, we will start with the beginning point of the new CDL by increasing youth investment. Following the circle to the left, we take the money and manpower to invest in aggressive outreach programs specifically aimed at reaching every 13-year-old within the church's footprint. Once a youth has become a follower of Christ, they are immediately put into a disciple-making program that helps them thrive in their faith (discussed below). As they continue to grow, after a year or two, they are trained to get involved in leadership development and make other disciples. We follow the circle around to the left and see attendance grow, which then flows into the Sunday morning service that feeds into a process. As you follow that circle around, you see that the average age

64 The New Generation & The Holy Spirit

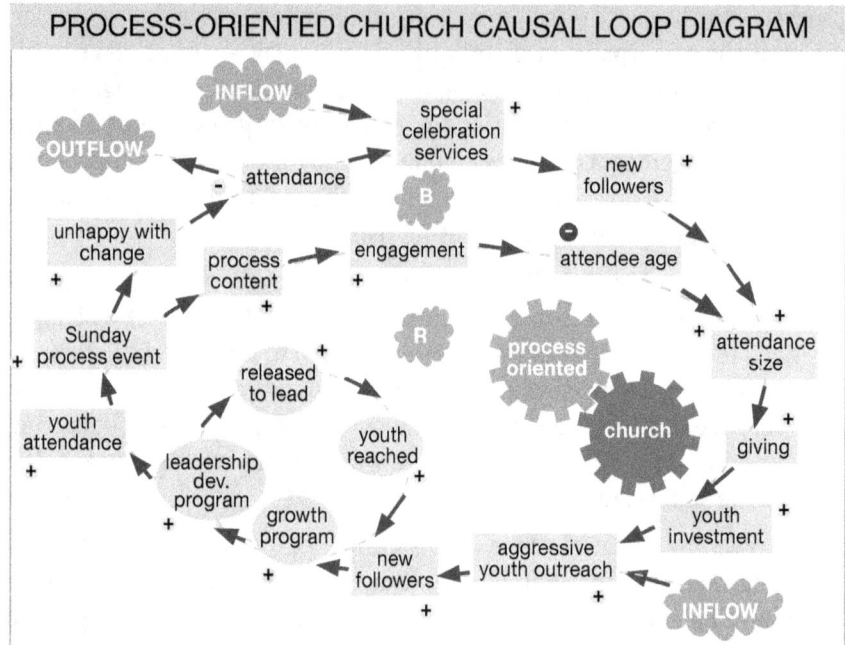

Figure 2: Luce, Ron., (2016). Growing Your Church Young; A new way of defining success in ministry. *Charisma Leader*

of attendees drops, which is the goal (noted with a green dot as a positive trend). Then, attendance begins to rise over time.

Also, the mini loop inside of the bigger loop is another self-reinforcing loop. As leadership capacity is developed among youth, they begin to lead small groups, which leads to more youth being reached. There is therefore a tornado of growth built into this system. As we follow the loop around, we still have special celebration events indicating that we do not have to completely change every facet of the event-oriented system. But it is possible to create this high-leveraged intervention within an event-oriented system, to shift it towards a process-oriented system. The variable that seems to provide leverage is youth investment, and that is what exponentially growing churches have chosen to do.

Training Young Leaders

Pastors of exponentially growing churches have broken the mental stronghold that reaching youth is simply an addendum to church. They have annulled the idea of the youth group and made reaching youth and developing them into disciple-makers a key component of their church growth strategy. Put a different way, they manufacture multipliers. Is it any wonder that Jesus chose mostly young people to be his disciples, to multiply and inaugurate his new movement called the church?[24]

These remarkable churches take very seriously the training and deployment of young people into leadership. The belief that Jesus wants to use everyone makes them begin to train and get youth involved in opportunities such as leading small groups. Our ministry has developed a tool called *Pathway to Leadership*[25] to train young adults in discipling middle school youth once they come to Christ. Exponentially growing churches have tools like these to help them spot youth in their church who demonstrate godly character, and then enlist them in a growth program to become a young leader.

The assumption is that everyone can get involved in the life-changing process of disciple-making. For too long we have heard stories like, "Johnny was really on fire for years, but then just disappeared. He stopped coming for no reason," mystified that maybe his spiritual pump was not primed enough to keep him engaged. Instead, maybe Johnny became like the Dead Sea. He was always receiving and never giving, as Christians are designed to do, and so became lifeless and dead on the inside.

Focus on Reaching Thirteen-Year-Olds in "The Exchange Zone"

The construct of youth ministry, as it has evolved over the past fifty years, is dead, ineffective, and threatens the future of the church. Time has revealed that the youth group model has not worked well at developing youth in the United States, nor has it worked as it has been exported and tried in nations around the world.

Importantly, a biblical view of ministry is intergenerational. God always thinks in generations, so ministry to the next generation should be defined as Abraham-Isaac-Jacob ministry or generation-to-generation ministry. Is it any wonder that when Jesus was commissioning Peter as the very first pastor, he exhorted him to "feed my lambs" (John 21:15, emphasis mine)?[26] In other words, "With all the ministry activities you are about to be immersed in, don't lose focus on the young ones. Don't let those whom everyone else overlooks starve to death right in front of you. They are the future of the church."

This concern is perhaps why the New Testament is replete with the metaphor of running a race. Paul declares in 1 Corinthians 9:24, "Do you not know that in a race all the runners run, but only one gets the prize? Run in such a way as to get the prize." Now, in an actual relay race, there is a zone in each runner's lane known as "the exchange zone," where it is legal to pass the baton to the next runner. This small area is the all-important focus of every runner and every coach. They work diligently to pass the baton right here, to win.

What is the baton, for the church? It is not simply leadership, for passing the baton of leadership does not mean that the baton of *the gospel* gets passed to the young generation; there are two different batons that must be passed. We have so far talked about leadership, but now I want to shift to focusing on the gospel—the message of life—passed to those most likely to receive it.

So, if the baton is the gospel, what is "the exchange zone"? This is the moment when people pass through and are most likely to grab the baton from the one who has it. According to surveys done by Barna and others, people in the age group 13–19 are more likely to embrace the gospel compared to any other age group.[27] This means that today there are approximately 1.8 billion youth in exchange zones, waiting to grab the baton of the gospel. A global study by the International Bible Society indicates that 83 percent of all Christians make their commitment to Jesus Christ between the ages of 4 and 14.[28] Another survey done by the Barna Group indicates that American children ages 5–13 have a 32 percent probability of accepting Christ; but youth or teens aged 14–18 have only a 14 percent probability of doing so. They also report that unbelieving adults, age 19 and above, have just a 6 percent probability of becoming Christians.[29]

In my survey of exponentially growing churches, I found leaders studying hard to discern where the sweet spot is in their region, for people most likely to come to Christ. For example, if 13-year-olds are the most probable, then they go after them. If college age is most probable, they focus on reaching them. I remember Pastor Tan Seow How (at Heart of God Church in Singapore) telling me, "Ron, we go after every 13-year-old in our footprint!" He continued, "I am not referring to the 13-year-olds in just our church—of course, we are going to reach them. I mean we find every school represented in our church, then discover how many 13-year-olds are in all those schools. *That* is our footprint!"[30]

Just imagine a massive crowd of 1.8 billion youth in the world crying out, "Pass it to me! Pass it to me, please I'm ready! I want it, pass it to me!" Many churches are running right by them with their programs, events, and conferences, with plenty of important activities but failing to look at the fruit of their activities through the lens of intergenerationalism.

Deep Dive Disciple-Making

One of the most profound aspects of exponentially growing churches is how deep and well-thought-through their tools are, to ignite ongoing growth in Christ in new followers. This strategy was embraced by Pastor Jason Lozano after expressing his frustration with his event-oriented model with, "Do you know how hard it is to pastor a thousand babies?"[31] Exponentially growing churches therefore set a goal of what they want their young people to look like as they arrive at their twenty-first birthday, and then set learning goals for each year from 13–21 years old. They literally scope and sequence the spiritual formation of young people for each year, to change the trajectory of students in the Lifeway Study that demonstrates 70 percent do not continue to go to church after college.[32]

These growing churches build a spiritual pipeline so they can have great hope for their future. Almost all of them use a trimester system (twelve weeks) with ten trimesters in their growth track, as well as small groups to help new followers process and apply what they have learned to their lives. These ten trimesters include memorizing lots of scripture; reading the New Testament, Psalms, and Proverbs the first year in faith; having quiet times every day; and discussing what was learned each week in a small group format. They are also taught to critically think through major issues in their culture and encouraged to connect with godly peers.

In addition, some exponentially growing churches have developed spiritual assessments for their youth to take, to get a glimpse of the intangible elements of spiritual growth in their lives. It is important to know if what you think is happening in small groups is indeed happening; a real rubric must surpass merely measuring attendance. This is not just a great plan for reaching the next generation, but for building a healthy church for the future.

The Kind of Gospel that is Presented

One of the most profound distinctives of youth-friendly churches is counterintuitive: instead of watering down the gospel to get people to come forward and pray a prayer of salvation, they go exactly the opposite direction and present a gospel that engages them far past the altar call. Instead of a casual acceptance, they present a provocative invitation to become a lifelong follower of Christ. The assumption is that, too often, churches fail to keep youth engaged because the message they present produces a variety of Christian-looking attendees who are not committed followers of Christ. Some of these under-discipled categories are summarized below:

- Mental Christians- those who have been mentally convinced to believe the right thing but still seem to be dominated by the disease of sin they were born with. They are shown things in the Bible that they ought to believe, and after enough sermonizing, choose to believe it. This is often called a "profession of faith." However, giving mental assent to the gospel is not the same as a transformational encounter with Christ who said it. Often, these mental Christians begin to live a life of sin management.
- Cultural Christians- those who grew up in a Christianized family or nation, who simply associate with Christianity as their religion. When asked what religion they are, they would quickly reason, "Well, I'm not Buddhist, Muslim or Hindu, so I guess I'm a Christian." Many of the people who attend church every Sunday in the United States would qualify as cultural Christians.
- Social Christians- those who have found that the people they like to be associated with self-identify as Christians. They go to or join a local church, and may be very active in volunteering at church activities. They try their best to help other people and work hard to be good upstanding citizens accepted by the community.

None of these categories are bad in and of themselves. However, Spirit-empowered transformation eludes them. The process of transformation is simple but also a profound mystery. All humans are born with sin, and the symptoms are everywhere including self-centeredness, brokenness, loneliness, power over others (which causes war), cruelty to others, jealousy, and others. The Early Church Fathers referred to our human condition as a fatal disease of sin we were each born with. Saint Cyril of Alexandria, for example, explains, "Our nature, then, became diseased by sin through the disobedience of one, that is, of Adam."[33] God, our loving Creator and Father, saw this disease and knew only one way to get rid of it. He did not create us to live like this. He knew a heart transplant was necessary because there was no way to repair the old heart. We will not rehash here all the theological realities that display the need and the evidence of a new heart, but suffice it to say that the innermost core of a person must be truly transformed. The surveyed youth-friendly churches are focused on keeping youth engaged in a lifelong journey of becoming more Christlike by actually following Christ. Hence, the messaging they employ is imperative. The gospel they preach includes the following emphases:

- Being a follower of Christ- In all the sermons and stories Jesus told, he never asked anyone to "become" a Christian; however, 32 separate times in the gospels, he exhorted people to "follow" him. Dallas Willard cautions that many people who call themselves Christians are not followers of Christ,[34] yet once we believe he is the way (John 14:6) and take our first steps towards following him, a miracle happens inside our hearts which Jesus describes as being born again or born from above (John 3:3). The word "follow" denotes pursuing him and taking action to continue in renewed pursuit.
- Access to our heart/will- You may have heard it said, "Ask Jesus to come into your heart." But what does that mean? What is the heart? Where is it? Certainly, it is not the physical heart, but referring to the inmost being or center of us. The heart is the "will" aspect of the personal reality, that is, its innermost core. Again, Willard explains that "[i]n biblical language, the will is usually referred to as the 'heart.'"[35] To trust Jesus is to give him our heart, our will, and everything we have command over in our lives.
- Living as an apprentice- An apprentice (or disciple) continues to learn, apply what they learn, and be transformed by Christ. Transformation begins with the miracle of a new heart but continues as we eagerly seek to learn and apply to ourselves the matters of our inward life. We are no longer dominated by sin or iniquity (Col 1:13), but as we enlist his grace to transform more of our inner life into his likeness, we then experience more of the freedom he intended and his kingdom expands within us (Luke 17:21).

As Jesus repeatedly called people to repent, he did not mean to just walk to the front of a church and feel bad about all the rotten things you have ever done. "Repent" (in Greek, *vmetanoia*) means to change your mind or the way you think.[36] Jesus wants us to change the way we think about life in every area. This is important because the gospel message presented is a big predictor of whether a convert continues to follow Christ. Youth-friendly churches are keenly aware that to make lifelong followers, it starts with the right invitation to become a whole-hearted disciple of Christ.

Pastor as Chief Strategist

Psalm 71:14–18 says, "So even to old age and gray hairs, O God, do not forsake me, until I proclaim your might to another generation, your power to all those to come." In this passage, King David focuses on the young generation even though he has gray hair. This role is taken seriously by leaders of youth-friendly churches that desire to grow exponentially. Moreover, the leaders of such churches have not delegated reaching the next generation to their youth pastor. The senior leadership leads the charge. Too many senior pastors are vexed by the thought, "But I am not cool. I am not relatable. What can I possibly do?" However, exponential growth leaders do not trouble themselves with these trivialities but leverage their experience, skill, and anointing to lead the strategy of their church to reach and disciple those most likely to come to Christ. The goal is for no one to think of the 13-year-olds in the church more than the senior pastor.

To see the impact of one strategy-minded leader, study Apostle Opoku Onyinah and how he grew the Church of Pentecost in Ghana from one million to two million in ten years by reaching out to youth.[37] Or, consider Bob Bakish, the CEO of Viacom, the parent company that owns MTV. He is not young, cool, or edgy. He is simply a strategist. He lives and breathes how he can get a mindshare of youth on every continent. In fact, years ago I had an opportunity to peek at some of MTV's marketing materials used to attract new advertisers. They boldly proclaimed, "We don't advertise to this generation, we own this generation." That is some kind of audacity.

The pastors who are leading exponential, youth-friendly churches are chief strategists who endeavor to carry this conviction: "This next generation is Christ's. I refuse to surrender any of the next-generation secular cultures." Jesus died for them, so like King David, the senior leadership's heart cry is, "Even when I am old and gray, let me impact this next generation." Let it not be said of the church that MTV wanted the youth more than we do. When it comes to the next generation, whoever wants them most will win their hearts.

Using Different Metrics for Success

Leaders of remarkable youth-friendly churches enlist a different kind of scoreboard as they think about what success looks like in five, ten, or twenty years from now. For example, we discovered exponentially growing churches monitor things like the average age (of those 13 and older) of the participants of their church. They are convinced that this is a more accurate way to measure the future vitality of their church. I have provided one acronym, AGILE, as a type of dashboard that can monitors these different priorities.[38]

Average age of church attendees 13 and up:
- Knowing how the average age compared to last year;
- Knowing the age and number of 13-, 14-, and 15-year-olds in your reach (within the influence of your church);
- Strategizing for youth whose parents go to the church, and also for any school that is represented in the church or local community.

Growth to track measurables for each disciple:
- Having a path laid out for 13–21-year-olds: how you want them to grow each year, how they will achieve that, and how to measure it;
- Assessing how many make it from the first level of growth to subsequent levels, and how to improve the funnel;
- Teaching new followers that church is not simply attending on Sundays but learning to do life together; this entails creatively assessing how well one's church is assimilating as a group;
- Small groups meeting each week to connect individuals in an ever-disconnected world: data has shown repeatedly that the more youth participate with modern technologies, such as online gaming and social media, the lonelier they are.[39]
- Churches teaching on how to have actual friends (not virtual friends), as well as how to forgive when offended (rather than just block or ghost people).

Inspiring future-fit vision:
- Encouraging horizon-scanning: where should your church go and how will it get there?

- Embracing new initiatives to leverage technology and keep from getting stifled in old paradigms;
- Asking why so many revivals have died? Why have so many denominations become irrelevant? Perhaps not understanding the times, or married to form rather than essence?

Leadership development of young disciples:
- Plans to recruit and train leaders as young as 14 or 15 years old. Instead of youth sitting on the sidelines, young people want to be on the field playing in the game—exactly what Jesus intended for all of his followers.

Engaging the entire church:
- Measuring the percentage of the adult congregation involved in impacting the next generation;
- Training adults to actively engage and feel the excitement of this vision: seasoned warriors are needed as mentors and volunteers, including those who would reach out to parents of youth from unchurched homes;
- Encouraging those with means to financially invest.

You have probably heard the expression, "What gets measured is what gets done." Exponentially growing, youth-friendly churches measure things that typical churches do not, and then keep focused on being effective at impacting the younger generations. What you look at ultimately determines where you go.

Conclusion

The proven track record of ten, twenty, and even twenty-five years of continuous impact on the young generation is a reason for *hope* for Christian leaders all over the world. Reaching and discipling is no longer an urban legend that cannot actually be realized. It is happening all over the world. Now pastors can implement these best practices even as they customize them to their own cultures and contexts. The promise of a bright future for Christendom is at our fingertips if an exponential growth strategy that prioritizes youth is embraced by the church as a whole. If only one million churches were engaged by 2030 in some form of exponentially growing, youth-friendly practices, it would ignite momentum that would produce fruit by 2050 that far outnumbers the current growth of Islam. As Spirit-empowered leaders, we must be willing to use new wineskins that will provide the systems and practices that are effective for this particular season in history.

Notes

1 Warren Bird June, "Not a Boomer Phenomenon: Megachurches Draw Twice as Many Under 45," Leadership Network, June 2014, http://leadnet.org/not-a-boomer-phenomenon-megachurches-draw-twice-as-many-under-45/, accessed March 22, 2022.

2 Michael Gryboski, "Teen Churchgoers Often Stop Attending as Young Adults, LifeWay Study Finds," *The Christian Post*, January 16, 2019, https://www.christianpost.com/news/teens-who-attend-church-often-stop-going-as-young-adults-lifeway-study-finds.htm/, accessed March 24, 2022.

3 Samuel Smith, "Religious 'Nones' Now as Big as Evangelicals in the U.S., New Data Shows," *The Christian Post*, March 20, 2019, https://www.christianpost.com/news/religious-nones-now-as-big-as-evangelicals-in-the-us-new-data-shows.html/, accessed March 24, 2022.

4 Andy Bloxham and Martin Beckford, "Average Age of Churchgoers Now 61, Church of England Report Finds," *The Telegraph*, January 2010, https://www.telegraph.co.uk/news/religion/7054097/Average-age-of-churchgoers-now-61-Church-of-England-report-finds.html/, accessed March 26, 2022.

5 Metropolitan Hilarion Alfeyev, in a personal interview with the author, March 14, 2018.

6 Korean Information Service, *A Handbook of Korea* (Seoul: Korean Overseas Information Service, 1993), 132.

7 Pew Research Center's Forum on Religion and Public Life, "Global Christianity: Regional Distribution of Christians," Pew Research Center, December 19, 2011, https://www.pewresearch.org/religion/2011/12/19/global-christianity-regions/, accessed June 2024.

8 Stephen Um, "TGC Korea Provides New Forum for Gospel-Centered Content," The Gospel Coalition, November 8, 2016, https://www.thegospelcoalition.org/article/tgc-korea-new-forum-gospel-content/, accessed June 2024.

9 Pastor Yeng Choe, in a personal interview with the author, November 2013.

10 Dr. Ronnie Mandang, in a personal interview with the author, July 2017.

11 Pew Research Center's Forum on Religion and Public Life, "The Future of World Religions 2010–2050," Pew Research Center, April

22, 2015, https://www.pewresearch.org/religion/2015/04/02/religious-projections-2010-2050/, accessed June 2024.

12 Yen Makabenta, "Protestantism: The Fastest-Growing Religion in the Developing World," *Manila Times*, November 2017, https://www.manilatimes.net/protestantism-fastest-growing-religion-developing-world/363522/, accessed June 2024.

13 Brittany Smith, "More Than 1 in 4 Christians are Pentecostal," *Charismatic Christian Post*, December 2011, https://www.christianpost.com/news/more-than-1-in-4-christians-are-pentecostal-charismatic.html/, accessed June 2024.

14 Pew Research Center's Forum on Religion and Public Life, "The Changing Global Religious Landscape," Pew Research Center, April 5, 2017, https://www.pewresearch.org/religion/2017/04/05/the-changing-global-religious-landscape/, accessed June 2024. Please note that many additional graphs appear here, to visually assess the startling demographic and religious landscape change in each continent between now and 2050.

15 Pew Research Center's Forum on Religion and Public Life, "Muslims," April 2, 2015, Pew Research Center, http://www.pewforum.org/2015/04/02/muslims/, accessed June 2024. Please note that many additional graphs appear here, to visually assess the startling demographic and religious landscape change in each continent between now and 2050.

16 Pew Research Center, "The Changing Global Religious Landscape."

17 Pew Research Center, "The Changing Global Religious Landscape."

18 Pew Research Center, "The Future of World Religions."

19 Lillian Kwon, "Total U.S. Churches No Longer in Decline, Researchers Say," *The Christian Post*, May 13, 2010, https://www.christianpost.com/news/total-us-churches-no-longer-in-decline-researchers-say.html/, accessed March 22, 2022.

20 Aubrey Malphurs, "The State of the American Church: Plateaued or Declining," The Malphurs Group, 2014, http://malphursgroup.com/state-of-the-american-church-plateaued-declining/, accessed, March 24, 2022.

21 Linda K. Stroh, *The Basic Principles of Effective Consulting* (New York City: Taylor and Francis, 2019), Kindle edition.

22 Ron Luce, "Growing Your Church Young: A New Way of Defining Success in Ministry," *Charisma Leader*, 2016.

23 Luce, "Growing Your Church Young."

24 Greg Stier, "Why Teenagers? A Case for the Importance of Youth Ministry," August 22, 2016, https://gregstier.org/why-teenagers-a-case-for-the-importance-of-youth-ministry/, accessed March 22, 2022.

25 Ron and Katie Luce, *Pathway to Leadership* (Dallas: Kindle Direct Publishing, 2021).

26 Unless otherwise noted, all scripture quotations are taken from the New International Version (NIV).

27 See, for example, Barna, "5 Things You Need to Know About Gen Z in 2024," Barna Research Group, September 12, 2024, https://www.barna.com/research/gen-z-2024/, accessed September 30, 2024.

28 Updated by Dan Brewster in August 2005. This article first appeared in a chapter entitled "The 4/14 Window: Child Ministries and Mission Strategy" in *Children in Crisis: A New Commitment*, ed. Phyllis Kilbourn (MARC, 1996), http://home.snu.edu/~hculbert/ages.htm/, accessed September 30, 2024.

29 George Barna, *Transforming Children into Spiritual Champions* (Ventura, CA: Regal, 2003).

30 Pastor Tan Seow How, personal interview with author at Heart of God Church, Singapore, 2017. For more on this mentality and approach, see chapter 14.

31 Jason Lozano, personal interview with author at Freedom Church, Whittier, CA, 2018.

32 Aaron Earls, "Study Confirms: Majority of College Students Drop out of Church," *The Courier*, February 13, 2019, https://baptistcourier.com/2019/02/study-confirms-majority-of-college-students-drop-out-of-church/, accessed August 8, 2024.

33 Cyril of Alexandra, "Commentary on Romans 74," 788–789, transl. Archimandrite Vassilios Papavassiliou, quoted in Michael Strickland, "Original Sin or Ancestral Sin?," Renew.org, https://renew.org/original-sin-or-ancestral-sin/, accessed August 8, 2024.

34 Dallas Willard, *Hearing God* (Grand Rapids: InterVarsity Press, 2012), 75.

35 Willard, *Hearing God*, 80.

36 "Repentance," *Baker's Evangelical Dictionary of Biblical Theology*, Bible Study Tools, https://www.biblestudytools.com/dictionary/repentance/, accessed August 8, 2024.

37 Ron Luce, *Faith at the Speed of Light* (Tustin: Trilogy Publishing, 2019), 183–197.

38 Luce, *Faith at the Speed of Light*, 221–228.

39 Mark Molloy, "Too Much Social Media Increases Loneliness and Envy," *The Telegraph*, March 2017, https://www.telegraph.co.uk/technology/2017/03/06/much-social-media-increases-loneliness-envy-study/, accessed March, 22, 2022.

5 Children's Stories in the Gospel of Mark: A Sermon[1]

Douglas Petersen

Receiving the Call to Children

Here at the Global Pentecostal Summit, I want to tell a couple of stories about the importance of children to Jesus. Many years ago, I wanted to be a scholar. My wife and I had gone overseas with our two young children to donate a year of our lives to missions, but my goal was to come home and go to graduate school.

So I did. I was pursuing my Ph.D. and filling out routine forms to continue my education, when God suddenly interrupted. It was Monday night, my wife was out, and I was watching football with the remote control in my hand. A commercial came on, I started changing the channel, and I saw a friend of mine singing on one of them. I stopped to listen until she was finished, but when she did, I found that she was singing for a World Vision special about helping children. I watched more, and I felt the Lord speak to me: "This is what I want you to do with your life."

It made absolutely no sense. I had no background. I didn't know anything about children, and I didn't have a developed social conscience. I was just a young man trying to keep things together. At that moment, I wanted to simply keep going with my life, but I knew I'd heard from the Lord.

When my wife came home that night, I said, "I have no way to explain this, but I know the Lord is going to change everything for us." I told her the story and we agreed that we would keep it to ourselves until we could explain it. Two or three weeks later, a friend and leader in Central America, John Bueno, called me and said, "Doug, let's get together for lunch." We had a wonderful lunch in Southern California where I lived, and at the end of the lunch, John said to me, "We have six schools in El Salvador, and we want to start our own program like World Vision. I'm sure you wouldn't have any interest, but would you want to start a program like that for us?" I responded, "John, I don't even need to pray about it. I've already had the experience with the Lord."

And so that was the beginning. We started with only a dream. I didn't speak any Spanish—I didn't even know five words—and I had no idea how we would complete the project. But we tried to be faithful, and as the years went by, the dream grew and grew until it became 300 projects with 100,000 kids going to ChildHope, our Latin American childcare program.[2]

The Gospel of Mark's Call to Children

Ministry to children and prioritizing children is biblical. Among other places, it is rooted in the stories about children in the book of Mark. We don't often think about the gospels as being about children's stories, especially Mark because it is so short. But there are six children's stories in Mark that ground ministry to the next generation in the heart of Jesus.

Jairus' Daughter (Mark 5)

First, in Mark 5:21–43, there is the children's story of Jairus, whose daughter is dying. Jairus comes to Jesus and asks, "Teacher, can you come with me and lay your hands on my daughter so she may be healed and live?" (vv. 22–23). Jesus starts towards his house knowing Jairus is a leader in the synagogue—an important person. But Jesus gets only a little bit of the way before a woman interrupts them, having thought to herself, as Mark writes it, that if she could just touch the hem of Jesus' garment she'd be healed. She had been bleeding for twelve years and spent all her money on doctors but remained ill. In the first century, she'd have been considered unclean and so could never have married or had children. Jesus stops, turns, and asks who touched him. The disciples tell him, we're in a crowd so everybody has touched you. But he says no, someone *touched* me—who touched me? The woman was afraid to come forward, but she did and told Jesus, "I just knew if I could *touch* you, I would be healed." And she was—Jesus healed her.

We know that story, but while this is happening, the news comes to Jairus that his daughter has died. Now any parent can imagine that feeling. People have been thronging to Jesus, wanting healing, with miracles happening everywhere. But when he gets close to your house, you miss it. It's too late, and your daughter dies. Jesus says not to worry, to just believe, but they get to Jairus' house where there is wailing, crying, and another crowd. During the commotion, Jesus proclaims, "The girl is not dead. She is only sleeping." The crowd laughs! They have been hired to wail and cry, so for them to start laughing is easy. They have nothing real in the relationship.

Jesus takes Peter, James, and John to go into the girl's room with Jairus. And all Jesus does is reach and take the girl *by the hand*, and say, "Little girl, be healed. Stand up." A miracle happens: the little girl stands up because Jesus touched her. Hear that word, *touch*. When Mark writes, he expects readers to tie stories together through his words. It is his technique. As one of the greatest writers, he clusters stories of the same kind and uses words to connect them, expecting the reader to notice. Remember that Mark also writes often in the present tense. He writes with dialogue because he wants the reader in his story. He wants you and he wants me to be in that story, have that experience, and make the connections to answer the same kinds of questions that were being answered back then. In this case, his touch extending to the child is important.

The Syro-Phoenician's Daughter (Mark 7)

Then Jesus meets a woman in Mark 7:24–29. In doing so, he's outside of his territory altogether. The Syro-Phoenician woman has a demon-possessed daughter, yet begs Jesus for help. Jesus says to go home and her daughter will be fine. She goes home, and, miraculously, her daughter is set free. This is the second children's story in Mark's gospel.

At this point, in his first seven chapters, Mark has strung together a series of spectacular miracles. In Mark 1, a demon-possessed man who recognizes Jesus cries out, "What do you have to do with us, Holy One of God?" Jesus casts the devil out of him. The crowd he had been teaching with remarkable authority is amazed and says, "Who is this that even the demons obey him?" Then crowds start coming from everywhere, Mark tells us. From the synagogue, Jesus goes to Peter's home where his mother-in-law is sick with fever. Jesus heals her, and the news spreads so that by night everyone is jamming the door. By the end of Mark 1, crowds have come from everywhere, bringing him their sick and afflicted, those bound by the devil, just so that Jesus would *touch* them.

He spends the evening touching, healing, making a difference. He follows that with walking on the water so that his disciples know he has power over nature. Jesus has power over illness. Jesus has power over the devil. Jesus has power over death. There isn't anything that Jesus cannot do. He is indeed the Messiah.

The Child Who Helps Feed the Crowds (Mark 8)

Therefore, by the time we get to Mark 8:1–8, we come to the third children's story. This is the feeding of the 4,000 through a little boy's offering of bread and fish. The disciples are confused because the book opened with Jesus announcing the kingdom of God and performing the signs that Isaiah prophesied about the kingdom: the lame walk, the blind see, the prisoners are set free. But Jesus has done nothing to establish his reign. Nothing has changed! The Roman oppression is still present, and the disciples are confused.

Yet everything shifts when Mark gets to this point, exactly halfway through his gospel. Mark divides his book into two parts with the first part showing Jesus' power and authority over sickness, storms, the devil, death. Then the second part shows that discipleship is not just about following a miracle worker. It's not just about following the sensational, beyond words—rather, discipleship comes at a price. To follow Jesus, every scholar who does anything with Mark knows the next two chapters are the two main chapters in the New Testament where Jesus teaches what it truly costs to follow him. He is clear: you must lose your life in order to gain it; you must be last to be first; you must answer, can you drink the cup? (Mark 8:34–38).

In context, in Mark 8, Jesus had just gone to Peter and asked, who do people say I am? Peter replied that some say Elijah, some say Moses. Jesus asks, but who do you say I am, Peter? And Peter announces, "You are the Christ, the Son of the Living God!" (Mark 8:29). And it's as if Peter has got it! But he doesn't. Jesus proclaims his own death and that he will have to go to Jerusalem. He will suffer there, he will die, and then he will rise again on the third day. Peter rebukes him and says, essentially, "Jesus, what are you thinking? I've just said you're the Messiah. What is this death talk?" And a wonderful scene follows where Jesus takes the three disciples up to the Mount of Transfiguration and they see Jesus in all his divine glory (Mark 9:1–12). His clothes are radiant; they see him in his rightful place like before he came to earth and became like them. They see this is what the future looks like, and they want to build tabernacles to stay there in his glory. But to follow Jesus is going to cost them everything, even this. And Mark makes this point with two children's stories at this very climactic moment. The first has been about feeding the people. The second comes next.

The Child Who Throws Himself into the Fire (Mark 9)

By Mark 9:14, the four have come down off the mountain. The night encounter is over, and they are going to go face-to-face with evil. A man brings his son who is demon-possessed and experiences convulsions. The father brings the boy to the disciples and asks if they can help, but they can't. So when Jesus comes, the man says, "I brought my son but your disciples couldn't help me. Can you help me? An unclean spirit seizes my son and throws him to the ground where he foams at the mouth and grinds his teeth. And sometimes the spirit even throws him into the fire or the water to destroy him" (9:22).

Now this is one of the most tragic stories that you could imagine if you are a parent. You've tried everything. This is your own son. If you could take his place, you would, but you can't. So Jesus says, "Bring me the boy." They bring him, and Jesus rebukes the unclean spirit. The boy convulses, throws himself to the ground, and the spirit comes out leaving the boy like a corpse (9:26). People think he is dead. Yet Jesus reaches down, takes the little boy by the hand—He has touched him! And the little boy is well and in his right mind.

"The Greatest in the Kingdom…" (Mark 9)

This event sets up Mark 9:33–36, where Jesus drills home with a children's story that if you want to be great, you will have to be the least. In Capernaum, Jesus asks his three disciples what they were talking about when they came down the mountain. Jesus knows what their discussion was, but they don't want to answer because they had been talking about who would be the greatest. In society, leaders have power and authority. They fight for position to keep their authority. They receive the biggest blessings, accolades, and positions. Jesus is going to upset the rules, so he says to bring him a child. He puts a child among them, in the center, and says if want to be first, they must learn to be last, and a servant of all (9:35).

These stunning words catch the disciples by total surprise. This is what it takes to follow Jesus? How you receive *a child* is how you receive the Lord (9:36)? In Mark, a child is not a symbol, a child is a person—a specific person. In Mark, a child is the new measurement. What it means to follow Jesus is seen in how you treat children. They should be first. They should have priority. They are defenseless. They are voiceless. They have absolutely no standing. They have no one to plead their cause. Jesus says to "receive" a child, and the word for "receive" means to "serve" or "welcome" or "love." When you do that, he says, that is how much you love him. Your discipleship is not measured by all the other things. Jesus isn't impressed by all the other things. He is impressed when we take a child, when we take the road that is uncomfortable, and we make them first. That's the new mark of greatness.

"Let the Children Come to Me" (Mark 10)

A few days go by, and we get to the sixth children's story in Mark 10:13–16. The crowds are still coming to Jesus; remember, throughout Mark the crowds are always coming. And they don't come just come to watch, they come with their sick. They come with their children who are sick. Parents are desperate and are coming with their children so Jesus can *touch* them.

The disciples have not yet learned their lesson about what it takes to love Jesus. He has held a child and told them it depends on how much they love, serve, welcome them, and become the least like they are. But now the disciples are actually pushing children away, aside, and not letting them get close to Jesus. So, Mark 10:14 says Jesus is "indignant." This means he is angry and incensed. There are only two times this word is used in relationship to Jesus, with the other being when he cleanses the temple from the moneychangers. Jesus is incensed with the disciples because he is thinking, "Don't you understand what I have been teaching you? This is not about power. This is not about you controlling who gets to see me. The kingdom is not about who is in charge. It is about who will reach out to a child and make a difference."

The kingdom of God belongs to the least of these. This means we just do not look after children. They enter the kingdom like we do, as redeemed people. They need to take their place in the life of our churches, and not just as little kids we chase around—but as those who are welcomed to the experience of being touched by Jesus. Jesus touched the lives of children, and now we can touch the life of a child. I have been involved in a lot of things in my ministry for more than fifty years, and I trust what I do is meaningful to the Lord. But this is what I know: when I touch the life of a child, I touch the heart of my heavenly Father. I make him glad. If we want to reach the world, that's where we need to be working. That's where our hands and feet need to be.

Conclusion

In Mark 10:38, before he dies, Jesus ends his instructions to the disciples with the great question, "Can you drink the cup?" He had started with losing your life and learning how to serve the least of these, but he closes with the question of whether they can drink the cup. He tells his disciples that he himself will drink it; that they are on their way to Jerusalem, and the Son of Man will be condemned to death. People will mock him, spit on him, flog him, and kill him. He asks his disciples if they too can drink the cup because, if they follow him, this is what being his disciple means.

As a contemporary disciple, our answer to the same question needs to be: yes, we can drink the cup. Mark's gospel is not a story just about the past, but the present. We must put ourselves into this story because we are the reader. Two millennia later, I can identify with the disciples' confusion over the question that Jesus asked Peter: "Who do you say that I am?" I struggle for the same reasons they did—sometimes I don't understand, or I don't want to understand. Sometimes I tailor Jesus' teachings to my own interests and read what I want.

But Jesus' rules remain a complete reversal of the order of things. In the twenty-first century, leaders still call the shots, and it's still a top-down world about who is in charge. In Mark's gospel, though, Jesus tips greatness upside down. The kingdom is like the plaque my wife gave me a few years ago: in a hundred years, it won't matter what car I drove, or the kind of house I lived in, how much money was in my account, or what my clothes looked like—just that the world was little better because I was important in the life of a child.

My prayer is that you would ask the Lord about what it means for you, that Jesus sees children as people and isn't using them as mere symbols of what it means to follow him. I pray that we will all ask what it will take for us to get more involved in the lives of actual children—for them to be first in our lives and in the lives of our churches. It will cost us. On our team, personally, sometimes it means we travel six or seven hours up the mountains to teach only a few children, to bring the good news to them, clothe them, and feed them. But when we love children, we're showing our love to Jesus. Let us pray and permit the Holy Spirit to come on us afresh, give us creative ideas, and impress upon our hearts the importance of the upside-down kingdom, about the very least of these.

Notes

1. This article has been adapted, with permission, from the live message given by Douglas Petersen to City Harvest Church at the 2023 Global Pentecostal Summit in Singapore. The full service can be found at Douglas Petersen, "Prof Doug Petersen: Children's Stories in the Gospel of Mark," YouTube, November 4, 2023, https://www.youtube.com/watch?v=PTb8j6iFfxw/, accessed June 28, 2024.

2. More about ChildHope's story, staff, and vision (which was shared in the original message in Singapore) can be found at "About Us," ChildHope, https://childhopeonline.org/our-mission/about-us/, accessed August 8, 2024.

Part II

Preserving and Reaching the New Generation

6 Born-Frees to Born-Again: A Look at the History of the Spirit-Empowered Movement in Namibia and its Appeal to the Post-Independent Generation

Caroline Polly Tjihenuna

Abstract

On March 21, 1990, Namibia gained independence from South Africa after decades of a blood-shedding struggle against the apartheid regime. The generation of Namibians born after independence (1990 and onwards) are therefore referred to as "Born-Frees." The Born-Free generation now makes up more than 60 percent of Namibia's population. They face many challenges that are distinct to their region (i.e., unemployment and poor education) and common challenges that Millennials and Generation Z face worldwide (i.e., poor mental health, gender identity confusion, etc.) With over 90 percent of Namibians as professing Christians, this paper will look at the brief history of Pentecostalism in Namibia, a general overview of what the Born-Free generation in Namibia is like, and what the Spirit-empowered movement has to offer the new generation of Namibians.

Introduction

Namibia is a vast country located in South West Africa and inhabited by 2.5 million people. This makes Namibia the second-least densely populated country in the world, just after Mongolia. This previous colony of the German empire has the shared African historical narrative of migration and colonization, as well as its own distinct history of genocide and apartheid. Traces of German colonization can still be seen not only in the architecture, schools, and cuisine, but also in the denomination that nearly half of the Christian population in Namibia affiliate with—Lutheranism.[1] Although Germany lost Namibia as a colony after their defeat in World War I, Lutheranism had spread through the country through missionaries sent prior to and during colonialism. Namibia now has the largest percentage of Lutherans in Africa.[2]

In light of Christianity's success among the Namibian people, Pentecostalism is taking ground rapidly. At the same time, globalization is also influencing many Namibians, particularly youth, towards Western thought and more left-leaning ideologies. At the speed at which the Spirit-empowered movement is growing in the Global South, Namibia has yet to take its place on the stage of global Pentecostalism. Until then, this paper aims to provide a glimpse of a nation that is twice as large as the state in which the Azusa Street Revival began, and holds promise unto that end.

The Involvement of Churches in Namibian Independence

Namibia was the last country in Africa to gain its independence at the turn of the last century.[3] The country was ushered into independence by a grassroots liberation movement that now is the country's most prominent political party, the South West Africa People's Organization (SWAPO). Although SWAPO had threatened to abolish the celebration of Christian holidays when in office, those threats fell flat as over 90 percent of the Namibian people affiliate with the church.[4] However, it is well worth mentioning that it was not SWAPO's efforts alone that gained the Namibian people their freedom but the joint efforts of Namibian churches as well. Today, the Namibian government believes that "the fear of God guides decision-making in Namibia and provides the driving force for the maintenance of a just and morally upright society."[5]

Christianity arrived on Namibian soil through European missionaries in the early nineteenth century. Lutheran missionaries from Finland and Germany settled in great numbers before colonialism began to take ground. The Albrecht brothers from the London Missionary Society established the first permanent mission station in the south of Namibia in 1806.[6] These missionaries planted churches and established schools to educate the youth and to promote local church leaders.[7] When colonialism was at its peak, however, missionaries began to side with colonial powers. During a genocidal retaliation against two tribes in Namibia, Lutheran and Catholic missionaries were said to have sided with the colonial power. Their reasoning was that the rebellion of the Namibians towards those in colonial power subsequently equated to mutiny against God.[8]

There were other missionaries who took this opportunity as a means of social work and established hospitals and missionary schools. According to Veikko Munyika, "Although missionaries accepted and even participated in the general structure of racial separation and even practiced it, these humanitarian services could be classified as a bold step indeed, and later served as a key element in the struggle for independence."[9] By the time the South African government took over Namibia, a few mainline churches had joined liberation movements to overthrow the apartheid regime. But there were also churches that were against the liberation of Namibia, and these were notably the primarily white churches, including the Dutch Reformed Church and the Pentecostal churches.[10]

During this period, the Pentecostal churches in South Africa were known to be vehemently aligned with the South African government. South African author Wynand J. de Kock describes the Full Gospel Church he grew up in as filled with racial discrimination and segregation.[11] When Namibia finally became independent, the favor was granted to the churches that took a stance against apartheid, whereas Evangelicals and Pentecostal-Charismatics were restricted in the ways they could operate.[12] However, that did not stop Pentecostal missionaries from flocking to Namibia following independence. Many of these missionaries and pastors came from other African countries, and a few from the United States.[13] Today, although only making up a small percentage, Pentecostal-Charismatic churches are continually gaining ground in Namibia.[14]

History of Pentecostalism in Namibia and the Apostolic Faith Mission

According to the *World Christian Encyclopedia*, in 2020, about 13.5 percent of the Namibian population was affiliated with Pentecostal-Charismatic denominations.[15] Although that number may not seem to be numerically significant, in the 1990s, Namibia's Pentecostal congregation only made up 2.5 percent of the population.[16] Unfortunately, Pentecostal-Charismatic churches have not had a great historical record in Namibia, at least when it comes to the country's fight for justice and independence, as previously mentioned.

South African Roots

Pentecostal churches in Namibia are often linked to South Africa because many of these congregations began in South Africa and made their way to Namibia through missionaries and church planters like P. J. Van der Walt. Van der Walt was a church planter who pioneered the establishment of three main Pentecostal denominations in Namibia: the Apostolic Faith Mission, the Full Gospel Church, and the Pentecostal Protestant Church.[17]

Today, however, the Apostolic Faith Mission (AFM) is the largest Pentecostal congregation in Namibia, having its beginning in South Africa out of the ministry of American missionaries John G. Lake and Thomas Hessmallach, in 1908. Although the AFM was multi-ethnic in membership and pastoral appointment, key figures of the AFM, including Lake and Jacob Lehman, saw the stronghold of prejudice among white members towards blacks and coloreds (the Afrikaans-speaking, mixed-race community); they noted that only the Holy Spirit could remove such deep-rooted prejudice.[18]

The color line that was said to be washed by the blood of Christ at Azusa was brought back to the surface by the AFM in South Africa when the decision was made to separate baptisms and church seating by race.[19] Unfortunately, Lake was said to be a proponent of the idea and played a role, though regretfully, in the segregation laws that were to be set in South Africa.[20] Since Namibia fell under South African rule near the end of World War I, naturally there were many similarities in the way native Namibians were discriminated against, both inside and outside the church.

Six Waves in Namibia

Louis F. Prinsloo, the President of the AFM at the time of this paper, gives a brief overview of the key figures who paved the way for the AFM in Namibia. However, no detail is given as to where they stood on segregation issues except for Van der Walt. Prinsloo succinctly breaks down the history of the AFM in Namibia in six waves.

The first wave of the Pentecostal movement was the arrival of a South African police officer by the name of A. J. Venter, who was a member of the AFM in South Africa. Venter arrived in Namibia in 1919 with a zealous witness that Prinsloo says "broke the ground for the movement of the Holy Spirit in Namibia and brought the message of Pentecost."[21]

The second wave was in 1928 through a group of white South African immigrants referred to as the Dorsland Trekkers. This group of people left South Africa and journeyed through the Kalahari Desert, eventually settling in Angola and relocating to Namibia, where they heard the message of Pentecost from Venter.

The third wave took place in 1942 through a pastor by the name of Andries de Kock, who planted an AFM congregation in Namibia's capital city, Windhoek. De Kock was known to minister to families, and his influence reached numerous towns in Namibia as he traveled and baptized many converts.

The fourth wave was in 1943, ushered in by the man known as the "Father of the Pentecostal Movement in Namibia," P. J. van der Walt, who was mentioned earlier. Van der Walt is perhaps granted this venerated title, not because he was the first to bring the message of Pentecost to Namibia, but because he and his wife were the first permanent missionaries stationed to the indigenous people of Namibia.[22] Van der Walt's approach to the Pentecostal mission was a holistic one: he believed in the salvation, physical healing, and healing of the community. Unlike many South African Pentecostal pastors at that time, Van der Walt's approach included the integration of all races and people groups. He was ostracized by fellow white leaders in the South African Pentecostal church because racial integration was contrary to the apartheid regime.[23] Unfortunately, it is noted that during the liberation struggle, Afrikaans-speaking churches such as the AFM, the Full Gospel Church, and the Pentecostal Protestant Church supported the apartheid regime and were in favor of the idea of having segregated places of worship, which is exactly what Van der Walt had worked against.[24]

The fifth wave occurred in 1975 when three Oshiwambo men established an AFM congregation in the northern part of Namibia. One of the three men, Paulus Nambindi, had fallen ill and traveled to an AFM congregation in Cape Town, South Africa, where he heard people were being healed. Nambindi received healing when members of the AFM prayed for him, and from there, he began preaching amongst the Xhosa people until the Lord told him to return to Namibia.

The sixth wave of the AFM in Namibia was among the colored community of Namibia and South Africa. According to Prinsloo, the colored community along the Namibian coast began an AFM congregation that spread to Windhoek and, from there, to other communities of color around Namibia.

The AFM Today

In the 1990s, the AFM began to reach out to the San community, which are the marginalized, indigenous inhabitants of Namibia. The AFM established a Bible school among this group, and today has five San-speaking congregations in Namibia.[25] The AFM in Namibia has evolved supporting apartheid and "stating that all the sections of the AFM opposed independence for Namibia," to its slogan today: "reconciled in Christ and with each other."[26] The AFM in Namibia now has a hundred assemblies across the nation with 93 branch assemblies, 92 pastors, five evangelists, and several counselors.[27]

My focus on the Apostolic Faith Mission is not only because it is the largest Pentecostal congregation in Namibia, but because my home church in Namibia, Emmanuel Church Windhoek, is one of the churches within the AFM congregation. I have attended this church with my cousins since I was 14 years old, and it was an essential part of my spiritual formation. A few days before I was set to fly to the United States to pursue my undergraduate studies, I went to the mall to run some last-minute errands by myself, and I saw the senior pastor and worship pastor of my church at a cafe. I worked up the courage to go talk to them, as I had not built a relationship with them during my years at Emmanuel Church, but I figured I had nothing to lose by going up to them and asking for a blessing before I left for college. As I thanked them for their leadership, the piece of advice my senior pastor gave me before I left was, "find a local church and serve." This was said with such weight.

According to Barna Group research, there is a decline of church involvement among up to two-thirds of young adults in the United States who have been raised in church.[28] Although these statistics are true in the USA, it would not be too much of a stretch to come to a similar conclusion among any group of young adults who grew up in a Christian home. When my pastor advised me to look for a local church, his words felt like the most important piece of instruction to ensure my spiritual safekeeping, even if I was going to a Christian university.

I have seen friends from Namibia go off to university, locally and internationally, and observed that those who have served in church are typically the ones who have remained steadfast in their beliefs and love for Christ. Some who were nominal Christians, or those who were not intentional in seeking and serving a local church, were the ones who began to deconstruct their faith or abandon Christianity altogether. According to David Kinnaman, one in ten young adult Christians are defined as a "resilient disciple" in their faith; that is to say that they ". . .

made a commitment to Jesus, who they believe was crucified and raised to conquer sin and death; are involved in a faith community beyond attendance at worship services; and strongly affirm that the Bible is inspired by God and contains truth about the world."[29]

In the case of young Namibian Christians, scholarly information regarding their faith is not readily available, but one can fairly estimate that the majority of them are affiliated with Christianity. The following section will contain information gathered from personal experience as a member of the Born-Free generation raised in Namibia, articles found in local newspapers, as well as Facebook posts regarding Born-Frees and the growth of Pentecostal churches in Namibia.

What is Known about the Born-Frees of Namibia

On July 19, 2022, a prayer request came to the International Missions Board from an anonymous individual from Namibia stating the following:

> Twenty-three years ago, some IMB missionaries started a youth outreach in their home in Windhoek as a means of sharing Jesus with Namibian teens. Hundreds of teens have been a part of this program, and many have come to know Jesus over the years. Today's teens, however, are facing a tremendously different world compared to that of their predecessors. The cultural pressures on these youth are exactly the same as what American teens deal with. Depression, eating disorders, gender identity confusion, self-absorption, and pornography addiction are just a few of the topics that are being addressed in the youth outreach Bible studies each week. Of course, the ever-pursuing love of Jesus is also shared each week. Please pray that the Holy Spirit will soften the hearts of these youths to the things of God and prepare them to someday say yes to the salvation that Jesus is offering to them.[30]

According to the National Youth Policy of Namibia, the term "youth" is used to classify anyone 15–34 years old.[31] This age group is now the majority amongst the Namibian population, the proportion being the highest ever recorded in Namibia's history.[32] The oldest of the Namibian Born-Frees are 32 years old at the time of this paper in 2022. Regarding the prayer request submitted to the IMB by this anonymous individual, the matters brought up ring true to the reality of Namibian young adults today.

A recent article released by a popular local newspaper, *The Namibian*, states that youth are turning to drugs and alcohol to cope with the issues they frequently face, such as unemployment, mental health challenges, and family troubles. One of the comments made by a 27-year-old Namibian is that youth are "dealing with stress, anxiety, and depression, among others, but don't feel like talking about it" out of the fear of being misunderstood and judged.[33] Thus, although Namibia is still a developing country, many of the issues that Gen Z and Millennials face in the West are being faced by many young Namibians. When I was in high school, there were a number of people, including myself, who struggled with some level of depression and anxiety; some were even on antidepressants. Eating disorders, gender identity confusion, substance abuse, and mental illness are nothing new to the Born-Free generation. Nowadays, the youth in Namibia are speaking up in favor of specific social matters such as LGBTQ+ rights, reproductive rights, the #MeToo movement, the destigmatization of sex work, and decolonialism.[34]

In 2020, right after Namibians celebrated thirty years of independence from South Africa, the following months were met with protests by Namibian youth, and activists marched in the streets of the capital. In October 2020, young people in Namibia were protesting against femicide and gender-based violence after it was reported that the body of a murdered young woman was found months after being reported missing. The reported passivity of the Namibian police department in carrying out an investigation before she was found enraged young people across Namibia and sparked months of protests in towns across the nation.[35]

Prior to the October protests, young Namibians also flooded the streets after the death of George Floyd in the U.S. during a police altercation in early June. In lieu of the protests, an article entitled "A Country on Fire," by author Heike Becker, states:

> ...protests under the Black Lives Matter banner were organised in Windhoek too. At the time Namibia's BLM activists focused on a statue near the Windhoek municipality of German colonial-era officer Curt von François, deemed the "founder" of Windhoek in colonial historiography. They demanded the removal of the statue with a widely circulated petition under the hashtag #CurtMustGo. Along with this local impression of activism against colonial iconography, the Namibian BLM protesters addressed other pressing demands of structural racism and social inequality.[36]

In observing this generation of young Namibians, one can easily draw similarities between them and other young people across the globe, especially when it comes to their vocality in civic engagement and social change.³⁷ The Born-Free generation in Namibia is seemingly following in the footsteps of the pre-independent generation who, Becker argues, made "enormous contributions to the political, though socially incomplete liberation of Namibia in the 1980s" with their protests and demonstrations.³⁸ It is well-documented that throughout history, young people have played key roles in political and social change in their countries.³⁹ However, the difference between the liberation movement that led to independence in Namibia and what the youth are fighting for today is the involvement of the church.

The Involvement of the Pentecostal Church

Finnish theologian Veli-Matti Kärkkäinen remarkably stated that a Spirit-filled individual is a person who "is impelled by that same Spirit to cooperate with God in the work of evangelism and social action in the anticipation of the new creation."⁴⁰ What Kärkkäinen has stated may be an answer to the "socially incomplete liberation of Namibia" that Becker brings up in her article.⁴¹ This socio-political dimension was still forming in the theology of individuals such as Van der Walt, evidenced by what he preached the gospel truly stood for, in light of politically-enforced segregation.

Renowned African theologian, J. Kwabena Asamoah-Gyadu, states that "what defines Pentecostalism is the experience of the Holy Spirit in transformation, radical discipleship, and manifestations of acts of power that demonstrate the presence of the Kingdom of God among his people."⁴² Although Lutheranism and Roman Catholicism are the two largest branches of Christianity in Namibia, perhaps the youth of Namibia need much more than "routine processes" such as infant baptism and confirmation (affirmation of baptism) as a means of being true followers of Jesus.⁴³ In an online article regarding the growth of Pentecostal churches in Namibia, it was written that "young people often claim that going to the more conventional church does not fulfill their spiritual hunger," and for this reason, many young Namibians are flocking to Pentecostal churches. Among those interviewed, a young man said, "The stage and the lights... have all just become white noise to those really seeking to encounter God. They are ear and eye candy for an hour, but they have so little relevance in people's daily lives that more and more of them are taking a pass."[44] Although the work of these mainline churches is significant in the history of Namibia, there is a need for a work that cannot be done through the doctrine and tradition of human beings alone but through the inner workings of the Holy Spirit. Therein enters the Spirit-empowered movement.

Pentecostals have a frame of reference for the role of the Holy Spirit to empower an individual for service. As de Kock puts it, God instills "Pentecostal power for a Pentecostal task."[45] The "Pentecostal task" that de Kock is referring to are the words Jesus reads from the prophet Isaiah in Luke 4:18, "The Spirit of the Lord is on me because he has anointed me to proclaim good news to the poor. He has sent me to proclaim freedom for the prisoners and recovery of sight for the blind, to set the oppressed free." The task is not exclusively for those who call themselves Pentecostals but those who have "the Spirit of the Lord" through a Pentecost experience—the baptism of the Holy Spirit.

In their well-renowned book concerning global Pentecostalism, Donald E. Miller and Tetsunao Yamomori coin the term "progressive Pentecostalism" as a form of Pentecostalism that attempts to meet both the physical and spiritual needs of individuals. When asked about the Pentecostal churches in Namibia, a local pastor stated that these churches have a "thirst for evangelizing, unlike the traditional church, they are able to capture those that are hungry for the gospel beyond tradition." Miller and Yamomori note that evangelism cannot be separated from meeting a person's other needs as well—this holistic approach is how Jesus ministered.[46]

In Namibia, there are multiple churches and parachurch ministries that focus on engaging youth. Notable organizations such as Campus Crusade for Christ, Scripture Union, and Youth for Christ are a few that play a role in actively going to local schools and universities to encourage youth with the gospel. Many of these ministries are interdenominational or Baptist, but only a few are affiliated with the Spirit-empowered movement, such as AFM Youth and an international campus ministry called Every Nation Campus. This may be due to Pentecostalism still being a relatively new and growing movement in Namibia.

Nevertheless, ministries like AFM Youth have been doing extensive work over the last year. In June 2022, they held a youth conference in the northern region of the country, where over a thousand young people showed up to the event. According to the AFM Youth chairperson, Patrick Molutsi, the AFM Youth organization has been active since 2014 with a national membership of 6,000 youth. It has also been involved in the Namibian Youth Council's conversation on ending the unemployment epidemic amongst Namibian young adults, and meeting practical needs by holding drives to collect and deliver hygiene products to youth whose families cannot afford them.[47]

Conclusion

Pentecostalism has undoubtedly found great soil in Africa and continues to thrive despite its complexities. As Pentecostalism continues to expand in Namibia, more scholarly research ought to be conducted as Namibia is a unique case study due to the following: nearly the entire population is affiliated with Christianity, the majority of the population now falls under the Born-Free generation, and it is ethnically and culturally diverse while having a population of only 2.5 million people. I suggest that Namibia is ripe to see a great movement of the Holy Spirit at work in the hearts of its people, shifting them from simply being nominal affiliates of Christ to resilient disciples of Christ, especially among the younger generation of Namibians.

Although this paper simply gives a general overview of Pentecostalism and the state of the Born-Free generation in Namibia, I believe that as more attention is drawn toward this distinctive nation, Pentecostal-Charismatic churches in Namibia will begin to focus more on raising up the next generation to be sustainable disciples who minister to people in a holistic, integral manner. The Born-Free generation in Namibia is similar to Millennial and Gen Z generations in other contexts in that social engagement is important. Michelet William makes a good point when he states that "Gen Z are more likely to participate and remain engaged when there is a strong focus on social issues."[48]

Although the younger generation of Namibians seems to be fighting with similar rigor as their predecessors when fighting for independence, the Born-Free generation perhaps needs the churches that claim to be Spirit-filled to come alongside them and not only meet their spiritual needs but prove they are against the tainted narrative and seemingly passive role during the struggle for independence. Perhaps progressive

Pentecostalism could be the way to win over the Born-Free generation, through displaying genuine care for both the spiritual and physical needs of individuals.

Notes

1 Todd M. Johnson and Gina A. Zurlo, *World Christian Encyclopedia*, 3rd ed. (Edinburgh: Edinburgh University Press, 2019), 561.

2 Patrick Johnstone, *Operation World: A Tool for Missions* (Grand Rapids: Zondervan, 1993), 403.

3 Linda Freeman, "The Contradictions of Independence: Namibia in Transition," *International Journal* 46:4 (1991), 687.

4 Nico Horn, "Religion and Human Rights in Namibia: Focus: The Foundations and Future of Law, Religion and Human Rights in Africa," *African Human Rights Law Journal* 8:2 (2008), 410.

5 Government of the Public of Namibia, *Namibia Vision 2030*, Office of the President, 2004, 40, http://the-eis.com/elibrary/sites/default/files/downloads/literature/Namibia%20Vision%202030_Chapter%204.pdf/, accessed July 19, 2024.

6 G. L. Buys and S. V. V. Nambala, *History of the Church in Namibia: An Introduction* (Windhoek, Namibia: Gamsberg Macmillan Publishers, 2003), 9–10.

7 Thorsten Prill, "Theological Controversies on the Mission Field in Southern Africa: Reasons, Implications and Responses," in *Mission Namibia: Challenges and Opportunities for the Church in the 21st Century*, ed. Thorsten Prill (Norderstedt, Germany: GRIN Verlag, 2012), 90.

8 Veikko Munyika, "Role of Churches in Namibia Before and After Independence," in *Changing Relations Between Churches in Europe and Africa*, eds. Katharina Kunter and Jens Holger Schjørring (Wiesbaden, Germany: Harrassowitz Verlag, 2008), 168.

9 Munyika, "Role of Churches in Namibia," 168.

10 Horn, "Religion and Human Rights in Namibia," 409.

11 Wynand J. de Kock, "The Church as a Redeemed, and Redeeming Community," in *Toward Pentecostal Ecclesiology*, ed. John C. Thomas (Cleveland, TN: CPT Press, 2010), 49.

12 Horn, "Religion and Human Rights in Namibia," 409.

13 Horn, "Religion and Human Rights in Namibia," 411.

14 Office of International Religious Freedom, "Namibia 2020 International Religious Freedom Report," 1, https://www.state.gov/wp-content/uploads/2021/05/240282-NAMIBIA-2020-INTERNATIONAL-RELIGIOUS-FREEDOM-REPORT.pdf/, accessed July 19, 2024.

15 Johnson and Zurlo, *World Christian Encyclopedia*, 560.

16 "Religion and Human Rights in Namibia," 410.

17 "Van Der Walt, P. J.," *Dictionary of African Christian Biography*, https://dacb.org/stories/namibia/vanderwalt-pj/, accessed September 28, 2022.

18 Allan Anderson, Spreading Fires: *The Missionary Nature of Early Pentecostalism* (London: SCM Press, 2007), 3–4.

19 Nico Horn, "Crossing Racial Borders in Southern Africa: A Lesson from History," *Cyber Journal for Pentecostal-Charismatic Research*, June 1991, http://www.pctii.org/cyberj/ cyberj3/nico.html#N_10_./, accessed July 19, 2024.

20 Horn, "Crossing Racial Borders."

21 Louis F. Prinsloo, "The Early History of the AFM Church in Namibia," Boet Prinsloo Ministries, http://www.boetprinslooministries.com/early-history-of-the-afm-church/, accessed September 14, 2022.

22 "Van Der Walt, P. J.," *Dictionary of African Christian Biography*.

23 "Van Der Walt, P. J.," *Dictionary of African Christian Biography*.

24 Horn, "Religion and Human Rights in Namibia," 414.

25 Prinsloo, "The Early History of the AFM Church in Namibia."

26 Horn, "Religion and Human Rights in Namibia," 414.

27 AFM Namibia, "The Apostolic Faith Mission of Namibia," https://www.afmnamibia.com/, accessed July 19, 2022.

28 "Church Dropouts Have Risen to 64%–But What About Those Who Stay?," Barna Group, September 4, 2019, https://www.barna.com/research/resilient-disciples/, accessed July 19, 2024.

29 Barna Group, "Church Dropouts Have Risen to 64%."

30 Anonymous, *Prayer Request, Windhoek, Namibia,* International Missions Board, July 19, 2022, https://www.imb.org/prayer/windhoek-namibia/, accessed August 21, 2022.

31 The Government of the Republic of Namibia, "Ministry of Sport, Youth and National Service," *National Youth Policy,* January 2020, https://www.civic264.org.na/images/pdf/National_Youth_Policy_III.pdf/, accessed July 19, 2024.

32 Ndeshi Namupala, "'One That Has Given You Little Has Your Soul Consoled'–Unemployed Youth on Surviving," *Journal for Studies in Humanities and Social Sciences* 5:1 (2016), 36.

33 Charmaine Boois, "I Don't Even Feel Like a Person I Just Pretend," *The Namibian Newspaper*, August 22, 2022, https://www.namibian.com.na/115154/read/I-dont-even-feel-like-a-person-I-just-pretend/, accessed July 19, 2024.

34 Ashley Currier, Erin Winchester, and Emily Chien, "#MeToo Activism in Namibia: Sex-Positive Feminism and State Cooperation in the Fight to Stop Rape," *Feminist Formations* 33:3 (2021), 271–280, https://doi:10.1353/ff.2021.0049.

35 Heike Becker, "A Country on Fire: Protests in Namibia," *A Review of African Political Economy*, November 3, 2020, https://roape.net/2020/11/03/a-country-on-fire-protests-in-namibia/, accessed July 19, 2024.

36 Becker, "A Country on Fire."

37 See Corey Seemiller, Meghan Grace, *Generation Z: A Century in the Making* (New York: Routledge, 2019).

38 Becker, "A Country on Fire."

39 See Michelet William, "Gen Z and Their Rights to Participation," in *Real. Deal. Heal.* Gen Z and Social Issues, ed. Steve Case (Lincoln, NE: Advent Source, 2021), 26.

40 Veli-Matti Kärkkäinen, "Are Pentecostals Oblivious to Social Justice? Theological and Ecumenical Perspectives," *American Society of Missiology* 29:4, (October 2001), 423, https://doi.org/10.1177/009182960102900402.

41 Becker, "A Country on Fire."

42 J. Kwabena Asamoah-Gyadu, "The Promise is for You and Your Children: Pentecostal Spirituality, Mission and Discipleship in Africa," in *Mission Spirituality and Authentic Discipleship*, Regnum Edinburgh Centenary Series, vol. 14, eds. Wonsuk Ma and Kenneth R. Ross (1517 Media: Fortress Press, 2013), 10, https://doi.org/10.2307/j.ctv1ddcsmf.

43 Kwabena Asamoah-Gyadu, "The Promise is for You and Your Children," 25.

44 The Patriot Namibia, "Love or Hate Charismatic Churches: Pentecostalism is on the Rise," Facebook, April 22, 2016, https://www.facebook.com/571400403038796/, accessed June 2022.

45 de Kock, "The Church as a Redeemed and Redeeming Community," 65.

46 Donald E. Miller and Tetsunao Yamomori, *Global Pentecostalism: The New Face of Christian Social Engagement* (Los Angeles: University of California Press, 2007), 59.

47 Patrick Karabo Molutsi, "On the 6 July 2022 the AFM Youth represented by the National Youth Chairperson Pastor Patrick Molutsi, Bill-Gatsby Iipinge and Jamal Brinkman, attended the Public Dialogue Program," Facebook, July 6, 2022, https://m.facebook.com/patrick.molusti/posts/pcb.6234376159922444/, accessed July 30, 2022.

48 William, "Gen Z and Their Rights to Participation," 29.

7   Reaching Burmese Americans with the Gospel: A Reflection on the Myanmar World Cup USA

Kham Khai and Samuel Khai

Abstract

This study is a reflection on the Myanmar World Cup USA soccer tournament as a vehicle for the gospel in reaching Burmese Americans. The first section describes the exodus of the Myanmar people to Europe and North America. The second section discusses the challenges of resettling in the United States as Myanmar immigrants. The third section explores the promises of living the American dream. Finally, the last section discusses the soccer tournament and its impact on the Burmese American community. The timeframe of this study on the tournament covers the ten-year period of 2011–2022.

Introduction

Our supposition in this chapter is that the Myanmar World Cup USA soccer tournament has impacted and transformed the Myanmar community with the gospel, including the younger generation. This study provides the necessary background to explore this supposition. The first section describes the exodus of Burmese people from Myanmar and discusses the extreme hardships of living in Myanmar because of ethnic, political and religious persecutions by the Burmese military in 1962, 1988, and 2021. Due to post-pandemic conditions and civil unrest in Myanmar, many people fled to neighboring countries for safety, peace, and freedom. But unexpectedly, many Myanmar refugees ended in North America with the help of the United Nations High Commissioner for Refugees (UNHCR).

The second section of this research examines the challenges of resettling in the U.S. as Myanmar immigrants. Culture shock includes adapting in all aspects of life: the language barrier, cultural barriers, transportation issues, raising children, adjusting to new food, and encountering prejudice.

The third section explores the promises of living the American dream as immigrants. Like most, Burmese Americans dream of having financial security through hard work and having a good life, as well as American freedoms without fear of persecution. Children of Myanmar immigrants are generally succeeding academically in public schools, colleges, and universities. As first-generation Americans, they tend to graduate with high academic achievements and work white-collar or highly respected jobs.

Finally, the last section contemplates the soccer tournament and how it has become a vehicle for the gospel with its motto, "For the Game, For the Gospel." Annually, during Myanmar World Cup USA tournament, community gatherings have become community fare where Burmese Americans from many U.S. cities gather just to eat ethnic food and fellowship with one another. This has had kingdom effects.

The Arrival of the Myanmar People

The First Odyssey

On May 27, 1917 at 10:00 a.m. (during World War I), 1033 Burmese men from 110 villages from Tedim and Tonzang townships in the Chin State of Myanmar moved to Marseille, France.[1] They travelled by ship and worked for the Zomi France Labour Corps for one year and eight months for the British monarchy.[2] They built railroads, carried military machinery, helped the wounded, buried the dead, and completed different tasks as needed.[3] King George V hosted a reception at Buckingham Palace in London[4] for the hill men of Burma, recognizing them as "among the most devoted and skillful works in their particular department."[5] He said, "I really want to see the people of Zomi (*Zomite mahmah mu nuam ing*), and gave them awards, medals, and certificates of good service.[6] Some of the Zomi died and were buried near the Blargies Communal Cemetery Extension in France.[7] Others returned to Burma (Myanmar).[8]

The Exodus

The exodus of the people of Myanmar refers to a later period when the Myanmar people immigrated to the U.S. from Malaysia, Thailand, India, and Guam. To break away from ethnic, political, and religious persecution by the Burmese military—which they had been experiencing since 1962—people groups from Myanmar first fled to neighboring countries for refuge.[9] The majority of Burmese refugees are from various minority ethnic groups, such as the Zomi-Chin, Kachin, Karen, Mon, Rakhine, Shan, and Wa.[10] According to the U.S. CDC report, since 1988, over 10,000 Myanmar

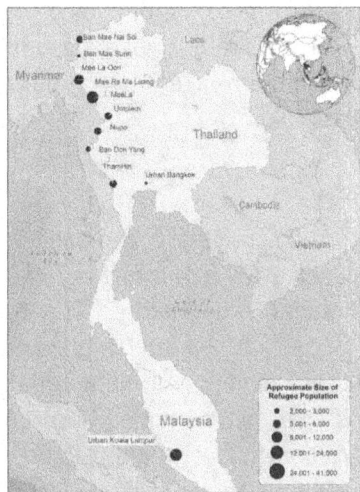

Figure 1: Location and Size of Burmese Refugee Camps in Thailand and Malaysia (December 2013)

people have moved to Thai refugee camps like Ong Phiam, Melah, Mesot, Nupoo, and others located on Thailand's border with Myanmar (Figure 1). Some ended up in Malaysia and got help from the UNHCR. Refugees in Malaysia reside mostly in the urban settlements in Kuala Lumpur (Figure 1).[11] As of August 2022, there were some 185,920 refugees and asylum-seekers registered with UNHCR in Malaysia. Some 159,190 are from Myanmar, comprising some 105,710 Rohingyas, 23,430 Chins, and 30,050 other ethnic groups fleeing conflict or persecution.[12]

In 2000, due to the continuing difficult circumstances in Myanmar, 1000 people migrated to the U.S. through Guam.[13] Then, from 2008 to 2014, tens of thousands of Burmese immigrated to the U.S. from Malaysian and Thai refugee camps (Figure 2).[14]

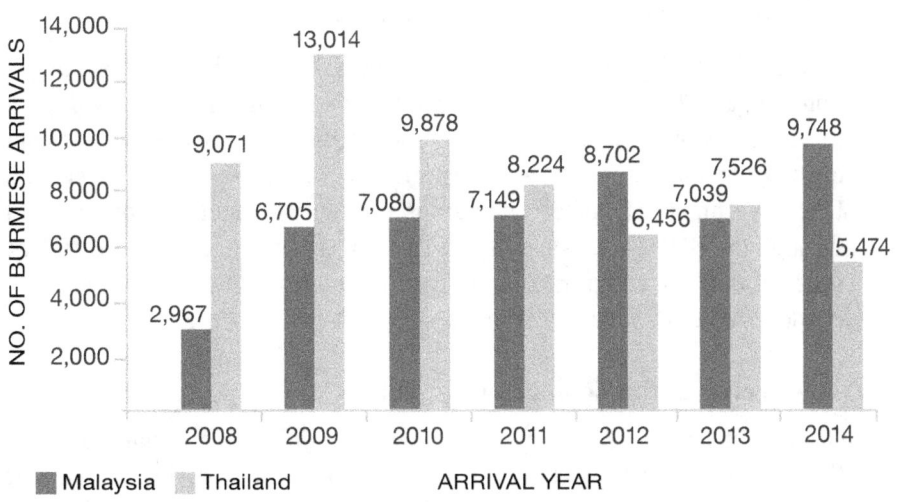

Figure 2: Number of Burmese Refugee Arriving in the United States from Malaysia and Thailand, 2008–2014 (N=109,033)

The exodus continued with 45.5 percent of Burmese immigrants being relocated to Texas, New York, Indiana, North Carolina, Georgia, and Minnesota.[15] Additionally, the majority of Burmese refugees resettling in the U.S. were young, ranging from 15–44 years old.[16]

The Present Situation: From Bad to Worse

A Burmese military coup seized power from the elected government of Aung San Suu Kyi on February 1, 2021, causing Myanmar to face what Russell Goldman has called the darkest moment in its history.[17] Having faced similar coups in 1962 and 1988, the decades of war and oppression made Myanmar one of the poorest nations in the world despite being full of natural resources including jade, rubies, gold, gas, petroleum, and teak. A handful of military leaders and their families benefit from these resources and make billions of dollars while the people of Myanmar struggle just to meet their daily needs in bamboo huts.

At present, the military continues seizing control of the country through force, and one cannot predict the end of the military coup in the foreseeable future. Many colleges and schools have been closed indefinitely, and masses of young people have escaped the country in search of safety, peace, and freedom. Unless world leaders listen to the urgent pleas and cry of the helpless, Gen Z and subsequent generations of Myanmar youth will end up dying in prisons.

Understandably, this has caused more refugees to Thailand and Malaysia. Some, since 2021, have gone to the Bangkok special shelter provided by the U.S. government. About 100,000 are still in Kuala Lumpur waiting to move to the United States, Australia, or Europe, as doors open. The U.S. government has helped numerous immigrants enter the country, and through the UNHCR in Asia, Myanmar refugees have been sent to different states in the U.S. and territories in Canada. Interestingly, most of the Zomi reside together in Tulsa, Oklahoma.

The Arrival of the Zomi People in Tulsa

The city of Tulsa was not well known by the people of Myanmar, however, those in the Burmese community who knew about it, knew about it through Oral Roberts University (ORU). Kham Khai first heard about

Oral Roberts' ministry from his principal teacher, Rev. Dr. Hau Lian Kham, when he was in college in Burma. In 1992, while his teacher and friend, Dr. Chin Do Kham and his wife, were studying for their Doctor of Ministry degree, Kham paved the way for Khai to go to ORU in 1994. During his studies, Khai arranged for his younger brother to come to ORU. In 1998, he married his wife while she was studying at Victory College. At that time in Tulsa, only five students and two families were known to be from Burma, and only Rev. Pum Za Thang Tombing's family were Burmese from India.

Establishing a New Myanmar Church

During that time, Myanmar Christian Church was established to bring together all ethnic groups from Myanmar and had its first Sunday worship in one of the rooms of Victory Church on December 7, 1997. This was possible as Pastor Khai got unmerited favor in the eyes of the Lord to use the building at no cost through the generosity of Victory Founding Pastors, Billy Joe and Sharon Daugherty.

As Pastor Kham Khai was studying at ORU and pastoring the church plant, he and his wife were praying together and asking God to bring many Burmese youth to Tulsa. People thought it was an insane idea and laughed mockingly at them saying, "How could people come to Tulsa when businesses are not good here?" However, they never slowed down their prayers.

Khai finished his Master of Divinity program, but his visa was expiring soon. So along with his wife, they applied for the Diversity Visa (DV) program, authorized by the U.S. State Department in November 2000. After filling out the applications, they laid hands on the forms and prayed over them before mailing them to Charleston Center. They said, "Almighty God, if you want us to serve you in the U.S., then please let us receive our DV."

Three months later, on March 19, 2001, Khai's wife Mary was surprised by a large brown envelope from the Department of State, Kentucky Consular Center. When she opened it, the letter read, "Congratulations." Neither one realized right away that it was related to the DV they applied for last November. As they continued to read, they found out that it was an approval for Mary's DV application form. They both rejoiced in the Lord with thanksgiving saying, "Our God wants us to serve him in the U.S.," and continued praising his grace that is sufficient upon them. Hallelujah!

At that time in Tulsa, Khai was the only one who pastored a church for the Myanmar community, and along with it, he continued pursuing his Doctor of Ministry, which he completed in 2007. (His oldest son, Samuel, would finish his B.S. in Psychology in 2022.) Because God did not forget the family's prayers since they started the church, the Lord himself brought many Myanmar refugees to the United States, many joined the church, and it has continued to grow to about five hundred members. Praise the Lord! Furthermore, Pastor Kham and Mary celebrated the Twenty-fifth Silver Jubilee of Myanmar Christ Church on December 2–4, 2022 with guest speakers Dr. William Wilson, President of Oral Roberts University; Dr. Ron Luce, Founder of Generation Next; and Pastor Sharon Daugherty of Victory Christian Center.[18]

Moving to a New Building

Because of their love for Christ, Pastors Billy Joe and Sharon Daugherty nurtured the Myanmar services for over twenty years without complaining, until it could stand on its own feet. They cared for the Myanmar community like the hen gathering and protecting her chicks under her outstretched wings (c.f. Matt 23:23). In 2016, with the help of God, Myanmar Christian Church purchased a 10 Gym-Fitness Center as its church building. The title company set the closing date on November 11, but it was moved to November 9. That was a remarkable day as it was the exact date when Donald Trump was elected U.S. President, and so we confirmed it by saying that "God gave us the building not on 9/11 but on 11/9." Additionally, the location was only one mile north of ORU's campus. We conducted the building dedication ceremony during Victory Christian Center's twenty-first anniversary on November 25, 2018, with Pastors Sharon and Paul Daugherty speaking.[19] Victory Church also made a generous donation to the building budget.

Thousands of Zomi moved to Tulsa, and now over 10,000 are living in Oklahoma. Around twenty Myanmar ethnic churches are in Tulsa, and two-thirds of them are Pentecostal-Charismatic.

The Challenges
Culture Shock
Coming suddenly from Myanmar, one of the poorest countries in the world, to America, with rich and high living standards, is like being a fish thrown out of water for a typical refugee. There are major challenges to adapt to in all aspects of life, including language, food, prices, transportation, and raising children. There are also cultural barriers and prejudice to overcome. Each immigrant faces social hardships of interacting, socializing, and connecting with Americans and their lifestyles.

The older generations who immigrated to the U.S. often have the hardest time adjusting because they can no longer drive or go anywhere by their own will, and end up staying home. Unable to find authentic Myanmar food anywhere made the first immigrants even more homesick. After some time, OK Asia Market,[20] KAI Burmese Cuisine,[21] and Asia Star Restaurant[22] were opened in Tulsa; now Burmese Americans can buy, cook, and eat their traditional food anytime, which helps ease homesickness. Since the pandemic, many Zomi-owned grocery stores have opened, and the Zomi community considers Tulsa their new home.

Spiritual Issues
Approximately 85 percent of Myanmar immigrants to Tulsa are Zomi, and they are all Christians. From their days in Myanmar, the Zomi is a minority ethnic tribe that has faced religious persecution, social injustice, and financial hardships. They live in the mountains on the sunset side of Myanmar, which is in the Northern Chin state bordering India. Deeply rooted in their Christian faith, they live by the Word of God wherever they settle. In Tulsa alone, over twenty Burmese churches exist now, and each individual worships the Lord freely, exercising their religious freedom unlike anywhere in Myanmar.

Yet, since the majority of Zomi church members do not speak fluent English, the pastor helps the community in transition. Everything from teaching and preaching, to social work, to helping with medical appointments, issuing ID in offices, applying for jobs, shopping, giving people rides, and translating are all part of the job. Additionally, since most church members are refugees, they have manual blue-collar jobs instead of high-paying jobs. Therefore, pastors ended up doing tent-making ministry and working outside or studying at the same time.

When our first son, Samuel, was born in 1999, our family faced many challenges. Mary worked daily from 7:00 a.m. to 11:00 p.m. Khai worked during the day assisting church members, driving his wife, and taking care of his kids, but also worked from 11:00 p.m. to 7:00 a.m. Even after their youngest son, Jonathan, was born, they continued serving the Lord and working daily in rain, snow, or sunshine. Rev. Dr. Thawng Khan Taithul said to us, "Your kids do not grow up in the house but inside the car." However, we continued serving the Lord faithfully, working overtime daily, and helping the needs of church members, especially refugees in any way possible, without any reservations. Some nights we spent at the Emergency Room or hospital, helping and translating for our members. Our children thought that serving the Lord in this way was incomprehensible. Since we always went out to help others, they said to us, "Will you always be out of the house?"

Twenty years later, Pastor Khai and his wife are thankful and grateful to have served the Lord in these circumstances. They served without giving up and enjoy it more than ever before. At present, their workload in helping their church members with social services has been much more manageable as their kids have grown. This enables them to assist their parents and siblings with their personal needs.

Mental Health Issues

As previously noted, adapting to the American lifestyle presents significant challenges for adult immigrants, particularly for those from Myanmar, as nearly every aspect of their lives is unfamiliar and vastly different from their previous experiences. Many individuals encounter considerable stress in the workplace, largely due to the pressure of managing demanding workloads within short timeframes. A tragic example occurred in 2018 in our local community of Jenks, where the father of one immigrant family suffered from severe mental illness as a result of work-related stress. This condition remained unrecognized by those around him, preventing them from offering the support he needed. Ultimately, he tragically took his own life and the lives of two of his young children.[23] This heartbreaking incident underscores a broader issue: numerous immigrants are grappling with similar mental health challenges, including clinical depression, as they navigate the complex process of adapting to life in the United States.

For the younger generation of Burmese immigrants, the process of adaptation to American society tends to be somewhat smoother. They often find their place more quickly, primarily through their participation in public schooling. These young individuals assimilate to the English language and American culture at an impressive rate, and increasingly integrate into mainstream social circles. However, balancing the influences of both American and Burmese cultures can present unique challenges. For instance, male Burmese American youths who are the eldest sons often bear significant familial responsibilities, including caring for their parents and managing household matters and finances. These expectations, while deeply rooted in cultural traditions, can place considerable pressure on young men. Nevertheless, the difficulties they encounter can be mitigated with the support of the Holy Spirit and through active involvement in a community of faith, where mutual support fosters personal growth and resilience.

Traditionally, mental health within the Burmese community has often been perceived through a lens of spiritual causality, such as being linked to the influence of evil spirits or attributed to past actions that might explain an individual's emotional or psychological state. However, the Burmese community is also deeply devoted to their faith, regularly attending church and participating in religious activities. Despite this strong spiritual foundation, recent tragedies have highlighted the critical importance of mental health alongside physical and spiritual well-being. For example, following the tragic incident in which a father took the lives of his two children,[24] and another case in which a young adult, active in both her church and community, attempted suicide by jumping off a bridge,[25] Burmese Americans have become increasingly aware of the need to address mental health issues. This growing recognition underscores the importance of mental health as a vital component of overall well-being, necessitating greater attention and care within the community.

Discipling the Next Generation

Most young individuals from Myanmar who immigrate to the United States with their families are between the ages of 6 and 18, which correspond to crucial developmental years in a child's life. According to psychoanalyst Erik Erikson, children within this age range undergo stages 4 and 5 of his psychosocial development theory.[26] Stage 4, known as "industry vs. inferiority," involves a child's exploration of their abilities and accomplishments in relation to their peers. During this stage, social interactions and parental encouragement are pivotal in shaping a child's sense of competence and self-worth. When children receive positive reinforcement, they are more likely to feel confident in their abilities to succeed. Conversely, the lack of such support can lead to self-doubt and a diminished sense of capability, causing them to question their potential to achieve their goals in life.

Erikson's theory is particularly relevant in the context of Burmese households, where there is traditionally a strong emphasis on the value of education. From a young age, children may face physical punishment for incorrect answers or failure to complete their homework, which can instill a sense of fear and aversion toward academic pursuits. On the other hand, some children may emerge with a sense of pride or heightened motivation to demonstrate their academic achievements. In Burmese culture, there is a widely held belief that success is largely contingent upon obtaining a college degree, which is seen as essential for finding one's purpose and securing financial independence to support oneself and one's family. However, this intense pressure to pursue higher education, often driven by the expectations of parents, can become burdensome. For many children, this pressure, coupled with a lack of emotional support or encouragement, can lead to feelings of inadequacy and self-doubt. As a result, some may give up on their educational goals, not due to a lack of effort or desire, but because they believe they are incapable of meeting the high expectations set for them. While this experience is not universal, it significantly affects the mental health and well-being of many young Burmese immigrants adjusting to life in the United States.

As a child transitions into Stage 5 of Erikson's psychosocial development, known as "identity vs. confusion," the process of forming a personal identity becomes central. At this stage, adolescents begin to seek answers to the fundamental question: "Who am I?" Their sense of self is heavily influenced by the social relationships they cultivate at home, in church, at school, and within their broader community. This is the critical period when young people start to define themselves, shaping their beliefs and determining their future career paths based on the influences around them. Stage 5 is closely connected to Stage 4, "industry vs. inferiority," because any alienation or lack of support experienced in Stage 4—whether at home or in church—can negatively affect the formation of identity. If a child has faced discouragement or disconnection during earlier stages, it may hinder their ability to develop a positive sense of self, potentially leading them to adopt beliefs or make choices that are less aligned with their true identity or well-being.

Unfortunately, some young people in the Burmese American community, having faced alienation or disconnection, have misused their newfound American liberties and freedoms. In an attempt to navigate the challenges of identity and belonging, many have turned to alcohol, drugs, and a lifestyle centered around self-indulgence, entertainment, and the avoidance of responsibility. These choices often lead them away from their cultural roots and, in many cases, from church involvement as well. The disengagement from religious and familial support systems compounds the difficulties many face during the critical stages of development. As a result, the community has witnessed a troubling trend where some youth abandon their spiritual and cultural foundations, seeking fulfillment in transient pleasures rather than in meaningful growth and connection.

In response, the Burmese American community yearns for a spiritual revival—one that would restore the minds, bodies, and souls of their youth. They hope for a renewal through the transformative power of the Holy Spirit and the guidance of the anointed Word of God. This revival is seen as essential not only for healing the psychological and emotional wounds that many young people face but also for fostering a cultural environment where faith, family, and personal responsibility are prioritized. Given the complexities of adjusting to life in the United States, including the pressures associated with education, identity formation, and mental health challenges, such spiritual renewal offers a potential pathway to restore balance, provide support, and help youth overcome the difficulties they encounter in both their personal and communal lives.

The Promises

Financial Security

When Myanmar immigrants move to the U.S., they dream of working hard and living the American dream. Life is so hard living in Myanmar, where they came from small villages and worked as impoverished farmers who cultivated the land. The majority of them had never seen a dollar before. Now, with perseverance and hard work, their livelihoods have changed dramatically. After working in big companies for several years, they can buy their own house, new cars, and many things they want.

Education for Children

Children of Myanmar immigrants thrive successfully academically as they enter public schools, colleges, and universities. As first-generation Americans, they graduate as engineers, lawyers, nurses, computer scientists, teachers, and preachers. In fall 2022, ORU had 56 Myanmar students, which is its highest enrollment among the Zomi population. An international admissions representative, Felipe Argolo, added that "These numbers are for residential programs on-campus and do not include online students taking online classes."[27] At present, 1,301 Zomi/Burmese Students are enrolled in Jenks public schools, which consists of 10 percent of the district's total population.[28] Myanmar Community School, which is under the ministry of Myanmar Christian Church, has taught Burmese and Zomi languages every Saturday since fall 2021. Its purpose is to teach through native speakers so younger students can read, write, and speak their tongue of heritage with correct pronunciation.

Reaching the Community Through Soccer

Reaching the community and beyond is the Great Commission of our Lord Jesus Christ (Matt 28:20–21). Myanmar Christian Church has many strategies to outreach locally and internationally, but the soccer tournament is one of our most effective outreach ministries because the people of Myanmar love soccer anywhere in the world. Wherever the people of Myanmar are—whether in rural or urban settings—there are also soccer games; they are soccer-crazy from the youngest to the oldest. Soccer is the national game of Myanmar and they are able to watch the European game league live on television or online. An American missionary to Myanmar wanted to use an illustration of Jesus Christ known by everyone by asking a little boy if he knew Michael Jordan. To his surprise, the boy replied, "No." He then asked if he knew any sports players and the boy quickly answered and said

"Beckham, Ronaldo..." The missionary then realized that the people of Myanmar are more much more interested in soccer than basketball.

How it Began

Our church youth started a soccer team in 2000, and during the season, they would travel from state to state to compete. Since the distances are far, the soccer leaders started brainstorming ways to have soccer games locally. Pastor Khai told the soccer leaders that since soccer players are more interested in playing on the soccer field than going to church, the leaders should begin going to soccer fields and leading players through prayer and reading the Bible there. In other words, we needed to bring church to them. We strategized to accomplish this. Our vision became, "To utilize soccer as a vehicle of the gospel of Jesus Christ." Our mission was threefold:

1. To provide soccer games for young adults of the Burmese American community.
2. To raise up young people to glorify God through their talents by becoming professional soccer players.
3. To have fellowship with Burmese people from different ethnic backgrounds who live in the United States.

Our core value was to "Empower one another through faith, friendship, and fellowship within the community."

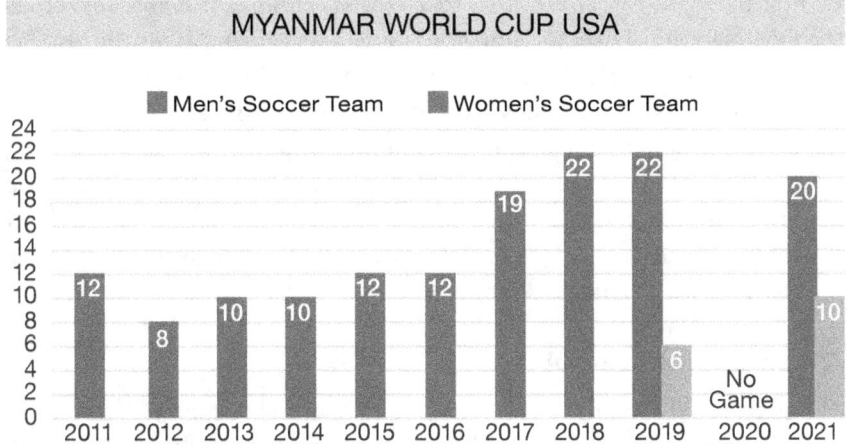

Figure 3: Number of Soccer Teams—Men's and Women's—Participating in Myanmar World Cup USA

The Game

Our first game began on May 30, 2011, which was Memorial Day. The tournament known as the Myanmar World Cup USA is now held annually in Tulsa during Memorial Day weekend. It started with twelve teams and has grown to twenty-four teams as of 2022; Myanmar people come from over twenty different states to attend. For seven years, Mr. Thang Sian Mang and Pastor Thangminlian Khai Dopmul led the tournament. Later, the sport ministry was registered as the Myanmar American Soccer Association by the Secretary of State of Oklahoma. The tournament was organized as an umbrella group under Myanmar Christian Church with the purpose of all Burmese young people coming together in Tulsa for friendship and for presenting the gospel of Christ to the fans and network.

Present Leadership

Do Khan Khup and his wife Cingh Pi have now led the tournament for the past two years, and it has been increasingly successful because both of them were part of the Myanmar National Professional League. Do Khup served as the CEO of Chin United FC in Yangon, and his wife serves the Asia Football Federation, which is affiliated with Myanmar Football Federation. As a professional club license holder, she served as the first female Match Commissioner of Myanmar Football Federation from 2015 to 2022. In 2008, Do Khup served as the OM National Director and Job Tuang was an administrator for the game. They invited a Brazilian professional soccer team to Myanmar in Pathein City where they got to share the gospel and testify to over 50,000 people consisting of Buddhist monks, military generals, government officials, and local people. It was the first open-air crusade ever permitted. Praise God that through soccer ministry, the people of Myanmar heard the story of the living God, and the seed faith of the gospel of Jesus Christ was planted.

A Vehicle for the Gospel

The soccer tournament has become a vehicle of the gospel with its motto, "For the Game, For the Gospel." In 2022, in only three days, over 5,000 people attended with some players and sports fans hearing about Jesus

Christ for the first time.[29] We were privileged to have the following distinguished guests: Dr. Wonsuk Ma, Distinguished Professor of Global Christianity from ORU; W. Kyle Tresch, Attorney at Law; Jim Davis, Director of Outreach at Asbury Church; and Thuzar Wint Lwin, Miss Universe Myanmar 2020. The game's opening ceremony was held on a Saturday morning and began with an opening prayer. After singing worship songs, the national anthem was sung. Ribbon-cutting was followed with a short motivational message from the guest speaker for the soccer players and spectators. Thousands of gospel tracts were distributed throughout the tournament to plant faith in the hearts of young people.

During the hour break of the final game, Pastor Khai and his son Samuel had an opportunity to share the gospel for about twenty minutes. Incidentally, that was when the soccer field had the largest crowd as everyone was anticipating who would go home with the trophy. Samuel led worship with contemporary gospel songs, and Pastor Khai preached in Burmese while his son preached in English. About 160,000 people were reached worldwide through the live broadcast. Church organizations and local businesses who believed in the vision sponsored the tournament.

The Benefits of Soccer

Through soccer, Myanmar youth learn not only about the Word of God but also the importance of having a disciplined life. Coaches are encouraged not to consume alcohol or drugs, and their right choices provide a positive example to players who have made poor choices. Since teams play within a certain slot of time, they are taught the importance of managing time efficiently and effectively. To maintain good health and stamina, the players regularly exercise. Some of the players even receive college sports scholarships while attending high school.

Community Gathering

Annually, during the Myanmar World Cup USA tournament, Burmese Americans from around the United States gather together just to eat ethnic food and fellowship with one another. The entire Myanmar community looks forward to this event as it brings everyone together through the game. Also, through attending the tournament, people from different parts of the U.S. come to know more about Tulsa and the Burmese American community. Most do not know that Tulsa has the largest Zomi population in the United States, according to Hau Suan Khai, the chairman of Zomi Innkuan Oklahoma (ZIOK), a local community organization.[30] During the tournament, young people meet and mingle, and some even end up falling in love and getting married. Consequently, many Zomi communities have ended up moving to Tulsa as they love the culture-friendly atmosphere.

Conclusion

Since their first odyssey as the Zomi France Labour Corps, the people of Myanmar have been known as nomads moving from one place to another in hope of finding safe refuge. As King George V earmarked them as "among the most devoted and skillful works in their particular department"[31] and wanted to see the people of Zomi personally,[32] the Zomi from Myanmar have continued to receive favor from the Lord. Although they have fled Burma as refugees from ethnic, political, and religious persecution—by the Burmese military, from 1962 to present—they remember their roots by doing their work with excellent spirit like Daniel in the Bible. Consequently, the Zomi diaspora has spread globally and they have become assets for the nations they inhabit. The first Zomi from Myanmar came to Tulsa in the early 1990s as theological students at ORU. Now Tulsa has the largest Zomi population in the United States with over 7,000 people and is proudly known as "Zomi Town" within the Myanmar community.

Furthermore, the Myanmar World Cup USA soccer tournament has impacted and transformed the younger generations and Myanmar community by being a vessel of the gospel. As a result, many have been edified and moved to Tulsa to find comradery. Most of all, thousands of youth have heard the message of Christ who would not have heard otherwise. Through this annual tournament, we hope and expect to help more youth from our local community, and the next generation of Burmese Americans more broadly, encounter God.

Notes

1. Don Ngaih Lian, *Ka Piantit Pai Sese [My France Odyssey]*, (Kalay Myo, Myanmar: U Nang Sawm Piang, Zomi Christian Literature Society, 2018), 71.
2. Lian, *Ka Piantit Pai Sese*, 167–194.
3. Lian, *Ka Piantit Pai Sese*, 308.
4. Lian, *Ka Piantit Pai Sese*, 308.
5. "Hillmen from Burmah," *The Guardian and the Observer News*, March 17, 1918.
6. C. Thang Za Tuan, "Zomite Pusuahcilna, Khanlawhna leh Khantohna," in *Golden Jubilee Commemorative Magazine* 1948–1998, 1 (1999), 173.
7. Lian, *Ka Piantit Pai Sese*, 200–221.
8. Lian, *Ka Piantit Pai Sese*, 71.
9. More details on this can be found in Chin Association of Maryland, "Two Years After the 2021 Military Coup," CAM, Inc., January 2023, https://chinmd.org/wp-content/uploads/2023/02/19484-2-Years-After-the-Coup-FIN.pdf/, accessed October 16, 2024.
10. United States Department of Health and Human Services, "Burmese Refugee Health Profile," Center for Disease Control and Prevention (CDC), April 27, 2016, 6, file:///C:/SnapVolumesTemp/Writable/Downloads/cdc_40149_DS1%20(1).pdf/, accessed July 5, 2024.
11. "Burmese Refugee Health Profile," 5.
12. The U.N. Refugee Agency USA, "Figures at a Glance in Malaysia," UNHCR, https://www.unhcr.org/en-us/figures-at-a-glance-in-malaysia/, accessed September 5, 2022.
13. Chin Association of Maryland, 4.
14. "Burmese Refugee Health Profile," 6.
15. "Burmese Refugee Health Profile," 6.
16. "Burmese Refugee Health Profile," 7.
17. Russell Goldman, "Myanmar's Coup, Explained," *The New York Times*, April 27, 2022, https://www.nytimes.com/article/myanmar-news-protests-coup.html/, accessed September 5, 2022.
18. Myanmar Christian Church, 2022, Facebook, https://www.facebook.com/mcctulsa/, accessed November 14, 2022.

19 Myanmar Christian Church, "MCC Tulsa–21 Anniversary Service," November 25, 2018, Facebook, https://fb.watch/fT0TCOgs-c/, accessed September 7, 2022.

20 OK Asian Market, 2022, Facebook, https://www.facebook.com/OKAsianMarket/, accessed September 7, 2022.

21 KAI Burmese Cuisine, 2022, Facebook, https://www.facebook.com/kaiburmese/, accessed September 7, 2022.

22 Asian Star Restaurant, 2022, Facebook, https://www.facebook.com/asianstartulsa/, accessed September 7, 2022.

23 Kelsy Schlotthauer, "Victims Identified in Jenks Murder-Suicide," *Tulsa World*, December 16, 2019, https://tulsaworld.com/news/victims-identified-in-jenks-murder-suicide/article_939f040f-4979-5472-b64c-8a4d378d7f68.html/, accessed September 10, 2022.

24 Schlotthauer, "Victims Identified in Jenks Murder-Suicide."

25 Victory Church, "Stories of Victory: Luan's Story," Facebook, https://fb.watch/fPhOu2ZRZU/, accessed September 12, 2022.

26 Kendra Cherry, "Erikson's Stages of Development," *Verywell Mind*, August 3, 2022, https://www.verywellmind.com/erik-eriksons-stages-of-psychosocial-development-2795740/, accessed September 12, 2022.

27 Felipe Argolo, International Admissions Representative, International Student Relations, Oral Roberts University, "Re: A Request of Myanmar Students Enrollment," email received by the author, September 21, 2022.

28 "Burmese Community Peer Educator Program: Sia Mah Nu," Community Service Council, https://csctulsa.org/sia-mah-nu-program/, accessed September 23, 2022.

29 Myanmar World Cup USA, 2022, Facebook, https://www.facebook.com/myanmarworldcupusa/, accessed September 7, 2022.

30 Priya Krishna, "In Tulsa, a Burmese Cooking Tradition Takes the Spotlight," *The New York Times*, June 27, 2022, https://www.nytimes.com/2022/06/27/dining/burmese-food-tulsa.html/, accessed September 7, 2022.

31 "Hillmen from Burmah," *The Guardian and the Observer News*.

32 Tuan, *Zomite Pusuahcilna, Khanlawhna leh Khantohna*, 173.

8 Children's Ministry from a Missional Perspective and an Online Strategy to Help Teachers with Children's Ministry on the Mission Field: A Case Study

Jane C. Kim

Abstract

This chapter explores the foundation of Christian education from a missional perspective and discusses the locus of children's ministry. It introduces an online platform aimed at aiding teachers in children's ministry as a missional strategy. The first part of the study focuses on the Great Commission in Matthew 28 and the outpouring of the Holy Spirit in Acts 2. In the second part, a case study provides survey outcomes to address ongoing challenges of children's ministry and explains how an online tool for Sunday school teachers can help in reaching the next generation.

Introduction

Churches worldwide are increasingly recognizing the importance of engaging the younger generations. A recent survey of American Protestant pastors has revealed that 40 percent of them have identified "reaching the next generation" as their top priority for future ministry.[1] In addition, a significant 65 percent of children's ministers have emphasized the crucial role of effective children's ministry in church growth.[2] In light of this growing concern, the Pentecostal World Conference 2022 in Seoul set a timely and relevant theme: "Pentecostal Revival in the Next Generation." These are promising signs that many church leaders understand the importance of engaging children and the critical role children's ministry plays in the church's future. However, a survey of leaders who are already involved in children's ministry reveals an ironic finding: 56 percent of them felt that "children's ministry is often forgotten in the church."[3] This data hints at a gap between the church's perception of the importance of children's ministry and the reality of what is happening.

This problem is confirmed in another survey taken in Korea. Senior pastors commonly rank education for the next generation as their top priority, with 35.4 percent identifying it as the most challenging aspect of current church ministry. Assistant pastors echo this sentiment, with 46.8 percent identifying "the problem of education for the next generation" as the most significant issue.[4] However, when the same pastors were asked which generation they would focus on in future ministry, 31.4 percent of them—the largest percentage—identified the middle generation of the church (individuals in their thirties and forties) as their top priority.[5] This indicates that while the importance of the next generation is recognized, the main focus of ministry is still the adult demographic.

This phenomenon is particularly evident in mission fields where there are many young churches. During church establishment, adult members are often valued more than children, and many churches are unable to start children's ministry because of practical obstacles such as lack of finances, space, and teaching resources. Understandably, pastors may prioritize adult ministry over children's ministry if both groups cannot be ministered to from the outset. Although environmental factors contribute to this problem, it is significantly rooted in churches' perspectives and values about children's ministry. To address this issue, this paper discusses the foundation of Christian education for children and introduces an online platform as a case study in providing practical assistance to children's Sunday school teachers.

The Foundation of Christian Education for Children from a Missional-Pentecostal Perspective

The Great Commission

The significance of Christian education for children has a strong biblical foundation.[6] However, Matthew 28:16–20 is particularly important as it proclaims the Great Commission to go into the world and make disciples of all nations. This passage is often valued for its missional encouragement to "go." Nonetheless, while interpreting the passage, Grant R. Osborne criticizes denominations and mission groups for prioritizing "winning new converts" over "anchoring them in the Christian faith."[7] Although the missional significance of the Great Commission should not be ignored, the missional emphasis on the urgent need of "going" has often resulted in a lack of attention to the pedagogical values embodied in the process of making disciples through teaching—including of children.

It is worth noting that there are two commands in the passage: going *and* making disciples. The primary emphasis of the Great Commission falls arguably on the latter. Regarding this, Craig Evans' grammatical and syntactical analysis is helpful: "The imperative 'make disciples' is the main verb in the commission of vv. 19–20. The commission is not so much fulfilled in the going but in the disciple-making."[8] Moreover, the command to make disciples is further described with two present participles—baptizing and teaching—as they characterize the process of discipleship. Thus, the predominant imagery of the teacher-disciple relationship in Matthew 28:16–20 underscores the centrality of educational values in Christian life from the time of conversion and baptism. Christian education is, therefore, not simply a means of training Christians or fulfilling God's command but is integral to the command itself. In this regard, Robert Pazmino rightly views the imperative to make disciples in Matthew 28 as an "educational commission."[9]

The interpretation of "all" in Matthew 28:18–20 has been a contentious issue, particularly the term *panta ta ethnē* ("all nations" or "all people"). The focal point of the discussion is an ethnographic question in terms of what comprises "all people." It is generally agreed that the term carries a universal sense, with D. A. Carson describing the commission as a universal principle for all humanity "without distinction."[10] N. Walter reiterates the same idea while arguing that the term *panta ta ethnē* could be "widely interpreted in reference to the totality of mankind."[11] It is therefore imperative to broaden the connotation of "all people" to all of humankind. Regarding this, Michael J. Wilkins' view is useful as he provides a specific definition of "all people":

> Jesus once again breaks down barriers to indicate that all of his disciples – women and men, Gentile and Jew, poor and rich – are to be taught to obey everything he has commanded....What Jesus has done in making disciples of his first followers, succeeding generations of the church will do in the making of new disciples of Jesus.[12]

If it can be argued that the term "all people" should not be limited ethnographically—as disciples should be comprised of men and women, regardless of ethnicity, social status, race, or economic condition—then it should not be limited to age either. The notion of human universality should be applicable not only culturally, but also generationally. Carson aptly points out an important aspect of discipleship when he says that

"These [disciples] in turn pass on the truth they received. So, a means is provided for successive generations to remain in contact with Jesus' teachings."[13] His point is a good reminder that children cannot be a viewed as a secondary group when it comes to church ministries. One should understand that the Great Commission to make disciples, characterized by teaching, centers on the equal value of all humanity without age distinction. Children's ministry is not subsidiary to adult ministry.

The Outpouring of the Holy Spirit

Peter's quoting of Joel 2:28 in Acts 2 reminds Pentecostals of what it means to be filled with the Holy Spirit. It signifies the missional call as noted by Eckhard J. Schnabel: "Peter clarifies that what follows in Joel's prophecy relates to the last days of God's history of salvation, which is now identified as the new age ushered in by Jesus."[14] That is why Pentecostal identity is normally appreciated for its missional origin and emphasis. However, it is often true that more attention has been given to the purpose of Spirit-baptism than to the qualifications of its recipients—who may receive it.

In fact, it is of paramount importance to understand that the Pentecostal identity is rooted in equality, which is highlighted with the term "all flesh." Regarding the interpretation of this term, many interpret Joel 2:28 to be referring to "all Judah," not "all humankind."[15] This perspective permits the misunderstanding that the baptism of the Holy Spirit is only for certain groups of people, since Spirit-baptism here appears to exclude Gentiles. However, even within this exegetical context, the point of the passage was to expand the promise of the Holy Spirit from a select group of people to all the people of Judah. In other words, Joel's prophecy initially foreshadowed universality, as Douglas Stuart explains:

> In the new age all of God's people will have all they need of God's Spirit. The old era was characterized by the Spirit's selective, limited influence on some individuals: certain prophets, kings, etc. But through Joel the people are hearing of a new way of living, in which everybody can have the Spirit. On this spiritual bounty compare Ezek 36:26–29; Hos 14:4–8; Micah 7:19; Zeph 3:9–13; Zech 8:16, 22. Even slaves will partake, on a par with the free, in the blessing of the Spirit's outpouring, no societal restrictions being able to limit the power of God to give himself to his people.[16]

Accordingly, despite any limited application of universality beyond Israel in the immediate context of Joel 2, Duane A. Garrett maintains it is still shocking that "in an era in which men (not women), the old (not the young), and the landowners (not slaves) ruled society, Joel explicitly rejected all such distinctions as criteria for receiving the Holy Spirit."[17] Joel's prophecy lays a foundation for human equality within all people of Judah, including the young.

Moreover, whether or not Joel's prophecy defines the outpouring of the Holy Spirit as the promise for all Judah, what characterizes the Pentecostal foundation of Christian education is Peter's interpretation of Joel's prophecy in Acts 2. According to Schnabel, "all flesh" in Acts is an inclusive term for "all the people who repent and believe in Jesus as the Messiah (v. 38)," including Gentiles (Acts 11:15–18).[18] Demetrius K. Williams also asserts that "in Acts the event foreshadows the eventual integration of Gentiles in the promise of the Holy Spirit."[19] F. F. Bruce maintains that the outpouring of the Holy Spirit in Acts 2:28 was "the beginning of the fulfilment" for all flesh.[20]

Thus, receiving the Holy Spirit is not a special privilege given to just a few, or a temporary privilege given just for particular leadership roles. Peter implies that when the Holy Spirit comes upon people, all distinctions of gender, social class, race, ethnicity, and *age*, will be removed. In view of the Pentecostal movement undergirding the rapid growth of Christianity, especially in the Global South, the Pentecostal message of universality for children should be acknowledged and valued so that church activities for children will be considered primary rather than secondary ministries.

Online Resourcing for Teachers as a Mission Strategy

To gain a better understanding of the reality of children's Sunday school ministry in the Global South, a survey[21] was conducted with the members of an online ministry called For Sunday School Teachers (FSST).[22] The first part of the survey asked members about the establishment date of children's Sunday schools and adult worship services in their respective churches. The survey results depicted in Figure 1 reveal that only 1.6 percent (4 persons) established Sunday schools before launching their adult worship services, while 28 percent (69 persons) of churches started both adult and children's services simultaneously in the same year. By contrast, 132 people (53.7%) reported that children's Sunday schools were established after the start of adult worship services.

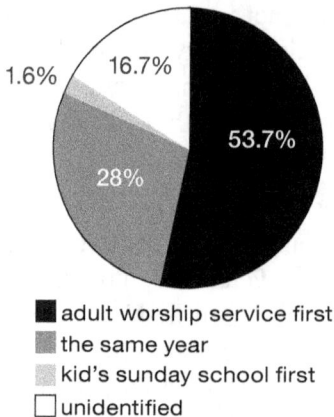

- adult worship service first
- the same year
- kid's sunday school first
- unidentified

Figure 1. Establishment Date of the Children's Sunday School and the Adult Worship Service in the Global South (n=246)

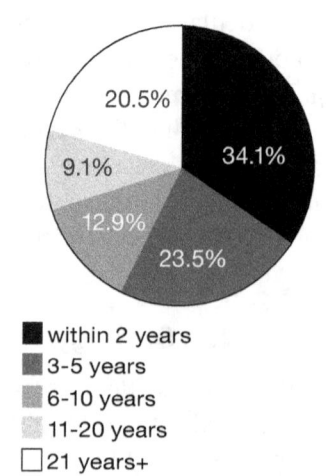

- within 2 years
- 3-5 years
- 6-10 years
- 11-20 years
- 21 years+

Figure 2: Time Taken to Establish Children's Sunday School (n=132)

Further analysis of the data reveals that for the 132 respondents who reported later establishment of Sunday schools, the time taken for Sunday schools to be established varied greatly, as shown in Figure 2. Of those, 34.1 percent started their Sunday schools within two years after the launch of their adult worship services. Additionally, 23.5 percent were established between three to five years, 12.9 percent between six to ten years, 9.1 percent between eleven to twenty years, and 20.5 percent after more than 21 years. It is quite alarming that it took 57.6 percent of churches two to five years to start a children's ministry, but even more alarming that 29.6 percent—almost one-third—took over one to two decades! This data shows that we need to give much more support and attention to children's ministry.

After overcoming the challenges of establishing children's Sunday schools, teachers often face the practical problem of finding suitable materials to aid their teachings. This can be difficult due to lack of finances and scarcity of materials. In addition to these challenges, the coronavirus pandemic brought about social distancing measures, which resulted in the suspension of church gatherings and worship services worldwide. To continue their mission, churches had to adapt to new technologies such as Zoom or YouTube Live for virtual worship services. However, the transition to move children's ministries online became a secondary objective again, because churches had to prioritize their resources for setting up online worship services for adults.[23] This made it difficult for children's teachers to continue their mission of helping children learn and grow in their faith. Furthermore, young children without suitable electronic devices often lack the capacity to use the internet without adult supervision, leading to further constraints on children's ministry.

Nevertheless, these limitations eventually created an environment that improved online accessibility, making the new environment an opportunity to adapt and progress. Despite the challenges that need to be addressed regarding children's online usage, online platforms have become useful tools for teacher preparation. This is confirmed through one notable example of the FSST.[24] This online group experienced significant growth during the pandemic. In May 2019, the group had only 50 members, but by January 2020 membership had increased to 650 (Figure 3). The group continued to gain members, adding 3,000 members between February 2020 and February 2021, and 4,400 from March 2021 to February 2022. As of February 2023, the group had approximately 12,400 members, an increase of about 5,000 from the previous year. The FSST experienced a significant increase in requests for permission to use sermons and craft activity materials so that children's teachers could provide resources to parents who had to teach their children at home during the pandemic.

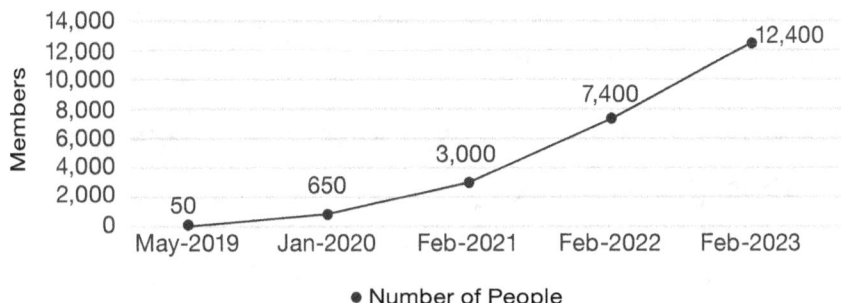

Figure 3: FSST Member Growth Rate

It is even more interesting to see that the need for the online ministry of the FSST was continually acknowledged even after the social distancing measures were lifted and in-person worship services resumed. There was an increase in requests for virtual training for teachers. Another notable trend during this period was an increase in views related to the administration of Sunday school and lessons for evangelism, as Sunday school activities resumed. Teachers who started looking online for children's materials during the pandemic still sought support for their children's ministry, which leads one to conclude that the pandemic drew teachers' attention to online resources, but they are increasingly finding them helpful.

This phenomenon has been, of course, facilitated by the smoothness of internet use globally. According to a survey of the Pew Research Center in 2020, more than half of those in 32 of the 34 countries surveyed reported that they own a smartphone and use the internet occasionally. Furthermore, the frequency of internet use was highest among young people 18–29 years old, with almost the same amount among those aged 30–49 in many countries.[25] Similar findings were discovered in the FSST study, which surveyed 276 respondents. Out of those surveyed, 63.5 percent (175 people) reported being able to easily access the internet as needed, while 31.5 percent (87 people) reported it being hard sometimes, and only 5.1 percent (14 people) reported not being able to easily access the internet. When asked about the availability of adequate internet speed and mobile data to easily watch tutorial videos for crafting and YouTube links for learning songs and motions, results were similar: 60.1 percent (166 people) said it was sufficient, 36.6 percent (101 people) said they sometimes have difficulties, and 3.3 percent (9 people) said they could not watch. When asked about the devices they use to access the internet, almost all respondents indicated cell phones as their primary device (94%), followed by laptops (44.2%), desktops (13.4%), and tablets (10.9%) (Figure 4).

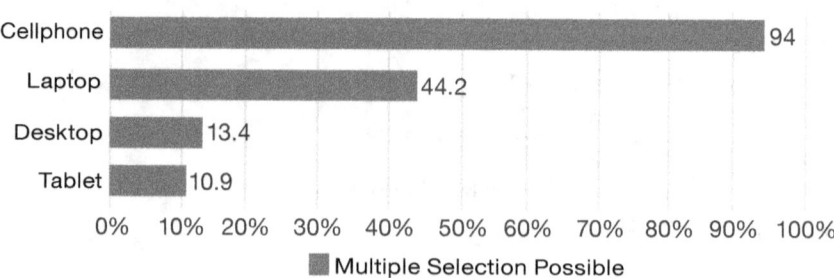

Figure 4: Devices Used to Access the Internet (n=276)

The group with the highest percentage of teachers using online platforms was the 31–40 age group, accounting for 38.8 percent. Following closely was the 18–30 age group, with 35.9 percent, trailed by the 41–50 age group and those aged 51 years or older (Figure 5).

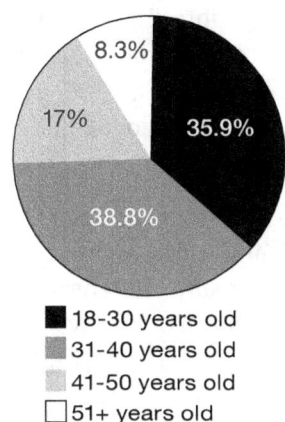

Figure 5: Age Distribution of Users Accessing Christian Education Materials Online (n=276)

This survey indicates that an internet-friendly environment is already well-established, and many people can easily access the internet today in many countries, including the Global South. This implies that offering continuous online support to teachers is feasible and can be a strategic resource for children's ministry. In fact, according to the FSST survey, the most common response given by teachers about the benefits of online information was that it is accessible (89.5%). Increasing the accessibility is the fact that FSST ministry can assist English-speaking and non-English-speaking teachers.

Consequently, online ministry of the FSST offers two significant advantages. First, it can alleviate language barriers to some extent. According to the FSST survey, 39.5 percent (109 people) of 276 respondents use Facebook's automatic translation feature to read materials. Although 60.5 percent (167 people) have no difficulty accessing resources written in English, it is noteworthy that only 31.2 percent (86 people) have English as their first language. This suggests that over a third of respondents (39.5%) who use the translation function represent a significant portion, indicating that online ministry has enormous potential in terms of translating materials into various languages with the aid of technology.

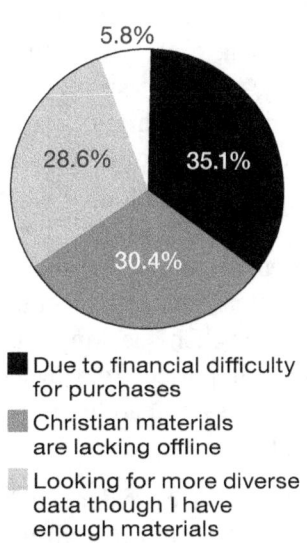

Figure 6: Reasons for Utilizing Free Resources on FSST (n=276)

Secondly, online ministry can offer immediate and realistic economic assistance for those in financial need. In the same FSST survey that asked about reasons teachers utilized free resources (Figure 6), 35.1 percent of respondents stated that they visit to use the free materials because of financial difficulties, while 30.4 percent mentioned that they lack access to Christian materials offline. Another 28.6 percent mentioned that they had enough data but were seeking additional sources.

We can conclude that providing free basic educational materials in children's Sunday school education is critical in delivering quality education and providing economic assistance to many churches on the mission field. Each church has the potential to create an online system for sharing educational information and materials that are no longer utilized in their Sunday schools. By doing so, they can extend a helping hand to Sunday school teachers on the field as well as exert educational influence on a weekly basis. And, they can do it at a lower cost than any other mission projects planned within the church.

However, churches must classify data suitable for the mission field's context, which is the most important factor in online ministry. The Third Mandate Program of the Theological Education Fund has presented a set of detailed questions regarding contextualization to assess the effectiveness of education. Among these questions, one inquiry regarding structural contextualization is particularly noteworthy: "Is the church, school, or program making an effort to establish an appropriate form and structure that caters to the distinct requirements of its culture within its specific social, economic, and political circumstances?"[26] This question is of immense importance since structural context plays a crucial role in educational success. In the realm of children's missions, even excellent organizations with high-quality programs often encounter challenges when attempting to expand globally. Language barriers are often a significant obstacle, but so is difficulty accessing a broad range of educational materials required to make schooling complete. For example, in the English-speaking mission field, many Christian education textbooks are imported from overseas. However, they are not always fully utilized because of inability to afford the additional materials necessary to prepare for their use.

In this regard, the FSST offers resources that consider teachers' financial limitations. A survey was conducted with 246 individuals in the Global South to gauge the financial support available for Sunday school in their churches. The findings are alarming, with

42.7 percent of respondents reporting that their churches are making efforts to secure sufficient financial support but have yet to achieve it. Additionally, a third (35.8%) of respondents have no financial support at all, and a significant minority (12.5%) are relying solely on their own expenses. Only one-fifth (21.5%) of respondents reported having adequate financial support for their Sunday school programs (Figure 7). This result illustrates the pressing need for greater financial support for teachers in the Global South.

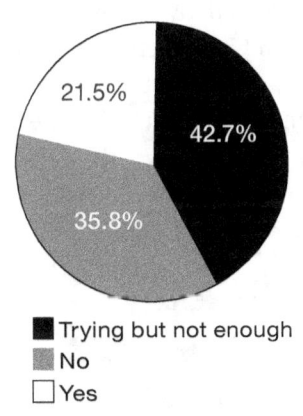

Figure 7: Financial Status of Children's Sunday School (n=246)

With respect to this matter, the way the FSST produces the program's resources provides a simple example of addressing this issue. The FSST provides free Sunday school lessons but also offers a variety of craft designs that come in both black and white and color options, to respect printer and ink availability. In another survey, almost two-thirds of respondents (64.2%) considered it financially difficult when they needed to print more than one page of craft design. Similarly, 67.1 percent of respondents claimed to face financial difficulties when additional materials such as straws, colored papers, or roundhead fasteners were required to complete the craft designs provided. For these reasons, when producing craft designs, the FSST produces designs that can be made with basic materials such as paper, scissors, glue, and crayons. Creating craft designs in line with the sermon but beyond simple coloring, not only piques children's interest but also effectively delivers the sermon content through the activity.

In fact, 82.5 percent of respondents confirmed that they use the resources provided by the FSST in their Sunday schools. Data analysis revealed that 64.2 percent of respondents visited the FSST less than five times per month after receiving a notification that a new lesson was uploaded weekly. A considerable number of respondents rely on notification systems, highlighting the effectiveness of online-based ministries. Additionally, 22.8 percent of participants visited between six

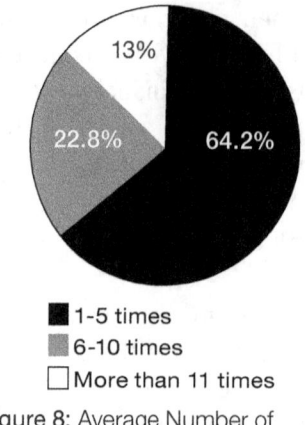

1-5 times
6-10 times
☐ **More than 11 times**

Figure 8: Average Number of Visits to FSST per Month (n=246)

and ten times, while 13 percent visited eleven times or more, indicating that around one-third of respondents visit the FSST at least six times every month (Figure 8).

In terms of resource use, crafts were the most common resource used by Sunday school teachers at 83.7 percent, followed by visual aids for sermons at 68.7 percent, sermons at 66.7 percent, songs at 61.0 percent, and administration at 31.7 percent (Figure 9).

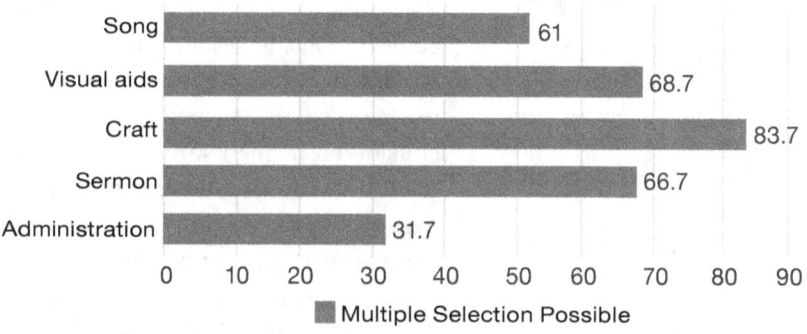

Figure 9: Resource Usage Status

It is also important that various active programs be developed, while considering the availability of suitable places for worship services. According to a survey of FSST, almost half (50.8%) of churches have an independent indoor space dedicated to Sunday school, while the other half (49.2%) are unable to provide this (Figure 10). Among those that cannot provide an independent indoor space, 27.9 percent use outdoor areas, and 17.6 percent use spaces at different times than the adult worship service. Other alternatives include using the homes of church members who live near the church, or the pastor's house. In such cases, the availability of a suitable place for worship service may be determined by the situation of the place provider, which can limit the stability of the

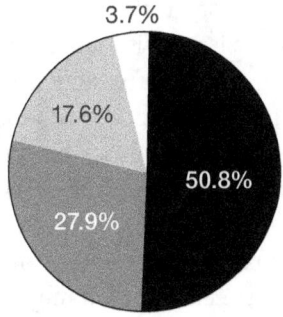

- There is a dedicated indoor space for Sunday School.
- We do not have an indoor space, so we hold it outside.
- We use the main hall because our adult worship service and Sunday School take place at different times.
- Other

Figure 10: Availability of Suitable Places for Children's Sunday School (n=246)

educational environment. Therefore, it may be necessary to develop worship services and curricula that take these spatial constraints into account more, to further promote the vitality of Sunday school ministry.

The Future Direction of Online Ministry of the FSST

FSST's first objective, to encourage beginners without teaching experience, is made possible through straightforward and easy-to-teach content. The worship components including songs, sermons, and activity sheets, are linked by the same theme, making lesson preparation easy for teachers. Additionally, the program offers information on various topics, such as how to initiate Sunday school, the importance of visual aids for children, effective seating arrangements, Bible reading plans, memory verse teaching techniques, and how to organize special events. To determine whether this program is being utilized effectively on the mission field, participants were asked the question, "What positive needs have you identified for your Sunday school through the FSST?" (Figure 11). The responses indicated that 37.3 percent recognized the need for an organized system, while 25 percent were confident in initiating a worship-based Sunday school, as opposed to a caretaking approach. Furthermore, 19.2 percent indicated that they had begun to build a systematic program based on the information obtained from this group, and 8.7 percent had launched a worship-based Sunday school. The realization and implementation of these teachers demonstrate significant progress in missionary work and the ripple effect of online ministry.

Second, for churches that are hesitant to start Sunday school because of financial difficulties, free provision lies at the heart of this ministry.

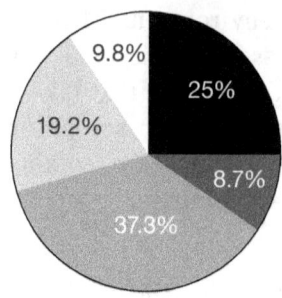

- I am confident in initiating a worship-based Sunday School.
- I actually launched Sunday School based on the information obtained from this group.
- I recognized the necessity of a systematic approach.
- I actually established a systematic program on the information obtained from this group.
- ☐ I am currently undecided.

Figure 11: Positive Needs Identified by Teachers through the FSST (n= 276)

The motivation for starting FSST was not a grand vision—it was simply the realization that, after creating a curriculum for the Sunday school of the local church, it could not be reused the following year. To avoid wasting the materials, this ministry began by sharing older resources freely online to help teachers in need. While it may seem small to share previously made materials in this manner, the fact is that it can have a significant impact on underprivileged areas. Daniel Topf highlights this significant disparity in the world today: in areas where theological resources are readily available, there is a decline in church attendance, resulting in a lower demand for ministerial training. Conversely, in regions like the Global South, where the church is experiencing growth, there is a scarcity of theological resources.[27] To address this imbalance, Topf emphasizes the need for "global partnerships." As such, it is worth considering online ministry as a viable platform for fostering these partnerships.

Lastly, Sunday school ministry is an essential aspect of cultivating the next generation of believers within church. Its significance cannot be overstated, as Christian education during childhood has a direct impact on the individual's faith in adulthood. According to a 2001 study by Barna, the majority (61%) of American adults who attended church during their childhood still attend services regularly today, whereas the majority (78%) of those who did not attend church as children often miss religious services.[28] These findings suggest that the experiences and teachings received in childhood play a crucial role in shaping one's religious beliefs and practices. They further indicate that individuals who attended church regularly as children are more likely to engage in church activities as adults. Another recent survey conducted in 2019 supports this theory, as 36.6 percent of adults active in Christian ministry reported accepting Christ between 12–19 years old. The survey also found that 32.1 percent accepted Christ between the ages of 7–11, while 15.1 percent accepted Christ at the age of six or younger.[29] These findings emphasize the importance of providing proper Christian education to children, particularly in Sunday schools.

In connection with this, utilizing online resources to assist local teachers is an efficient way to contribute to the church's long-term vision for revival in the mission field. This approach meets immediate needs with minimal expenditure. Therefore, it is imperative for Sunday school teachers to employ effective resources to maximize their reach and provide quality Christian education to children through online platforms. From an integrated perspective, the terms "hybrid" and "all-line" have become increasingly familiar in the post-pandemic reality characterized by the coexistence of online and offline educational modalities. Consequently, it is paramount for FSST to optimize its comprehensive system through the online platform, thereby fostering seamless teacher preparation. Simultaneously, teachers should carry it offline to achieve the benefits of forming relationships with children and providing education that is adapted to their level. These considerations provide valuable insights and future directions for the advancement of FSST. Many teachers have expressed the need for FSST to enhance its educational programs in the future. According to the most frequent feedback, teachers would like to see an improvement in the segmentation of sermons. It is suggested that subdivided sermons for kindergarten, elementary, and youth groups with the same theme should be provided. This will help teachers cater better to the needs of each age group offline. Furthermore, FSST currently only provides craft designs for activities, but there is a need for workbooks with questions and answers for older students. However, it is important to note that teachers find it difficult to print multiple pages, so any forthcoming workbooks should be designed accordingly.

Conclusion

Christian education has placed a great deal of emphasis on what to teach but has often overlooked the importance of ensuring equality across all age brackets, especially children. While the method of education should vary based on the age of the child, age should never be used as a criterion for evaluating the effectiveness of education. With the realization that children's ministry is not a secondary objective, the church now has a responsibility to actively engage in its belief that the next generation matters.

Whether accepted or not, technology has generated a completely new measure of influence and autonomy, especially in a post-pandemic era when online technology has proliferated. While it has its downsides, technology has the potential to engage people across generations, social, economic, and physical boundaries,[30] making it a valuable tool for the church to deploy Christian education for children that may have been previously overlooked. By utilizing technology to augment children's ministries, the church can make a systematic impact on the education of Sunday school children, especially on the mission field. One of the ways to do this is by providing online platforms like FSST that freely share information and resources, making them accessible and affordable to teachers worldwide. Through this approach, churches can make valuable contributions to the development of a more equitable and effective education system for all children.

Notes

1 Aaron Earls, "The 9 Greatest Concerns Pastors Have for Their Church," Lifeway Research, February 13, 2020, https://research.lifeway.com/2020/02/13/the-9-greatest-concerns-pastors-have-for-their-church/, accessed June 27, 2024.

2 "Children's Ministry is Crucial, but its Impact is Hard to Measure," Barna Group, May 25, 2022, https://www.barna.com/research/childrens-ministry/, accessed June 27, 2024.

3 Barna Group, "Children's Ministry is Crucial, but its Impact is Hard to Measure."

4 Yong-geun Ji et al., *Hangug Gyohoe Teulend 2023* [Korean Church Trends in 2023] (Seoul: Kyujang, 2022), 198.

5 Yong-geun Ji et al., 151.

6 See Proverbs 3:1–2, 22:6, Matthew 19:14, Ephesians 6:4, Isaiah 54:13, and 2 Timothy 3:14–15.

7 Grant R. Osborne, *Matthew,* Zondervan Exegetical Commentary on the New Testament, vol. 1, ed. Clinton E. Arnold (Grand Rapids: Zondervan, 2010), 1080.

8 Craig A. Evans, *Matthew*, New Cambridge Bible Commentary, ed. Ben Witherington III (New York: Cambridge University, 2012), 484; also see D. A. Carson, "Matthew," in *The Expositor's Bible Commentary*, vol.8, ed. Frank E. Gaebelein (Grand Rapids: Zondervan, 1984), 595.

9 Robert W, Pazmino, *Foundational Issues in Christian Education*, 3rd ed. (Grand Rapids: Baker Academic, 2008), 141, 276.

10 Carson, *The Expositor's Bible Commentary*, 596. He notes that the words have been interpreted in two ways: "all Gentiles except Israel" or "all people, including Israel."

11 N. Walter, *"ethnos,"* in *Exegetical Dictionary of the New Testament*, vol.1, eds. Horst Balz and Gerhard Schneider (Grand Rapids: Eerdmans, 1990), 383.

12 Michael J. Wilkins, "Matthew," in *Zondervan Illustrated Bible Background Commentary*, vol.1, ed. Clinton E. Arnold (Grand Rapids: Zondervan, 2002), 190.

13 D. A. Carson, *The Expositor's Bible Commentary*, 599.

14 Eckhard J. Schnabel, *Acts*, Zondervan Exegetical Commentary on the New Testament, ed. Clinton E. Arnold, (Grand Rapids: Zondervan, 2012), 136.

15 John Barton, *Joel and Obadiah* (Louisville, KY: Westminster John Knox Press, 2011), 96.

16 Douglas Stuart, "Hosea–Jonah," in *Word Biblical Commentary*, vol. 31, eds. David A. Hubbard and Glenn W. Barker (Waco, Texas: Word Books Publisher, 1987), 260–261.

17 Duane A. Garrett, "Hosea, Joel," in *The New American Commentary*, vol. 19A, ed. E. Ray Clendenen (Nashville: Broadman and Holman Publishers, 1997), 369.

18 Schnabel, *Zondervan Exegetical Commentary* on the New Testament, 136.

19 Demetrius K. Williams, "Acts as a History of the Early Church," in *The Gospels and Acts*, eds. Margaret Aymer, Cynthia Briggs Kittredge, and David A. Sanchez (Minneapolis: Fortress Press, 2016), 319.

20 F. F. Bruce, *The Book of The Acts*, The New International Commentary on the New Testament, rev. ed. (Grand Rapids: Eerdmans, 1988), 61.

21 The survey was conducted through a questionnaire distributed to 276 children's Sunday school teachers from 45 countries who are members of the "For Sunday School Teachers" (FSST) on Facebook. The survey took place between December 21, 2022 and February 18, 2023 and was conducted via Google Forms, consisting of 32 questions and taking

approximately 8–10 minutes to complete. Of the 276 participants, 89.1 percent (246 people) were from the Global South, 9.4 percent (26 people) were from the Global North, and 1.4 percent (4 people) did not have a recorded nationality. It is worth noting that this survey only represents the views and experiences of those who participated in the FSST Facebook group and may not necessarily reflect the views of the wider population.

22 FSST is a nonprofit mission organization established in May 2019 by a Korean missionary with 50 initial members, mostly from the Philippines, to support children's ministries worldwide. It is an interdenominational ministry that provides practical help and educational training programs for Sunday school teachers from approximately 50 countries. FSST's major vision is to expand God's kingdom through missional collaboration with local churches in mission fields for children. The organization upholds two major values in its missions: contextual sensitivity and educational simplicity. To make its resources easily accessible, FSST uses a Facebook Group as their major platform to collect, prepare, and produce songs, sermons, and crafts based on a single weekly theme. The crafts are designed to be made using the most available materials in mission fields such as paper, scissors, glue, pencils, and crayons. Moreover, every material is offered for free to address the financial challenges faced by many churches in the Global South.

23 Hyun Joo Oh and Kyungwha Hong, "A Case Study of Online Children's Ministry in South Korea during the COVID-19 Pandemic," *Christian Education Journal* 18:3 (December 2021): 477, https://web.p.ebscohost.com/ehost/pdfviewer/pdfviewer?vid=3&sid=29310a27-6e8a-4230-baca-706af85c6256%40redis/, accessed June 27, 2024.

24 This online group offers a comprehensive collection of free resources including sermons, craft designs, links to YouTube for worship songs, and visual aids for sermons, all conveniently accessible in one place.

25 Shannon Schumacher and Nicholas Kent, "8 Charts on Internet Use Around the World as Countries Grapple with COVID-19," Pew Research Center, April 2, 2020, https://www.pewresearch.org/fact-tank/2020/04/02/8-charts-on-internet-use-around-the-world-as-countries-grapple-with-covid-19/, accessed June 27, 2024.

26 Theological Education Fund, *Ministry in Context: The Third Mandate Programme of the Theological Education Fund* (1970-77) (Bromley, U.K.: Theological Education Fund, 1972), 31.

27 Daniel Topf, "Ten Characteristics of Pentecostal Theological Education in the Twenty-first Century," *Pentecostal Education: A Journal of WAPTE* 5:1–2 (2020): 46, https://wapte.org/wp-content/uploads/2020/10/pentecostal-edu-vol-5.pdf/, accessed June 27, 2024.

28 "Adults Who Attended Church as Children Show Lifelong Effects," Barna Group, November 5, 2001, https://www.barna.com/research/adults-who-attended-church-as-children-show-lifelong-effects/, accessed June 27, 2024.

29 "Kids and Salvation Survey," Ministry-To-Children, 2019, https://docs.google.com/forms/d/e/1FAIpQLSegmKVK5CTvzJqtL9M9lxyYaKS8WGyEagSYeK52lP63kNhvJw/viewanalytics/, accessed June 27, 2024.

30 "Technology Study: Social Networking, Online Entertainment and Church Podcasts," Barna Group, May 26, 2008, https://www.barna.com/research/barna-technology-study-social-networking-online-entertainment-and-church-podcasts/, accessed June 27, 2024.

9 Individualized Faith, or What? A Reflection on the Pressure of Shaping Christian Faith in the Swedish Context

Ulrik Josefsson and Fredrik Wenell

Abstract

Swedish society has undergone major changes during the twentieth century, especially concerning its relationship to Christian faith. The last wave of revival movements emerged in a society characterized by Lutheranism and associate values, but that is no longer the case. In this chapter, which draws on several recently published empirical papers, we discuss these changes in relation to young adults in conservative and Charismatic congregations. We highlight three areas where the faith has changed. The first concerns the understanding of conversion which is increasingly seen as a protracted process rather than an instantaneous conversion. The second is about the church community taking on a different meaning that the individual relates to. The third is that faith needs to become one's own and not just something that is handed down. We conclude by suggesting that the challenge for contemporary churches is to create places where faith can become meaningful, and to use modern worship music as a kind of language school to shape the worshipper's theology and language about their faith.

Introduction

There is no doubt that Swedish society has undergone profound cultural changes since the late 1960s. To meet these changes, congregations and Christian movements need to find new ways to be Christians. It is the relationship between the new situation in Swedish society and what it means to be a Christian that this chapter deals with. The chapter is largely based on the studies presented in the research report *Kristen tro på glid? [Christian Faith on the Slide?]*, where the faith among young adults in the Swedish Free Church is analyzed. The overarching question for the project as a whole concerns how young adults in or from Free Church contexts understand their Christian faith.

The group in focus of the study are those commonly referred to as "young adults." Young adults are in a stage of life characterized by protracted formation in which crucial choices in life need to be made; but it is also the group that today lives with the consequences of the changes that congregations have made to face a changing societal context. The congregations and respondents included in these empirical studies come from different parts of the Swedish revival movement. Theologically speaking, they are not uniform but share the revival movement's emphasis on personal conversion, Christocentric preaching, and an emphasis on the affective side of faith. The fact that faith is personal does not necessarily mean that it is individualistic. On the contrary, the earlier revival movements assumed that a person who had been converted participated in common practices such as congregational prayer, worship, Bible reading, and a jointly maintained morality. Conversion was personal but formed in community, and the content of the faith was collective.

The purpose of this chapter is to discuss the findings of the various articles in the underlying project, to answer the question of how young adults in Sweden understand their Christian faith.

Sweden and Religion

It is a well-known fact that Swedish society is secular. Religion has little meaning and, if it matters, is part of private life. The global World Value Survey still ranks Sweden in an extreme position in relation to the rest of the world.[1] Japan, Hong Kong, Macau, and South Korea are placed higher on the secular scale than Sweden, but when individual values are added, it is reasonable to describe Swedish secularism as just as extreme. Religion is not expected to have any influence on economics, education, or politics. However, a spiritual search is affirmed in the private sphere. Radical secularization does not necessarily mean that interest in spirituality has decreased, but rather that it has gone in an individualizing direction.

The Canadian philosopher Charles Taylor has described three kinds of secularization in Western societies.[2] His view of secularization can be interpreted as a process in which the first leads to the second, leading to the third. The first is characterized by the fact that the public space has been emptied of references to God. This leads to people increasingly underrepresenting themselves in ecclesiastical practices such as religious services, which in turn leads to a more pervasive cultural transformation in the second phase. Taylor describes the third stage of secularization as "a move from a society where belief in God is unchallenged and indeed, unproblematic, to one in which it is understood to be one option among others, and frequently not the easiest to embrace."[3]

Secularization becomes no longer just about personal beliefs or participation in religious gatherings, but about the fact that the cultural conditions for people to believe have changed. When religious belief no longer creates a framework for people's interpretation of life, it encourages what Taylor calls a "nova effect."[4] This means that different ideologies, interpretations, and attitudes to life are thrown out and clash with each other. Against this background, personal faith is subject to questioning and requires justification both for oneself and before others.[5] No one can be sure or take their own interpretation of life as self-evident, but everyone must justify their conviction or belief.

If Sweden is an extreme country when it comes to its level of secularization and individualization, it is reasonable that this also changes the conditions for the young adults who will shape the faith into adulthood. It is not natural to be a believer, but it can rather be perceived as suspicious. The believer must constantly justify his life stance and negotiate with surrounding society.

When the Free Church identity was formed within Swedish culture in the mid-1800s, the Christian faith was self-evident. The Bible was still a textbook in elementary schools, where days began with devotionals and hymn-singing. In congregations, revival meetings were invited to awaken the faith that was slumbering in the population. Faith was based on the Bible and belief in its absolute authority. Based on Pietism, within the Free Church there was a strong focus on Jesus and conversion to a life of Christlike discipleship. This discipleship would, of course, be lived out within an active life in the congregation.[6]

Given the characteristics of a revivalistic Christian faith—a personal belief lived out in community—it aligns with the cultural traits of individualization by which the rest of Swedish culture is characterized. But a different dimension of the revivalist Christian faith—the Free Church tradition of common ethics and collective practices—counteracts this and makes it unique in comparison with secularism. It is in this cultural context that young adults from Free Church revival settings should shape their faith.

In the following sections, the results of various empirical investigations from the "Christian Faith on Slide" project will be shortly presented and discussed. We apply the results from these different studies to the overarching question of how young adults from Free Church settings understand their Christian faith.

Young Adult Faith in the 2020s

In the project, five empirical studies were conducted. The results from these form the basis of this section:

1. Martina Björkander interviewed six people who were Bible school participants between 2005 and 2010. So they are now around 35 years old.[7]
2. Maria Karlsson interviewed four young adults in a multicultural congregation about how they handle the three cultures they interact with.[8]
3. The Danish theologian Henrik Holmgaard has, within the framework of a doctoral project, interviewed people about the conditions for their coming to faith in relation to Free Church congregations.[9]
4. Jakob Svensson and Ulrik Josefsson, together with six congregations within the Pentecostal movement, the Swedish Alliance Mission, and the Evangelical Free Church, conducted an action research study. The purpose of this study was to increase knowledge about what causes some young adults to remain within the congregational environment while others leave it. Eleven group interviews were conducted in the six participating congregations.[10]
5. The project also includes a survey conducted by the Norwegian sociologist Roald Zeiffert. The survey was sent to all students in Bible schools run by the denominations included in this study.[11]

In this chapter, the results are not presented in full, but they are brought together in order to draw overall and synthesizing conclusions.

Repentance: From Moment to Process

In Free Church revival tradition, personal faith has been fundamental. It is through an individually received faith that people are saved and join a Free Church community. Previous research on Free Church tradition shows that the salvation experience itself is often associated with strong emotional experiences, as well as a dateable event.[12]

When young adults in today's Free Church, however, describe how they come to faith, the picture is less clear than the traditional one. The experience of having a specific "moment of salvation" still has bearing, and some cite it as absolutely crucial to their ongoing journey in faith.[13] In Björkander's study of young adults who had reached early middle age, they still describe being saved in emotional terms and as very important—as an experience of being seen by God or enveloped in God's love.

But this differs from the results of the younger group that Zeiffert examined. There, it is strikingly unusual for them to describe a salvation experience in emotional terms. A majority describe it rather as a personal process of coming to faith. This slightly younger group does not describe a specific dateable event but a protracted time in which faith has matured. Also around 15 percent report not having made any decision at all but simply growing into the faith. The paradox is that these respondents do not indicate their parents as the most important factor in growing into faith, but rather worship and personal Bible reading.

When compared to previous generations within the revival movements, moreover, there is a significant difference. In the 1910s, the importance of salvation assurance built on a clear experience was emphasized.[14] In the revival movements of the 1930s, the kind of Christian faith in which children and young people grew into the faith was referred to as "upbringing Christianity." It was considered deeply problematic because a personal conversion was perceived as crucial to a personal Christian faith. Without an identifiable conversion experience, the power and opportunities of faith were perceived to be lost.[15]

Holmgaard's study of Danes who come to faith confirms that it is now common to have a long-term process to become a Christian. One of his respondents tells of a spiritual experience that did not immediately lead to a lasting faith, but rather the respondent needed time to understand what had happened in order to make the experience his own. Here, then, a specific experience was combined with a longer process of acquiring the faith.[16] Björkander notes that her respondents similarly express a need for faith to be internalized in themselves through conscious decision.[17]

It is thus a multifaceted picture we encounter. Of those in the young adult bracket, the elder indicate a crucial experience, while the slightly younger ones lean towards describing it as a process. In contrast to early Swedish revivalism, there has been a shift where experiences are still important but as part of a repentance process over time, or that young ones have simply grown into the faith. This could be understood from the angle of increased secularization, which puts more pressure on people with religious beliefs, or with Taylor's concept of *cross-pressure*. Or, process-oriented salvation could be partly based on reduced prior knowledge of historic Christian faith, which leads to a lack of cognitive tools to both interpret the experiences and make them theirs.[18]

Changing Community

Revivalistic Free Church faith was personal but it was not individualistic. The very reception of salvation most often took place in community, and, normally, within the framework of a worship service. This has led several scholars to speak of the service or community as a Free Church sacrament.[19] Being saved also meant becoming part of a believing community in a congregation. It was in that community that you grew in the faith and met Jesus.[20] At the same time, there was a common commitment to reading the Bible on one's own, which was almost a prerequisite for many of the Free Church's practices of joint decisions. They believed in anchoring personal experiences in a common culture and governing through the participation of members in collective processes that sought to discern God's will.[21] Simply put, the faith was shared within the community in which the personal convert was included.

This meant, among other things, that those who were part of a Free Church community shared moral beliefs and lifestyles, but also practices such as church services and revival meetings. This no longer seems to be self-evident, according to Josefsson and Svensson. For, in cases where the community agrees or expresses strong beliefs, it can rather lead to young adults slipping away from the congregation because they perceive that the space to think otherwise is too small.[22] It is clear that faith is still mediated by the Christian community, and so remains absolutely crucial to a person's faith. In fact, faith seems to be transmitted above all through encountering other believers in various forms of groups. It is often characterized by a positive experience of community. One problem in our action research project was that people who felt hurt by their time in a congregation were not willing to participate in interviews, which means that the results do not include problematic experiences. But those who responded tell us that the community was the most significant factor in coming to faith, and this applies to both those who remain in the church today and those who have left it. So, the emphasis on community that has always been prominent has changed, but still exists.[23]

On this point, many of those who left a congregation state that there were really no strong reasons for leaving, but the congregation became irrelevant and increasingly peripheral to eventually no longer being a part of their lives. In most cases, social factors such as changes in social interaction are pointed to as reasons for this migration. But for those who made conscious choices to leave or remain, the choice was often oriented around how they dealt with cognitive dissonance that arose in the content and convictions of faith, or the moral implications of it. For those who stayed in a congregation, Björkander emphasizes that it was crucial that they were able to get answers to their critical questions: questions that could be about how they were treated in a congregation, family, by other Christians, or other substantive issues. Young adults still had questions left but had received enough satisfactory answers such that new questions that arose were no longer acute or reasons to leave.[24]

Those who left, on the other hand, did so because they failed to bridge the cognitive dissonance that often surrounded ethical issues.[25] The difference between what they perceived the congregation to believe in different moral areas, and the ethical beliefs they encountered in mainstream society became too great, which finally led to their departure. They could no longer stand within the morality that was perceived to be normative and to some extent limiting.

Zeiffert's survey also showed that Bible school students remain strikingly traditional in their theology but more liberal on ethical issues.[26] There is a tendency among them to make a distinction between the ethics one affirms for society in general and what one believes should apply in the congregation. For example, a majority believe that homosexuals living in a relationship cannot have leadership positions in the church, while a majority also think that same-sex couples should have the opportunity to adopt children. Most believe that all religions should have the same rights in society as well, even while having chosen one for themselves as truth. Most of Zeiffert's respondents, then, seem to make a distinction between moral beliefs for Christians and what should apply more broadly in society.[27]

The Content of Faith has Changed

When the Swedish revival movements emerged, they were within the framework of a Lutheran society.[28] This naturally affected the conditions for coming to faith and continuing to live in this faith. That repentance has become a process that takes time, for more and more people, is therefore not so strange. Holmgaard shows in his analysis that the vast majority of people who have been converted to Christianity already have some kind of knowledge of, or relationship to, Christian faith and yet committing to it takes time.[29] He also notes that the context of community has changed so that basic Christian faith is no longer a collectively held belief to be transmitted, so to speak. One's congregation rather acts as a help and a support for the individual in the process of interpretation to make faith meaningful.[30] It seems, then, that the church has taken on a different function. From previously being the vessel for truth, carrying and transmitting the cognitive content of faith, it is now rather a place that the individual uses to put into words his personal beliefs. Holmgaard's respondents therefore relate eclectically to the faith they encounter in the congregations.

Another characteristic feature of the early Free Church revival movement was its Christocentric orientation. Repentance was about being saved by Jesus and for him. In the interviews conducted in the context of this study, Jesus is conspicuously absent. Respondents in several of the sub-studies link their involvement in church to different dimensions of community rather than to encounters with, or teaching about, Jesus.[31] It is the positive or negative aspects of the community that feature in their anecdotes. It is therefore reasonable to ask: how has the view of the church—which has changed with increasingly expanded youth activity, organized in the form of associations— affected the view of the community's relationship with Jesus? In the

Pentecostal movement and in the Örebro Mission there was widespread criticism of the so-called "association system."[32] They felt it would take away the focus on personal conversion and centering on Jesus. Were these reasonable concerns of the early movements? Has the way youth work been organized meant that community has been prioritized at the expense of a Christocentric faith?

There has been another shift in the content of faith, to the emotional parts being given precedence. When respondents were asked to estimate what is important to their faith, just over 80 percent stated that worship is important—referring to music.[33] Personal Bible reading was almost as important. This denotes a shift towards certain practices that can be collective but also individual. The songs of the revival movement have always been emotional and catchy, but also bearers of a clear theological foundation and, in this sense, formative to the content of the faith.[34] The importance given to the faith by these respondents today should probably be perceived as a change in which personal devotion and communal expression are emphasized more than the theology of which they are the bearers.

The core of Christian faith thus seems to have changed. It is no longer a canonized faith passed on through the life of the church, but the individual uses the church in shaping their own faith. The Christocentric aspect seems to be toned down in favor of the importance of community as a social place. Likewise, cognitive content does not seem to have the same primary function as, for example, the individual's experience in singing praises.

Implications and Synthesis

The question we wanted to seek answers to is how the faith of young adults in the Swedish Free Church is understood by them. In the last section, we showed some trends and shifts identified by the different studies. Young adults today grow up in a society that has undergone major changes, especially as it comes to the Christian faith. Faith no longer has the same privileged status as before but is now one of several possible positions. In some studies, the picture therefore emerges that actively believing young people perceive themselves as exposed.[35] We have also seen a shift towards faith being an individual project rather than a collective tradition that is transmitted. Correspondingly, repentance as a process rather than a specific conversion moment is more prominent. Experiences of God as seeing and caring for the individual are described as significant. Some report that repentance has not even happened but through a personal process, they have simply grown into the faith.

We therefore conclude that the faith among the young adults in these studies partly share the same dimensions as the Free Church of previous generations—community, emotionality, the Bible, morality—but how these are understood and related to has undergone significant changes. The next section will analyze and discuss the theological challenges that these results may give rise to. We also discuss the consequences for Free Church congregations in these traditions.

Theological Challenges

Earlier, we mentioned that Taylor argues that the kind of secularization that the West now finds itself in means that all people are subjected to an ideological trial. The way of life they have chosen needs to be justified. One factor that should be added to the Swedish context is that our culture was previously strongly discipled by Lutheran values. According to theologian Mattias Martinson, the culture in which young Swedes live in still has "a Lutheran deep identity."[36] Swedish culture does not necessarily maintain belief in a Christian God, but it still carries the values that come out of having done so. In a sense, then, the kind of secularization that Sweden is characterized by is a Lutheran type of secularization.

In Swedish culture, Christianity's previous position of power expressed, among other ways, through the state church, has led to religiously motivated morality being perceived as oppressive. Although the state and society are now professedly secular, they still bear the imprint of Christian identity. Thus, a negative view of religiously motivated people and their lifestyles seems to have been transferred to Free Church youth, some of whom agree that the church's moral view is limiting. By contrast, in his work, Barry Saylor claims that American young adults do not perceive the same problem. This may be because the American church has been disestablished for a long time. Thus, religiously motivated morality is only part of the expression in a congregation and, for American young adults, there is not the same need to turn against what could be perceived as oppressive structures.[37] Saylor's depiction of curiosity and simpler relationship between an American Christian identity and the surrounding culture is not what Holmgaard found in his study of Danes who have been converted. On the contrary, Holmgaard shows that there is a wide gap between a Christian way of understanding life and how the ordinary Dane perceives life.[38] The question therefore becomes: what does it mean for a congregation's work to shape Christian identity if young adults have identity-based practices, but the basis and conditions for these practices have changed with secularized Swedish culture?

Create Meaningful Spaces

It is a basic fact that Western society today is multicultural. We will not return to the time when there was a monoculture around which everyone could unite. Not even the Christian faith has a single way of understanding existence: although the Christian church shares basic teachings, it interprets them in different ways and they have different meanings for how life is lived. Since young adults can no longer assume a uniform culture, this necessarily means that in their everyday lives they are exposed to a variety of options.

Fredrik Wenell argues that the variety of options that meet us in society can be understood in the same way as what Paul calls "powers and dominions."[39] These powers are spiritual powers in the sense that they draw people to or away from Jesus. As highlighted above, different empirical investigations show that there are several such powers that could potentially do both. The congregation in some cases draws young adults to Jesus and into the community, but in other cases the design of the community and beliefs leads to some abandoning the faith. Family, partners, and other interests can also work in a similar way.

Taylor does not use the term "powers" but describes the multiplicity of options as individuals being in a situation where it is no longer possible to refer to a transcendent authority.[40] In a society where different cultures coexist, young adults must constantly fend off and negotiate with other ways of understanding life based on the beliefs that they themselves need to be the guarantor of. This negotiation often seems to be either too simplistic or too difficult in the congregations. Several of those who have disengaged from church feel that, as young adults, they did not receive the support and help they needed to deal with the issues they faced. This includes, for example, various forms of ethical dilemmas and positions. The other options offered in a society marked by a secular, Lutheran-deep structure did not help them to be drawn closer to Jesus either. In the end, the distance became too great and they slowly drifted further from community and faith.

There may also be cognitive dissonance associated with the amount of options. The answers young adults previously settled for are now no longer enough to make faith meaningful. What distinguishes those who leave and those who remain in church is often that the latter have managed in different ways to negotiate the faith in such a way that it remains meaningful. Congregations need to be spaces where questions can be asked and answers are given so that conversations about a Christian interpretation of life can be conducted without blind obedience being demanded.

Maria Karlsson shows that the multicultural congregation from which her respondents come constitutes such a place for them.[41] Her respondents not only negotiate between Swedish secular culture and church culture, but also family and homeland cultures. This group can be seen as a forerunner in the negotiation of life interpretation that all young adults face in the Swedish context where everyone is in negotiation with other life attitudes. It turns out that a multicultural congregation helps young adults to do that. It's not about a well-thought-out strategy but rather a result of a congregation where different cultures come together and agree on how congregational life should be lived. It seems to be in the DNA of a multicultural church to have to find a common ground to keep the community together. For young adults from immigrant families, the local congregation becomes the meaningful space that helps them negotiate that.

Therefore, what needs to happen is for churches to become places where young adults have the opportunity to negotiate different positions so that faith can continue to be meaningful. Swedish culture is individualized, and therefore, the church needs to take that into account and become the place where people receive support for their negotiation. As Holmgaard shows, the language at the church's disposal can help individuals understand what they have been through and how it should be interpreted. The next section explores this further.

Worship as a Language School

In Roald Zeiffert's survey study, a large portion of respondents maintain that worship is key to their faith. This report may seem strange and perhaps even startling, given the prominent role that the Bible and preaching have played in most revival movements. A natural reaction would be to resist the prominent position currently given to worship music. A more constructive approach would probably be to acknowledge the situation and use it. It is not as alien as it might first be perceived.

The experience of worship that the young adults in the study refer to is not only message-carrying songs but also a holistic, identity-shaping experience that creates space for the believing person.[42] Nor is this a new phenomenon in the Swedish Free Church, where singing, albeit in different forms, has helped shape Christian identity for a long time.[43] The function of worship can thus rather be understood within the context of a tradition in which the affectional aspect of faith has been prominent. Faith speaks not only through the cognitive, but equally through emotions and participation; in this way, worship becomes an important experience in maintaining the faith.

Nor is it necessary to interpret worship music as an antithesis of the cognitive content of faith. One of the congregations that has the clearest expression in this area and has contributed many modern songs is Hillsong. A characteristic feature of their worship songs is that the lyrics often contain more advanced theology than their sermons. The sermon is often characterized by a direct address and is shaped to be easy to understand, while the worship lyrics have an elaborate and advanced theology. In this way, the songs shape an in-depth theological understanding and help strengthen the cognitive content of the faith. One example of how Hillsong conveys a knowledge of Christology in an in-depth way, is their song "What a Beautiful Name."[44] In the text, there is a clear theology of Jesus' pre-existence that is linked to the doctrine of salvation. "Broken Vessels,"[45] as another example, alludes to the classic hymn "Amazing Grace" and frames a message about the need for the individual to be saved and established in Jesus.

It seems, then, that Hillsong has used a deliberate strategy of allowing more in-depth theological messages to be conveyed through worship songs rather than through preaching. Moreover, worship songs from

Hillsong are something many young adults have in their headphones on their way to work or at their workouts. Given this broad usage, it is probably a wise strategy to let the songs be the language school that the congregation uses to create room for the negotiation that is necessary in the present time. This, as previously shown, is not too different from the early revival tradition known for its easy-to-sing and compelling songs. If we now live in a time where the individual's own choice and formation is the center, songs can constructively be what conveys the knowledge that the Christian faith presupposes.

Conclusion

This chapter, as well as the broader research project it draws from, has been guided by the question of how young adults in and from Free Church congregations in Sweden understand their faith. It can be stated that they understand their faith within the context of a secular culture that bears traces of a Lutheran culture. Personal conversion has changed character and so is no longer primarily about an instantaneous emotional experience, but a process over time where the social context exerts a certain pressure that is dealt with.

There is also a surprisingly high percentage of Christians today who have not made a decision at all, but state that they have grown into the faith. They have a faith that is nourished above all by fellowship with other people. The risk with a faith that is primarily rooted in social relationships is that relationships can change, people can fail, and faith can then slowly slip away. The emphasis on community that the revival movement has traditionally had and maintains is thus both a strength and a weakness.

This study points to and analyzes challenges for young adults to form stable Christian identities. How this should be handled and addressed needs to be shaped in the conversation within congregations and denominations. There is an obvious need for clear and concrete steps to be taken, to find a foothold for a Christian faith on the slide.

Notes

1. "Findings and Insights," WorldValuesSurvey.org, https://www.worldvaluessurvey.org/WVSContents.jsp/, accessed September 1, 2222.
2. Charles Taylor, *A Secular Age* (Cambridge: Belknap Press, 2007), 2–3.
3. Taylor, *A Secular Age*, 3.
4. Taylor, *A Secular Age*, 299–313.
5. Taylor, *A Secular Age*, 20–21.
6. As explained well in Oloph Bexell, *Sveriges Kyrkohistoria. Väckelsens och Kyrkoförnyelsens Tid* (Stockholm: Verbum, 2003).
7. Martina Björkander, "En andra naivitet," in *Kristen tro på glid?*, eds. Ulrik Josefsson et al. (Stockholm: IPS-forskningsrapporter, 2022), 93.
8. Maria Karlsson, "Att forma sin tro i mötet mellan kulturer," in *Kristen tro på glid?*, eds. Ulrik Josefsson et al. (Stockholm: IPS-forskningsrapporter, 2022), 161.
9. Holmgaard, "It is Easy! Really?" in *Kristen tro på glid?*, eds. Ulrik Josefsson et al. (Stockholm: IPS-forskningsrapporter, 2022).
10. Ulrik Josefsson and Jakob Svensson, "Should I Stay or Should I Go?" in *Kristen tro på glid?*, eds. Ulrik Josefsson et al. (Stockholm: IPS-forskningsrapporter, 2022), 123.
11. Roald Zeiffert,"Vad tror unga vuxna på?," in *Kristen tro på glid?*, eds. Ulrik Josefsson et al. (Stockholm: IPS-forskningsrapporter, 2022), 69.
12. Ulrik Josefsson, *Liv och över nog* (Skellefteå: Artos, 2005); Fredrik Wenell, *Omvändel-sens skillnad* (Uppsala: Uppsala universitet, 2015).
13. Björkander, "En andra," 93.
14. Josefsson, *Liv och över*, 85–86.
15. Wenell, *Omvändelsens skillnad*, 47–71.
16. Holmgaard, "It is Easy" 181.
17. Björkander "En andra," 93.
18. Taylor, *A Secular Age*, 676. See further reasoning in Andrew Root, *Faith Formation in a Secular Age: Responding to the Church's Obsession with Youthfulness* (Grand Rapids: Baker Academic, 2017), 113–117.
19. Sune Fahlgren "Frikyrkligt gudstjänstliv—ett försök till historisk orienteering," in Fahlgren and Klingert, *I enhetens tecken* (Örebro: Libris,

1994), 187; Ulrik Josefsson, "Bilder av församlingen," in Josefsson and Wahlström, *Svensk frikyrklighet under pandemin* (Stockholm: IPS-forskningsrapporter, 2022), 83ff.

20 Ulrik Josefsson, "Doppraxis i samtida svensk baptism," in Stephan Borgehammar, *Dop. Svenskt gudstjänstliv 86* (Skellefteå: Atros, 2011).

21 Mats Larsson, *"Vi kristna unga qvinnor": Askers Jungfruförening 1865–1903—identitet och intersektionalitet* (Uppsala: Uppsala universitet, 2015).

22 Josefsson and Svensson, "Should I Stay," 123.

23 Josefsson and Svensson, "Should I Stay," 123.

24 Björkander, "En andra," 93.

25 Josefsson and Svensson, "Should I Stay," 123.

26 Zeiffert, "Vad tror unga," 69.

27 Zeiffert, "Vad tror unga," 69.

28 Wenell, "Omvändelsens Skillnad," 47–71.

29 Holmgaard, "It is Easy," 181.

30 Holmgaard, "It is Easy," 181.

31 Björkander, "En andra," 93; Josefsson and Svensson, "Should I Stay," 123.

32 Wenell, *Omvändelsens skillnad*, 61–71.

33 Zeiffert, "Vad tror unga," 69.

34 Sven-Åke Selander, *Den nya sången: Den anglosachsiska väckelsesångens genombrott i Sverige* (Lund: Gleerups, 1973); Inger Selander, *O hur saligt att få vandra* (Stockholm: Gummessons, 1980); Jernestrand Lennart, "Aven ateisterna kan hans sånger utan- till" in Claes Waern, *Pingströrelsen, Verksamheter och särdrag under 1900-talet* (Örebro: Libris, 2007).

35 Fredrik Wenell, *Unga troende i samhället. Varannan kristen ungdom upplever sig kränkt för sin tro* (Stockholm: Sveriges kristna råd, 2020).

36 Mattias Martinson, *Postkristen teologi: Experiment och tydningsförsök* (Göteborg: Glänta produktion, 2007).

37 Barry Saylor, "The Emerging Church," in *Kristen tro på glid?*, eds. Ulrik Josefsson et al. (Stockholm: IPS-forskningsrapperter, 2022), 197.

38 Holmgaard, "It is Easy," 181.

39 Fredrik Wenell, "Andliga makter och ung vuxen tro" in *Kristen tro på glid?*, eds. Ulrik Josefsson et al. (Stockholm: IPS-forskningsrapperter, 2022), 47.

40 Taylor, *A Secular Age*, 567–571.

41 Karlsson, "Att forma sin tro," 161.

42 As articulated in Nick Drake, *A Deeper Note: The 'Informal' Theology of Contemporary Sung Worship* (Cambridge: Grove Books, 2015).

43 See, for example, Selander, *Den nya sången*, or Thorsén Stig-Magnus, *Ande skön kom till mig: en musiksociologisk analys av musiken i Götene Filadelfiaförsamling* (Göteborg: Göte-borgs universitet, 1980).

44 Ben Fielding and Brooke Ligertwood, "What a Beautiful Name," Hillsong, https://hillsong.com/lyrics/what-a-beautiful-name/, accessed October 1, 2022.

45 Joel Houston et al., "Broken Vessels (Amazing Grace)/Life," Hillsong, https://hillsong.com/lyrics/worship/broken-vessels-amazing-grace-life/, accessed October 1, 2022.

Part III

Forming and Empowering the New Generation

10 Global Christianity and Gen Z: What is the Hope for the Future of Faith?[1]

Antipas L. Harris

Abstract

Although Generation Z tends to distance themselves from religion, this study suggests that they exhibit a strong spiritual inclination amidst rapid societal changes. It is crucial to recognize their unique spiritual hunger and consider their spirituality as a valuable asset to society. From a clinical perspective, spirituality is associated with the search for supernatural meaning and purpose. The Holy Spirit can provide meaningful guidance and purpose to a generation seeking such answers. This chapter explores four main areas of interest in Gen Z's pursuit of meaning: spiritual, technological, social-psychological, and personal-communal aspects, including family dynamics. Further, this study presents five recommendations for how the church can adapt its approach in addressing the needs of Gen Z and recognizing its value as a vessel of the Spirit: integrating advanced technology into congregational life, fostering meaningful communities, dedicating time for earnest prayer, involving young people in reimagining church practices, and connecting faith to the relevant needs of everyday life.

Introduction

This study offers a global perspective on how Generation Z engages with Christianity. Gen Z is often defined as comprising those born between 1996 and 2012 and identified as the most disengaged from religion in modern history. This global observation necessitates further investigation beyond the scope of this chapter to comprehend the diverse racial, cultural, and contextual settings that shape their generational characteristics. On the one hand, this generation is religiously disaffiliated. On the other hand, this study reveals that Gen Z possesses a deep spiritual hunger amid fast-paced societal changes.

As Spirit-filled people of God, it is important to remain aware of cultural and contextual realities while acknowledging spirituality as a unique gift to society. Clinically, spirituality is about one's hunger for supernatural agency, meaning, and purpose. The Holy Spirit offers meaning and purpose to a generation in such a quest.

This chapter explores four significant concerns in this generation's search for meaning: spiritual, technological, social-psychological, and personal-communal, which includes the family. The role the church plays as the agency of the Holy Spirit to "serve this present age" (*a la* Charles Wesley) requires a revised approach to faith to address Gen Z's needs. This study proposes five suggestions: normalize advanced technology as part of congregational life, develop communities of meaning, commit to diligent prayer, involve young people in rethinking the way we do church, and connect faith to relevant needs in everyday life.

There are dynamics pertinent to generational examination. The next section outlines the precautions. In summary, several dynamics play a role in sociological realities. Also, generations do not exist in neat and distinct categories. With these dynamics in mind, all living generations in various ways participate in the current religious landscape to be discussed in subsequent sections in this chapter.

Five Precautions

Pew Research Center's president, Michael Dimock, offers five important precautions in his generational study apropos to this discourse on global Christianity and Gen Z.[2] The first is that generational categories are not scientifically defined and thereby remain imprecise. Second, categories can lead to over-generalizations and stereotyping; groupings violate the fullness of human personhood and diversity. Third, categorizing generational differences tends to get more attention than generational commonalities, i.e., "Millennials are like this, and Gen Z's are like that." Therefore, comparisons may be false methods of assessment. Fourth, generational research is often "skewed toward the experiences of the upper middle class." Some research does not capture a full picture of socio-economic, racial/ethnic, and perhaps gender diversity. Lastly, people change over time. Dimock aptly notes, "Young adults have always faced a different environment than their parents, and it's common for their elders to express some degree of concern or alarm."[3] Categorizing people based on their generation demarcates human behavior with oblivion to similar behavior in previous generations.

A Changing World Affects All Generations, with Gen Z in the Vanguard

From the digital revolution to changing views on sexual morality; from climate change to war and terrorism; from the uptick in violent behavior to post-pandemic stress and more, the world is rapidly changing. Many adverse experiences result from a fast-moving world where people have little time to process before other adverse experiences occur. Psychologists observe trauma amid unprocessed personal and societal adversity. Some of the changes, such as with digital technology, advance society. Others like climate change, the threat of nuclear and biological war, and the sexual revolution raise philosophical, theological, and anthropological questions of identity, the meaning of life and death, the role of spirituality, and hope. At the same time, faith is not the obvious resource to quench the thirst of this generation. While all living generations are affected by these issues, the younger generation experiences the brunt of it.

To consider the future of faith in the face of so many global issues, this chapter analyses the situation of faith and Gen Z from a position of concern about the future of the church. American Millennials came of age at the peak of American secularism. Because of this, Pew labels Millennials as drivers of religious disaffiliation.[4] They are tagged "the generation of 'nones,'" popularizing "spiritual, but not religious."[5] Gen Z scholar, Ryan P. Burge,[6] as well as Christian historian, Dale M. Coulter,[7] and others point to several attributes for the stark decline of faith affiliation. Some have to do with political ideology, a bolder confession of disaffiliation, growing multiple secularisms,[8] and demographic issues such as increased formal education, challenging questions about Christianity's participation in racial histories, racialized nationalisms, marital status, sexuality, and matters related to gender. Moreover, some of the reasons are not merely cynicism about Christianity as much a slow, long-term shift of priorities more crystalized in this generation. Therefore, such concerns must not be discussed independently of living generations such as Baby Boomers, Gen Xers, and Millennials.

When making value comparisons between generations, however, we must note that times are changing more than generational comparisons reveal. *All* generations participate in and are impacted by the changes. Thus, comparisons are more fluctuant than static. As Dimock aptly notes:

[G]enerational thinking can help us understand how societies change over time. The eras in which we come of age can leave a signature of common experiences and perspectives. Similarly, historical advances like desegregation, effective birth control, the invention of the internet, and the arrival of artificial intelligence can fundamentally change how people live their lives, and the youngest generations are often in the vanguard.[9]

Sociology observes emerging trends in human behavior incalculable to hard science. This means that one must not take a hard stance such as, "this generation is about this, and that generation is about that." All generations are experiencing shifts at the same time, even if one generation behaves differently than another when they were *this* or *that* age. As we consider Gen Z, therefore, we might find ourselves saying, "That's not really unique to Gen Z." Or, "We were kind of like that in my day," as if "our day" no longer exists. Actually, there are probably more youth trends across generations than not. Yet, paradoxically, generational attributes contribute to the lived reality and views of faith. Much of what impacts Gen Z are ripple effects from previous generations. At the same time, studies show evidence of discontinuities in which one generation moves in the opposite direction of another.[10]

An Ipsos Global Advisor study revealed some surprising twists regarding generational religious affiliation. Researchers surveyed twenty-six countries and found that overall, younger people are less likely than older adults to identify as Christian, especially Catholic.[11] Religious young people are more likely to identify as Muslim or other religions.[12] The same study indicated an even more notable shift—the difference in religious affiliation among Boomers in comparison to Gen Z.[13] While in nearly all countries at least one-third of all adults believe in God as described in holy scriptures, Gen Zers are the ones less likely than Boomers to hold such beliefs.[14] However, that trend is reversed in less religious countries. Samantha Saad claims that Gen Zers tend to gravitate towards faith in countries where older adults are less religious. She also observes that in countries where religious practice is low, young people tend to have higher participation rates.[15]

Critical Factors Impacting Gen Z's Faith Participation

Several crucial factors currently impact the global Christian situation: (1) elements of secularisms mixed with non-religious spirituality, (2) continued decline in traditional family systems, (3) modern technology, and (4) social isolationism. While these crucial elements are listed separately, they are interwoven.

Secularisms Mixed with Non-Religious Spirituality

First, the decline in religious affiliation in Gen Z exists as a byproduct of multiple generational shifts away from holding church affiliation as essential to faith formation. A three-hundred-year rise of multiple iterations of secularism, post-secularism, and the resurgence of secularism is coming to a head, impacting a diverse world in multiple ways. The latter, the resurgence of secularism, is complex. On the one hand, it comprises a variety of secularisms rather than the traditional Western one. On the other hand, contemporary secularisms are unique because they are not absent of spirituality but rather integrate non-traditional spiritualities. Thus, calling this a resurgence of "secularism" proves problematic.

However, the new secularisms are hard to define. For the sake of discussion, I will mention a few perspectives. White South African scholar, B. J. van der Walt, defines secularism in the following manner:

> Secularism, born from the atheistic notions of three centuries, is a subjectivist, relativist and utilitarian view—as well as the resulting state of affairs—according to which [hu]man[kind] is so-called free, independent and having come of age. Because of the part the particular powers which [human beings] ha[ve] at [their] disposal, [humanity] has taken the place of God, who in [their] view has become superfluous, so that [human beings] can now live solely out of, by, and toward this life which is closed off in itself.[16]

While van der Walt provides insights into an anti-religious, anti-God version of secularism, other scholars argue for a more nuanced view, pointing out many secularisms as opposed to a single Western version. Another definition, for example, hails from The Center for Inquiry. Their definition bootstraps secularism with humanism in the following manner: "Secular humanism is a nonreligious worldview rooted in science, philosophical naturalism, and humanist ethics. Instead of relying on faith, doctrine, or mysticism, secular humanists use compassion, critical thinking, and human experience to find solutions to human problems."[17] An attempt to define many approaches to secularity is evident in this definition.

The research is a mixed bag. Some secular humanisms are anti-religious and anti-God. Others are not concerned about God so much as they are with understanding the human situation. The human-focused secularists may be where many "nones" are. They are neither atheists nor religious. Many expressions of secularism emerge from contextual social struggles. José Casanova explores this from a global-comparative perspective: "[M]ore importantly [than a European comparative analysis] is the further recognition that with the world-historical process of globalization initiated by the European colonial expansion, all these processes [of secularization] everywhere are dynamically interrelated and mutually constituted."[18] Although there are variations of secularisms, they maintain a common focus on responding to the human condition. They tend to account for highly diverse experiences, globalization, social environments, and human history in all its complexity.[19] This means that secularism is not all a reaction to religion or God per se. Some secularisms even critique Western ideals and how religion has wielded oppression, privileging some human persons over others. In this sense, any reasonable religious person would laud global secularity for its needed critique of historical Western religious overreach and abuse.

Decline in Traditional Family Systems and Values

The second factor impacting the global Christian situation pertaining to Gen Z is the continued decline in traditional family systems and values. Failing systems include the disintegrating family nucleus (e.g., father, mother, and children). Declining values refer to regular family time, playing games, talking about life and faith, sharing family dinners, taking trips with, and going to church as a family. A report from Daniel A. Cox at the Survey Center on American Life of the American Enterprise indicates that previous generations produce more religious detachment in the next generation.[20] The detachment may also be described as a break from the secular-sacred divide while also detaching from traditional forms of religion. The new form of religion ("spirituality") is more fluid, culturally syncretic, ever-changing, employs divine love as an affirmation of human-centered interests, and is less concerned about traditional religious routines unless they are mysterious (otherworldly), meaningful (shedding light on personal inklings and affectivity), and practical (adding positivity to how one feels about themselves and the world).

The evolution of religious engagement, detachment, and new forms of engagement is an incremental process from one generation to the next. It often appears reasonable, empowering, and harmless. Examples are as follows: Busyness has pushed family meals down the priority list. They are no longer centerpieces for family life with prayer being part of the daily or even weekly family table fellowship. The Survey Center on American Life reports that:

> For as long as we have been able to measure religious commitments, childhood religious experiences have strongly predicted adult religiosity. They still do. If someone had robust religious experiences growing up, they are likely to maintain those beliefs and practices into adulthood. Without robust religious experiences to draw on, Americans feel less connected to the traditions and beliefs of their parents' faith.[21]

The trajectory is set. Without another societal Great Awakening, the future will continue in the direction of secularism and church disaffiliation. Sunday school is almost obsolete. There is often a justifiable reason to choose work, leisure, or sports over regular church attendance. The separation between church and state has construed a false notion of divided human consciousness when we are, in fact, holistic beings. Like everyone else, Christians are just trying to keep up in a fast-paced world. Subsequently, they participate in *secularization* while also rejecting *secularism*. As a result, young generations are moving further away from fidelity to faith or affiliation with the church.

Modern Technology and Social Isolationism

Third, while modern technology is an asset in many ways—enhancing the spread of the Christian message through digital means (apps, YouTube, GodTube, streaming technology, and social media outlets)—the digital age has, nevertheless, challenged the role of faith in contemporary times. A world made smaller through technology amidst social isolationism is a perfect storm for mental health challenges and to stifle communal formation in a generation that is hungry for community and belonging.

In Jean M. Twenge's book, *iGen*, she notes that the problem of loneliness is much deeper than merely a popular desire for belonging or seasonal depression. She says that "More young people are experiencing not just symptoms of depression, and not just feelings of anxiety, but clinically diagnosable major depression."[22] That depression has led to a growing epidemic of self-injury such as cutting and even suicidality. Twenge highlights comments from New York psychiatrist Fadi Haddad in Time Magazine, where Haddad laments, "Every single week we have a girl who comes to the ER after some social-media rumor or incident that upset her."[23] Those ER visits are almost always caused by girls cutting themselves. According to a report from the Center for Disease Control, "[P]oor mental and health remains a substantial public health problem, particularly among adolescent females."[24] Twenge points out, "Many parents have no idea what their children are doing on social media, and many feel helpless."[25] Particularly, girls often cry out for help in subtle ways, even on social media.

In an article in The Gospel Coalition, Sarah Eekhoff Zylstra points out that Gen Z is anxiously digital.[26] Twenge asserts that Matt Carmichael, *Advertising Age's* former director of data strategy, agrees that more than "Gen Z," this generation is more accurately described as "iGen."[27] They seek approval and validation, and they express their opinions and cry for help in digital spaces. Zylstra explains: "Part of the problem is that every social media platform is like a stage on which Gen Zers both perform and compare themselves to others."[28] They create social media pages and soon delete them. Or they create multiple pages and make them private for select friends in each one. Twenge points out that New York psychiatrist Haddad reports, "One mother found that her self-harming daughter had seventeen Facebook accounts, which the mother promptly shut down. 'But what good does that do?' asked Haddad. 'There will be an eighteenth.'"[29] Or they create public pages, post photos, and soon delete the pictures and start over.[30] Image insecurity is blatant in a culture of bullying and a generation with an unprecedented desire for peer acceptance. Zylstra quotes from her interview with Malisa Ellis who has worked in various parts of the world with the youth ministry, Cru: "The level of panic is high. Everything is out there all the time on social media. . . . As this generation leans into that, their anxiety goes up. But as they disengage from it, they feel like they're missing out. They're constantly battling back and forth between deleting and reinstalling their social media."[31] One might conclude that in this way, Gen Z has a love-hate relationship with digital resources.

The current digital age offers many assets, but at a time when social isolation and anxiety are at an all-time high, what once was a source of human progress is adding to social ills. For example, on the one hand, Bible apps are conveniently available for the smartphone as are many preaching videos and opportunities for virtual community. Most Christians would say these are great things. On the other hand, so too are negative things immediately and freely available such as anti-religious thought, porn, and damaging misinformation. The virtual good, bad, holy, profane, and propaganda all flood the digital audience at the click of a button. A world ravenous for more and more vices, more and more success, and more and more attention is overwhelming Gen Z. So, they engage a bit and then want to pull back for self-preservation.

Selected Global Cases

The following four global cases—the Netherlands, U.S., Ghana, and Singapore—shed light on Gen Z and its potential to lead a revolution of faith. Admittedly, these cases do not reflect all the continents and are thus an inadequate representation of a global context. Notwithstanding, they demonstrate the urgent need for a more robust conversation to examine faith's relevance in a global context, revealing both the challenges and the potential for a revival of faith.

The Netherlands

For centuries, a type of Euro-secularism matured across Europe and influenced other parts of the world. In 2002, Dutch scholars, Manfred Te Grotenhuis and Peer Scheepers, studied why, since 1937, the Netherlands is one of the most secular countries in the world.[32] Most Dutch people do not attend church regularly, and most of the population does not affiliate with any church. They found that people are introduced to rationalization at a young age. As people deepen their analysis of life with logical reasoning as the primary tool, the role of faith in their lives fades into shadow. In other words, for the Dutch populace, religious disaffiliation did not suddenly drop in the Millennial and Gen Z generations. As structures of logical reasoning have taken center stage, the role of faith has been pushed to the margins. This process has been underway for decades.[33]

Ipsos Global Advisor's study, mentioned earlier, offers a glimmer of hope. In most religious countries where Boomers are more religious, younger generations tend to be less religious. But, where older generations are less religious, younger people are more likely drawn to religion. With this trend in view, the Netherlands may be positioned for revival. As the current generation is largely secular, Gen Z may be the key to a forthcoming Great Awakening in the Netherlands!

The United States of America

The United States is also experiencing an ongoing faith erosion. As in the Netherlands, this did not start with Millennials but accelerated among them and continues in Gen Z. Christian historian, Dale Coulter, points out that "The tag 'none' has been used since the 1960s as shorthand for those who consider themselves 'spiritual but not religious'."[34] Pew Research Center reports that in 2017, 27 percent of cross-generational adults (Boomers, Gen Xers, Millennials, and older Gen Zers) said they are "spiritual but not religious"—an 8 percent increase over five years.[35] The arc is sharply bent toward increased religious disaffiliation in this generation, including women and men; whites, blacks, and Hispanics; varying educational levels; and a mixture of political affiliations. Much could be said about what happened in preceding generations that facilitated this.[36] Notably, older adults cultivate the environment for Gen Zers. They are the parents, leaders, teachers, and influencers.

Norfolk State University sociologist of religion, Aprilfaye T. Manalang, explains: "Although Gen Z and minority millennials feel ambivalent about their relationship to the church, they do not regard unbelief as either atheistic or religious per se, but a more nuanced negotiation in their daily lives."[37] They respect religion and would likely say they believe in God. This stems from their sense of loyalty to their family. In communities of color, integration of faith and God-talk remain part of the cultural fabric that binds parents, children, grandparents, grandchildren, etc.

The spread of spiritual exploration intermingled with elements of secularism accelerates through the virtual halls of high-speed internet. One observes emerging challenges related to the digital revolution in Gen Z. For example, Zylstra discusses the "anxiously digital" generation with Craig Millard, College Ministry Pastor at Redeemer Church in New York, who says:

> When we announce we're doing a 24-hour ministry-wide fast, they immediately think of fasting from social media. When I first started, I thought that was an easy way out of fasting from food. But now I can see how hard it is for them [...]. Students are more aware of how damaging it is to be constantly online, but it's so wrapped up in how they think of the world.[38]

In other words, Gen Z has a love-hate relationship with the digital age. Food is not the source of Gen Z's most serious gluttony. Social media is! It keeps them up at night. As Twenge observes,

> Smartphone use may have decreased teens' sleep time: more teens now sleep less than seven hours most nights. Sleep experts says that teens should get about nine hours of sleep a night, so a teen who is getting less than seven hours a night is significantly sleep deprived. Fifty-seven percent more teens were sleep deprived in 2015 than in 1991. In just the three years between 2012 and 2015, 22 percent more teens failed to get seven hours of sleep.[39]

Differently than reading a book or watching TV, electronic devices and social media are addictive. Twenge explains that "[t]he allure of the smartphone, its blue light glowing in the dark, is often too much to resist."[40] As part of Gen Z's everyday life, digital technology is both an asset and a challenge. The world acknowledges the digital age as a gift in human advancement. However, more attention must be given to the impact of modern technology on Gen Zers' mental health.

A similar observation exists related to digital media and worship. Many Gen Zers have greater attraction to cathedrals and traditional worship spaces than to worship spaces inundated with digital screens and flashing lights. Notwithstanding, the complexity is that Gen Z is not completely averse to all digital assets.

Millard's point above is that, while Gen Zers seem lost in the crevice of the worst fractures in the structures of faith, they are crying out for a better way. To say this is an "anxious" generation is an understatement. A current mental health crisis exists, exacerbated by the aftermath of the COVID-19 pandemic, Gen Z is in search of spiritual and mental betterness. Yet, "better" is not a return to some previous generation's way. It is a search for a way forward that includes the digital age but with more guidance and temperance. It is a search for holistic treatment of mental, spiritual, and physical wellness. Christian spirituality has internal norms to satisfy this thirst if only the church rethinks the role of the Holy Spirit in the everyday life of the believer with Gen Z's interests in mind.

Ghana

Countries like Ghana, where Christians make up 71.2 percent of the populace,[41] boast more Gen Z religious affiliations than many countries. Ghanaian scholar and pastor Mensa Otabil explains two important factors in strong faith participation: family and African spiritual culture. First, Otabil says Ghanaian parents continue to heavily influence young people's faith practices.[42] The central role of faith incubated in the home cannot be overstated. The influence and authority of the family remain strong in Ghana and other African countries. Second, Otabil points out, "Even the most secular African is also spiritual."[43] So, a Ghanaian Gen Zer may be less likely to say, "I am spiritual and not religious," since spirituality is inherent to the persisting pan-African culture. Notwithstanding, one wonders what the future of faith will look like for Africa. Certainly, they struggle with forms of secularism and the infiltration of Western versions of secularism as indicated above in South Africa. However, Ghanaian Gen Zers, for example, do not seem to have significantly wavered amid the global resurgence of secularisms.

It is not surprising that Spirit-filled Christianity fans the flames of young African spiritual excitement. Pentecostal expressions of the faith find home amid cultural spirituality. So, while family nurtures faith in children, Ghanaian theologian J. Kwabena Asamoah-Gyadu observes that when they come of age, they make their faith commitment in Christian high schools and post-secondary schools.[44] That is when they often deepen their faith commitment and experience the baptism of the Holy Spirit. Because the younger generation feels excited about their experience Spirit-baptism, Pentecostal spirituality permeates many denominations as well as Catholicism.

Nor does Christianity in the Global South seem to be tapering off any time soon. However, Asamoah-Gyadu points out a brewing rift between older generations and Gen Z, based on what he calls "denominational uprootedness."[45] Gen Z pulls away from traditional denominational approaches in search of church experiences more aligned with contemporary culture, which is largely informed by normalized high-speed internet, new forms of music, Western influence on dress, as well as personal and societal trauma and victories. Nigerian business leader, Tunji Adegbite, aptly notes:

> Gen Zs [sic] were born during the dot com era and were raised on technology. They witnessed the election of Barack Obama, rise of gender equality, sexual orientation equality, shared family responsibilities, and collective volunteerisms. However, they were born into a deeply troubled system, a time of worldwide terrorism attacks, Arab uprisings, effects of climate change and a great recession. This generation (c.32% of world's population) have come of age to shape policies and open doors they were locked out of.[46]

Fast-paced technological advancements stimulate excitement for innovation and hope for material success. Ghanaian and other churches must keep reimagining ways to bridge faith with Gen Z where they are—socially, spiritually, aspirationally, etc. The global trend is that young people tend to lose interest in faith that they deem disconnected from their complex experience of self and the world at large. Churches in countries like Ghana, parts of Nigeria, and other places where Gen Z remains highly connected must invest more in hearing their voices and ideas as well as including them in leadership roles.

Singapore

Singapore is experiencing shifts amidst the maturing digital revolution and other related cultural shifts. A version of Western-like secularism is affecting Singaporean views about self, life, family, morality, sexuality, and faith, with Gen Zers raised in both a far less religious world and a society resistant to traditional values. The challenge presents itself not only in Christian families but also in other religions and non-religious families.

Reflecting on Gen Z and the church in a *Christianity Today* article, Pearlyn Koh writes, "Many young people's views on issues like sexuality or what comprises a family unit are no longer defined by Asian societal norms."[47] She points out that a 2020 census revealed that a growing number of Gen Zers have joined the Western "nones"—from 21 percent in 2010 to 24 percent in 2020.[48] Pew reports that the rise of "nones' in Singapore is "uniquely high" along with other countries.[49] This, in part, results from the influence of the Western world. Parents encourage education and new experiences, not gauging how they might lure youth away from tradition. It is, however, not surprising that Gen Z has benefitted from exposure to cultural and ideological diversity. Gen Z has also been impacted by varying parental decisions about faith and church attendance, changing family systems, modern technology, isolationism compounded by COVID-19, and more.

Opportunities

Many opportunities exist to engage the younger generation. The first—education—is a key shaper of culture. There is, therefore, a need for more Pentecostal scholarship and Christian education, which must engage the whole person. When considering human beings, there really is no separation of secular and sacred. Pentecostal-sponsored education must show concern about the mind, soul, body, and spirit.

The second opportunity has to do with leadership. Gen Z is a generation of leaders. Empowering young people to lead through experiential learning is key to capturing their faith interest. Koh points out that Heart of God Church in Singapore has "succeeded in attracting a hard-to-capture demographic: the average age of its congregants has remained steady at 22 years old."[50] They employ an effective strategy to host Gen Z-led main services. The church's co-founding pastor, Cecilia Chan, explains: "Youths need to be invited, included, [and] involved, before they can be influenced and impacted."[51] This also suggests that to capture the innovation and spiritual energy of this generation is to centralize space for experiential congregational leadership and experiential spirituality.

As in many other contexts, ministries in Singapore struggle to adjust to a generation where change is their new norm. Change challenges traditional forms of normalizing communal practices. Yet, to reach this generation effectively, creating new norms of change remains crucial for the future of faith. Cru Singapore published an article called the "Future of Youth Ministry" by Deborah Ng, who sums up an interview with a Singaporean youth leader who observed that "one of the main weaknesses highlighted by youth leaders […] seemed to be a resistance to change. That ministry was 'running in the same way when the culture is changing,' and 'just struggling to hold on to certain forms of discipleship, certain programs.'" The same report explains a similar issue in varying proportions globally: "Young people are thinking about questions like meaning, purpose, identity, and sexuality. These questions are not new, but in a post-truth world where they've been told to think with their feelings, they are facing more uncertainty in dealing with these questions than ever before."[52] The relationship between Christianity and everyday life is in question. Ministries in Singapore must continue to learn and creatively adjust approaches to ministry to capture the imagination of this generation while remaining faithful to the core tenets of faith. This is no small task. Yet, we have hope!

Ng quotes Max Jeganathan, Director of Thinking Faith, who says, "It makes sense to me, why issues like anxiety and loneliness are at an all-time high among young people."[53] From the article, it is not altogether clear why Jeganathan draws such a conclusion. However, reading between the lines, it seems that his conclusion is based on what he perceives as a gap between this generation of digital natives and previous generations. The digital age, coupled with the social isolation effects of the COVID-19 pandemic, has created the perfect storm for anxiety and loneliness for everyone, particularly Gen Z. Moreover, Ng understands Max to believe that conditions are ripe to respond to Gen Z's search with a gospel of belonging, community, meaning, and purpose. Singaporean youth need a renewed presentation of the person of Jesus Christ whose life and teachings have more relevance to them.[54] When the church's vision of Christ is renewed, the faithful are more authentically equipped to extend a relevant Jesus in this generation. Revisioning is necessary for the future of the church.

Conclusion

This chapter provides only a snapshot of the complexities related to the current crisis of faith. There are no quick fixes. There remains insufficient research to capture all contemporary nuances pertinent to a survey of Christianity and Gen Z. Yet, this birds-eye view ponders important characteristics to begin that study.

Importantly, Gen Zers are growing up as "nones" but are searching for spiritual awareness. I teach many of them in my "Life, Death, and Meaning" course at Old Dominion University. One of the gifts of teaching in a secular university is that students are often either not affiliated or only loosely affiliated with a religious tradition. When I lecture on religion, it is as if I have them in the palm of my hands. A student recently asked me to start a podcast. Another immediately commented, "It will be very popular!" Every week, I rediscover a hunger for meaning and identity formation. Students have questions about life and death, and wonder whether faith can give sufficient answers. Podcasts and YouTube are the new pulpits. Millennials, as well as Gen Zers, look for answers there rather than at church. It might also be argued that they bring their search to the classrooms, whether online or in person.

Gen Z and the Non-Faith-Based Spiritual Search

Often, my students share their admiration for their grandparents' religion and are curious to learn more. Some don't see the point of going to church but do believe in God. Others grew up in church and are questioning whether a church is the best expression of God in the world. Yet others believe in something out there but are not sure whether "God" is the best way to describe that "something." Some are exploring other faiths like Wicca, Indigenous religions, the science of consciousness, and expanded consciousness. Some agnostics question the validity that there is a "God" or "something out there" altogether. Then, there are those holding on to their faith but weary with questions about faith and life that the church does not answer adequately. They are exploring how to follow Jesus differently than traditional approaches. They want a Jesus who cares about the things they care about and who navigates the world the way they do. They want to know that Jesus is for their cause: he attends to brokenness in the world, affirms love in whatever forms people claim it, includes everyone, and incorporates digital reality and social media as social and religious norms.

Notwithstanding, the same bout with faith manifests itself in the neighborhood. Gen Zers everywhere are asking the same questions. I was pleasantly surprised when I visited Barnes and Noble: young people's heads were buried in books. There is no denying their hunger for truth and deeper understanding. A closer examination observes an unprecedented spiritual search. This means the search for truth is no longer purely a scientific one. Gen Z may be dubbed a generation of creativity—not because previous generations were not—but because they are most unrestrained by the rules of what's right and wrong, appropriate, and inappropriate. So, even in their spiritual search, there are no rules; nothing is off-limits. They are more creative, more "in-touch" with today's times, it seems. Integration is premium, even the integration of religious thought, signs, and symbols with scientific ones.

Gen Zers are looking for something scientifically supported but that also brings peace, joy, love, identity, community, and a sense of belonging. This means that affectivity is just as sacred as anything else. Feelings, motivation, emotions, and belief systems must exist in tandem with that which is cause-driven, affirming, non-discriminatory, and non-sectarian. They care about social evolution: why should things remain the way they have always been? They also value art, science, ecology, climate change, peace, fairness, and communities that both affirm and include each person's gifts. The salient theological-anthropological questions sum up their search:

- Who am I?
- Why am I here?
- Is there a power greater than me?
- Does that ultimate being care about what's going on in the world?
- Can life be better for me?

These are complex queries. The answers must not be cookie-cutter but contextual and must include Gen Z in the discovery of truth. Importantly, such complex questions require a deeper analysis of the questions. Where are they coming from? Why are the questions important to this individual, and why now? Understanding where questions are coming from sheds light on ways to arrive at answers in a meaningful and inviting manner. Many times, probing questions reveal abuses and trauma embedded in the life of the questions. All of this is important to reimagining faith and local church ministry for greater engagement with Gen Z—and any other generation for that matter.

What Should Churches Do About the Gen Z Crisis of Faith?

Churches attuned to what's important to Gen Z are best positioned to attract and cultivate a faith environment to produce a Great Awakening amidst a generation of spiritually hungry, spiritual but not religious, unchurched young people. Thom Rainer offers the following helpful observations for pastors around the world interested in evangelizing and retaining Gen Zers:

- Positivity: Churches who are negative and fight often will not even be considered by Gen Z: "Gen Z will quickly walk away from churches fighting over such trivia as times of worship services, styles of music,

and facility preferences. They hate the divisiveness and pettiness they see when church members complain about their pastors. They've had enough negativity! They are wondering if any church members really remember the gospel is good news!"55
- Simplicity: Gen Z will strongly prefer churches that are focused and simple. Says Rainer, "They detest activity-driven churches. They will not hang around long if you ask them to attend a plethora of events and activities that make no sense to them. The simple church will be the church of choice."56
- Adaptability: Change-resistant churches will not attract Gen Z. This generation is not stuck in a rut of "it's always been this way." Rainer continues, "This is a generation of digital natives. They understand constant change. They live in a world of technological disruption. Change is their norm. Gen Zers, therefore, have no concept of the pettiness of many church issues."57
- Integrative: Additionally, churches that invite Gen Zers into worship and administrative leadership roles are more likely to attract and retain them. This is a generation of innovators accustomed to navigating life more independently.

The search for community amidst an epidemic of isolation, the desire for meaning, the hunger for spiritual awareness within a generational religious draught—all these must not be taken lightly. The atmosphere is set. The harvest is ripe. We must pray to the Lord of the harvest to send laborers like the children of Issachar who understand the times. A Great Awakening is just beyond the horizon!

Glimmers of Hope

Pockets of Gen Zers are rekindling the flames of revival, providing glimmers of hope. Globally, Pentecostal-Charismatic Christian spirituality is leading the charge. As a recent article in the *Washington Examiner* asserts:

> Younger generations of Christians are particularly drawn to the Charismatic experience today. So it is with Holy Spirit-led churches each week around the world. The Asbury Revival and others like it embody a universal desire to experience the more supernatural, metaphysical faith that has been absent in many of the churches that are hemorrhaging [sic] members. Headlines often declare the loss of religion in the United States, a notable trend toward those who identify as "nones." That shift, however, is being slowed dramatically by the rise of Charismatic movements found partially in the influx of immigrants from Latin America, Africa, and Asia to the U.S.[58]

Congregations unafraid to engage in ongoing, re-imaginative ministry remain on the cutting edge of youth attraction. Some examples are referenced above; other examples are the Ghanaian prayer gatherings in secondary and post-secondary schools, and the sparks of congregational enthusiasm at Heart of God Church in Singapore.

Another is the 2023 Asbury University Outpouring,[59] which sparked during a chapel service that lasted twenty-four hours, seven days a week, for a few weeks. Local news in Louisville, Kentucky, reported that approximately 50,000 to 70,000 people from around the world gathered at Asbury University to attend a worship service that started at 10:00 a.m. on Wednesday, February 8, 2023, and continued uninterrupted until February 24, 2023, when the university officials ended it.[60] Notably, the revival was at a Christian university and not a secular one. As stated earlier, the Pew Research Center reports Gen Z as the highest generation of "nones." Most Gen Zers attracted to the Asbury experience—on campus and beyond—seem to have been among the declining remnant of Gen Z Christians. Not many of the testimonies were from people who converted from being a "none" to the faith. For example, Anneli White is a student at the University of Kentucky and a member of Immanuel Baptist Church. She journeyed to Asbury for the revival experience and commented, "The Holy Spirit was tangible in the room. Chains were broken, confession happened, and God was praised as holy, holy, holy."[61] While White and others touched by the revival were already Christians, their experiences represent the need for a fresh wind of the Holy Spirit among the remnant of believing Gen Z. Hope is harbored in their renewed excitement about the faith. Their congregational participation and leadership inspire new ways of communicating the relevance of faith in their generation.

Churches worldwide that include young people in the ongoing work of theological re-imagination—bridging faith, higher education, business, care for the environment, community formation, and technology—will prove more effective in attracting and retaining young people most affected by secularism. Faith integration in the pursuit of meaning in everyday life produces fresh religious excitement in this generation.

Notes

1. This study was originally presented at the Global Pentecostal Summit hosted by City Harvest Church, Singapore in November 2023, and subsequently published in Kong Hee, Byron D. Klaus, and Douglas Peterson, eds., *Voices Loud and Clear: Understanding the Spirit's Movement Worldwide* (Oxford: Regnum Books, 2024).

2. Michael Dimock, "5 Things to Keep in Mind When You Hear about Gen Z, Millennials, Boomers and Other Generations," Pew Research Center, May 22, 2023, https://www.pewresearch.org/short-reads/2023/05/22/5-things-to-keep-in-mind-when-you-hear-about-gen-z-millennials-boomers-and-other-generations/, accessed May 7, 2024.

3. Dimock, "5 Things."

4. Michael Lipka and Claire Gecewicz, "More Americans Now Say They're Spiritual but Not Religious," Pew Research Center, September 6, 2017, https://www.pewresearch.org/short-reads/2017/09/06/more-americans-now-say-theyre-spiritual-but-not-religious/, accessed May 7, 2024.

5. Lipka and Gecewicz, "More Americans."

6. See Ryan P. Burg, *The Nones: Where They Came From, Who They Are, and Where They Are Going* (Minneapolis, MN: Fortress, 2021). Also Daniel A. Cox, "Generation Z and the Future of Faith in America," Survey Center on American Life, March 24, 2022, https://www.americansurveycenter.org/research/generation-z-future-of-faith/, accessed May 7, 2024.

7. See Dale M. Coulter, "Thoughts on the Future of American Christianity," *Firebrand*, October 3, 2023, https://firebrandmag.com/articles/thoughts-on-the-future-of-american-christianity-firebrand-big-read?fbclid=IwAR3azTAmv3axMdffq9uQJ277a9Ppe0-yAo_Uozj1C3ukx0HpXw8PdA-0_h8/, accessed May 7, 2024.

8. The academic conversation has moved beyond European secularism that compartmentalizes religion as non-essential in public discourse. Post-secularism and post-liberalism consider religion important for private life but not public discourse. However, my usage of secularisms seeks to capture Jose Casanova's insights of local challenges with religion rather than an import of European long-known secularism. Also, this chapter's reference to secularisms pushes Casanova's views towards new insights into how this generation separates institutional religion from spirituality. See Clayton Crockett, "What is Postsecularism?," *American Book Review* 39:5 (2018), 6–14, https://doi.org/10.1353/abr.2018.0062.

9. Dimock, "5 Things."

10 "Global Religion 2023: Religious Beliefs across the World," Ipsos Global Advisor, May 11, 2023, 2:1–39, https://www.ipsos.com/sites/default/files/ct/news/documents/2023-05/Ipsos%20Global%20Advisor%20-%20Religion%202023%20Report%20-%2026%20countries.pdf/, accessed May 7, 2024.

11 Nicolas Boyon, "Two Global Religious Divides: Geographic and Generational," Ipsos Global Advisor, https://www.ipsos.com/en-us/two-global-religious-divides-geographic-and-generational/, accessed May 7, 2024.

12 Boyon, "Two Global Religious Divides."

13 Ipsos, "Global Religion 2023."

14 Ipsos, "Global Religion 2023." Also see Samantha Saad, "Where Boomer Faith in God is Low, Gen Z Belief is Up," *Christianity Today*, July 24, 2023, https://www.christianitytoday.com/news/2023/july/ipsos-global-religion-survey-boomer-gen-z-belief.html/, accessed May 7, 2024.

15 Saad, "Where Boomer Faith in God is Low."

16 B. J. van der Walt, *Transforming Power: Challenging Contemporary Secular Society* (Potchefstroom, South Africa: ICCA, 2007), 298, quoted in T. Derrick Mashau, "A Reformed Missional Perspective on Secularism and Pluralism in Africa: Their Impact on African Christianity and the Revival of Traditional Religion," *CJT*, 44:110 (2009), 108–126, https://www.calvin.edu/library/database/crcpi/fulltext/ctj/2009-441-108.pdf/, accessed May 7, 2024.

17 "What is Secular Humanism?," Center for Inquiry, https://centerforinquiry.org/definitions/what-is-secular-humanism/#:~:text=Secular%20humanism%20is%20a%20nonreligious,find%20solutions%20to%20human%20problems/, accessed May 7, 2024.

18 José Casanova, "Rethinking Secularization," *Hedgehog Review* 8:1–2 (Spring/Summer 2006), 11, https://hedgehogreview.com/issues/after-secularization-special-double-issue/articles/rethinking-secularization, accessed May 7, 2024. Also see Aprilfaye T. Manalang, "Generation Z, Minority Millennials, and Disaffiliation from Religious Communities: Not Belonging and the Cultural Cost of Unbelief," *Interdisciplinary Journal of Research on Religion* 17: 2 (2021), 1–24, https://www.religjournal.com/articles/article_view.php?id=159/, accessed May 7, 2024.

19 Casanova, "Rethinking Secularization," 1–2.

20 Daniel A. Cox, "Emerging Trends and Enduring Patterns in American Family Life," Survey Center on American Life, February 9, 2022, https://

www.americansurveycenter.org/research/emerging-trends-and-enduring-patterns-in-american-family-life/, accessed May 7, 2024.

21 Cox, "Emerging Trends."
22 Jean M. Twenge, *iGen: Why Today's Super-Connected Kids are Growing up Less Rebellious, More Tolerant, Less Happy – and Completely Unprepared for Adulthood* (New York: Atria, 2017), 108.
23 Twenge, *iGen*, 109.
24 "Emergency Department Visits Involving Mental Health Conditions, Suicide-Related Behaviors, and Drug Overdoses among Adolescents–United States, January 2019–February 2023," *Morbidity and Mortality Weekly Report* 72:19 (2023), 502–512, Center for Disease Control and Prevention, May 12, 2023, https://www.cdc.gov/mmwr/volumes/72/wr/mm7219a1.htm?s_cid=mm7219a1_w/, accessed May 7, 2024.
25 Twenge, *iGen*, 109.
26 Sarah Eekhoff Zylstra, "6 Things Christians Should Know about Gen Z," The Gospel Coalition, https://www.thegospelcoalition.org/article/gen-z/, accessed May 7, 2024.
27 Twenge, iGen, 7. Twenge explains: "The prominent magazine *Advertising Age* has backed iGen as the best name for the post-Millennials. 'We think it's the name that best fits and will best lead to understanding of this generation,' Matt Carmichael, *Advertising Age's* former director of data strategy, told USA Today."
28 Zylstra, "6 Things."
29 Twenge, *iGen*, 109.
30 Zylstra, "6 Things."
31 Zylstra, "6 Things."
32 See Manfred Te Grotenhuis and Peer Scheepers, "Churches in Dutch: Causes of Religious Disaffiliation in The Netherlands, 1937–1995," *Journal for the Scientific Study of Religion* 40:4 (2001), 591–606, JSTOR, https://www.jstor.org/stable/1387654/, accessed May 7, 2024.
33 Te Grotenhuis and Scheepers, "Churches in Dutch," 591–606.
34 Coulter, "Thoughts on the Future of American Christianity."
35 Lipka and Gecewicz, "More Americans."
36 Racism, misogyny, and Christian nationalism to name a few.
37 Manalang, "Generation Z," 1–24. Manalang examines faith disaffiliation and unbelief among Gen Zers and Millennials in American communities of

color, specifically, Filipino Americans (the second-largest Asian American group), African Americans, and Hispanic Americans.

38 Zylstra, "6 Things."

39 Twenge, *iGen*, 114.

40 Twenge, *iGen*, 115.

41 Ghana Statistical Service, "Introduction: Africa, Ghana," The World Factbook, https://statsghana.gov.gh/docs/countrypdf_gh.pdf/, accessed May 7, 2024.

42 Mensa Otabil (Pastor of International Central Gospel Church), personal conversation with the author, September 21, 2023.

43 Otabil, personal conversation.

44 J. Kwabena Asamoah-Gyadu (President of Trinity Theological Seminary), personal conversation with the author, September 15, 2023.

45 Kwabena Asamoah-Gyadu, personal conversation.

46 Tunji Adegbite, "Tapping into the Chutzpah of Nigeria's Generation Z," *This Day Live*, https://www.thisdaylive.com/index.php/2020/10/18/tapping-into-the-chutzpah-of-nigerias-generation-z/, accessed May 7, 2024.

47 Pearlyn Koh, "To Keep Gen Z in the Pews, One Singapore Church Lets Them Run the Service," *Christianity Today*, February 10, 2023, https://www.christianitytoday.com/ct/2023/february-web-only/singapore-youth-church-gen-z-ministry.html/, accessed May 7, 2024.

48 Koh, "To Keep Gen Z in the Pews."

49 William Miner, "In Singapore, Religious Diversity and Tolerance Go Hand in Hand," Pew Research Center, October 6, 2023, https://www.pewresearch.org/short-reads/2023/10/06/in-singapore-religious-diversity-and-tolerance-go-hand-in-hand/, accessed May 7, 2024. See his comment: "Among Singaporean adults, 26% identify as Buddhist, 18% as Muslim, 17% as Christian, 8% as Hindu, 6% as a follower of Chinese traditional religions like Taoism or Confucianism, and 4% as some other religion, including Indigenous religions. Another 22% do not identify with any religion."

50 Koh, "To Keep Gen Z in the Pews."

51 Koh, "To Keep Gen Z in the Pews."

52 Deborah Ng, "The Future of Youth Ministry in Singapore," Cru, https://www.cru.org/sg/en/stories/helping-others-grow/the-future-of-youth-ministry-in-singapore.html/, accessed May 7, 2024.

53 Ng, "Future of Youth Ministry in Singapore."

54 Ng, "Future of Youth Ministry in Singapore."

55 Thom Rainer, "3 Significant Issues for Churches to Reach Gen Z, Teenagers," *The Pentecost*, October 5, 2021, https://thepentecost.ng/2019/12/3-significant-issues-for-churches-to-reach-gen-z-teenagers/, accessed May 7, 2024.

56 Rainer, "3 Significant Issues."

57 Rainer, "3 Significant Issues."

58 Ericka Andersen, "Charismatic Christian Movements Offer Hope for Gen Z," *Washington Examiner*, April 12 2023, https://www.washingtonexaminer.com/opinion/charismatic-christian-movements-offer-hope-for-gen-z/, accessed May 7, 2024.

59 "What Happened at Asbury University?," Asbury University, https://www.asbury.edu/outpouring/, accessed May 7, 2024.

60 "Asbury University Student Uses Map to Track Worshipers Who Came to 'Revival' Services," *WDRB.com*, February 24, 2023, https://www.wdrb.com/news/asbury-university-student-uses-map-to-track-worshipers-who-came-to-revival-services/article_a5e03506-b459-11ed-b30e-474a6ca5ff8b.html#:~:text=Over%20the%20past%20couple%20of,for%20more%20than%20a%20week/, accessed May 7, 2024.

61 Mark Maynard and Hannah Julian, "All Eyes Focus on (Another?) Asbury Revival," *Kentucky Today*, February 13, 2023, https://www.kentuckytoday.com/baptist_life/all-eyes-focus-on-another-asbury-revival/article_6994621a-a9b0-11ed-9cf7-67c841f9b6a3.html?fbclid=IwAR1tq3P_4dntYTur7ipKOPbi7w3zGoBLB_-t2ishqBEjSQRdzB2OUxOT6dg/, accessed May 7, 2024.

11 A New Wave of the Spirit: Second Generation African Pentecostals in the West and Their Contribution to Pentecostalism

Caleb Nyanni

Abstract

Pentecostalism and its progeny—Charismatics, neo-Pentecostal, and neo-Charismatic movements—arguably represent the fastest-growing churches globally. Within this Spirit-empowered movement is a new paradigm shaping Pentecostal praxis in innovative, inclusive ways. This chapter focuses on defining this next generation of Pentecostals as it intersects with the African diaspora, and discusses the nature and contributions of second and third-generation Afro-Westernism to traditional African Pentecostalism. Throughout this chapter, I use the phrases "second generation" and "Millennial Pentecostals" interchangeably to refer to the second generation of African Pentecostals in the West, especially in the U.K. and Western Europe.

Introduction

Pentecostals are generally known for their keen emphasis on the doctrine of the baptism of the Holy Spirit, as well as their attention to the manifestations of the works of the Spirit in their lives and worship services. With events of Pentecost providing a springboard for the basis of their beliefs, some Pentecostals place a high premium on receiving the power that comes with the promised Holy Spirit, often accompanied by speaking in tongues.

Though Spirit-baptism and power are Pentecostal traditions worldwide, African Pentecostals have perspectives of the Holy Spirit and power which are comprehensible only within an African worldview and understanding. African perspectives of Pentecost have shaped the pneumatology and ecclesiology of most African Pentecostals both at home and in the diaspora. Generally, first-generation African Pentecostals in the diaspora have sought to maintain their African worldview and practices even though they live in the West. However, the rise of second and third-generation African diaspora Pentecostalism has contributed to a new and emerging brand of Pentecostalism that is an amalgamation of African and Western practices and beliefs. This convergence of African and Western concepts is creating and shaping a new form of Pentecostalism that requires attention. This paper discusses how the beliefs and practices of second-generation African Pentecostals in the West are contributing to the changing face of global Christianity.

Defining Three Generations of African Pentecostals

Defining concepts, groups, and organizations is not always easy. Indeed, there is no consensus on how Africans view the Spirit, and there are several ways of approaching the Holy Spirit and spiritual matters among Africans. With this caveat in mind, however, a traditional African understanding of the Holy Spirit can be proposed as an empowering, pervading, personal Spirit who is vital for life, success, fruitfulness, and productivity. This traditional understanding of the Spirit permeates African theology and liturgy. The Holy Spirit makes it possible for Christians to be engaged with God daily, fight demonic and evil spirits, achieve their life goals, live a holy life, and become powerful witnesses and missionaries.[1]

That said, dealing with Millennials and Gen Z of African origin in the diaspora, especially in Europe, is a task that involves not only careful observation but also calibration of concepts and ideas. William Strauss and Neil Howe have provided some helpful indicators of generational cohorts and characteristics. However, the complexities of second and third-generation African Westerners make it difficult to generalize their character, behavior, and nature. From my own research conducted in 2020, one hundred young people between the ages of 18 and 35 did not even agree on how to describe their own generation. Half the participants used different words and phrases to describe their own generation and cohort, which suggests that any attempt to describe Millennials and Gen Z must be nuanced and done in context.[2]

Notwithstanding, a new wave of the Spirit and approach to the Holy Spirit is detectable among Millennials of African descent in the U.K. and Western Europe. I refer to these Millennials as Afro-Western Millennials, born between 1982 and 2004, and currently between 20–42 years old. I myself am in this generation. Though it is difficult to categorize this broad age range, there are certain practices and emphases common among this group. In particular, we have bridged cultural and religious gaps before and after the diaspora. In a sense, we are transitional: caught between first-generation and third-generation worldviews.

First-generation African immigrants were born and raised in Africa before the 1980s and immigrated to Europe and the West with an already-formulated and robust religious framework. Their understanding of the world was solidly dualistic. Their worldview was influenced by spirit manifestations and their effect on matter and physical beings, including humans. For first-generation African Pentecostals, the Holy Spirit and matters regarding cosmic spiritual battles were key in their conversion, church practices, and liturgy. These first-generation immigrants have since produced a second generation of Pentecostals in the West: Millennials like myself caught between their parents' beliefs and practices and Western philosophies and ideologies. Many of us were born in Africa but immigrated to the West at a young age. Although our foundational beliefs and practices remain African, we have had to quickly assimilate and adapt to Western practices and philosophies.

Now the third generation of individuals, Gen Z, are maturing into their late teens and emerging with new forms of church practices based on their socio-spiritual understanding of the world. Allan Anderson observes that, specifically, the first generation's approach to the Holy Spirit, which was primarily to empower them for life and serve as an antidote to spiritual attacks, is not largely shared by their children and grandchildren in the West.[3] While the Holy Spirit remains key to Pentecostal emphasis among the newest generation of Pentecostals—and emphasizing spiritual matters has been key to the growth of Pentecostalism in both Africa and the diaspora—many young Africans in the West struggle to identify with the same emphasis of the Holy Spirit as their parents and grandparents did. Education, social media, secularization, new forms of spirituality, and social movements have all bolstered and enhanced new ideologies that are impacting the youngest generation of Pentecostals both positively and negatively.

Pentecostal Practices and the Next Generation

In a discussion on how Christianity transmits from one generation to another, Andrew Walls espoused what he called "the pilgrim principle" of Christianity, in which he suggests that as Christianity moves from one territory to another, and one generation to another, each invariably adds fresh ideas to the understanding of Christ, humanity, and culture.[4] Therefore, no culture or generation can hold the gospel captive perpetually. The same could be said of Pentecostalism specifically.

Pentecostals, Pentecostalism, and Pentecostal practices have all become increasingly difficult to describe in recent years. Any description of Pentecostalism as a movement that simply believes in the work and baptism of the Holy Spirit is inadequate. Wolfgang Vondey asserts that such "identifiers" are no longer sufficient to describe the contemporary Pentecostal movement.[5] Anderson has described the origins of Pentecostalism as "polynucleated" and argued for the recognition of Pentecostalism as a multidimensional missionary movement.[6] Crucially, although Anderson points to various roots of Pentecostalism, he acknowledges that the Azusa Street Revival was by far the most pivotal in creating ". . . a distinct Pentecostal identity."[7] This Pentecostal fire seems to have taken different trajectories with the emergence of neo-Pentecostals, the Charismatic movement, neo-Evangelical churches, and—in this paper—Afro-Western Pentecostal Millennials and Gen Z. Among Pentecostals, there are further nuances and categorizations of practices and beliefs that make pneumatological consistency incredibly difficult.

The reality is that Pentecostalism is a movement with complex strains.[8] The orality and experiential bases of this movement mean that there is no clearly defined doctrinal statement guiding global Pentecostal practice and pneumatology. For example, the Assemblies of God in Britain states in their beliefs: "We believe in the baptism in the Holy Spirit as an enduement of the believer with power for service, the essential, biblical evidence of which is the speaking with other tongues as the Spirit gives utterance (Acts 1:4–5, 8; 2:4; 10:44–46; 11:14–16; 19:6)"[9] But the Elim Pentecostal Church puts it this way: ". . . and that the believer is also promised an enduement of power as the gift of Christ through the baptism in the Holy Spirit with signs following."[10] Here, although Elim states the importance of signs, they do not specifically mention tongues.

The entire process of trying to define Pentecostalism has been complicated by the emergence of Charismatic movements. Arguably, these "new Pentecostals" have recalibrated the emphasis on tongues and Spirit-baptism with spiritual gifts, demonology, prosperity teachings, healing, and deliverance. These Charismatic-Pentecostals stress not only the need for spiritual gifts but also spiritual warfare, which underpins the believer's ability to fight against the underlying causes of illness and misfortune, and be prosperous in life.

Further complications in describing Pentecostal pneumatology is the rise in indigenous Pentecostalism from sub-Saharan Africa, Asia, and South America. These indigenous worldviews, like first generation African Pentecostalism, presuppose the great cosmic battle between God and satanic forces. Subsequently, for most of these Pentecostals, the Holy Spirit is essentially power over witchcraft, vindictive spirits, and demons. In contrast to mainstream Western churches, these Pentecostals believe in the direct influence of witchcraft and evil spirits on human endeavors and that through the power of the Holy Spirit, they can confront these malevolent spirits.

All of these different strains and concepts have helped shape and create the most recent chapter of emerging Pentecostalism. On one hand, the traditional emphasis on Spirit-baptism and power in the warfare of this world is still very visible. In England, for example, cases of diaspora Pentecostal-Charismatic churches engaging in exorcisms and deliverance practices have soared.[11] This idea of power, Opoku Onyinah articulates, is associated with a powerful Jesus who enables Christians to have a powerful encounter with the Holy Spirit, who in turn empowers believers to overcome poverty, sickness, and witchcraft.[12] The holistic idea of power is appealing to numerous communities who see the Holy Spirit as a life-giving power that gives them the same ability and capacity that Jesus had to fulfill his mission. Emerging Pentecostals also share with first generation Pentecostals that the descent of the dove is the moment of empowerment for Jesus, and that Pentecost is the occasion where the Spirit empowered the disciples.[13] Also, like early twentieth-century Pentecostals, many Millennial and Gen Z Pentecostals today continue to see the world as a cosmic battle.

On the other hand, the emphasis on experiencing the Spirit means that the context of power has become contextualized in the various forms of Pentecostalism around the world. For emerging Pentecostals, power is still needed, but more for daily life struggles and issues rather than the demonic battle. These modern Pentecostals still engage in spiritual warfare prayers, but ask for and place the power of the Holy Spirit in becoming successful in their education, careers, and life choices. Since they do not always blame misfortune on evil spirits, they see Jesus' life-giving power as empowering them in life's practical issues. It could, therefore, be argued that the emphasis on power has dwindled among second-generation Pentecostals in Britain and in the West. And it appears that, in some cases, secularization, advancement of technology, and well-organized, decorously designed churches and programs have taken the place of the power needed by the Holy Spirit to counter the powers of Satan. Yet, I have argued elsewhere that second and third-generation Pentecostals do not assume they need less power from the Holy Spirit, but rather, their flexibility in matters of the Spirit means there is enough room for conversations with the modern and religiously pluralistic society it finds itself in.[14] Though the severity of the dualistic cosmic worldview may have lessened among emerging Pentecostals in the West, their heritage from their African, Asian, or indigenous parents continues to ground a superstructure of belief that has a place for a world inhabited by demons that influence spirituality and progress in life. Thus, Pentecostals from the developed world and those in the diaspora continue to seek the Holy Spirit for power over demonic and evil spirits.[15]

Lastly, but importantly, a new chapter of Pentecostalism is emerging as second and third-generation diaspora Pentecostalism asserts itself. These Pentecostals are an amalgamation of European-African or European-Asian heritage and are less interested in the categorization of denominations and institutions. Indeed, some do not know or even seem interested in knowing the differences between Pentecostals, Methodists, and Anglicans. Their church attendance is largely based on the fulfillment of their spiritual and physical needs rather than denominational loyalty. This means their theology, pneumatology, and church practices are an amalgamation of borrowed liturgy from their parents, but also Anglican, Evangelical, Charismatic, and Pentecostal streams. Given that three-quarters of the world's Pentecostals are now from Africa, Asia, and Latin America, it is vital that we take the beliefs and practices of this group seriously. Globalization, transnationalization, and immigration have all contributed to the increase of multicultural societies in the U.K. and the West in general and are therefore also poised to be a central influence in defining Pentecostalism for the future.[16]

A Fresh Approach to Mission

A key element of Pentecostal pneumatology is the emphasis on mission. For Pentecostals, Spirit-baptism and the power that comes with it is primarily to equip them to proclaim Jesus. Although the reception of power is personal, the results have wider implications: the purpose of receiving the Holy Spirit's power is to serve the church and community.

Traditionally, Pentecostalism's approach to mission has been based on an eschatological orientation that frames the power of the Holy Spirit to witness through Spirit-baptism. Based on Peter's application of Joel's prophecy in Acts 2, Pentecostals believe that they have been called in these last days to preach to the world before the *parousia*. Characteristically, some streams of Pentecostalism have emphasized an imminent *parousia* and placed "getting souls saved" high on their agenda, as Gary B. McGee describes it.[17] As Douglas Petersen notes, some also embrace the ability to speak unlearned languages from other cultures to evangelize the world, through Spirit-baptism and evidential *glossolalia* and *xenolia*.[18] The message has been, "Repent, for the kingdom of heaven is at hand" (Matt 4:17), which is heavenly-minded, evangelistic, and eschatologically motivated.

This has caused some, like Keith Warrington, to report "limited social involvement" as a trait in Pentecostal missions.[19] David Hilborn also notes that other denominations have developed public theologies to match the mission agendas in their societies, while Pentecostals still see missiology in terms of salvation and evangelism.[20] Yet, whilst Pentecostals continue to see evangelism as the mainstay of their missionary agenda, emerging second and third-generation Pentecostals are now expanding their missiological praxis to include social action. Increasingly, observes Wonsuk Ma, they have moved from the fringes of Pentecostalism, where its members were generally seen as poor and marginalized, to wealthier backgrounds where they can now help the less privileged in society.[21] Thus, there has been a broadening of Pentecostal missiology in recent years which is not only based on evangelism and salvation but also on social engagement and ministry to the poor. Heaven remains the goal for most modern Pentecostals, but the ministry on the street has taken on a more vital role.

In this context, contemporary Pentecostals are finding and joining different initiatives, such as the Anglican-initiated "Fresh Expressions"

(FX), to engage people outside the church. Though the aim of initiatives such as FX is to reach the unchurched, it is done in a more relational way than perhaps the traditional evangelistic way of some Pentecostals.[22] For example, while some first-generation African diaspora Pentecostals continue to give out tracts and engage in open-air evangelism, their children and grandchildren are increasingly involved in social engagement interventions such as feeding the homeless and helping those with addictions. They have embraced supporting the poor and providing supplies and services to the needy and unchurched in their communities.

Additionally, Afro-Western Millennials and Gen Z are engaged in a new mission agenda involving the internet and social media. While first-generation African Pentecostals and Charismatics have mainly used digital means to connect with various institutions in Africa, including receiving special prayers and ministries from home churches, second and third-generation Afro-Western Pentecostals are employing new media technologies to enhance church preaching, singing, announcements, and notices. Visits to African diaspora churches where there are significant numbers of second-generation Pentecostals show the youth using PowerPoint presentations in their sermons and projecting songs onto screens. Announcements that took ten minutes for one of the leaders to speak are now condensed into two-minute video clips. Or they are posted on Twitter, Instagram, and WhatsApp platforms. These are visible demonstrations of how second and third-generation communities are seeking to change the way church is conducted. Their ideas are undoubtedly borrowed from other churches through various media networks.

Fortunately, the second and third generations' indulgence in new media technologies has also enhanced their evangelistic inventions. The rise of media technologies has made the world a competitive place. From the marketplace to churches, people use online tools to gain attraction and followers. The recourse to new alternatives to evangelism is therefore facilitated and necessitated by the emerging generations' understanding of the power and influence of media technologies. The second generation employs fewer conventional forms of evangelism such as door-to-door, open-air, and tract evangelism. Significantly, they are using the internet—a perceived impersonal medium of communication—to achieve personal and spiritual results. With social media language and pictures, most of these second-generation Afro-Western Pentecostals are attracting other people to their churches and their faith. Most African diaspora churches that are flourishing have second-generation web designers and communicators who operate and manage their websites and social media feeds. The youth connect with their peers and the world through the church's websites or Instagram, and they often stream services live on Facebook and YouTube. Through these avenues, Afeosemime Adogame documents, church programs, and events have local and global reach.[23] Some churches even have apps that can be downloaded on mobile phones to stream, chat, or give real-time information. Unlike the first generation, whose structures attract other Africans, the second generation uses online media to highlight the relevance of the African church in the diaspora.

Pentecostal Pneumatology: Encountering the Spirit

For some Christians, acceptance of the Holy Spirit simply means acknowledging he is present. However, for Pentecostals, the presence of the Holy Spirit must be tangible, heard, felt, or in some way experienced. In other words, Pentecostals like to know through some perceptible manifestation, one way or the other, that the Holy Spirit is in their midst. This is what Warrington describes as a theology of encounter.[24] Indeed, all Christian worship is through the Spirit; however, traditionally Pentecostals have placed a high emphasis on the active and lived experience of the Holy Spirit in their worship services to the extent that, until the Spirit is felt, the service is not over. In this context, if the Holy Spirit fails to move, traditionally the leader must "move the Spirit."[25]

This is the case in many Pentecostal services, especially among African and Asian diaspora churches, where services often go on longer than planned because of the "active" presence of the Holy Spirit. This active presence of the Holy Spirit is often felt in their prayers, singing, dancing, and, significantly, the expressions of charismatic gifts including prophecy, words of knowledge, healing, and deliverance. In serving the church, the emphasis is on the gifts of the Holy Spirit especially as described in 1 Corinthians 12. Emerging African Pentecostals in the West are expectant and seek the Holy Spirit's power in these visible manifestations. For some of these young Pentecostals, the visible manifestations of the Holy Spirit's power, such as healing, prophecy, and working of miracles, encourage their faith and belief in God.

With reference to scriptures such as "where the Spirit of the Lord is, there is freedom" (2 Cor 3:17), Pentecostal worship becomes open to the moving of the Spirit in the sense that the leaders and congregation allow the Holy Spirit to take control. It is within this freedom in worship that leads to vibrant prayers, ecstatic praises, and exuberant celebrations within Pentecostal services. Simon Chan describes this celebration or "play" within Pentecostal worship as a blend of free worship and spontaneity: The Spirit provides freedom in worship, and the community's tradition provides the framework within which to celebrate.[26] Referring to John 4:23 and Luke 11:2, J. E. Alvarado explains that for many Pentecostals, the understanding of worship is a dual engagement of the Spirit and the flesh, as well as a connection between heaven and earth. Subsequently, there is a constant desire to connect with the Holy Spirit who is the link between these two vicinities.[27]

It is during such encounters with the heavenly realm that Pentecostals make room and anticipate hearing the voice of God through prophecies and words of knowledge, and to see the manifestations of God's power through healings and miracles. It is, therefore, common to see people falling, shaking, shouting, laughing, or expressing physical manifestations during Pentecostal worship services. Some worship services turn into healing and miracle services where people come forward for prayer for healing or deliverance. Others experience miracles during the service because of the tangible presence of the Spirit. In some cases, as I have noted, ordinary members, and not the clergy, stand and prophesy as led by the Holy Spirit.[28]

Regarding second and third-generation Pentecostalism specifically, Hilborn accurately documents that in some Pentecostal churches, open charismata are seen less.[29] The modern trend of carefully orchestrated worship teams who take control of most of the service is visible, especially in larger churches where the worship leader or pastor controls events during the services.[30] However, even among such Pentecostal congregations, there remains the element of emotional, passionate, vibrant, and ecstatic worship. For emerging Pentecostals from African and Asian backgrounds, there still appears to be a desire for and a blend of spontaneous worship—filled with charismatic activities of the Spirit—in addition to a measure of orderliness. Second generation Pentecostals may talk of "feeling the Spirit" in church or worship, by which they mean perceiving the active presence of the Holy Spirit through manifestations such as prophecy, healing, miracles, deliverance, or ecstatic praises and dancing. However, due to the influence of globalization and their sociocultural environment, they also seek to maintain some form of order in the service, including finishing on time.

Conclusion

Afro-Western Millennials like me, who have grown up in the U.K. or Western Europe, have been heavily affected by postmodern, secular, multicultural society. Their complex identities, multicultural environment, and other influences such as secularization and globalization make exploring their theologies an enormous task. One can no longer categorize the children of first-generation immigrants into a single theological framework, and so this paper does not aim to speak for all Afro-Western Pentecostals.

However, based on participant observation research, interviews, and surveys, certain cautious conclusions can be made based on observational findings. Generally, second-generation Millennials have not totally adopted the theology of their Western colleagues. Neither have they embraced their parents' understanding of the Holy Spirit or the spirit world from Africa. Observations of Afro-Western Millennials have shown that most of them are now caught between African and Western theological ideas. Since most of these Millennials did not suffer the extent of oppression and racism suffered by their Caribbean counterparts, the basic ideas of liberation and black theologies do not resonate with them. However, they still appear to be influenced by the concepts of spiritual warfare in their parents' African theological and cosmological orientation, and neo-Western spiritualities. Thus, argues Israel Olofinjana, second-generation diaspora Pentecostals are immersed in an Afro-Western pneumatology that is an amalgamation of African and Western influences.[31] Chike Chigor likewise notes this trend when he concludes that there is a growing transition of beliefs and practices between Africans in Africa, and Africans in the diaspora, due to the influence of Western culture and theology.[32] The hallmarks of this new and emerging understanding of the Spirit can be defined in three categories: the experience of power, a new missionary approach, and empowering worship. This is in many ways like Warrington's definition of Pentecostal theology, which he describes as a theology of encounter.[33] Furthermore, from the African perspective, there is an emphasis on experience in church, the marketplace, and every aspect of life. The universality of the Spirit's presence is an essentially African expression of Pentecostal theology.

The convergence of African and Western theology is therefore reflected in Millennials' admiration of the African way of expressing themselves in church liturgy, including intensive prayers, exuberant praises, and dancing—while at the same time embracing Western ways of communication, structure, and mission. Significantly, these Millennials do not attribute the same power to demonic spirits as their first-generation parents. Millennials generally do not blame evil spirits for many of life's incidents, and most of them do not spend time engaging in spiritual warfare prayers for protection against evil spirits. However, a reluctance to blame every occurrence on malevolent spirits does not mean that Afro-Western Millennials are oblivious to the work of Satan and his emissaries. This is what one respondent meant when she said, "It's not that we don't believe in evil spirits. Of course, we do believe in them. But we also believe things happen without the interference of evil spirits."[34] Another respondent explained, "It's not that we don't believe in the demonic forces, but we simply don't give them more attention than they deserve."[35]

In other words, unlike some of their parents and grandparents, second and third-generation Pentecostals do not believe that their world is full of malevolent spirits. Their understanding of the spirit world, coupled with the socio-cultural influences of Britain and Europe, produces in some of these young Pentecostals, a form of spirituality that transcends the sterility of demonic powers and fearful spirits. Subsequently, diaspora Pentecostals do not link every misfortune and life struggle to the presence, power, or influence of evil spirits. Their pneumatology is nuanced, with most Millennials seeking power from the Holy Spirit for practical living rather than protection from witchcraft. For most diaspora Millennials, evil and malevolent spirits appear to be the least of their worries. Finding good jobs, life partners, and living Spirit-filled lives in their communities seemed to be the mainstay of their quest for the Holy Spirit. This has been attached to mission, evangelism, and community. Globalization, multiculturalism, and secularization have shaped the Pentecostal understanding of mission to be not simply winning souls for Christ, but making an impact in one's community through media and social action.

Finally, the active presence of the Holy Spirit has been transformed by second and third-generation communities to mean being lived out daily rather than experienced only by "the power and the fire on Sundays." To this effect, although Afro-Western Millennials believe in the power of the Holy Spirit through healing and miracles, their emphasis in prayer is more on seeking wisdom, direction, and guidance for life than it is for breaking the demonic activities around them. Diaspora pneumatology appears to be shifting from one based on radical power against evil spirits and forces, towards one that focuses primarily, but not exclusively, on the quality of life produced in Christians by the power of the Holy Spirit and the effects of this power in their communities.

Notes

1 As described in Allan H. Anderson, *Spirit-Filled World* (Palgrave: McMillan, 2018), 219.
2 Caleb Nyanni, *Second Generation Diaspora Survey: African Diaspora Churches U.K.* (unpublished, 2022).
3 Anderson, *Spirit-Filled World*, 219.
4 Andrew F. Walls, *The Missionary Movement in Christian History: Studies in the Transmission of Faith* (Edinburgh: T & T Clark, 1998), 8–9.
5 Wolfgang Vondey, "Christian Amnesia: Who in the World are Pentecostals?" *AJPS* 4:1 (2001), 22.
6 Allan Anderson, "The Emergence of a Multidimensional Global Missionary Movement," in *Spirit and Power: The Growth and Global Impact of Pentecostalism*, eds. D. Miller, K. Sargeant, and R. Flory (Oxford: Oxford University Press, 2013), 25–33.
7 For a full discussion of Anderson's assumptions see Anderson, "The Emergence of a Multidimensional Global Missionary Movement," 30–31.
8 Donald E. Miller and Tetsunao Yamamori, *Global Pentecostalism: The New Face of Christian Social Engagement* (Berkeley: University of California Press, 2007), 1.
9 "What We Believe," Assemblies of God Incorporated, https://www.aog.org.uk/about-us/what-we-believe/, accessed June 6, 2024.

10 "What We Believe," Elim Pentecostal, https://www.elim.org.uk/Articles/417857/Our_Beliefs.aspx/, accessed June 6, 2024.

11 Harriet Sherwood, "'Spiritual Abuse': Christian Thinktank Warns of Sharp Rise in U.K. Exorcisms," July 5, 2017, *The Guardian*, https://www.theguardian.com/world/2017/jul/05/christian-thinktank-warns-of-rise-in-exorcisms-mental-health/, accessed March 19, 2019.

12 Opoku Onyinah, *Pentecostal Exorcism* (Dorset: Deo, 2012), 99; Joseph Quayesi-Amakye, *Christology and Evil in Ghana: Towards a Pentecostal Public Theology* (Amsterdam: Rodopi, 2013), 251–252.

13 For more, see Robert P. Menzies, *Spirit and Power* (Grand Rapids: Zondervan, 2000); also Roger Stronstad, *The Charismatic Theology of St. Luke* (Peabody, MA: Hendrickson, 1984).

14 Caleb Nyanni, *Second Generation African Pentecostals in the West* (Eugene: Wipf & Stock, 2020), 182; Richard Burgess and Kim Knibbe, *Pentecostalism in Europe: A Sketch of the Dynamics* (Roma: Edizioni Borla, 2013), 154–161.

15 As described in Cephas Omenyo, "African Pentecostalism," in *The Cambridge Companion to Pentecostalism*, eds. Cecil M. Robeck Jr. and Amos Yong (Cambridge: Cambridge University Press, 2014), 140–141.

16 For more on this subject, see J. H. Logan Jr., "Black Pentecostalism," in *Encyclopaedia of Pentecostal and Charismatic Christianity*, ed. S. Burgess (London: Routledge, 2006), 60–64; also Anderson, *Spirit-Filled World*, 3.

17 Gary B. McGee, "Pentecostal and Charismatic Mission," in *Towards the Twenty-first Century in Christian Mission: Essays in Honor of Gerald H. Anderson*, eds. James M. Phillips and Robert T. Coote (Grand Rapids: Eerdmans, 1993), 42.

18 Douglas Petersen, *Not by Might not by Power: A Pentecostal Concern for Social Action in Latin America* (Oxford: Regnum Books, 1996), 9.

19 Keith Warrington, *Pentecostal Theology: A Theology of Encounter* (London: T & T Clark, 2008), 263.

20 David Hilborn, "Anglicans, Pentecostals and Ecumenical Theology," in *The Many Voices of Global Pentecostalism* (Cleveland: CPT, 2013), 260.

21 Wonsuk Ma, "Asian Pentecostalism in Context," in *The Cambridge Companion to Pentecostalism*, eds. Cecil M. Robeck Jr. and Amos Yong (Cambridge: Cambridge University Press, 2014), 165.

22 "What is a Fresh Expression?" September 10, 2018, Fresh Expressions, http://freshexpressions.org.uk/about/what-is-a-fresh-expression/, accessed March 20, 2019.

23 Afeosemime Adogame, *The African Christian Diaspora: New Currents and Emerging Trends in World Christianity* (London: Bloomsbury, 2013), 156.

24 Warrington, *Pentecostal Theology*, 32.

25 Described in Babatunde Adedibu, *Coat of Many Colours: The Origin, Growth, Distinctiveness and Contributions of Black Majority Churches to British Christianity* (London: Wisdom Summit, 2012), 142.

26 Simon Chan, *Pentecostal Theology and the Christian Spiritual Tradition* (Sheffield, U.K.: Sheffield Academic Press, 2000), 117–118.

27 J. E. Alvarado, "Worship in the Spirit: Pentecostal Perspectives on Liturgical Theology and Praxis," *JPTS* 2:1 (2012), 144.

28 Nyanni, *Second Generation Pentecostals in the West*, 150.

29 Hilborn, "Anglicans, Pentecostals and Ecumenical Theology," 262.

30 See Calvin Johansson, "Pentecostal Worship," in *New SCM Dictionary of Liturgy and Worship*, ed. Paul Bradshaw (London: SCM Press, 2005), 370–371.

31 Israel Olofinjana, "Introduction: Towards African Theology in Britain," in *African Voices Towards African British Theologies*, ed. Israel Olofinjana (Carlisle: Langham, 2017), 11.

32 Chike Chigor, *African Christianity in the Diaspora* (Oxford: Author House, 2007), 56.

33 Warrington, *Pentecostal Theology*, 27.

34 Sarah (from Birmingham, England), in discussion with the author, April 15, 2020.

35 Jude (from Birmingham, England), in discussion with the author, August 27, 2020.

12 Rejuvenation of a Denomination: The Experience of the Church of Pentecost, Ghana

Charles Prempeh

Abstract

Focusing on the Church of Pentecost (CoP), this chapter argues that the Christian religion is not established for ritual and cultural atavism, but for flourishing and responding to the human existential condition. It must, therefore, respond to modernization and the changing social context which create those conditions. Thus, the CoP—under multiple chairpersons since the 1930s, but consolidating under Apostle Professor Opoku Onyinah since the 1990s—has embarked on a course of rejuvenation. As a result, it has emerged as the largest Protestant church in Ghana. My paper is structured socio-historically: it privileges the socio-historical implications of the church's claim of a covenantal relationship with God, as well as the socio-cultural and economic shifts in the late 1970s locally and globally. I explore how socio-cultural realities in Ghana informed rejuvenation in Ghana's CoP. I then discuss Onyinah's cultural creativity and theological innovativeness in reforming the CoP. Finally, I draw conclusions with an assessment of Onyinah's rejuvenation of the CoP. In all, I conclude that reforms have helped the CoP's efforts at legitimizing its identity and demonstrating the capacity to measurably accommodate Ghana's changing socio-cultural climate.

A Critical Engagement: God's Covenant with the CoP, or Holiness Theology?

Background

I begin my discussion of CoP's rejuvenation from the perspective of the church's claim of a divine covenant: a major subject in the church's quest for rejuvenation since the 1930s. I engage the CoP's claim to its covenant with God, not as a theological issue, but as a sociological one. In particular, I argue that the CoP did not make a claim of divine covenant from the time of its founder, James McKeown, until the very last days of its third chairman, Prophet Martinson Kwadwo Yeboah.[1] This is important for historical reasons.

Importantly, at the time of the disputed covenant in 1931, the CoP had not been formed. The church's founder, McKeown, was not in Ghana until

1937.[2] So while Yeboah identified the CoP with a 1931 covenant at the end of his ministry in the 1990s, no divine covenant is discussed in the authoritative account by CoP historians, academics, and theologians that was published in 2004.[3] Moreover, Onyinah, one of the highest-ranking members of the CoP and the church's foremost scholar, has so far not mentioned the CoP's covenant with God in his peerlessly extensive research and publications on the church.

Thus, with the covenant being anterior to McKeown, it makes sense that he hardly appealed to it. Possibly, McKeown and his immediate successors did not want to claim an elitist entitlement that would undermine Christian unity. After all, McKeown's mission was decidedly about evangelism and hardly any claim to theological uniqueness. His later receptivity to the Latter Rain in 1953, against the Bradford Apostolic Church (the International Missions Headquarters of the Apostolic Church), is telling.[4] It indicates that he did not cherish the theological idiosyncrasies and church polarization that marred the Christian mission in the late nineteenth century and the Pentecostal movement in the early twentieth century.

Even so, just when Prophet Yeboah was nearing the end of his ministry, he presented before the CoP members the divine covenant I will discuss subsequently. It is unclear why Yeboah decided to talk about the covenant towards the end of his tenure, and more importantly, the end of his life. I surmise that Yeboah's action had sociological importance: his reclaim of a divine covenant that preceded the CoP is identifiable with how new religious movements curate legitimacy and longevity.

New Religious Movement Sociology

New religious movements tend to have credibility issues. As new movements, they are often profiled pejoratively as cults. They may also be disdained and considered a breakaway, syncretic, or superficial expression of a "true" religious group. As a result, new movements have at times deployed the paradigm of established religion to carve an acceptable image for themselves.

Incidentally, established religions, especially in the case of Judaism, lay claim to having special covenants with God. This makes them a group chosen to undertake a special assignment. The idea of "chosen-ness" by

God, divinely mediated by prophets, is an established pattern of premodern established religions. For this reason, many new religious movements claim to have a covenant with God. In contemporary Christian history, Jehovah's Witnesses, Seventh-Day Adventists, and the Church of Jesus Christ of Latter-Day Saints all claim uniqueness founded on a prophet mediating God's special relationship with them. The Seventh-Day Adventists refer to themselves as the "remnant church" with a special end-time message to the world, symbolized by their faithfulness to an established religious paradigm, the Sabbath. Jehovah's Witnesses similarly claim to retain the ancient name of God, Jehovah. The names each movement chooses signals their identity and continuity with established religions to claim legitimacy away from the label of cult.

Covenant and CoP Legitimacy

The 1930s were highly crucial for Ghana's (the Gold Coast's) Pentecostal holiness doctrine, orthopraxy, and the CoP's claim to a unique covenant with God. For this reason, post-2004 CoP historians claimed and identified the CoP with a covenant that was made prior to the church's establishment. The account claims that, during a prayer meeting at Akroso in the Eastern Region of Ghana, a prophetic message in the form of a divine covenant came to the church. This was through Reverend J. S. Gyimah. According to this prophet-mediated covenant, God promised to sustain the Church of Pentecost, to claim it as his own, and use it to reform the moral contours of the world.[5] The church had a role to play, which was to uphold holiness.[6]

With no intention of watering down the CoP's covenantal claim, I argue that divine covenant was hardly mentioned until the 1990s. Thus, its absence is revealing and significant. It is often said—and I heard this from my mother several times—that Prophet Yeboah was overly concerned about the future of the CoP. As I discuss later in this chapter, he was particularly wary of modernity, with good reason. As Ghana and the world were preparing for the turn of the millennium, under Yeboah's chairmanship significant changes were taking place. Ghana had re-democratized, the media had significantly liberalized, and the country had become a "mecca" or migratory destination of Western African citizens who escaped from the dictatorial regimes of Sani Abacha of

Nigeria and Gnassingbé Eyadéma of Togo. Consequently, towards the end of Prophet Yeboah's tenure, Ghana had become highly cosmopolitan. It had all the local and imported cultural traits that threatened Pentecostal holiness theology. As I remember, during the 1990s, modern feminism was gaining traction in Ghana with figures such as Grace Omaboe, then a renowned actress, encouraging women to wear whatever they wanted. There was a decade of young women wearing short, skin-tight outfits that exposed the private parts of their bodies—locally called *Apuskeleke*, or "I'm aware," after the response young women allegedly gave when the older generation drew attention to their immodesty.[7]

This context is essential to the discussion of CoP's reforms and whether they have breached the original divine covenant, especially for first-time readers of CoP history. The terms of the covenant—to uphold holiness—were not especially unique to the general command given to the Christian church since the apostolic era in the first century (c.f. 1 Pet 1:16). Among early Christians, non-Jewish Christians had to decide whether to continue with Jewish practices of ritual purity. Also, the Corinthian church incorporated headscarves as a mark of holiness for women. Through the centuries the church has had to wrestle with maintaining holiness within changing standards. Thus, the ideas of holiness theology, which were part of Pentecostalism's debut in the early twentieth century and wedded to the CoP's founding, means the CoP leadership has had to wrestle with the practical expression of holiness since the 1930s.

Initially, the CoP instituted every first Wednesday of each month as Missionary Day, for prayers and offerings to be made for the expansion of missions work. The Women's Movement set aside every first Tuesday of the month to pray for the growth and expansion of the church spiritually, morally, financially, and numerically. The Women's Movement also adopted as its slogan, "Holiness unto the Lord," because of the covenant of holiness; this is still in practice today in places. Finally, callings and elections were to be confirmed through divine intervention and the general consensus of the people.[8] All of these were offshoots of McKeown's sermons and the basic theme of holiness.

As part of fulfilling its commitment to holiness theology, the CoP profiled adultery and fornication as specific indices of unholiness. The church was to suspend members who fell or lived in sin, and the oral history of the CoP is replete with McKeown strictly applying the rule of suspension against violators. Yet, because adultery and fornication are somewhat culturally defined, the CoP had to find culturally relevant canons to determine moral boundaries. And to do so, the church intentionally looked to its immediate context of Akan culture, which had very strict rules regarding men and women. Towards the end of the nineteenth century and the beginning of the twentieth, Christian missionaries had conceded significantly to indigenous cultures, partly, as Brian Stanley reasons, as a result of the cultural crisis that World War I caused.[9] Similarly, around this time, notable African Christian elites, including J. E. A. Casely Hayford (1866–1930) and J. Mensah Sarbah (1864–1910), began the agenda of cultural nationalism—centering the African worldview around Christianity rather than traditional Akan religion.[10] By the time McKeown arrived in Asamankese, David Kimble describes how cultural nationalism had strongly shaped Gold Coast politics.[11] However, McKeown—possibly informed by his own idiosyncrasies—had a favorable view of Akan and indigenous culture. He was famously reported to have said that he did not come to the Gold Coast to plant an English oak tree, and therefore paved the way for creative incorporation and assimilation of selected Akan cultural ethos into the CoP.[12]

McKeown adopted a cross-cultural mission strategy. The church incorporated Akan women's wearing of headscarves as well as segregation by gender as marks of holiness. Concerning headscarves, I have described elsewhere that among the Akan, older post-menopausal women sometimes wear headscarves as a mark of seniority.[13] Old age is often believed among the Akan to come with wisdom and purity, as the aged no longer discharge the culturally tabooed menstrual blood as impure.[14] Conflating headscarves with purity, the CoP readily accepted the practice of head covering for all its adult women.

Segregation by gender in the church was also borrowed largely from the Akan. Emmanuel Akyeampong describes how, among the Akan, adultery was so strictly defined that even touching a married woman was considered adultery.[15] This appealed to the CoP's narrow idea of holiness, so they encouraged gender-segregated seating during church services. Women and men similarly had to appear visibly different in costume. The CoP outlawed the wearing of trousers for its female constituency. Another mark of holiness included avoiding artificial nail extensions as, one elder reports, these were considered unholy.[16] While leveraging the

Akan worldview for holiness theology, Rev. Oppong Asare-Duah notes that the CoP remained largely antagonistic to chieftaincy.[17]

Strict holiness theology helped the CoP to choreograph its identity as the end-times chosen church of God, but it suffered cultural backlash when it relocated its headquarters to Accra in 1948. The city had become very cosmopolitan since its inception as the administrative capital of the Gold Coast colony in 1877. Its multilingualism found commonality in the country's retention of the English language for use in governance. Onyinah explains that the widespread use of English and its social signifier of elitism helped in the explosion of parachurch movements and neo-Pentecostalism which were in English.[18] Parachurch groups such as the Ghana Fellowship of Evangelical Students, Christian Fellowship, Inter-College Camp, Joyful Way, the Scripture Union—of which Onyinah was a member during his tertiary education days—set the pace for linguistic reform in Ghanaian Pentecostalism. The movement united Ghana's ethnic plurality with the English language for religious rejuvenation.

The cultural plurality of Accra also impacted religious evangelism. Around the 1960s, the Catholic Church, through Vatican II, also conceded more to indigenous cultures as a means of evangelism. This development, observes Onyinah, resulted in several Catholic Charismatic renewal movements.[19] Similarly, by the 1970s, the economy of Ghana atrophied, which complexly coincided with the rise and flourishing of the neo-Pentecostal movement. According to George M. Bob-Milliar it was also during this period that chieftaincy revitalized its socio-cultural and political significance.[20] Around this same period, Ghana witnessed a progressive rise in Reformist Islam, including the Ahlu Sunna Wal'Jamah, and other streams like Shi'a and Elijah Mohammed's Nation of Islam.[21]

As Ghana's public sphere became increasingly enchanted, local and international pressures compelled Flight Lt. Rawlings, who had led Ghana as a military leader since 1981, to re-democratize the country. As Ghana re-democratized, political and religious freedoms attracted several "oppressed" West African citizens to the country, which added more to the complex cultural texture of Accra and major cities. These cultural crosscurrents converged on a segment of young men and women in the CoP who were agitating for linguistic and sartorial reforms.

Holiness Theology and the Challenge of Religious Rejuvenation

Beyond biblically ethical boundaries which are universally shared across the church, the CoP's strict holiness theology gave it a sense of being divinely selected for its mission. Its rules and theology impressed on the church to have a unique, visible presence in public. It was largely for this reason that the CoP ritualized Akan notions of holiness formulated around sartorial practices, hairstyles, and clear gender boundaries between men and women.

As human-made cultural idioms and social conditions for the message of Christ are highly osmotic, the CoP's fossilization and investing of Akan cultural practices with divine validation hindered theological innovation.[22] The inertia in theological innovation was complicated by the CoP's drawing parallels between a hermeneutically complex text in 1 Corinthians 11:2–13 and the legitimization of women's head covering. As the CoP retained, essentialized, and universalized Akan cultural practice into its branch ministries, the socially upward-mobile youth profiled the church as fronting Akan hegemony. I have met several individuals, particularly women, who left or did not join the CoP because they felt their sartorial choices did not correspond with the CoP's head coverings for women.

The CoP's lag in religious rejuvenation was consequently influenced by several factors. First, the church fell short in seeing religion or faith in general as part of human efforts at explaining what life all is about, who human beings are, and what is expected of them. Faith is not just about rituals, but about consolidating ethical and ontological boundaries as part of human beings keeping and tilling the land for human flourishing. Second, the church confused the fact that beliefs are not just informed by theology and philosophy, but by social conditioning.

Thus, for the church to have failed to recognize its own Akan/southern Ghana cultural biases, the issue of rejuvenating the church for robust cross-cultural and transnational missions suffered. Beyond the above challenges, the aspect of divine election into leadership, which Apostle Michael Ntumy, the immediate predecessor of Onyinah, called "theomocracy,"[23] proved problematic. For example, the nomination and election of Apostle Onyinah became a complex mixture of church politics and manipulation of prophecies—a situation that rendered Onyinah's rejuvenation of the church difficult. This will be discussed below.

Rejuvenating the CoP since the 1980s

Apostle Safo (1982–1987)

In 1982, Apostle Fred Stephen Kwasi Mensah Safo took over the chairmanship from founder James McKeown. During the five-year regime of Apostle Safo, the CoP had to deal with influences from non-denominational and Charismatic churches that were restructuring the Christian landscape in Ghana. Given Safo's personal closeness with McKeown, he was noted for shielding the church from cultural influences from the outside. He was therefore, according to Matthew L. Wettey, reported as a good disciplinarian who kept the principles of McKeown and pushed forward the spiritual uplift of the church.[24] On the other hand, Safo was amenable to pro-English reforms in the church and, overall, a well-informed person and level-headed leader who was abreast of time.

As the CoP became keenly aware of its cultural atavism that obstructed its socio-cultural relevance in the 1980s, Apostle Safo and his general secretary Apostle Daniel Kwabena Arnan began the process of rejuvenation. In 1984, they introduced the English Assembly concept into the church.[25] The main characteristic of the English Assemblies was their use of English for church services. The rationale was to attract youth and foreigners who could not speak the local dialects. However, these could not be materialized until the formation of Pentecost International Worship Centers, which I shall discuss later in this chapter.

Prophet Yeboah (1988–1998)

Unfortunately, Apostle Safo served only for five years before passing away. From 1988–1998, the CoP was headed by Prophet Martinson Kwadwo Yeboah, who was elected to office through "directive prophecy,"[26] During this period, the constitution of the CoP permitted the consideration of directive prophecy during leadership selection. A directive prophecy was, however, to be endorsed by an electoral college made of all apostles and prophets of the church and ratified through election by the General Council (the highest decision-making body of the church), which at the time was made up of all ordained pastors and elders' representatives.

The fusion of prophecy and election in nominating and electing a new leader of the church—Apostle Ntumy's "theomacracy"—is not unique to the CoP and has a tendency to create greater reliance upon prophecy. The CoP's reliance on prophecy resonates with, according to Keith Warrington, the Pentecostal practice of looking to prophecy as a means of determining direction or confirmation in decision-making and for encouragement.[27] Nonetheless, as I will discuss later in this chapter, it was this deployment of prophecy in appointing the chairman of the church that partly prompted the backlash against the 2010 reforms of the CoP.

As mentioned, Yeboah's regime proved less receptive to modernizing reforms within the church. Yeboah had worked closely with McKeown as a high-ranking officer in the CoP until McKeown left Ghana in 1982 (The latter died seven years later, at Ballymena in Northern Ireland). Interestingly, McKeown was pro-modernization inasmuch as he believed in the leading of the Spirit. But Yeboah became a key player in shielding the church from modernization in the sense of not allowing the influence of the Charismatic movement to infiltrate the church.

Given Yeboah's interest in shielding the CoP from negatively perceived influences from other churches, his regime did not see significant reforms. However, some significant changes occurred during his era, including a restructuring committee of the church, chaired by Onyinah. Onyinah's recommendations led to the establishment of area executive committees, district executive committees, an international missions office, a women's directorate, a finance and administrative director, and a youth and evangelism directorate. Furthermore, it was during his time as the International Missions Director that Onyinah initiated the establishment of the Pentecost International Worship Centre (PIWC), which paved the way for future rejuvenation.

In 1997, towards the end of his regime, most of Yeboah's recorded sermons (many of which I have listened to on the CoP's public Facebook handle)[28] focused on retaining the Pentecostal culture that constituted the foundation of the CoP. He is best remembered for keeping the traditions of the church and for his loyalty to classic Pentecostal doctrines promulgated by McKeown. His chairmanship, along with

Safo's, were relatively conservative regimes that introduced important pro-English reforms but provoked the need for more significant reforms in the following years.

Perhaps ahead of its time, under Yeboah's leadership, the CoP's Pentecost Students and Associates (PENSA) had become a careful blend of Charismatic Christianity and traditional Pentecostal Christianity. Given that PENSA branches were set in secular universities, they did not enforce many of the CoP's most rigid holiness rules. For example, during communion service, no one was barred from "dining with the Lord," and male and female students could freely mix and sit together during worship services. Young adults were also allowed to take up roles as Sunday school teachers, cell leaders, and service coordinators. There were also vibrant Bible studies that allowed members to freely voice their opinions about church teachings. While speaking in tongues remained key in the CoP, PENSA did not necessarily enforce it during their meetings. Above all, church services were conducted in English.[29]

In my interview with Apostle Professor Opoku Onyinah in January 2019, his view was that the CoP would be stunted in its growth if it failed to engage "modernity" in Ghanaian culture as a whole. He said that the CoP must protect the sanctity of Christian doctrines but must also, at the same time, seek to shun any attempt to render itself a church averse to modernization.[30] Onyinah's theology is grounded on the view that "doing theology is a difficult task that needs the leading of the Spirit to speak to the times and also the willingness of the individual to yield to the Spirit."[31] Thus the church must often review its practices and see whether they are addressing contemporary issues. Above all, Onyinah maintains, the church should not be static and resistant to change.[32]

It was, therefore, during Onyinah's tenure as the International Missions Director (1991–1996) that he established the Pentecostal International Worship Centers (PIWCs), which provided well-organized, cross-cultural communities for people of non-Ghanaian cultural backgrounds, as well as educated Ghanaians who preferred churches of excellence conducted through the medium of the English language. Accordingly, under Onyinah's apostolic leadership, the entire CoP would proactively respond to the rapidly changing socio-economic and political landscape to retain its members.

Apostle Ntumy (1998–2008)

From 1998–2008, the CoP was led by Apostle Dr. Michael Ntumy, who was at that point the youngest chairman the CoP had ever appointed and did not have any personal connection to McKeown. Ntumy built on the foundation laid by his predecessor, Prophet Yeboah, in terms of retaining key cultural values of the CoP, like the wearing of headscarves by women and gender segregation in church seating arrangements. However, since his regime coincided with the liberalization of politics and media in Ghana, following the country's re-democratization in 1992, he encouraged the use of media—in particular, radio and television—to make the church more visible on a national stage. Ntumy also encouraged the use of English, as he broadcasted most of his sermons on national television in English, as well as concurrently translated into Twi (Akan). In his ten-year leadership of the church, the total membership of the CoP globally increased from 869,889 to 1,788,114. The number of nations in which the CoP operated also rose from 38 to 70.[33]

Apostle Professor Onyinah (2008–2018)

However, it was during the chairmanship of Apostle Professor Opoku Onyinah that the church experienced its most transformative reforms, made more estimable because they followed the dramatic social and political shifts of the 1990s. Onyinah was one of the church leaders who had worked with McKeown, having been called into pastoral ministry in 1976. His formal theological education began in 1986, when he enrolled at Elim Pentecostal Church in London, and Elim Bible College in Capel, Surrey.[34] He also held various leadership positions within the CoP before becoming chairman. Besides serving as International Missions Director from 1991–1996, he was a member of the Executive Council, the highest body that runs the daily activities of the church.

In 1996, Onyinah enrolled at Regents Theological College in England to pursue a master's degree in applied theology, validated by the University of Manchester. The CoP sponsored Onyinah to study in the U.K. because Regents College, which is the training center of the Elim Pentecostal Church, shared the same theological teachings with the CoP. The Elim Pentecostal Church was also the affiliated church of the CoP in the U.K. After completing his program at Regents College, Onyinah enrolled at the

University of Birmingham for his doctoral research in Pentecostal studies and missions, which he completed in 2002 under the supervision of Allan Anderson.[35] His research explored innovative approaches to witchcraft and exorcism within the CoP. He thus became the first pastor of the CoP to earn a Ph.D. in theology.

Kwabena J. Asamoah-Gyadu explains how the need to establish branches of the CoP that resonated with the diverse cultural needs of both Ghanaians and new immigrants became a priority for Onyinah. He had already begun this path when he pioneered the PIWCs, which appealed to youth and newcomers. The PIWCs ran as parallel "parishes" of the CoP and were officially under the same theological umbrella as other branches of the CoP. However, in addition to relaxed holiness rules and services in English, there were other important ways in which the PIWCs differed from the local-language churches of the CoP. For example, at the PIWCs, songs were (and still are) English-language translations of CoP songs, but many extensively draw upon a type of American music popular in many Charismatic churches. The other major difference between the PIWCs and non-English speaking branches of the church (known within the church as "local churches") was that, unlike the pro-English churches, the local churches retained most of the traditional practices such as headscarves and gender-segregated seating. Furthermore, the pro-English PIWC churches were mostly located in multilingual urban areas of Ghana whereas the local churches continue to be located in rural or peri-urban areas that have some degree of monolingualism. The PIWC model has become the CoP's main strategy for retaining the upwardly mobile, highly educated, and younger generation in the church—the demographic who are most attracted to the newer Charismatic churches.[36]

Additionally, as part of the reforms in 2014, the CoP through its novel organization of the Royal Conference—held at its Pentecost Convention Centre, Gomoa-Feteh, Central Region of Ghana, from June 10–13, 2014—formally incorporated chiefs into its practices. This implied that, until 2014, the various leaders of the CoP in different parts of Ghana were to decide, based on their own understanding of chieftaincy in their respective areas of administration, whether a member of the church could take up a chieftaincy office.

Another way Onyinah revitalized the CoP was his creative incorporation of the young generations into church ministry. Apostle Ntumy's campus visitation was a watershed in later youth involvement in pastoral ministry. However, CoP leadership was essentially gerontocratic—against young people's passion to change the world for good. Historically, complex and traditional forms of gerontocracy invested power and resources in the hands of the older generation which created a wedge, usually conflictual, between the younger generations and the older group. This nationwide-shared gerontocratic culture had been complicated by Ghana's economic turn since the 1990s because, as young men and women increasingly received education and became economically empowered, gerontocratic threats of losing power polarized the two generations. The tendency has been for the older generation to blame young people for being lazy, intemperate, and responsible for radical economic and social change. Admittedly, while young people have sometimes been quite revolutionary in their demands, the exaggeration of their zeal has often resulted in multidimensional social exclusion from the older generation. Meanwhile, social media at the turn of the millennium marked a major shift in young people's role in change.

Against the backdrop of these actions, Onyinah involved young people in leadership positions. He mentored them and engaged with them on social media, allowing them to ask questions at church services and meetings. He also officially recognized those who excelled in examinations or other life-affirming endeavors during church general council meetings and actively encouraged pastors and church leaders not to discourage young people from pursuing education.[37] It is no surprise that he is the founding rector of Pentecost University. Additionally, Onyinah increased church finances and building projects, emphasizing the importance of physical discipline.[38] These changes reinvigorated the active participation of young people in church activities.

Yet the most controversial of Onyinah's reforms—which threatened internal schism—was his decision to relax rules regarding headscarves for women, granting permission for women to wear pants, and allowing men with dreadlocks to worship with the church freely. On the whole, Onyinah's regime signaled a decisive shift of the CoP on the issue of modernization and reform. Concomitantly, his regime has been described by Ntumy and others as "the Opoku Onyinah era."[39]

Concluding Thoughts on CoP's Rejuvenation

Many CoP leaders have hailed the Onyinah reforms as key to the continued success of the church within modern Ghanaian society. Onyinah's general secretary and right-hand person during his first term as the chairman was Apostle Alfred Koduah, whom Onyinah credits as one of the key persons behind his success. In a personal interview with Koduah, he indicated that the reforms have contributed to the church retaining its youthful constituency and attracting new ones from the Ghanaian populace. He supported his claim with the assertion that the youthful constituency of the church in 2020 stood at 73 percent.[40]

CoP leaders, including Koduah, subsequently attribute much of the demographic growth of the church to the reforms. For example, the church's population in Ghana in 2010 (when the reforms were introduced) was 1,703,585. By June 2018, the number had boomed to 2,660,012.[41] Additionally, in 2014, the youthful population of the CoP was 624,647, while the general church population was 2,407,545. However, by 2018, youth had increased to 1,046,114, while the general population of the church stood at 3,147,939.[42] Koduah also believes that publicity about the reforms in the media helped the church grow as a whole and increase its youthful constituency.[43]

Nevertheless, Koduah's positive evaluation of the 2010 reforms has not been shared by many members of the CoP. For example, in 2010 when the CoP relaxed its dress code—and while I was pursuing my postgraduate studies at the Institute of African Studies, University Ghana—on my way to campus, I met a female member of the CoP at the 37 (a suburb of Accra). Seeing she was clad in the uniformed cloth of the Women's Movement of the CoP, I greeted her with the usual greetings of the Movement. "Holiness unto God," she replied. She followed up with a question, "Gentleman, are you with the church?" Responding in the affirmative, she replied, "You, the young educated ones, are those destroying the church. What we inherited from the founders, the covenant (*apam*), you with your education are messing up the legacies of our founders." She added with an imprecation, "God will punish anyone who seeks to destroy the covenant the Lord has with the church." After she said this, I was speechless and only managed to assure her that, "God is in control of his church," and left.[44] This woman's anger is shared by many church members. As I have mentioned above, the leadership of the Executive Council and General Council have been cursed, insulted, and prayed against.

The CoP rejuvenation, however, should be carefully considered because the church needs to retain its covenant, but the discursive social condition of the covenant implies the need for reinterpretation. This is because while the words of the covenant remain canonized, the world of the covenant changes. On this, I find Onyinah's wisdom for religious rejuvenation for mission insightful: "An understanding of postmodern tendencies and the continuous development, adaptation, and deployment of relevant evangelistic strategies in fulfilling and obeying the Great Commission is extremely crucial."[45] This conclusion is very apt because McKeown did not found the CoP or write theological theses to build a static personality cult around himself. Nor has Onyinah led under this intention. In all this, Onyinah has succeeded because, as David Osei Nimoh rightly assessed, "Onyinah is a Spirit-empowered leader who, with extraordinary dexterity in merging effective mentorship and charismata, significantly impacted modern-day Pentecostalism."[46]

I conclude with Onyinah's own evaluation of his religious rejuvenation, which he shared on Facebook after the CoP's Royal Conference in Ghana, June 1–3, 2022. He said:

> As I sat down in worship, enjoying the Closing Service, my mind was taken back to reflect on some of the issues the Lord has used me to initiate or contribute to in the Church. I realized that most of the things have been controversial issues that people did not easily understand. To God's glory, the issues have now settled with many praising God for their timeliness. These include understanding of ancestral curses, the establishment of Pentecost International Worship Centers, Christians' involvement in Chieftaincy, Christians' understanding of witchcraft, and the release of a communique dealing with various issues including head covering, sitting arrangement in church, and dressing. I do not do these things out of my own volition, but somehow the Lord does impress them on my heart or gets me involved through His sovereignty. As a retiree of the full-time ministry of The Church of Pentecost, one of the controversial issues I am now fully involved in is the putting up of a National Cathedral with a Bible Museum and Biblical Gardens. Today, Apostle Ekow Badu Wood preached at the funeral service of Apostle Blessed Bonney and stressed, "Execute the purpose for which the Lord has raised you up." Then, out of the blue, the family head of Apostle Bonney commented on the Cathedral and assured us of the Lord's leading. What words of encouragement from these people for such a time as this. May the will of God for each one of us be accomplished.[47]

Notes

1. For acquaintance with Prophet Yeboah's mention of the CoP's divine covenant, see Martinson Kwadwo Yeboah, "God's Covenant with The Church of Pentecost," YouTube, April 24, 2021, https://www.youtube.com/watch?v=VUUug6b-v-0/, accessed July 5, 2022.
2. Opoku Onyinah, ed., *James McKeown Memorial Lectures: 50 Years of the Church of Pentecost* (Accra: Church of Pentecost, 2004).
3. See Onyinah, *James McKeown Memorial Lectures*.
4. Yaw Bredwa-Mensah, "The Church of Pentecost in Retrospect, 1937–1960," *James McKeown Memorial Lectures: 50 Years of the Church of Pentecost*, ed. Opoku Onyinah (Accra: Church of Pentecost, 2004), 1–27.
5. This theme is conveyed in National Literature Committee, *Tell the Next Generation: Lecture Notes on the Annual Themes of the Church of Pentecost* 1 (Accra: The Church of Pentecost, 2007).
6. National Literature Committee, *Tell the Next Generation*, 20.
7. Brigid, M. Sackey, "*Apuskeleke*: Youth Fashion Craze, Immorality or Female Harassment?" *Etnofoor* 16:2 (2003), 57–69.
8. National Literature Committee, *Tell the Next Generation*, 21.
9. Brian Stanley, *The Bible and the Flag: Protestant Missions and British Imperialism in the Nineteenth and Twentieth Centuries* (Leicester: Apollos, 1990), 135.
10. For more, see Bengt Sundkler and Christopher Steed, *A History of the Church in Africa* (Cambridge: Cambridge University Press, 2000).
11. David Kimble, *A Political History of Ghana: The Rise of Gold Coast Nationalism*, 1850–1928 (Oxford: Clarendon Press, 1963).
12. Christine Leonard, *A Giant in Ghana* (Chichester, U.K.: New Wine Press, 1989), 69.
13. Charles Prempeh, "Religious Reforms and Notions of Gender in Pentecostal Christianity: A Case of the Church of Pentecost," in Nimi Wariboko and Adeshina Afolayan, eds., *African Pentecostalism and World Christianity: Essays in Honour of J. Kwabena Asamoah-Gyadu* (Eugene: Pickwick Publications, 2020), 75–87.
14. See Prempeh, "Religious Reforms"; also Mary Douglas, *Purity and Danger: An Analysis of Concept of Pollution and Taboo* (London: Routledge, 1966).
15. Emmanuel Akyeampong, "Sexuality and Prostitution among the Akan of the Gold Coast c. 1650–1950," *Past & Present* 156 (1997), 144–173.

16 Elder Godfried Asante (of the Birmingham CoP, England), in a personal interview with author at Birmingham Christian College, February 2, 2022.

17 Rev. and Mrs. Oppong Asare-Duah, *The Gallant Soldiers of the Church of Pentecost: History of the Fathers of Old Whose Relentless Efforts Gave Birth to the Church*, vol. 1, 2nd ed. (Accra: Wise Image, 2014).

18 Opoku Onyinah, "African Christianity in the Twenty-first Century," *Word & World* 27:3 (2007), 305–314.

19 Opoku Onyinah, "Catholic Charismatic Renewal and Pentecostalism," *PECANEP* 1:3 (2020), 60–66.

20 George M. Bob-Milliar, "Chieftaincy, Diaspora and Development: The Institution of *Nkosuohene* in Ghana," *African Affairs* 108:433 (2009), 541–588.

21 See De-Valera N. Y. M. Botchway and Mustapha Abdul-Hamid, "'Was It a Nine-Day Wonder?' A Note on the Proselytisation of Efforts of the Nation of Islam in Ghana, c. 1980s–2010," in *New Perspectives on the Nation of Islam*, eds. D. Gibson and H. Berg (London: Routledge, 2017), 95–117.

22 See Opoku Onyinah, "New Ways of Doing Evangelism," World Council of Churches, *International Review of Mission* 103:1 (2014), 121–128.

23 The use and definition of this term by Ntumy can be found in Gibson Annor-Antwi, *Myth or Mystery: The 'Bio-autobiography' of Apostle Professor Opoku Onyinah* (U.K.: Inved, 2016), 353.

24 Matthew L. Wettey, *The Legacy of Pastor James McKeown* (Tema: Faustag Ventures, 2017), 27.

25 Earlier in the late 1970s, Brother J. S. Gyimah, Elder Joshuah Adjabeng, Elder Ntre, Apostle Abraham T. Nartey, Brother Joseph Kwamina Paintsil, Elder Badu Wood, Brother Peter Ohene Kyei, and Elder Lawyer J. A. Larkai introduced Pentecost Students and Associates (PENSA) into the church. This was the students' wing of the church that ministered to students in tertiary education. English was the medium of expression.

26 A prophetic message which gives directives to the leaders or the congregation.

27 Keith Warrington, *Pentecostal Theology: A Theology of Encounter* (New York: T & T Clark, 2008), 82.

28 The Church of Pentecost, Facebook official page, https://www.facebook.com/thecophq/videos/660764648094098/?mibextid=rS40aB7S9Ucbxw6v/, accessed June 1, 2024.

29 Steve Nyarkotey Quao, personal interview with author, August 2, 2019.

30 Opoku Onyinah, personal interview with author, January 2, 2019.

31 Opoku Onyinah, "African Christianity in the Twenty-first Century," *Word & World* 27:3 (2007), 205.

32 This theme is evident in Onyinah, "New Ways of Doing Evangelism."

33 Annual Statistics Report, 2018, Statistics Office, Church of Pentecost Headquarters.

34 L. Elorm-Donkor and Clifton R. Clarke, eds., *African Pentecostal Missions Maturing: Essays in Honor of Apostle Opoku Onyinah* (La Vergne: Wipf & Stock, 2018), 1.

35 Elorm-Donkor and Clarke, *African Pentecostal Missions Maturing*, 2.

36 Kwabena J. Asamoah-Gyadu, "Rooted in the Spirit," in *African Pentecostal Missions Maturing: Essays in Honor of Apostle Opoku Onyinah* Donkor, eds. E. Lord and Clifton R. Clarke (La Vergne: Wipf & Stock, 2018), 196.

37 Opoku Onyinah, "Raising Vibrant Youth for Ministry: The Example of the Church of Pentecost, Ghana," paper presented at the Global Pastors Congress on the Next Generation in Manila, Philippines (August 8, 2019), 1–21.

38 Onyinah, "Raising Vibrant Youth for Ministry."

39 Michael Ntumy, "Forward," in *African Pentecostal Missions Maturing: Essays in Honor of Apostle Opoku Onyinah,* African Christian Studies Series 14, eds. Donkor, Lord Elorm, and Clifton R Clarke (Eugene: Pickwick Publications, 2018), xiv.

40 Alfred Koduah, personal interview with author, June 8, 2020.

41 Annual Statistics Report, 2018, Statistics Office, Church of Pentecost Headquarters.

42 Annual Statistics Report, 2018, Statistics Office, Church of Pentecost Headquarters.

43 Alfred Koduah, personal interview with author, on June 8, 2020.

44 Anonymous, informal communication between the author and a female member of the CoP, July 15, 2010.

45 Onyinah, "New Ways of Doing Evangelism," 128.

46 David Osei Nimoh, "Profile of a Spirit-Empowered Leader: Opoku Onyinah, the 'African Paul'," *Spiritus* 7:2 (2022), 199–210.

47 Opoku Onyinah, Facebook, June 4, 2022, https://www.facebook.com/Aps.opokuonyinah/, accessed June 6, 2022.

13 *Hikikomori* Ministry: The Possibilities of Empowering Japanese Young Adults

Chaa Chaa Ogino and Michio Ogino

Abstract

The present chapter analyzes case studies of *hikikomori* (those suffering from acute social withdrawal) at a local Pentecostal church in Japan.[1] We set the scene of our case studies by briefly describing ourselves and the context of Japanese Christianity in Galilee Maruko Christ Church. After that, we define *hikikomori* and describe their phenomena. We introduce existing *hikikomori* supports and their problems. We state our strategy that is based on 1 Cor. 9:19–23, both in theory and in practice. Then, we anonymously introduce three *hikikomori* and why they are noteworthy to be studied. We explain: 1) the struggles of each; 2) what kind of ministry has changed their lives, and in what way; and 3) further issues that need to be dealt with.

Introduction

The Jesuit missionary Francisco Xavier introduced Christianity to Japan for the first time in 1549. Since then, the population of Christians in Japan has held steady for nearly five centuries at about 1 percent of Japan's population. This chapter introduces the possibility that *hikikomori* ministry may play a part in reviving Japan since this ministry follows closely Jesus' model of ministry to social minorities in Galilee.

After the previous Japan Assemblies of God pastors decided to retire, we, Rev. Chaa Chaa and Rev. Michio Ogino, were assigned to pastor Galilee Maruko Christ Church (GMCC) in 2013. We have been pastoring this church for over eight years. The wife of the church founder, Pastor Rieko Matsuyoshi, told us that it is difficult to pastor a church in a rural district. GMCC is located in Ueda city in the Nagano prefecture where the 1988 Winter Olympics were held. Nagano is rural countryside surrounded by mountains. As mentioned, for centuries, the Japanese have resisted the gospel, but this is especially true among a rural population who are almost completely unwilling to accept this foreign religion.

According to GMCC's official records, before we came to this church, the average service attendance between 2008 and 2012 was a little less than 20 people. In 2021, the average attendance at GMCC was 35 people. Statistically, during our tenure, the congregation has grown twofold. Taking the COVID-19 pandemic since 2020 into consideration, our ministry, by the grace of God, has been successful so far. Notably, four or five ex-*hikikomori* attend our weekly service. These ex-*hikikomori* started attending in 2016 after Chaa Chaa became bi-vocational and started working for Samurai Gakuen as a regular employee. Samurai Gakuen is an institution that helps *hikikomori* re-establish relationships with people and society. It should be noted, however, that Samurai Gakuen itself is not officially affiliated with Christianity.

Hikikomori and the Problems in Existing *Hikikomori* Supports

What exactly is *hikikomori*? According to Tamaki Saitō, who created the term, *hikikomori* is defined as: "A state that has become a problem by the late twenties, that involves cooping oneself up in one's own home and not participating in society for six months or longer, but that does not seem to have another psychological problem as its principal source."[2] This phenomenon may continue into middle adulthood (thirties, forties). Minami Misono reports that the latest research reveals that in Japan, 1 out of 24 households have [*hikikomori*].[3] Although the term *hikikomori* was coined in Japan and was considered a Japanese culture-bound syndrome, there are reports of cases in Spain, Ukraine, Hong Kong, Oman, France, Italy, the U.S., Australia, Bangladesh, Iran, India, South Korea, Taiwan, Thailand, and China.[4] Nonetheless, Japan's *hikikomori* is unique in the long persistence of the condition among them, with many of them aging through their lifecycles as *hikikomori*.

In "Re-examination of Discussion about 'Hikikomori' Support: The New Aspect for Support," Takashi Matsumoto categorizes existing supports into six types and concludes that the problems with existing supports lie in all of them maintaining a supporter-centered orientation.[5] In other words, existing supports have been implemented without carefully listening to the voices of *hikikomori* themselves. As a result, the supporter's theory or hypothesis determines the type of help offered, and a "solution" that does not include the voices of *hikikomori* becomes arbitrary and problematic.

The Strategy of Our *Hikikomori* Ministry
Theory

Matsumoto's article exhorts us on the pivotal issue of listening to the voices of *hikikomori*, but he admits that practical methods for helping the *hikikomori* lie beyond the scope of his article.[6] Our theory and practice build on Matsumoto's foundational insight, but are viewed through the lens of scripture.

Biblically speaking, we adopt the methods of the Apostle Paul described in 1 Corinthians 9:19–23.[7] Because Jesus, the Son of God, became flesh, he can listen to us, understand us, and empathize with us perfectly. Although no human humility compares with Jesus' infinite humility, the humility of his incarnation provides a model for us to imitate. Indeed, David E. Garland claims that Paul "imitated Christ's self-emptying humiliation and suffering for others."[8] Therefore, both Paul and Jesus give us models that urge us to make ourselves slaves to the *hikikomori* and his/her family so that we might win more of them.

Importantly, Paul uses the word "as" when he speaks of becoming like a Jew and like one under the law (vv. 20–21). However, "as" does not appear when the apostle speaks of becoming weak. Apparently, Paul did not completely equate himself to the Jews when he became "as" one under the law. In other words, he would not cross the line separating justifiable flexibility in mission strategy from infidelity to Christian doctrine. In Galatians chapter 2, Paul scolds Peter for returning to Jewish dining customs and separating himself from gentile table fellowship. At that time, Peter crossed a doctrinal red line by becoming a Jew. Peter unwittingly violated soteriology by acting as if circumcision were needed for complete salvation or sanctification. Wisely enough, by inserting "as" when he talks about winning a Jew, and one under/outside the law, Paul limits himself and the Corinthians to stay within the sphere of missional strategy rather than the sphere of doctrine.

Second, Paul's use of "as" supports the objective stance of a pastor or counselor who offers help with empathy by entering the perspective of his or her parishioner/counselee. Carl Rogers (1902–1987) describes the art of listening and understanding as follows: "Real communication occurs . . . when we listen with understanding . . . [U]nderstanding *with* a person, not *about* him—is such an effective approach that it can bring about major changes in personality."[9] He adds that the counselor aims to "sense the client's private world as if it were your own, but without ever losing the 'as if' quality."[10] It is therefore important to listen to *hikikomori* and his/her family members emphatically. However, objective detachment also remains necessary. Although we intend to listen to and understand *hikikomori*, if we are emotionally involved too much, or depressed with him/her, we cannot help.

On the other hand, why does Paul omit "as" when he says, "To the weak I became weak" (v. 22)? First, to become weak does not conflict with Christian doctrine. Unlike becoming a Jew or one under the law, becoming weak does not cause doctrinal problems. In all his expressions, the incarnated Jesus took on all fleshly weaknesses but never committed sin. Paul followed Jesus' example, and his humble self-recognition made him able to equate himself with being weak (e.g., 1 Cor 2:3, 11:29, 12:9–10).

In summary, our actions should not violate Christian doctrine, and we should always have an "'as if' quality" in order to support *hikikomori*. As long as it does not conflict with Christian doctrine, we can identify ourselves with the *hikikomori* in order to win them over to Christ.

Practice

In this section, we will detail our concrete strategy to follow 1 Corinthians 9:19–23 in our efforts to evangelize the *hikikomori*. In certain ways, we apply a missional strategy that does not conflict with doctrine to win some. Personally, Michio does not want his wife to talk on the phone after 10:00 p.m. because it interferes with family life. But *hikikomori* are more or less night owls, and they often make bad decisions in the middle of the night. If one should become as a *hikikomori* (as Paul became as a Jew, or as one under the law), he/she needs to be ready to help at night time. With the consent and understanding of her husband to talk on the phone or go out in the middle of the night, Chaa Chaa is ready to help the *hikikomori* twenty-four hours a day.

For example, if a *hikikomori* was missing at midnight and his mother called Chaa Chaa, she would go out and look for him. Quite often *hikikomori* has contacted her instead of his/her own family members. On such occasions, she has persuaded him to go home or back to the Samurai Gakuen dormitory. One mother felt embarrassed and sorry because many people had looked for her son in the wee hours of the morning. Chaa Chaa advised her not to be embarrassed and not to be sorry but just say, "Welcome home," to her son. According to Chaa Chaa, the mother's embarrassment and anxiety caused her son to feel depressed. In the end, his mother cried, agreed with Chaa Chaa, and did what she was advised. In this way, Chaa Chaa, with the help of the Holy Spirit, learned to become "as a *hikikomori*" in attempting to win some of them over to Christ.

Some of the *hikikomori* are schizophrenic and suffer auditory hallucinations. For example, one man believed the Japanese government was eavesdropping on him and radio broadcasting his secrets. His mother was so discouraged and kept telling her son that it was a hallucination. Out of love and worry, his family members kept telling him that his "experiences" were not true. However, the more his family tried to persuade him, the more stubborn he became. On one occasion, one of the *hikikomori* told Chaa Chaa that he was being chased by an unidentified car. She did not tell him that it was a hallucination. She simply said, "Next time when that car chases you, please write down the car registration number and call me. I will come and help you." Chaa Chaa's strategy is to accept the *hikikomori*'s experience as true. In this sense, it does not matter whether what a *hikikomori* has experienced qualifies as an objective fact or delusion. For one truth is certain within it all: this man felt lonely and believed that no one understood him. By becoming as a *hikikomori*, Chaa Chaa had success in stabilizing them. On some occasions, after Chaa Chaa took a *hikikomori*'s experiences seriously, interestingly the *hikikomori* himself admitted that his experience had been a hallucination.

Having discussed our general approach and strategy, we now turn to three case studies through which we wish to evaluate the effectiveness of our methods.[11] We chose the following three cases because these cases are (to some extent) successful, and because each case is quite different. One is a man in his thirties who is a highly educated individual but so far struggles to cope with inward suffering. Another is a man in his twenties who is a junior high school graduate and is now gradually learning to put emotions and thoughts into his own words. The other is a man in his twenties who has been diagnosed with ADHD but is slowly learning to overcome what he had been previously unable to cope with. We also chose these particular three cases because we believe that without the Holy Spirit's help on behalf of both the *hikikomori* and the ministers, these three cases would never have been successful. In terms of outcomes, two of them profess belief in Jesus Christ, and one of them is not yet a Christian. None of them have been baptized by the Holy Spirit in the sense of classical Pentecostalism (Acts 1:8). Nonetheless, the Holy Spirit's role has been crucial in coming this far, and his work will be indispensable for them and for us as we move on from here.

Case Study 1: Thirty-One Year Old, Male

When he is doing well, this man appears to be a gentleman without any obvious problems. He attended one of Japan's top universities, and his future looked promising. He was working at a barbeque restaurant as a part-time worker. However, he was diagnosed with depression which persisted for two years and caused him to be hospitalized twice. Eventually, his depression made it impossible for him to study or work. He enjoys listening to music, reading, and writing novels. According to him, he is not good at getting along with people. He becomes nervous, oversolicitous, and shy when he meets people. He is afraid to go outside because he sometimes has heart palpitations. When he feels too stressed, he confines himself to his bed. He worries about his future, is unmotivated, tends to be pessimistic, and is sometimes suicidal. He would like to learn how to relax and get used to working every day. He would like to pursue a job that helps people, such as counseling.

He successfully graduated from Samurai Gakuen in 2018. The period of his attendance at Samurai Gakuen was three years.[12] Those who heard his speech at the graduation were so touched. He went back to his hometown and worked at city hall, but could no longer continue after three months because of a heart condition. We were praying for him. Chaa Chaa suggested to him and his parents that he should come back to Ueda City where we live. Chaa Chaa promised him and his parents that she would take care of him his whole life. His parents told Michio that meeting Chaa Chaa has been their son's deliverance.

So, he came back to Ueda City. He lived in an apartment, and Chaa Chaa had him teach kids and work as a counselor. When he was in good condition, he enjoyed doing this work. However, sometimes he could not continue due to his mental condition or heart palpitations. Chaa Chaa encouraged him to take 英検 (Eiken's Test in Practical English Proficiency), Grade Pre-1 (intermediate college level) and Grade 1 (advanced college level). He successfully passed both tests. Although he is not a Christian yet, he sometimes did consecutive interpretations of Chaa Chaa's sermon at church when Michio went to the U.K. for several weeks to write his dissertation. So, this gentleman is good at studying and is a hard worker, even though his mental condition does not allow him to have a stable life or hold down a job.

On one occasion, when he had lost the will to live, Michio referred him to Matthew 6:25–34. Michio expected these verses to encourage him to live at least today (day by day). He seemed to be encouraged. Later on, when he gave a speech at Samurai Gakuen, he shared Matthew 6:25–34 and my annotation. To prevent him from being alone when he was depressed and sometimes suicidal, we let him stay at our house (at church) for a few months. However, as an independent personality, he also needed space to be alone. So, he basically stays in an apartment. Chaa Chaa asked him not to decide to kill himself on his own but to inform her before taking his own life. He has kept this promise so far. When he is tempted to commit suicide or has heart palpitations at midnight, Michio's parents watch our son while we go to the gentleman's place and stay with him until he regains equilibrium.

To assign a job to him and other *hikikomori*, Chaa Chaa, this gentleman and one of the board of directors of Samurai Gakuen, started a company called Quietude. Quietude provides "translation, proofreading, and interpretation services available for English and Japanese," "a variety of design services," "individual teaching," "counseling," and "luxury goods."[13] The parents of Chaa Chaa's counselee voluntarily invested and provided the land and building for Quietude. A quiet old house was remodeled and became the Quietude office. It was opened on March 25, 2022. Chaa Chaa then had the gentleman move from his apartment to one of the rooms at the Quietude office. He can now work at Quietude whenever he feels able to work. Since this is their company, he is not required to work eight hours a day, five days a week. Of course, if he can, he should do so, and all of us would be happy for him. He still has problems with his mental condition and his heart, but gradually he is learning how to cope with his conditions.

Further issues that need to be dealt with are that although he has attended services at our church from time to time, he is not a Christian yet. He still has mental issues and is sometimes suicidal. He needs Jesus. We believe that Jesus alone can completely heal him and set him free.

Case Study 2: Twenty-Five Year Old, Male

This young man graduated junior high school but did not enter high school. His father has a gambling addiction, causing his parents to divorce. According to the young man, his aunt continually tells him that his father is a gambler and so he will become the same. He was arrested twice because of stealing and holding up a store. He was sent to a youth detention center. He worked for a few years but quit his job because of financial troubles and interpersonal difficulties.

Once he quit his job, he became unable to go out of his house for a year. He lived the life of a vampire, waking up at 6:00 p.m. and going to sleep at 8:00 a.m. He likes to watch television dramas and anime. He is unbothered by meeting people. On the other hand, there is nothing he wants to do. He was worried about his life because he had an unplanned life. He felt he needed to work a plan intentionally for his future. He also felt it necessary to talk with his family members since he had lost communication with them except for his twin brother.

He came to Samurai Gakuen with the hope that he could talk to various people and learn how to relate to people and how to control his mind. He hoped that he could continue his job for a long time after graduating from Samurai Gakuen. He is physically healthy and not suicidal, but felt a kind of brain fog and had no purpose in his life when he came to us.

Chaa Chaa had him read novels. She hoped that reading would teach him more words to express his inner thoughts and emotions. Chaa Chaa also taught him how to play the bass guitar. She hoped that he could expand his hobbies and interests by playing music. He now regularly plays the bass at Sunday service. Since our son Kibō likes him, she has him stay with Kibō. They talk about iPhone games and TV games. He says that Chaa Chaa, Michio, and Kibō are his family. So, it was natural for him to come to church and learn about the Christian faith. He continues to attend church regularly even now. He studied catechism with Michio for several months. We waited until he himself wished to be baptized. Since he expressed his will to be baptized, we baptized him on Christmas in 2021.

He looked stable. People trusted him at Samurai Gakuen and at his workplace (a part-time job in Ueda City). Therefore, he graduated from Samurai Gakuen in one year. Previously, he thought he would go back to his hometown and asked Michio for help finding a church there. However, returning home was a concern. Whenever he would go home for a few days, he looked different and became stubborn. On one occasion, when he was asked to come home to talk about his debts to his mother and aunt, he looked extremely nervous. Therefore, although it involved a 13-hour car drive, Chaa Chaa and Kibō went together to his hometown with him. Chaa Chaa and Kibō stayed at a hotel while the young man met with his family and relatives. The fact that Chaa Chaa and Kibō were near him made him relax. Knowing that he could see them if he felt panicked made a huge difference.

The young man decided to keep living in Ueda City where we live. He needs family, and therefore we have become his family. He lives in an apartment, but our family frequently meets him, and we see him every Sunday in our time of Christian fellowship. Chaa Chaa calls him every morning because he has an issue with oversleeping. By the grace of God, though oversleeping was a long-standing issue that was hard for him to overcome, he is recently becoming much better than before. Chaa Chaa also reads the Bible and prays together with him every night on the phone. According to her, he does not have a good vocabulary, but he is transformed when he prays—becoming able to speak well (Rom 8:26). Chaa Chaa teaches him, and she also arranges for others to teach him high school subjects. She has been helping him prepare to take the Certificate for Students Achieving the Proficiency Level of Upper Secondary School Graduates. If he passes this test, he will be officially recognized to have the ability of a high school graduate. In order to pass, a test-taker needs to pass seven subjects. He took this test and passed five subjects in 2021. So, he has two more subjects to go. Chaa Chaa lets him teach English classes at a beginning level. This way, he studies English and learns to get along with people. By so doing, Chaa Chaa expects him to gain confidence. We allow Kibō to stay over at his apartment every weekend. We hope that he will experience having a family.

The young man sometimes regresses to his previous state after talking with his family or facing financial issues. In the worst cases, he disappears and never picks up the phone. We visit his apartment, but he is not there. When we cannot catch him, he sometimes plays *pachinko* (Japanese slots) and uses all his money and savings. We thank God that he has not committed suicide during these times. Usually, we can finally get in touch with him a few days later. He repents and starts a new life with Jesus. He might feel discouraged to have fallen back into old habits like oversleeping or squandering all his savings with *pachinko*. However, we have stayed with him, encouraged, scolded, and helped him.

He needs to open his heart more to us. It is understandable that he could not share his emotions with us because he did not know how. It takes time for people to become family, but we hope that he can become sensitive to his emotions and learn how to express his feelings and thoughts in his own words instead of running away. Jesus will help him, especially if he chooses to be intentionally empowered by his Spirit.

Case Study 3: Twenty-Four Year Old, Male

Although this young man graduated from junior high and high school, during his elementary years, he was diagnosed with pervasive developmental disorder and hospitalized periodically in relation to this disorder. When he was in fourth grade, he finally met a family doctor who prescribed prescription drugs to treat his condition. He held a mental disorder certificate grade 2, which means "Mental disabilities that severely limit (or force a person to severely limit) their daily activities."[14]

This young man likes taking photos and taking care of kids. He abhors hearing violent words. He would be confused if he heard ambiguous or just verbal work instructions. He has great difficulty meeting new people. When he meets someone for the first time, his hands and feet shake. It is difficult for him to work when he cannot properly catch the information. If he feels the provided information is vague and not concrete, he does not have the confidence to work. He would like to do a job related to computers, cameras, people, and kids. Even if the salary is not that high, he is grateful if he is not forced to hurry. He feels like he can work if he develops his physical strength, acquires professional skills, communicates well with people, is mentally healed, and is helped by co-workers who understand his condition.

He struggles with communication; he misunderstands or cannot understand what people say. To let others know about him, he thinks he needs to know himself and speak out about the fact that he is worried about communication. He does not complain about his life, family, or past. But he is not well physically and mentally: he does not have an appetite, he has headaches, he wants to die, and does not feel happy with anything.

He graduated from Samurai Gakuen in two and a half years. Along with going to Samurai Gakuen, he was coming to our church in 2018. It is well known to people who know him that by going to church, he became stable and could work in society. Wherever he goes in Samurai Gakuen, he carries a small Bible and reads it. He had difficulty regarding his relationship with his father but gradually became able to get along with him. His father thought that church had something to do with his son's good change, so his father attended church services twice. He thanked us and entrusted his son to us. His mother also thought that her son became non-violent after beginning church. The young man studied catechism with Michio and was baptized at Christmas in 2020.

Before graduating from Samurai Gakuen, he was working a part-time job where one person harshly attacked him. He might not have been able to continue his job if he were in his previous condition. But he read the Bible saying, "Love your enemies and pray for those who persecute you" (Matt 5:44). Therefore, he prayed for his mean co-worker. According to him, his mean co-worker's attitude toward him obviously changed after his prayer. He was surprised that prayer could actually change a co-worker. He was further surprised as Michio preached on the same subject the next Sunday. In this way, his reading of the Bible was not just reading. Reading the Bible helped him to overcome his weakness and changed his circumstances and life.

Since he believes he can work if he has skills, he now intensively pursues obtaining various licenses. Chaa Chaa does not stop him and allows him to pursue any license he wants. Though he had various licenses already, he desired to obtain a driver's license for large-size vehicles. He made a prayer request in the church and took an exam. He successfully obtained the license. He testified at our church that God heard his prayer request and thanked the congregation for their prayers. The new license makes him more useful at his workplace. He is also now trusted there, and some operations cannot be done without him. He and both of us believe that reading the Bible has made him smarter (Ps 119:130).

Further issues that need to be dealt with are the fact that he was diagnosed with ADHD. ADHD is a part of his personality and may not be curable. However, he overcame some areas that he previously could not cope with, so we believe that he can grow more. We do not need to impose the label "normal" on a certain individual. But he can improve in some areas such as speaking loudly enough in front of people and attending services regularly.

Conclusions

It is our strength to work with diversity. We do not force *hikikomori* and ex-*hikikomori* to adjust to Christian or Japanese culture. We respect their subjectivity; therefore, it is sometimes hard to lead them moving forward. We are thankful for this opportunity to write about our ministry in this chapter. Observation, analysis, and writing increase our ability. Everyone is so unique. Knowing and serving each *hikikomori* makes us realize how much each person is quite different. With the power of the Holy Spirit, we can allow them to be the way they are. "Now the Lord is the Spirit, and where the Spirit of the Lord is, there is freedom" (2 Cor 3:17). And we believe where the Spirit of the Lord is, there is twofold freedom: one is to set the *hikikomori* free (Isa 61:1); the other is to allow Christians to freely serve *hikikomori*. As Gordon Fee notes, "This is the glorious freedom of the children of God, made available through the Spirit."[15]

However, we admit that our approach has weaknesses. It is challenging to guide and lead unique individuals. It takes time. In a sense, it is easy to *write* about our ministry but difficult to *practice* it. It is not always easy to work with different people. Without the Holy Spirit and without fully letting Jesus be in charge, we cannot transform the *hikikomori*. Again, we hope in the Spirit who Michael Welker aptly calls, the "patient 'teacher.'"[16] As a temple of the Holy Spirit, we need to let the Spirit be fully in charge so that we may be able to surpass our impatience and bear the fruit of patience (Gal 5:22). The Spirit, who is the most patient teacher, will never forsake the *hikikomori* and can certainly guide him/her to become whom the triune God has designed him/her to be.

One may wonder. Isn't it ineffective to take so much time and customize ourselves for each *hikikomori*? After all, the population of Christians in Japan has remained at 1 percent for nearly five hundred years. Should we even use our energy for such an inefficient ministry? Why not find a way that gets many more involved, such as mass evangelism in Tokyo?

These are valid questions. In our introduction, we likened our *hikikomori* ministry to that of Jesus of Nazareth. Jesus prioritized the marginalized in Galilee. The four gospels record that Jesus preached in front of mass audiences only six times. However, he talked to individuals 114 times.[17] E. P. Sanders asserts, "It is a strong possibility that virtually all of Jesus' active ministry, except the last two or three weeks, was carried out in Antipas' Galilee. Jesus was not an urbanite."[18] So, Jesus' ministry was mainly to individuals in rural areas. And is there a ministry on the earth more effective than Jesus' own ministry? We are proud to take time for each *hikikomori* in Nagano, surrounded by mountains because this is Jesus' way. If revival should take place, it may very well come through a ministry that follows the steps of Jesus. We believe that the *hikikomori* ministry at GMCC, and any ministry to young people imitating Jesus' earthly pattern, has that potential.

Notes

1 All data is as of October 11, 2022.
2 Tamaki Saitō, *Social Withdrawal: Adolescence without End*, trans. Jeffrey Angles (Minneapolis: University of Minnesota Press, 2012), 24.
3 Minami Misono, "Tokyo Ward Finds 1 in 3 Recluses Don't Want Government Help to Reintegrate" in *The Japan Times: Independent Voice in Asia*, August 19, 2022, https://www.japantimes.co.jp/news/2022/08/19/national/social-issues/recluses-tokyo-help/, accessed September 26, 2022.

4 Marcus P. J. Tan, William Lee, and Takahiro A. Kato, "International Experience of Hikikomori (Prolonged Social Withdrawal) and its Relevance to Psychiatric Research," *BJPsych International* 18:2 (May 2021), 36.

5 Masashi Matsumoto, 「ひきこもり」支援論の再検討—新たな支援への視点 ["Reexamination of Discussion about 'Hikikomori' Support: The New Aspect for Support"], 日本社会分析学会 [*Japan Sociological Association for Social Analysis*] 35 (2008), 89.

6 Matsumoto, "Reexamination of Discussion about 'Hikikomori' Support," 94–95.

7 Unless otherwise noted, all scripture references are from the New International Version.

8 David E. Garland, *1 Corinthians*, Baker Exegetical Commentary on the New Testament (Grand Rapids: Baker Academic, 2003), 436.

9 Carl R. Rogers, *On Becoming a Person: A Therapist's View of Psychotherapy* (Boston: Houghton Mifflin Company, 1961), 331–332, emphasis in original.

10 Rogers, *On Becoming a Person*, 284.

11 Needless to say, *hikikomori* recovery would be impossible without the efforts and patience of him/herself, his/her family members, Samurai Gakuen, our church members, and people in various positions who support *hikikomori* in various ways. Without them, there is no ministry. But to stick to the theme of the present chapter, we describe only our ministerial role here.

12 Fixed attendance period is not required at Samurai Gakuen. When *hikikomori* become independent mentally and financially, he/she can graduate. Staff and *hikikomori* decide together when to graduate.

13 "Quietude," QT Quietude, https://quietude.jp/en/home-english/, accessed September 26, 2022.

14 "Getting a Mental Disability Certificate (*Seishin Shogaisha Techo*) in Japan," Tokyo Mental Health, https://www.tokyomentalhealth.com/getting-a-mental-disability-certificate/, accessed September 26, 2022.

15 Gordon D. Fee, *God's Empowering Presence: The Holy Spirit in the Letters of Paul* (Peabody, Massachusetts: Hendrickson Publishers 1994), 314.

16 Michael Welker, "The Holy Spirit," in *The Oxford Handbook of Systematic Theology*, eds. Kathryn Tanner, John Webster, and Iain Torrance (Oxford: Oxford University Press, 2011), 244.

17 Masaharu Watanabe, 個人伝道に励もう「なぜ 伝道するのか」 ["Let Us Be Zealous in Personal Evangelism: Why Do We Evangelize?"] in 教団ニュース　アッセンブリー [*Denominational News: Assemblies of God*], eds. Yoshinobu Ishihara and Kazuo Kikuyama, Japan Assemblies of God 424 (January 1991), 5.

18 E. P. Sanders, *The Historical Figure of Jesus* (Middlesex, U.K.: Penguin Press, 1993), 12.

14 Five Universal Strategies to Grow a Church Younger and Stronger: A Journey with the Heart of God Church, Singapore

Tan Seow How and Cecilia Chan

Abstract

This reflection examines the concept of "GenerationS" as the answer to the global challenge of a graying church. "GenerationS," as defined by Heart of God Church (HOGC) Singapore, is not a 20–40 year age gap, but a 3–5 year age gap between cohorts of young leaders in the church. HOGC, founded in 1999, has an attendance of 5,000 and an average church member's age of 23 years old. It is a youth church run by youth, for youth, to reach youth. More than 80 percent of the congregation actively serves in a ministry, and over 70 percent are first-generation Christians. In this chapter, two founding pastors (How and Lia) reflect on their two decades of experience reaching GenerationS, to make sure there are always 13–16-year-olds in the church. To date, they have trained seven GenerationS of young leaders who have built the church alongside each other, with a vision to keep raising future GenerationS. They share their journey and provide five lessons to keep a local church younger, which, as a result, grows it stronger.

Christianity is Only One Generation from Extinction

Pastor How: We have all heard about the great South Korean revival in the previous generation. My jaw dropped when Lia and I attended the fiftieth-anniversary service of the world's biggest church, Yoido Full Gospel Church. There, in the Seoul Olympic Stadium, 80,000 South Korean Christians came to worship and pray—and that was just a small portion of their members. If they had all been permitted, they would have filled the stadium ten times over! The massiveness of it all made me think this was what heaven would be like. When everyone began praying together, I then thought of the Early Church in Acts 4:31 where "the place where they were assembled together was shaken; and they were all filled with the Holy Spirit, and they spoke the word of God with boldness."[1]

Before the Korean War (1950–1953), only 4 percent of South Koreans were Christians. By 1985, that number went from 4 percent to 34 percent.[2]

Revival had caused one in three South Koreans to convert to Christianity! But by 2015, the number professing faith had declined to 22 percent. Worse, the number of South Korean Christian youth between 10–19 years old had plunged to 3 percent.[3] This was even lower than before the war. My heart sank as I realized the great Korean revival had lasted only one or two generations.

In another twenty years, when the current post-war, pioneering, and praying generation passes on, Korean Christianity could be worse off than before the war. If nothing miraculous happens to pull back this nosedive, by the next generation, the Korean revival is over. I can imagine the demons in Satan's war council high-fiving each other and saying, "We let them have their revival for one generation, but we played the long game. We couldn't stop them from building their cathedrals, but we won their children and grandchildren." While Korean Christian leaders were good at growing churches big, far, and wide, they did not grow them younger.

Sadly, the graying church is not limited to South Korea but is a global pandemic. Indonesia, for example, experienced a revival in the 1960s and 1970s, similar to Korea. The number of Christians doubled from 6.7 million to 12.8 million,[4] and their churches experienced growth rates of about 15 percent, believed to be the highest in the world.[5] But today, they are also losing the next generation. One Indonesian pastor told me that his denomination, which has over 100,000 churches, is seeing 85 percent of its youth ministries decline or close down.

In the U.S., the average age of a typical churchgoer is 53 years old.[6] Millennials are leaving with a rate of 6 out of 10 young people who grew up in church walking away. The Pew Research Center notes that many youths 13–17 years old who are attending church are following their parents.[7] The downside is, that when they gain their independence, they do not necessarily keep attending.

Australia is blessed with Hillsong, Planetshakers, and other global ministries that have impacted the entire world. It would, therefore, be easy to assume that Aussie churches are overflowing with young people. Yet the average age of church attendees is also 53 years old.[8] While 53 percent of Australians call themselves Christian,[9] only 38 percent of those 13–18 years old do so.[10] Based on data, it is projected that by 2050, the percentage of Christians in Australia will drop by 20 percent.9

Thus, there are a few bright spots in the world, but these are the exception rather than the norm. In churches all over the world, the average age of the congregation is growing older and revival fires have dimmed. What the church world is going through is akin to a war scenario, when all the young men become casualties, don't come home, and entire towns are left with children and old people. Our young people are casualties, and we have lost a generation. This is not a criticism but a cry: Christianity is one generation away from extinction.

The Heart of God Church Story

Pastor Lia: Against this backdrop of graying churches, Heart of God Church (HOGC) stumbled onto youth as its sweet spot. Our church name has its roots in the biblical character of King David. We want to be a church that expresses God's heart and desires on the face of the earth. We started pioneering with that intent. After twenty years, we recognize that God really wanted a youth church that builds what we call "GenerationS" to exist. I believe a church will always live out its name. Now we are so privileged to be able to tell the story.

When we started HOGC, my ministry partner and husband, How, ran an adult service while I ran a children's church service concurrently. It was in those children's church services that I noticed a group of teens who were either too cool to be engaged or too cold to be enlivened; they were definitely not on fire for Jesus. At first glance, you knew they were too old for children's church and too young for adult services. I was burdened for them. Everything in my heart went out to those bored faces.

I took nine of these teens and started a teen small group in my father-in-law's office, which was unused during the weekends. Taking out these nine to pioneer a youth group was a monumental step. They were a monument in themselves. I called them "the Nine Stones" because they would not worship, would not pray, refused to respond when you spoke to them and did not smile. Their grand silence made them aloof and alone, a terrifying monument indeed. They were a stony-faced bunch of teenagers, but Jesus said that even the rocks would cry out and praise his name! Thank God that they began to grow spiritually. In fact, since that time, several of our homegrown senior pastors and full-time staff have emerged out of these Nine Stones.

Eventually, the entire youth group exploded in growth. So that was how our church started: in a small industrial park, with all kids. Many of our well-meaning pastor friends and relatives urged us to reconsider building a youth church. Everyone said that youths had no money to contribute. It was not sustainable. It was just not possible. To some extent, they were right. Money was not the only thing lacking. We had no musicians, no millionaires, no mature leaders. We had to kick and punch just to stay above the water.

Undeterred, we plowed on. For the first few years of pioneering the church, we did not take a salary. Living in a dream and fresh air is what Asians call it. We had a vision that we could build a church operated by youths, for youths, to reach youths. I used my savings to bus in more students. The small group of adults in the church also gave generously to the church. We invested limited finances into the youths but poured limitless time into discipling and training them. Little did I know that out of that first small group of nine teenagers would come the strong youth church of thousands we have today!

Running Down an Upward Escalator

Pastor How: In 2019, we celebrated our twentieth anniversary as a church. Lia and I were seeking God for his plan for the next ten to twenty years for HOGC. Was it to plant churches globally? Host a mega-conference in stadiums? These were the usual routes and typical next steps for church growth. Then God asked me a question: "What is the average age of congregants at HOGC now?" I did not know exactly, so I got my team to calculate. Our average age was 22.3 years old. I was unpleasantly surprised because we used to be closer to 16–19 years old. We were no longer a youth church . . . ouch! Then God spoke: "For the next ten to twenty years, the vision of HOGC is to bring down the average age." I was honestly thinking, "God, that's not very spectacular. Other megachurches are running conferences and planting churches. Bringing down the average age is not exactly an impressive vision."

Nevertheless, we attempted it. Lia and I shared the vision with the church, calling it "HOGC21: Bring down our average age from 22.3 to 21." This sounded easy enough, but not when we had to figure out how to do it. We mobilized the entire church to bring youths. For a whole year, our church brought 4,147 unchurched youths to our services. In the end, 1,528 of them made decisions for Christ, and 379 of these youths stayed and were planted. It was fantastic. One year later, I was excited when the team presented me with the latest statistics. Then they announced it: our average age was . . . 22.17 years old. What!? After all the hard work, we only managed to bring it down from 22.3 to 22.17! I was demoralized.

Then, I realized the difficulty of bringing down a church's average age. In order to bring it down by just one year, you actually have to bring it down by two years—because every year, the church ages by a year. It is like running down an upward escalator. So even after our effort and focus, and after 4,000+ youths came with 1,500+ decisions, we only managed to stem the tide. We essentially kept our average age.

Most pastors and churches are not monitoring this number. While we want to grow bigger, we must not neglect to grow younger. We do not realize how time flies. Many churches start with pastors in their thirties and a congregation around the same age. Typically, the church will grow old with the pastor. By the time the church is established, everyone is in their forties or fifties. This is when pastors realize that they have been blindsided. I strongly encourage pastors to take a first step against this trend by calculating the current average age of their churchgoers. Then, make a simple mathematical plan to maintain or lower the average age. This "average age down" exercise has shown me that it is much harder to grow younger than to grow bigger. If the majority of the church is middle-aged, the friends they reach out to will naturally be around the same age. So, even as a church grows bigger, it tends to grow in the same demographic group.

However, I have seen for myself that our God is a genius. Most successful churches have already discovered their own formula for growing bigger or planting new churches that essentially replicate a template, similar to franchising. But reaching the next generation is ever-evolving. Every ten years, the youths of that generation are different. Reaching youths is, therefore, a moving target that forces leadership to figure out what works. A youth church needs to be constantly reinventing itself and finding new methods. Strong GenerationS churches do not fight tomorrow's war with yesterday's strategies.

Five Lessons in Reaching, Retaining, and Releasing GenerationS

Pastor How: When I talk to pastors about bringing down their church members' average age, they ask a very good question: "When married couples give birth to children, doesn't that naturally and mathematically bring down the average age of the congregation?" Yes, that is true. However, while the average age temporarily lowers, there is a camouflaged problem. Many pastors plant their church in their thirties. Typically, their congregation will be around the same age or slightly younger, as reflected below in Figure 1.

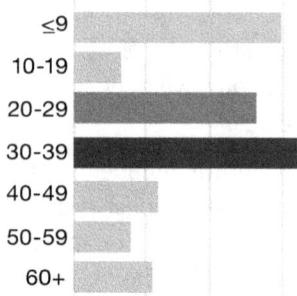
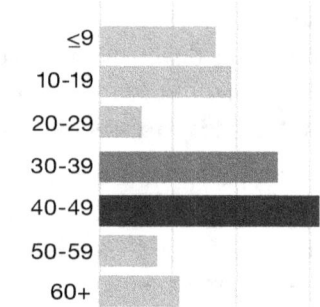

Figure 1: Church Plant Demographics Reflecting the Typical Age of the Pastor, Parents, and Small Children.

Figure 2: Same Church Plant Demographic, Ten Years Later

In ten years, however, the church demographic will shift to look like Figure 2. The pioneer congregation ages from twenties and thirties to thirties and forties.

During this phase, people in their thirties and forties have children in their teens or younger. The church goes through a cute stage with babies born every month, a children's ministry with their hands full, and a youth group of kids who grew up together. On the surface, all seems fine at the family church.

But if you look carefully, you will see the problem—a generation gap in the twenties. These young men and women typically power the volunteers in a church, so this causes a problem common in family churches. I know because I was a university student when I saw my former church suffer from what we call "Family Church Syndrome." This is illustrated below, in Figure 3.

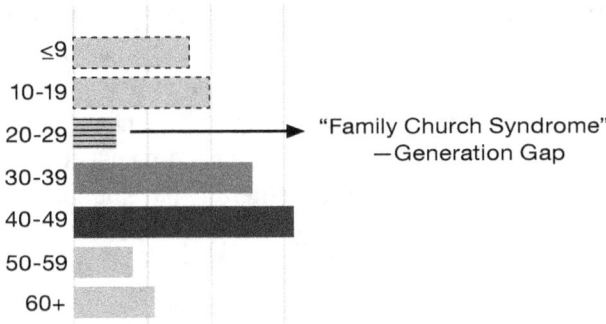

Figure 3: The "Family Church Syndrome" (Generation Gap)

Most churches do not intentionally focus on reaching and retaining youth and young adults. They simply leave the demographics with their gaps in the organic cycle of life. However, the gap between parents and children is typically between 25 to 35 years; the church actually cannot afford this gap. A strong church needs a cohort of leaders and church builders every ten years. If the church is big, like in the thousands, then you may have a spread of age groups that might mitigate the problem. But if your church is in the hundreds, you will feel the adverse impact of this gap. The lack of manpower will be felt even more if your church is located in places where young people commonly move away for university or work. So what is the stopgap measure, literally? GenerationS.

Pastor Lia: What is the difference between GenerationS and other widely adopted philosophies of reaching youth? Many churches pioneered youth groups in the late 1990s and early 2000s, which were brilliantly successful with young people. But if you look around now, these youth groups are no longer youth movements. They only went with the flow of one youth generation. In the typical scenario of their church history, they arduously reached other youths in their generation or, at most, the next generation. Twenty years later, those youth and young adults have become parents and are now generally reaching other parents. Understandably, they are reaching those of their own kind. But sadly, the church no longer has a vibrant youth ministry, which was their original strength. They have not reproduced more than one or two generations of young leaders.

The difference with GenerationS is that we do not just focus on reaching "my generation" or even "the next generation," but we keep going back down for another generation, and another generation, to make sure there are always 13–16-year-olds in the congregation. In HOGC, we do not define a generation as a forty-year gap or even a twenty-year gap. We treat every generation as if it is about three to five years apart. This means that every few years in HOGC, we start a new youth group as the preceding generation grows up. Every generation gets to grow up and grow old together. With each cohort, we literally have hundreds of leaders and volunteers serving together and growing up together. Currently, we are already in our seventh generation. This is how we ensure longevity, renewal, and an endless pipeline of ignited youth.

All pastors know it is hard work growing a church bigger. But, it is even harder to grow a church *younger.* As How mentioned, to keep your church young is a moving target, like running down an upward escalator. You will pant, you will plant the next group, but you will never have time to pat yourself on the back.

Still, God has been good to us. Right now, we have seven GenerationS of young HOGC leaders serving God all at the same time. Homegrown senior pastors, associate pastors, leaders, staff, and young parents have all come out of the first generation, while the seventh generation is our youth who became leaders when they were as young as 12 years old. The beautiful thing is that the average age of our church is still 23 years old… after twenty years! At this point, I see the seventh generation still carrying the torch to produce GenerationS beyond theirs. They have joined us on the escalator run. This is what our rally cry has been for the last two decades: *GenerationS are not replacements. GenerationS are reinforcements.* The following are five specific lessons that we have learned from building a youth church and pastoring our youths.

Lesson 1: Youths need to be invited, included, and involved before they can be influenced and impacted. But we try to impress . . . in vain.

Pastor How: I have spoken to countless pastors, politicians, and business leaders about youth, and every one of them has agreed with me enthusiastically about their importance. Many reiterate that "Youth are the future," and "Youth are the leaders of tomorrow." But for Lia and me, the road diverges here. Yes, it is obvious that youth are the leaders of tomorrow, but our crusade is that youth would be leaders *today*!

Youths need to be invited, included, and involved before they can be influenced and impacted. But we try to impress...in vain. How did Lia and I raise up thousands of young people to serve God? It is not rocket science. We do not have a special anointing. We just invite, include, and involve youths in ministry. If you were to ask any 10-year-old boy if he would rather watch soccer or play soccer, almost all of them would jump off the couch to kick the ball to play. Therein lies the problem for the church. Traditional youth ministries are set up for the kids to "watch soccer" rather than to "play soccer." They advertise: "Come to youth group where we have a really cool band, brilliant lights, and humorous preaching. Join us because we have fun and crazy games." But the games, the band, lights, screens, and preaching are all played onstage with only a few participants, and everyone else is watching. Youths are just spectators watching others "do" church. Then we try so hard to impress them with what's going on onstage.

HOGC's secret is to let the *youths* "do" church while we "watch." We turn it around. We let the youths be onstage. Let them run the whole show (use professional equipment and run all aspects of our services). We let them impress us, and then we celebrate them.

In one sense, this is normal. Parents go to school to watch their kids act in dramas, compete in sports, or perform in the arts. The church is the only youth organization that does it the other way around. Imagine if the schools did it like us, with the parents in school playing soccer, and then inviting their kids to watch. (You are laughing now.) Imagine a 40-year-old dad acting in the school drama or a 40-year-old mom dancing ballet, and then trying to get their kids to come watch. It would be a ridiculous sight. The kids would never come to watch the adults play.

It is no wonder that youth ministry is not working. Again, it is as simple as getting the youths involved. Stop putting on a show and trying to impress them. You will never beat Hollywood and pop culture.

This brings me to the next benefit of involving youth and not impressing them: smaller and less-resourced youth ministries do not have to compete with social media or big churches. When you involve your youth, you do not need big budgets, big productions, or big names. During the first ten years of HOGC, Lia grew the youth from nine members to hundreds with one guitar and an overhead projector and simply involved them in the ministry. Once they are "in the ministry," then you can influence and impact them. This is where discipleship begins. It's always on the job, on the go, not a lecture-style Bible study. Again, isn't that how it works elsewhere? When teachers try to get students to run during P. E. lessons, they are lethargic and disinterested. However, when they sign up for the school basketball team, a coach can push them to train hard. When youths are "in the team or ministry," then you can influence and impact them.

Lesson 2: Empower, don't entertain.

Pastor Lia: The problem with most youth ministries is that they are built on entertainment. Most youth pastors feel a great need to be a clown, fire-eater, and juggler all in one. Empower youth, don't entertain them!

This is good news for pastors who know they can never be a comedian or entertainer. I am not saying that basketball, games, Xbox, etc., do not have a place. In fact, we need those to attract new friends who are not yet Christians. But we cannot build a youth or young adult ministry on entertainment. We must build it on empowerment.

I always tell our youth leaders, "If you babysit the youth, you will get babies. If you lead the youth, you will have leaders." Do not just love them. Train them, lead them, guide them. Give them a vision for God and train them towards fulfilling that vision. If you visit Heart of God Church, you will see youths running the weekend services for youth. They are trained to be leaders and handle the operations: screens, cameras, lighting, sound, and music. You might spot a 9-year-old photographer zipping through the congregation, stealthily capturing moments in the service. You will see 16-year-old leaders boldly praying for pastors. During our "Reinforcements Weekend," we up the ante: the entire service in all departments is run by those 16 and under!

When COVID-19 hit and the church went into online mode, we did not lose momentum. The youth made the jump online with such finesse because, from day one, our church had always been about training and empowerment. When COVID-19 descended, the youth did not wait around to be entertained by church online programming. They knew it was not about entertainment. Instead, they jumped on board to create captivating content for online services. It was surreal watching them make the digital plunge! During COVID-19, the youth used technology for empowerment and enrichment, not entertainment.

Remember this: empowered youths become producers. Entertained youths become consumers. Empower, and do not entertain your youth and young adults today!

Lesson 3: The younger generations are not here to push you OUT but to push you UP.

Pastor Lia: One of the toughest hurdles of developing people in church is when those with ministry experience view the new, younger crew as a threat to themselves. From the usher ministry to platform ministry, you see veterans holding tight to their posts, refusing even an inch of space for the younger people. Why is this? Because older individuals fear being replaced. Replacement is such a commonplace fear that it has become part of the cultural wallpaper in most churches. It is time for churches to have an epochal advance in ministry by having a seismic shift in mindset. We say it this way: "GenerationS are not replacements but reinforcements!"

We also tell the young crew that seasoned leaders do not *have* to give time to train them, but are choosing to. So, they ought to be grateful and not act entitled. We then tell the older generation that the young ones are not there to replace them, but to reinforce them. No one is waiting for an older leader to slip up or die (whichever comes first) so that a younger leader can take their place. In our church, it is not uncommon to see three GenerationS serving together. For example, a first-generation drummer might train a new, second-generation trainer who trains a young third-generation drummer. Nobody has to be replaced. The young generation is not here to push people out but to push them up!

It is important to keep assuring both older and younger generations. If you can assure veterans that the younger generations are there to reinforce, not replace, then you start having layers and levels of equally skilled team members serving alongside each other.

Lesson 4: The house of God must be a home for youth.

Pastor Lia: A house is built by hand, but a home is built by heart. This is why we are called the Heart of God Church. We believe the hand of God will build this house, and the heart of God will build this home. House has to do with "where," while home has to do with "who." Home is where family and friends are. A home has warmth, love, and relationships. The same is true for church— it is not so much "where" is church as much as it is "who" is in church.

Traditionally, for a person to join a church, he or she goes through this sequence:

Believe → Become → Belong.

They must first *believe*, then *become* a Christian. Let me add another "B" word, Behave. We expect the youth to behave to our standards and expectations. Then when we are satisfied, we extend our fellowship and offer them church membership. Only after probation do we open our circle for them to *belong*. This is not going to work for the young generation. Youth want to know and feel that they belong first, before deciding if they want to believe and become a Christian. They tend to follow the sequence:

Belong → Believe → Become

In HOGC, after the youths feel like they *belong*, they tend to take the next step to *believe*. In case you have not noticed, kids are not really into theology. They do not really care if your church teaches pre-tribulation rapture or recites the Nicene Creed. When they *belong*, they just find it easier to believe in Christ. Additionally, Christianity is not just believing but also belonging. Jesus died for us not just so that we believe, but so that we belong. We are now part of God's family. He is now our Father. We now belong to a spiritual home (the church) and ultimately belong to an eternal home.

We have found at HOGC that when the youths *belong* and *believe*, they will almost naturally *become* and *behave*. For all the pastors, preachers, and leaders reading this, this mindset shift is a game-changer. It relieves us of the pressure to "get them saved" on their first visit. You are no longer on a forty-minute countdown to "close the deal." Instead, your goal is to make youths initially feel that they belong so that they will keep coming back.

When church members feel strongly that they belong, then something beautiful happens. They mature from *membership* to *ownership*, and from *fellowship* to *stewardship*. They move from a mentality of "I belong to

HOGC" to "HOGC belongs to me." If you have never had a warm, loving home and never had true, uplifting friendships, then when you find it, you will protect it with all your might. When the church becomes a youth's home, they will build it, defend it, and fight for it.

Lesson 5: Be a king-maker, not just a king.

Pastor How: Our next generation should be greater than us. They should stand on our shoulders and see further and dream bigger. Lia and I went to Bible school, but we never had the opportunity to get our Masters of Divinity degrees. When we were pioneering our infant church, there was neither time nor money to further our theological studies. When the church became more established, the option was on the table, but instead of enrolling ourselves, we decided it would be better for us to hold the fort so that the next generation of pastors could pursue their advanced degrees. Our young pastors started their education while still carrying their full responsibilities in church. They flew frequently to Oral Roberts University for classes and back, hitting the ground running. When they graduated, Lia and I attended their commencement ceremonies at ORU. We felt like proud parents. They were 28–33 years old and had already completed their theological studies. Subsequently, they were ordained as the next generation of pastors in HOGC.

When Lia and I were that age, we only preached to a group of a few people. The first time I preached to over 2,000 people, I was already in my late thirties and my legs shook—not from anointing but anxiety! But when our next-generation pastors first started preaching, they were already preaching to hundreds. Today, Senior Pastors Garrett, Lynette, and Charleston are our main preachers who deliver world-class, life-changing sermons to thousands every week. They have also preached in Bible schools and conferences in Southeast Asia, Hong Kong, Taiwan, Australia, and Europe. The best part is, that because they are still so young, they connect so well with Gen Z and Gen Alpha.

Subsequently, we sent another batch of next-generation pastors to get their divinity degrees. And, just as we brought our first batch of homegrown pastors overseas when they were youths, they now bring teams of youths with them when they preach. This leaves me hopeful that the next generations will stand on their shoulders as they have stood on ours. Let's be the king-makers.

Bishop Bronner said it this way: "Legacy is not what you have achieved but what you set in motion."[11] Some successful people think, "My accomplishments and achievements are my legacy." No, if it dies with you, it is not legacy—it is history. Only if it continues beyond you, does it become legacy. Some successful people might leave behind a great history but not a legacy. Consider Psalm 127 in *The Message*:

> Don't you see that children are God's best gift?
> the fruit of the womb his generous *legacy*?
> Like a warrior's fistful of arrows
> are the children of a vigorous youth (Ps 127:3–4, MSG)[12]

This verse is crystal clear: our legacy is in our children and spiritual children. Legacy is about who, not what. Legacy is about the future, not the past. Our legacy is what we set in motion after we hand over, retire, or die. Legacy is about movement. From a worldly perspective, Jesus did not achieve much when he ascended to heaven: there was no megachurch or global denomination. But he started a movement that cannot be stopped. Now, a significant portion of the planet are his followers.

Final Thoughts

Pastor Lia: Some people ask incredulously: "Can my church still be relevant to youth when I am in my thirties, forties, and fifties?" Yes, it can, if you keep building GenerationS and never let up. Every generation will have a slightly older generation to lead them. In that sense, the youths you have built earlier will be your hands, feet, ears, and heart on the ground, leading the younger youths. They embody your heart, vision and values to the next generation. Our three homegrown senior pastors and pastors from our first generation of youths carry our heart and vision down through the pipeline. It is so crucial to have each generation just a few years apart, not forty years!

Then some ask: "Can *I* still be relevant to youths when I am in my thirties, forties, and fifties?" Yes, you can. I personally am still ministering in youth services. I am still writing some of my sermons just for young people. I am still meeting youths to disciple them on a regular basis, or going crazy with them at the batting cages. I am still relevant. But I believe this is because I have never related to them just based on trends or cool looks. I can still relate to them because spiritual principles are timeless. Love, belief, and passion for young people cannot be eroded by time. Vision and values are never the victims of passing epochs. I have been doing the same thing for over twenty years. I am still doing it. Yes, I am boring that way, but like I always say, "There are miracles in the mundane, beauty in the banal, and riches in the routine!"

Pastor How: As of today, we have been banging the drum for GenerationS for over two decades. When we started in the 1990s and early 2000s, as far as I know, there was not excitement or brouhaha about youth churches. Then, around the middle of the 2010s onwards, something changed globally. By God's grace, there was a shift to greater emphasis on youth and young adults. Lia and I quietly rejoiced when we witnessed this pivot.

With this increased attention, leaders globally asked for more details and in-depth teachings—essentially the how-to's. So we launched the GenerationS Pastors Conference in 2009. At the time of this writing, we have run it 35 times. For pastors willing to go all in, they see fruit. One pastoral couple in Sydney started implementing the Strong Church Model after they attended our GenerationS Pastors Conference. Lia and I also gave them access to the inner workings of HOGC and showed them how we disciple our leaders. They were moved to tears and determined to build the same kind of Strong Church with layers and layers of leaders. They took the heart, passion of discipleship, and Deep Bench back to their church and grew from 30 to 65 connect groups. They did not just get a bigger crowd but added more connected and committed people.

Another pastor from Hong Kong went back after attending a GenerationS Pastors Conference and started eleven new ministries for youths to serve in. Then he empowered his youths to run evangelistic events and 200 new students came. That had never been done before in his church, and the best part was that the adults didn't have to lift a hand except to clap.

I could go on and on talking about Russia, Scandinavia, South America, Europe, Thailand, Indonesia, Taiwan, China... The principles of GenerationS are both universal and timeless. They work in every culture. They work for every generation—X, Y, Z, and even Alpha generations. They are duplicable and doable. In the same way God brought a revival in Heart of God Church, he can bring a revival in every church, city, and nation.

Notes

1 Unless otherwise noted, all scripture references are the New King James Version (NKJV).

2 "Census Bureau, Province/Age/Gender Religious Population (1985)," Statistics Office, Korean Statistical Information Service, https://kosis.kr/eng/statisticsList/statisticsListIndex.do?parentId=A.1&menuId=M_01_01&vwcd=MT_ETITLE&parmTabId=M_01_01/, accessed July 20, 2024.

3 "Census Bureau, Province/Age/Gender Religious Population (2015)," Statistics Office, Korean Statistical Information Service, https://kosis.kr/eng/statisticsList/statisticsListIndex.do?parentId=A.1&menuId=M_01_01&vwcd=MT_ETITLE&parmTabId=M_01_01. Also Detlef Pollack and Gergely Rosta, *Religion and Modernity: An International Comparison* (Oxford: Oxford University Press, 2017), 340; "World Population Prospects 2019: Volume I: Comprehensive Tables," Department of Economic and Social Affairs, Population Division, United Nations, https://population.un.org/wpp/publications/Files/WPP2019_Volume-I_Comprehensive-Tables.pdf/, accessed August 1, 2024.

4 Jan Aritonang and Karel Steenbrink, *A History of Christianity in Indonesia* (Leiden: Brill, 2008), 202.

5 Edward Plowman, "Demythologizing Indonesia's Revival," *Christianity Today*, March 2, 1973, https://www.christianitytoday.com/ct/1973/march-2/demythologizing-indonesias-revival.html/, accessed June 20, 2022.

6 Warren Bird, "Not a Boomer Phenomenon—Megachurches Draw Twice as Many Under 45," *Christian Post*, June 25, 2014, https://www.christianpost.com/news/not-a-baby-boomer-phenomenon-megachurches-draw-twice-as-many-people-under-45.html/, accessed June 20, 2022.

7 "U.S. Teens Take After Their Parents Religiously, Attend Services Together and Enjoy Family Rituals," Pew Research Center, September 10, 2020, https://www.pewresearch.org/religion/2020/09/10/u-s-teens-take-after-their-parents-religiously-attend-services-together-and-enjoy-family-rituals/, accessed June 20, 2022.

8 Australian Bureau of Statistics, "A Demographic Snapshot of Christianity and Church Attenders in Australia," McCrindle Research: National Church Life Survey, April 18, 2014, https://mccrindle.com.au/app/uploads/images/A-Demographic-snapshot-of-Christianity-and-church-attenders-in-Australia_McCrindle.pdf/, accessed June 20, 2022.

9 "The Future of World Religions: Population Growth Projections, 2010–2050," Pew Research Center, April 2, 2015, https://www.pewresearch.org/religion/2015/04/02/religious-projections-2010-2050/, accessed June 20, 2022.

10 Australian Bureau of Statistics, "Census Reveals Australia's Religious Diversity on World Religion Day," *Media Release*, January 2018, https://www.abs.gov.au/ausstats/abs@.nsf/mediareleasesbytitle/8497F7A8E7DB5BEFCA25821800203DA4?OpenDocument, accessed June 20, 2022

11 Dale C. Bronner, "Extravagant Love," Weekend Worship Service Sermon at Heart of God Church, Singapore, October 4, 2014.

12 Eugene H. Peterson, The Message: *The Bible in Contemporary Language* (Colorado Springs: NavPress with Tyndale House Publishers, 2018).

15 Planetboom: A Case Study in the Effects of Youth-Led Revival in Australia

Clayton Coombs, Andrew Harrison, and Susannah Harrison

Abstract

Historical accounts of revivals past have typically documented not just conversion statistics, but also broader societal effects of the revival. The present study documents the revival that is currently gathering momentum in Australia, and the unique role that youth (under 30) are playing. Data has been gathered from interviews with leaders and participants in Planetboom, the youth ministry of Planetshakers Church. At a time when many churches have struggled to rebuild attendance post-pandemic, evidence is presented of a youth-led, prayer-fueled revival that is not only seeing thousands of young people respond to the gospel, and an unprecedented number of miracles, but an impact beyond the church that cannot be ignored. This study will examine testimonial evidence in five key areas: church, welfare, culture, crime, and cross-cultural missions.

Introduction

As both a student and teacher of church history, as well as a minister at Planetshakers Church, it has long been my observation that we are witnessing at Planetshakers a revival comparable to any revival in modern or ancient times. Present are countless testimonies of encounter, the pervasive sense of God's presence, thousands upon thousands of documented conversions, numerous supernatural miracles of healing, missionaries and ministers released, and a lasting impact on culture. If not entirely unique, what is uncommon about this revival is the fact that it has endured for nearly two decades and shows no signs of waning in influence.

Furthermore, since the beginning, it has been a revival that is occurring primarily among young people. Eyewitness accounts from a recent camp for Planetboom (the youth ministry of Planetshakers church), gathered from Instagram posts and personal interviews, detail a heavy sense of awe that was present in the meetings. This manifested in repentance, experiences with God's Spirit that resulted in a greater love for God and his

Word, greater confidence, a sense of being touched by the fire of God, being overcome with God's power, and slain in the Spirit. This multi-ethnic teen gathering experienced a unity of Spirit that is nothing short of miraculous.[1]

The stories from revivals past are only known because they have been told.[2] Later generations have been blessed both by eyewitness and firsthand accounts, and also by secondary works of synthesis. For this reason, I have had a growing conviction that our own story of revival needs to be told. What follows is one telling of it, mostly by Andrew and Susannah Harrison, both of whom encountered God in significant and transformative ways as young people at Planetshakers Church, and who went on to become youth pastors at Planetshakers. Their account focuses on Planetboom, which is not just a microcosm, but an engine room of Planetshakers Church. Though they take no credit for it, God has used both Andrew and Susannah powerfully in being carriers of revival. From their perspective, and in the words of a recent Planetboom song: "This is a move of God. We didn't start it, and nothing can stop it..."[3]

Andrew Harrison's Testimonial

I'm backstage and taking a moment in the green room to have a drink of water and catch my breath after preaching and ministering over the last hour. But the sounds from within the meeting spill out and urge me to take another look. My eyes are still stinging from the tears and my throat is raw from preaching and praying, but I've come to love this familiar "end of a youth conference" feeling. Now as I near the back door to the sanctuary, the muffled sounds become clearer. Young people of every background, race, and color are singing at the top of their lungs, "You are holy, holy, holy!"

I circle back behind the large LED walls to look toward what's taking place below. Singers and dancers, no longer neatly spaced across the front of the stage, are scattered randomly. Some are on their knees, weeping but still singing. Some are jumping and shouting with microphones discarded to the side. Others are in pairs, doubled over as they pray for one another. Most are so caught up by this time that they haven't noticed me. I carefully step around them, moving slowly forward, and my eyes look toward the young people below. What a beautiful mess. Neat rows of chairs and the lines of a congregation are long gone by now. There's no delineation between where the altar starts or ends. The whole room has become the response. Groups stand huddled together praying. Young people lie on the ground around them, under the power of God. Leaders throughout the room are still laying hands on people and praying. And young people everywhere are caught up in worship. Earlier, I preached from Esther 4:14, "For such a time as this," and then we prayed for every teenager in the room. We had young people respond if they felt called by God to ministry or leadership in some area of society. We had pastors praying, prophesying, and giving words of wisdom and knowledge—and now, somehow, that has led to this.

Pastor Russell Evans, attuned to the Holy Spirit, quiets the band and begins to talk about the fire of the Spirit and a burden for others. The band roars back and another level of worship kicks in: "Our generation has been searching for You. Our generation has been thirsting for You God. Show us Your glory." What a sound and what a heart cry. This is the last session of Planetboom Conference 2023, and it is a move of God. But it didn't start here. It's just more fuel thrown on a fire that has been burning among young people for some time now.

Eyewitness testimonies from the visitation of the Holy Spirit that occurred at this camp converge on three key themes: Life change, experiencing the presence of God, and new boldness.[4] Sophie Mauger testified, "It was so life changing and I will never be the same again." Sophia Escuro said that camp "took me to a future full of hope... A few weeks ago I turned 16, proving what I said long ago [about not making it] wrong and I'm grateful for where I stand today." Lilly Tobgui felt God calling her to ministry: "God revealed why I had such a passion for the Bible, which was then later on revealed to me that He has called me to teach theology." Others felt empowered to minister. Ava Ching spoke of the experience of her encounter with God as, "Before camp, I was really afraid to step out and pray over others, however during and after some of the sessions, I was able to pray for some people and see them be touched by the power of God!!" Josh Creek likewise gained renewed confidence saying that "God moved in a way I have never experienced before. He reassured me that I don't need to be afraid and that He would be with me in every situation." Joanna Kuku, to her surprise, experienced a new level of confidence and fruitfulness in praying for others. Sebastian Licciardi described the collective touch by God in the room as follows:

Teenagers and leaders alike were being touched by the fire and calling of God. All the regional leaders of our youth ministry were called up on stage during ministry time, and as these leaders received, teenagers were touched deeply vicariously through the impartation of the Holy Spirit their leaders got. It felt like there were not just a lot of individual encounters, but almost like a "hive mind" kind of feel to the encounter. Everyone felt each other's encounter, and there was a supernatural unity amongst complete strangers of all ages, races, backgrounds and spiritual and social circumstance. Many just dropped to the floor, cried in repentance, kneeled, yelled and shook as they encountered him.[5]

Lavei Tukuafu likewise recalled feeling "a weight of glory...like I never wanted to leave that room." She was convinced that the encounters experienced that day would have generational effects, and journaled this excerpt from a longer poem:

People step out of who they are in the ordinary
and operate through the Spirit and be extraordinary
People kneel before God
An army rises up
A generation won for God.[6]

The Story of Planetshakers

So where did it begin? To answer that question properly, we would have to go all the way back to Pentecost or, at the very least, Azusa Street. However, to hone in on this little chapter of that great story, we begin in 1997. Pastor Evans, then the youth pastor of Paradise Community Church in Adelaide, Australia, received an interrupting thought from the Holy Spirit while attending a revival meeting in Melbourne. The Spirit told him, "Start a conference and call it Planetshakers." With no bearing for what would take place and no precedence for how this kind of youth conference should look, he simply obeyed.

It started small with only 300 delegates the first year, but the power of God was displayed, the Holy Spirit poured out, and word began to spread. Over the coming years, Planetshakers would grow to become over 30,000 young people gathering across seven separate conferences in Perth, Adelaide, Melbourne, Sydney, and Brisbane every January. Pastors Russell and Sam Evans took the flame that God had given them and passed it on to the new generation.[7]

Arguably though, the real impact was not the scale or size of the meetings, but the explosive passion and potency of the ministry moments. Youth groups would line up from the early hours of the morning, already chanting and singing in expectation of the move of God. Salvations, Spirit-baptism, deliverance, signs, wonders, and miracles broke out in every meeting, along with a new expression of praise and worship. Radical giving and generosity among young people also marked these services as the kingdom of God got a hold of people's lives.

The impact of the conferences began to change the landscape of youth ministry across Australia. Youth groups were exploding and doubling each year from the overflow of what the Holy Spirit did. Young people were stepping out in the power of the Spirit on the streets and in their schools to reach others with the love of God. Today, pastors and leaders across Australia and the globe would testify that it was at a Planetshakers conference, as young people, that they encountered God and received his call to the ministry in which they are now active today. I am one of them.

My own little youth group had combined with some other local groups to bring about a hundred people from Tasmania. To keep expenses low, we traveled overnight by boat and then another twelve hours by bus to get across to Adelaide. I was as just another 16-year-old in the crowd, caught up in the hunger for an encounter with God. It was 2004, right in the heat of everything that was happening at Planetshakers conferences. I had attended them for the previous two years and was baptized in the Spirit in one of those meetings. However, this was the year a significant encounter with God would leave me with no doubt that he had called me to a life of ministry. I don't remember the preacher and I don't particularly remember the response call; I just recall being compelled to race down from the balcony along with hundreds of other young people to get as close to the altar as I possibly could. I knew my heart was burning with a desire to know God and make him known, and I wanted to respond to that.

I don't know how long the service went on, or how long I spent on the ground under the power of God, but I do know that the flame that had been entrusted to Planetshakers to win a generation was, that day, passed on to me as well. I wrote down in my little paper journal after the service what I believed I had received from God: "You are Mine! I want to do something great in your life. Don't worry about your weaknesses and the things that you lack. I am giving you My power to live for me and win others for me."

Back in 2003, Pastor Evans had felt the Holy Spirit's clear prompting to plant a church called Planetshakers in Melbourne, Australia. In April of 2004, the first services began, and later that same year, their youth ministry Planetboom took shape. The flame that had set young people and youth groups on fire all across Australia now had another torch. Over the coming years, Planetboom blazed a trail for youth ministry in Australia with schools in Melbourne opening up to the gospel, buses full of teenagers lining the streets for youth services on Friday nights, and thousands responding to Christ.

With the Holy Spirit moving this way, it would be impossible to quantify those who have been reached and converted on the streets, in schoolyards, or over phone calls as youth leaders and young people reached out to witness to those around them. However, within Planetboom services themselves, there have been thousands of such decisions recorded and accounted for. In 2014 alone, there were 1,055 recorded salvation responses from Friday night services and small group meetings. From that year onward, there was a rapid increase in souls being saved within Planetboom services, with an average of 2,000–2,500 souls per year since then. In 2015, there were 239 recorded decisions in one meeting alone, and in 2018 there were 880 teenagers saved in Planetboom services over one school term. Across this last decade, there have cumulatively been over 20,000 recorded salvations within Planetboom services in Melbourne. Each of these teenagers represented in that statistic has been prayed for, discipled, and encouraged in their faith after making this decision. Many of the current youth leadership team of Planetboom are accounted for within this number and carry on the discipleship process, now leading teenagers to Jesus themselves.

Missions and Impact on Communities

One of the teenagers who received salvation during this period was Audrey Tandiokusuma-Fakhrsadeh. Audrey's testimony, in her own words, is as follows:

> At 14 years of age, I moved to Australia as an international student and initially enjoyed the freedom of doing whatever I wanted, being far from the influence of parents. However, across my first year in Australia, I began to grow distant from God and to experience loneliness. In July 2013, I attended Planetshakers Church, rededicated my life to God and was introduced to the

most hungry for God, passionate teenagers I'd ever known. I went on to use the rest of my high school years to prioritize being in God's house, taking every opportunity I had in Planetboom to grow in God.

It was during these years of being mentored by leaders and building a strong foundation in God that I felt God calling me to lay down my life to go into the nations and make disciples (Matthew 28:19). Prompted by this call, I decided to do Planetshakers Bible College after high school and during my first mission trip went to Papua New Guinea, where I felt God speak to me about full-time ministry. Over the course of five years, I continued to volunteer in the Believe Team whilst completing a degree in International Development Studies. Unsurprisingly, this course was a set-up by God for the work that God would ultimately lead my husband and me to do in Papua New Guinea where we are currently part of building community hubs in rural areas across the nation. I came to Australia as a teenager to pursue academic excellence and prepare myself for a career, but God met me along the journey and set me up for the calling He had for my life to empower and win the nations.[8]

The "Believe Team," to which Audrey refers, is one of the missions projects of Planetshakers Church. Commencing in 2016 with students from Planetshakers College, Believe began what would become a long-term missions engagement with the nation of Papua New Guinea. Initially, Planetshakers sent short-term teams at least once a year. These teams toured primary and high schools, visited hospitals and prisons, and facilitated mass evangelism campaigns at the national stadium. The first of the latter campaigns was attended by around 100,000 people and recorded 40,000 conversions. In the ensuing years, the school program developed a national curriculum, which is now taught in every school in the nation. Mass evangelism encouraged tens of thousands more recorded conversions, countless miracles were witnessed by teams, and a training center was established at Port Moresby's Bomana prison to rehabilitate and educate prisoners. Central to the ethos of this center is the strong belief in God's power to transform the lives of offenders.

But perhaps the most significant thing to come out of this sustained partnership was a plan to establish ninety community hubs cross Papua New Guinea. Audrey Tandiokusuma, along with her husband, Mohammed Fakhrsadeh—who escaped Iran having been converted to Christianity and was later educated at Planetshakers College— were responsible for establishing the first of these hubs in Papua New

Guinea's Gazelle district in April 2023.[9] They now manage a halfway house for troubled young men that is seeing great impact just outside Port Moresby.

The same department that manages Believe Teams also run a community ministry out of our Melbourne Campus called Empower. Empower offers English classes to immigrants and refugees, and a food bank for those in need. Prior to the COVID-19 global lockdowns, in response to a word from God, Empower radically upscaled its capacity in the foodbank. When the pandemic hit, Empower was ready. In 2021, Empower distributed one million meals to the needy in our city.[10]

Susannah Harrison's Testimonial

It was 2005, and as a 14-year-old, I found myself at the very first Planetboom camp. I'd never experienced anything like this: teenagers hungry, desperate even, to get into sessions where praise was explosive, worship was intimate, and preaching led to hours of encounter and ministry. I had recently decided to follow Jesus, and while I didn't understand everything that was happening in the sessions, my heart was stirred. I wanted the kind of relationship with God that I saw others demonstrating, I wanted to be used by God in the way they spoke about, and I wanted my friends to experience this too.

On the second day of camp, Pastor Evans preached about David and how the world judges by outward appearance while God looks at the heart. I postured myself, ready to receive, and asked God to give me a heart like David. As I began to worship, Pastor Evans singled me out of the crowd and began to prophesy: "God has given you a gift of leadership, and He wants to use you to lead your generation, but He's asking you to give Him your whole life, your whole heart. He's asking you to say yes to Him and to use the gifts He's given you to serve Him. He loves you so much." Not quite understanding everything that had happened but being overcome by the presence of God, I wrote these words down in the journal I was handed as I arrived at camp. Eighteen years later, I still have that journal. As I look back and reflect, I know it was moments like this that changed the trajectory of my life. Little did I know what was on the other side of my yes to God's call at fourteen years of age.

Revival Impact on Community Develops

Planetboom youth ministry has always reflected the multiculturalism that is present in Melbourne and has grown and developed with it. Australia's 2021 Census found that 27.6 percent of Australians were born overseas, with nearly half the population (48.2%) having one or both parents born overseas.[11] Consequently, Planetshakers Church in 2023 boasts 155 nationalities represented in its congregation. But, at its conception in late 2004, Planetboom youth had less ethnic diversity present. Then, in 2010, the youth ministry received a prophetic word about African teenagers coming into Planetboom specifically from the South Sudanese community. At this point in time, there were around ten African teenagers in Planetboom who got on fire for God. Over the next few years, a move of God took place in the South Sudanese community, with over 500 young people coming into Planetboom.

This coincided with the migration influx of refugees settling in Melbourne, seeking refuge from the South Sudanese civil war. As this community immigrated to Melbourne, they brought their lived experiences of war, disorder, trauma, and struggle to integrate into society. Many Sudanese youth formed gangs, incited violence, and earned a reputation in Australia as violent assailants or lost causes involved in criminal gangs.[12] There were even calls from government ministers to deport them *en masse*. From 2010 onwards, Planetboom reached out to and discipled South Sudanese young people in a way that was viewed as exceptional to unbelievers.

Then, in 2014, Planetboom received a prophecy about Pacific Islanders coming into the youth ministry. At this time, Boom began to see a great increase in its general cultural diversity. A key group of the original teenagers from the South Sudanese and Pacific Islander communities took on leadership roles within the youth ministry and, ultimately, across different spheres of society. High schools, police departments, and welfare agencies sought help from Planetboom, who acted as consults to schools, welfare departments, and the Victoria Police in their engagement with this community. To provide context, youth crime had become a salient problem in Melbourne, culminating in violence-fueled brawls between youth gangs breaking out on the streets of the city at a major public festival in April 2016. These gangs, mostly comprised of African and Pacific Islander teenagers, were deemed as responsible for rampages across the city involving motor vehicle thefts, aggravated burglaries, and assaults on both civilians and police.

Yet, Pastor Evans' prophetic vision for Planetshakers was "healing the waters of the city." He began to cast a vision about Planetshakers being "a church for all." Inspired by this, the Planetboom youth team began to pray and seek God for greater influence in the city and for opportunities where they could bring healing and restoration to youth within Melbourne. As a result of this, and the increasingly multi-ethnic leadership team of Planetboom, a connection with Victoria Police was divinely formed that grew into a partnership to overcome youth crime. The first step in this partnership with Victoria Police was when they requested to come and observe a Planetboom youth service. Those in attendance were amazed at what they saw: hundreds of youth and young adults from diverse backgrounds interacting with great love and affection for each other. This evolved into regular meetings with police to strategize how they could combat youth crime at future events in the city, and engage and reform individual youth offenders.

In 2016, Planetboom was invited to meet with the Police Chief Commissioner at his personal Youth Crime Summit where leaders and influencers of youth culture were gathered to strategize solutions for the rising youth crime rates. Several plans were enacted, and the Chief Commissioner reported in the year following, that there was a significant drop in crime levels.[13] One of the key strategies employed was creating "community engagement teams," which were comprised of volunteer youth leaders from Planetboom who would patrol the city at all major events, including New Year's Eve and cultural festivals such as White Night and Moomba Festival. After the first event where community engagement teams from Planetboom were engaged to patrol the crowd of 500,000+ in attendance, the Police Inspector reported back that there was a 41 percent decrease in crime compared to the previous year's event. The inspector shared that they had observed that the teams' ability to connect with multicultural youth was as effective as approximately 100 detectives on the street with regard to crime prevention.[14]

In subsequent events in 2017, a significant decrease in crime was recorded. Intelligence came back that this was a result of the leaders of the youth gangs pledging not to act if members of Planetboom youth leadership were present—such was their reputation and rapport amongst these groups. Detectives responsible for the behavioral profiling of gang members also noted that when gang members interacted with Planetboom youth leaders, their behavior was entirely different and did not match anything they'd seen in the profiling and monitoring of these teenagers up to that point.[15]

The success of community engagement teams was publicized widely in a documentary by SBS as well as in news reports and articles in the *Herald Sun*, Channel 9, and *The Age* newspaper.[16] The inspector responsible for this initiative and the formal partnership between Victoria Police and Planetshakers wrote of it, saying, "I firmly believe that the concept of community engagement teams is an initiative that is effective and must continue in the future, particularly at these major events. I understand that my superiors were very impressed with our partnership and the commitment demonstrated by your staff."[17] The youth leaders who took part in these teams were able to pray with, minister to, and witness to hundreds of teenagers—as well as the Melbourne Police on the streets each time they went out. In response, many came to Planetshakers Church and were led to Jesus on the streets in those moments.

In the Victoria Police Annual Report of 2016–17, which was presented to Parliament by the Minister for Police, Lisa Neville MP acknowledged Planetshakers' valuable partnership in preventing crime, detecting and apprehending offenders, and improving public safety.[18] From 2017–2019, Planetshakers also received an annual award acknowledging their work in multicultural youth communities and were invited to march with Victoria Police and emergency services at Moomba Parade in 2019 in front of 100,000+ as a display of partnership. The Police Inspector responsible for our partnership and initiative was awarded the Australian Police Medal at Government House in 2019, acknowledging his work and strategy in engaging groups like Planetshakers to combat youth crime and edify multicultural youth communities.[19]

Planetboom's success with the police opened the door for them to consult with leaders of juvenile prisons as well as the Department of Corrections and Justice in Victoria, policy writers, social workers, and Children's Court Diversion Coordinators. We were also able to engage and divert many youths involved in low-level crime, reform those who had come out of prison, and reintegrate them into the church community, as well as support the families and communities involved. Planetboom has since raised up young leaders who specialize in juvenile detention, corrections, the media, and the education system. The first group of South Sudanese teenagers to come into Planetboom have emerged as leaders in these areas as well as the arts, sports, and ministry.

For example, in 2020, a partnership was established between one of Australia's largest football clubs and Planetboom to speak about anti-racism in high schools across Victoria. Two of the key speakers include Emmanuel (EJ) Jakwot, Planetboom's first South Sudanese youth pastor (one of the original teenagers to come from this community), and Noah Walker, Planetboom's first Pacific Islander youth pastor. The miracle of the influence that has taken place in both of these ethnic communities has come full circle due to these two young men who were saved and discipled in Planetboom, which is now facilitating the program. This anti-racism program is the first of its kind and leading in the space of sports culture and school curriculum. Subsequently, EJ has gone on to become a youth spokesperson in schools and the media, appearing on a national left-wing television program to speak about his faith, salvation story, and the goodness of God.[20] EJ's life and words present just one of the exemplary testimonies that are possible because of the transformative power of the gospel.

A Healing Testimony

Further evidence of revival has been recorded in the many miracles and healings that have taken place in the lives of young people during this time. There are too many to recount here, but whole families have experienced salvation as the result of the change and healing they have witnessed in their teenagers' lives. One particular testimony that affected our community was of a 14-year-old boy from Planetboom who was diagnosed with leukemia in 2020.[21] Only his mother could visit him in the hospital while he received treatment during lockdown, and after several months, he was put into an induced coma to try to save his life. After a few weeks in this state, his prognosis was dim.

Doctors exercised a compassionate exemption to invite the entire family to say goodbye at the hospital, predicting he would not last the weekend. This was the first time that his siblings, including his older sister who was a leader at Planetboom, had been able to see him in months. After being confronted with the reality of his condition, this young woman responded to the doctors' news by saying that she had faith to speak to this mountain and see it. She believed that her brother would not die but would be healed. She invited the doctors to join her as she prayed with her family for a miracle. Then our church began to rise up and pray, with young people organizing prayer meetings online to ask God for a miracle.

From the moment his older sister first prayed in the hospital ward, little miracles began to happen. Doctors were astounded to see the young man's red blood count begin to slowly rise and his eyelids begin to flutter when they spoke to him. He began to gain strength and fight the infections that were crippling his body. A few weeks later, he was eased out of the coma. Upon waking, he told of the dreams that he had during the coma of voices praying over him. He testified that he knew it was only by the prayers of others that he was alive. Doctors came back to his older sister after his astounding recovery and acknowledged that they had seen a miracle take place, just as she had prayed for. Several months later, this young man was declared cancer-free and has been so since. There were more testimonies that came out of this hospital of other children and medical staff who were reached as a result of this amazing testimony.

Conclusion

It is difficult to capture all that has happened in our church community in one short chapter or to know which story arcs to follow. But perhaps the story of Noah Walker is a fitting conclusion because it brings us up to the present. As a promising young footballer with a Pacific Islander background, Noah was far from God but attracted to Planetshakers by encountering his presence here. Later, before Noah committed his life to Christ and completed his diploma at Planetshakers College. During that period, he met and married Aimee Evans, the founding pastors' daughter. Andrew and Susannah Harrison subsequently moved into an oversight role, and Planetboom has been entrusted to Noah and Aimee to lead. As youth pastors, this new couple typifies the move of God that has been happening at Planetshakers for years: Christian heritage meets a new generation hungry for God with the presence and power of the Holy Spirit, and the revival passes to yet another set of hearts and hands. Indeed, "This is a move of God. We didn't start it, and nothing can stop it."

Notes

1. Our Instagram handle, "pbdevotions," continues to record many spontaneous testimonies.
2. I think in particular of firsthand accounts from the Azusa Street revival, and others that circulated in the years following in publications like *The Apostolic Faith*. But I also have in mind Augustine's frustration: that accounts of contemporary miracles that he was personally aware of were largely unknown because they had not been told. In *City of God* 22.8, Augustine tells of a woman who was supernaturally healed from cancer. When he realized that the church in her city did not know of the miracle, he was indignant and invited her to testify so that God might receive glory.
3. Planetboom, "Move of God: Planetboom Official Lyric Video," YouTube, December 4, 2022, https://www.youtube.com/watch?v=fh3fv0andas/, accessed August 20, 2024.
4. The following accounts were gathered from personal interviews and from the Planetboom Devotions feed on Instagram (user name: "pbdevotions"), Instagram, February 20, 2022.
5. Sebastian Licciardi, observations from Boom Camp as told to the authors, September 27, 2022.
6. Lavei Tukuafu, personal correspondence to the authors, September 29, 2022.
7. See also Clayton Coombs and Scott Lim, "Planetshakers," in *Brill's Encyclopedia of Global Pentecostalism Online*, eds. Michael Wilkinson, Connie Au, Jörg Haustein, and Todd M. Johnson (online edition, 2019), https://doi.org/10.1163/2589-3807_EGPO_COM_044872.
8. Audrey Tandiokusuma-Fakhrsadeh, personal interview with the author (Susannah Harrison), September 30, 2023.
9. "Community Hubs," Believe Global, https://believeglobal.org/community-hubs/, accessed November 20, 2023.
10. "Empower Australia: 1 Million Meals Distributed to Victorians in 11 Months," CrowdInk, February 22, 2021, https://crowdink.com/food/empower-australia-1-million-meals-distributed-to-victorians-in-11-months/, accessed November 20, 2023.
11. "2021 Census: Nearly Half of Australians Have a Parent Born Overseas," Australian Bureau of Statistics, June 28, 2022, https://www.abs.gov.au/media-centre/media-releases/2021-census-nearly-half-australians-have-parent-born-overseas/, accessed November 5, 2023.

12 Paul Karp, "Peter Dutton Says Victorians Afraid to Go Outside Because of 'African Gang Violence,'" *The Guardian*, January 3, 2018, https://www.theguardian.com/australia-news/2018/jan/03/peter-dutton-says-victorians-scared-to-go-out-because-of-african-gang-violence, accessed August 20, 2024.

13 David Hurley, "Melbourne Youth Summit 2017: Police Chief Launches Push to Get Young Criminals to Work," *Herald Sun*, October 25, 2017, https://heraldsun.com.au/news/law-order/melbourne-youth-summit-2017-police-chief-launches-push-to-get-young-criminals-work/news-story/da9a8abdf415e48118f7d48b164b3a9b, accessed August 20, 2024.

14 Inspector Stephen Mutton, in personal interview with Susannah Harrison, March 2, 2017.

15 Inspector Stephen Mutton, follow-up interview with Susannah Harrison, March 29, 2017.

16 See for example, Tammy Mills, "Forget Shootings and Sieges, This Cop Leaves a Better Legacy," *The Age*, May 24, 2019, https://www.theage.com.au/national/victoria/forget-shootings-and-sieges-this-cop-leaves-a-better-legacy-20190507-p51ky4.html/, accessed August 20, 2024; also "Victoria Police and Planetshakers at Moomba 2019!," Facebook Video, March 10, 2019, https://www.facebook.com/victoriapolice/videos/victoria-police-at-moomba-2019/556072128240238/, accessed August 20, 2024; and Planetshakers being acknowledged in "We're Live with Deputy Commissioner Andrew Crisp and Police Minister Lisa Neville RE. Moomba Festival," Facebook Video, March 11, 2017, https://www.facebook.com/victoriapolice/videos/were-live-with-deputy-commissioner-andrew-crisp-and-police-minister-lisa-neville/1458877474184384/, accessed August 20, 2024.

17 Inspector Stephen Mutton, business email to Susannah Harrison, March 18, 2017.

18 Graham Ashton, *Victoria Police Annual Report* (Melbourne: Victoria Police, 2017), 37.

19 Linda Dessau, "List of Australia Day Honours," Australian Honours and Awards (Government House, Victoria: Government of Victoria, April 5, 2019), https://www.governor.vic.gov.au/sites/default/files/2019-03/Australian%20Honours%20and%20Awards%20Friday%205%20April%202019.pdf/, accessed January 1, 2022.

20 "Keeping the Faith," *Insight (episode 33, season 2022)*, SBS, https://www.sbs.com.au/ondemand/watch/2074704963548, accessed August 20, 2024.

21 The following testimony about Oback Chol was shared with Susannah Harrison, by his sister Marna Chol, in September 2021. It was subsequently shared with the church and leadership on September 28, 2021.

16 *Kata Pneuma*: European International Churches and Next Gen Immigrant Youth

Anthony J. Gryskiewicz

Abstract

As immigration increases in Europe, cultural hybridization seems to be accelerating. How will sociologists and anthropologists classify a child with a father from one culture and a mother from a second culture, with the child being raised in a completely different third culture? How will missiologists and practitioners engage with cultural hybrids? Pentecostal international churches in Europe are engaging immigrants, refugees, globalized Europeans, and, arguably, cultural hybrids. Examining the praxis of the two most prominent models of Pentecostal International church within the Fellowship of European International Churches (FEIC)—the mono-congregational and the multi-congregational models—this paper offers suggestions on how to better reach cultural hybrid youth in Europe's vast urban areas.

Introduction

One Sunday morning, as I turned to greet the people sitting next to me, I noticed several new faces in the crowd happily chatting in Romanian with some church members. As I approached the group, several turned to me and effortlessly code-switched to American English and greeted me. At the same time, an Austrian church member came to welcome the visitors, and some code-switched to Austrian German to speak to him. A few minutes later, the music faded, and the countdown ended, indicating the end of the give-and-greet time. The entire congregation code-switched from whatever language they were using—German, Romanian, Mandarin, or Igbo—and began to sing in some variation of World English.

I was distracted by the thought: why do people choose to worship in a language not indigenous to them? There are many Austrian and Romanian churches in the city; why choose an English-speaking one? One of the characteristics of international churches (ICs) that scholars have discussed is that they use English yet draw people from many different cultures and nationalities.[1] This brief essay will examine the praxis of Pentecostal international churches in Europe through the postmodern lens of cultural hybridity and will explore how ICs can adjust their praxis to more effectively reach what Jan Nederveen Pieterse calls the "global *mélange*"[2] of culturally hybrid youth present in Europe's urban areas.

Multicultural Church Literature

Heterogeneous churches in the United States are arguably "multiethnic" rather than "multicultural." While there are certainly differences between various co-cultures in the United States, there are also shared commonalities. To state it succinctly, there are more cultural commonalities between African Americans, Chinese Americans, and Anglo Americans in an American church than among Nigerians, Spaniards, and Filipinos in a German IC. Therefore, while "multiethnic" may be the best word to describe churches in the United States, "multicultural" may be a better descriptor for ICs. Nevertheless, multiethnic church literature offers insights useful to ICs, especially the studies regarding immigrant churches in the U.S. and Canada that indicate a change in praxis,[3] and how the contact hypothesis has produced positive results in interracial churches.[4]

Immigrant Churches

When an immigrant church starts, it usually uses the immigrants' first language. For example, Latino churches often use Spanish while Korean immigrant churches usually use Korean. The choice of language is understandable since the target audience of immigrant congregations is immigrants. Some language-based immigrant churches are multicultural. It would not be uncommon for an immigrant Latino church to attract Mexicanos, Venezolanos, or people from other Latin American countries. Due to the nature of language distribution, other immigrant churches may be more limited in their reach—e.g., Korean and Ethiopian immigrant churches. Few people outside Ethiopia would be fluent enough in Amharic to participate in worship, and neither Amharic nor Korean are generally taught in Western schools.

The language barrier has led to a unique challenge in immigrant and some international churches: how do these churches retain their youth and reach the population of their new country with the gospel? Daniel Rodriguez observes that some Latino churches in the U.S. have responded by becoming bilingual—using Spanish and English in the same service.[5] As a result of this change in praxis, Latino churches retain their non-Spanish speaking youth and reach their English-speaking neighbors with the gospel.[6]

Similarly, in Canada, some Korean immigrant churches use Korean while others use a combination of Korean and English. Nam Soon Song found that Korean immigrant churches that integrated their youth services and used English and Korean in the church functioned well together and "appeared much happier than those groups separated by language."[7] Perhaps this unity is a byproduct of the contact hypothesis and propinquity effect, which will subsequently be explained.

The Contact Hypothesis

Simply stated, the contact hypothesis suggests that group contact among different ethnic or cultural groups can reduce prejudice. Closely related to the contact hypothesis is the propinquity effect—that people tend to develop friendships and romantic attachments with those with whom they spend significant time. George Yancey found, for example, that church participation promotes primary relationships and interracial contact in a religious setting that corresponds "with more responsive attitudes with Whites" (per APA guidelines) towards African Americans."[8] In other words, as individuals continue group contact with people from other cultures and ethnicities, they begin to see the other as a part of their in-group. As a result, Yancey reports, "bias toward former outgroup members tends to become dramatically reduced."[9]

The contact hypothesis and the propinquity effect are positive outcomes in multiethnic churches in the U.S. It would also seem that this is the case in ICs. A common theme among multiethnic churches in the U.S, and presumably among European ICs, is the reconciliation that occurs. Multiethnic churches fall into two broad categories regarding reconciliation. The first group, what Gary L. McIntosh and Alan McMahan have termed "reconciliation churches,"[10] prioritize reconciliation and social justice among ethnic groups. The second category of multiethnic church focuses on reconciling God and humanity, with reconciliation between people occurring as an intentional byproduct: as people are reconciled with God and start living out a biblically informed worldview, they become reconciled with others.[11]

While there appears to be tension among multiethnic churches in the U.S. regarding prioritizing social justice, reconciliation, and the gospel, this tension has not been observed in the Pentecostal ICs in Europe. McIntosh and McMahan posit that "Biblically speaking, the number one priority for a disciple of Jesus Christ is not doing social justice. The primary purpose in relation to the world is evangelization."[12] Perhaps because the Pentecostal ICs in Europe are missional churches focused on evangelism, the tensions over reconciliation are not an issue or, at least, are not apparent.

The Fellowship of European International Churches

The Fellowship of European International Churches (FEIC) is a relational network of Pentecostal International Churches. In its mission statement, the FEIC offers its members support, resources, and leadership training "specific to international ministry."[13] Pentecostal ICs are not required to join the FEIC but volunteer to associate themselves with the network. The data Larry Henderson provides indicates that, as of 2018, 82 FEIC-affiliated churches existed in 38 European countries.[14] Our more recent demographic study of the FEIC indicated that 152 nationalities were represented in the 31 churches that responded to the survey.[15] Findings from the European IC demographic study and insights from Stephen D. Dye and Paul Dreessen that are pertinent to this project include the ubiquitous use of English and the presence of Europeans, immigrants, and refugees within European international churches.[16]

The Use of English

Michael Crane and Scott Carter observe that "English is the *lingua franca* of the world."[17] Dreessen concurs that the prevalent presence of the English language has helped international churches spread across the globe.[18] One participant in Dye's study commented that "English is a language that unites many people because [even though] many people don't have it as a mother tongue, they still speak it, so that many people can come here (to worship)."[19]

In Europe, English is taught in most schools, and approximately 94 percent of students in the European Union learn English.[20] The international churches belonging to the FEIC have leveraged the prevalence of English in Europe to their advantage to reach out to immigrants, refugees, and

Europeans. Interestingly, Dreessen found that speaking English was one of the few commonalities found among the socially, economically, and culturally diverse people in international churches.[21] It should be noted, however, that while English is the primary language used in European ICs, many English-speaking congregations often translate the services into other languages.[22]

The Presence of Immigrants and Refugees

The creation of the Schengen area—an agreement among 29 European nations to forego internal border controls—has dramatically facilitated the ease of travel among EU member states.[23] For example, a resident of Slovenia can immigrate to Spain, Norway, or Germany as easily as a New Yorker can move to Florida or a Californian to Texas. Furthermore, immigrants from outside Europe who receive permanent residence status in one EU country can do likewise. Many people from Africa, Asia, and Latin America can, therefore, be found within the Pentecostal ICs of Europe.[24] Our research found that the average number of nationalities represented in international churches of Europe was 30.42, with 96 being the highest number of nationalities reported in one European international church.[25]

Within the FEIC, 61 percent of the churches reported having refugees in attendance.[26] Many refugees originate from areas closed to the gospel, but they are exposed to the good news for the first time when arriving in Europe. According to Henderson's research, numerous refugees have responded to the evangelistic efforts of the European international churches.[27]

In summary, immigrants, refugees, and Europeans are attending international churches. The data indicate that ICs reach many cultures, including cultural hybrids. The participants in Pentecostal ICs come from various socio-economic, ethnic, and cultural backgrounds and, for the most part, prefer to worship in English rather than their indigenous language or mother tongue of the country. International churches also provide space for ethnic groups to worship in culturally contextualized ways—whether in an ethnic congregation, small group, or special gathering.

Cultural Hybridity

Arising in urban areas with large immigrant populations is what many postmodern scholars identify as "cultural hybridity." Cultural hybridity is defined by Pieterse as "the mixing of Asian, African, American, European cultures." In his words, "Hybridization is the making of global culture as a global *mélange*."[28] James A. Banks further notes that:

> Cultural hybridity constitutes the effort to maintain a sense of balance among practices, values, and customs of two or more different cultures. In cultural hybridization, one constructs a new identity that reflects a dual sense of being, which resides both within and beyond the margins of nationality, race, ethnicity, class, and linguistic diversity.[29]

The theory of cultural hybridity suggests that the binary way that anthropologists, sociologists, and missiologists have categorized people may no longer be relevant in today's rapidly globalizing world, as argued by Pascal-Yan Sayegh.[30] How do we categorize people who have a Nigerian father and an Irish-Chinese mother? What impact will cultural hybridization have on Ralph Winter's "People Group framework," or the often-discussed "Homogenous Unit Principle" within the missions community? More to the point, how can ICs adjust their praxis to better reach the cultural *mélange*[31] that will only continue to develop in the urban centers of Europe?

Models and Praxis of European International Churches

As previously noted, there are two primary models of an IC—mono-congregational and multi-congregational models. Both models have their advantages and disadvantages. In Europe, the mono-congregational model is more prevalent than the multi-congregational model. In the mono-congregational model, one congregation creates spaces for ethnic expressions of worship, as illustrated in Figure 1.

In the mono-congregational model, there is excellent potential for intercultural contact. The participants meet regularly to worship, thus creating a great opportunity for the contact hypothesis and propinquity effect to operate. However, participants can still meet in mono-cultural ministry groups for worship, prayer, and extended fellowship. The mono-congregational model allows for easier service scheduling and less competition for space than the multi-congregational model. The mono-congregational model would also seem to function with less staff and produce less sideways energy than the multi-congregational church.

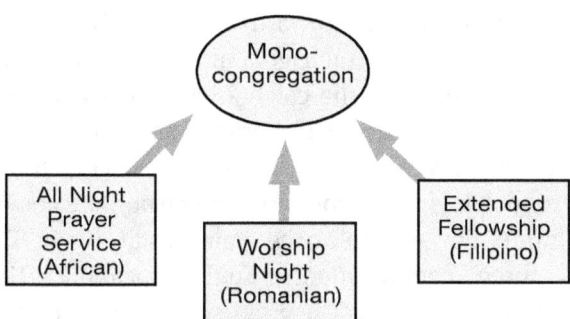

Figure 1: Mono-Congregational Model of an International Church

While the mono-congregational model does provide space for weekly expressions of cultural worship, a weakness of the model is that it does not provide for church services in different indigenous languages and styles. Since the operational language of ICs in Europe is English, often but not always translated into the indigenous language of the host country, participants must have some fluency in English or the national language. This limitation excludes people from mono-congregational ICs who lack enough fluency in English or prefer to worship in their native language.

The multi-congregational model of the international church can be somewhat challenging to depict depending on if it uses Manuel Ortiz's rental, celebration, or integrative model.[32] Figure 2 illustrates the rental and celebration models. In the multi-congregational model, different congregations operate all under the umbrella of the IC. While the church has one lead pastor, each sub-congregation often has its own pastor, lay leaders, and leadership team.

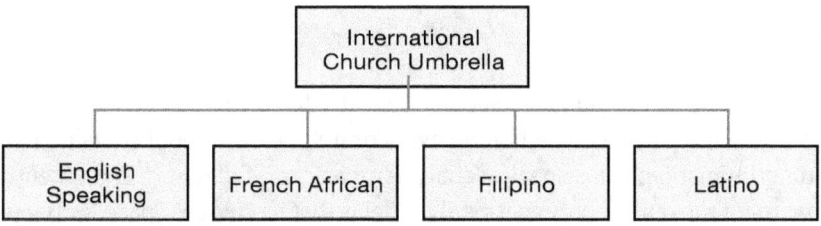

Figure 2: Multi-congregational Model (Rental-Celebration) in an International Church

While a few ICs are moving toward an integrative style, no data indicate that they have realized their goal at this time. Few, if any, ICs use the rental model; however, the celebration model is quite popular. A celebration model has different ethnic congregations that come together several times a year for a celebration service.[33] In the multi-congregational model, it is not uncommon for one or more congregations to be multicultural. For example, the Pentecostal IC in Bucharest, Romania, has three congregations—English-speaking, Romanian-speaking, and Nepali-speaking. The English and Romanian-speaking congregations have people from different cultures, while the Nepali congregation is homogenous. Vienna Christian Center (VCC) in Austria likewise has eight congregations, and all but two are multicultural, as illustrated in Table 1.

Congregation Name	Primary Language	Worship Style	Homogeneity	Translates Services
International Fellowship (IF)	English	Western	Multicultural	Yes
JesusZentrum (JZ)	German	Western	Multicultural	Yes
Filipino Fellowship (FF)	Tagalog	Ethnic	Monocultural	No
African Fellowship (AF)	English	Ethnic	Multicultural	No
French African Fellowship (FrF)	French	Ethnic	Multicultural	No
Latino Fellowship (LF)	Spanish	Ethnic	Multicultural	No
Farsi Fellowship (FaF)	Farsi	Ethnic	Multicultural	No
Ethiopian Fellowship (EF)	Amharic	Ethnic	Monocultural	No

Table 1: Vienna Christian Center Congregations (Multi-Congregational IC)

As Ortiz notes, language seems to be the factor that drives at least the above congregations to be homogenous or not, i.e. few people outside their ethnolinguistic groups speak Nepali, Amharic, or Tagalog.[34] The essential feature of the multi-congregational model is that it provides space for people to worship in their indigenous language using familiar worship structures.

Two prominent strengths of the multi-congregational model are that it provides space for the church to grow and reach people who may not be drawn to the mono-congregational English-speaking model, and the strength of their numbers. The different congregations of the church can pool their resources and do things they could not do independently such as purchase property, build a church, marshal large numbers of people for community projects, and make their voices heard in the community. Globally, several Pentecostal ICs are classified as megachurches.

A significant weakness of the multi-congregation model, however, is that it limits cross-cultural contact with people in other congregations. While the staff may be in constant contact, there are few opportunities for members of the different congregations to meet each other except for quarterly or biannual celebration services.

To mitigate against the weakness of limited contact between the congregations, some ICs are developing cross-congregational ministries. Examples include youth, student, men's, and women's ministries that are open to people across all the sub-congregations. These ministries increase contact with people from other cultures and help reduce sideways energy by reducing replicated ministries. Ministries that meet weekly, such as students and youth, should see more significant results from the contact hypotheses and propinquity effect. Future studies would be helpful regarding this data.

Reaching Cultural Hybrids

If cultural hybridity is increasing, then it would seem that ICs would be well-suited to reach cultural hybrids. It could be argued that they are reaching them already since many of the participants in the English-speaking worship services appear to be cultural hybrids. At first glance, the worship services of ICs may seem identical to those found in the United States. However, a deeper analysis would reveal that they have adopted practices from many different cultures. These changes could include the length of service, extended greeting and singing times, or other elements not usually found in Anglo-American churches. Yet, these elements would be familiar to many cultural hybrids.

The mono-congregational model of the IC would need minimal, if any, adjustment to reach hybrids since their structure is formatted to minister to immigrants, refugees, and globalized Europeans in one congregational setting. On the other hand, the multi-congregational model may need some adjustments to facilitate reaching hybrids. Using the structure of VCC in Table 1 as an example, it would appear that the International Fellowship (IF) and JesusZentrum (JZ) are attracting hybrids. The IF is drawing hybrids who wish to worship in English, and JZ is attracting hybrids who want to worship in German. However, much like the immigrant churches studied by Rodriguez[35] and Song,[36] other congregations draw primarily first-generation immigrants and refugees.

Furthermore, there is tension among second and third generations of immigrants—the cultural hybrids, who may want to worship in English or the national language, but feel pressure from their parent's collectivistic cultures to stay in the ethnic congregations. Both Rodriguez and Song note that cultural hybrids, the youth, and second-generation immigrants are leaving church.[37] Helen Rose Ebaugh and Janet Saltzman Chafetz find that the more an immigrant congregation focused on "recreating the ethnic ambiance of the old country," that the same were "the most likely to alienate their youth."[38] Some of the chief complaints were that hybrids did not speak the parent's indigenous language well (or at all), and they did not identify culturally with the older generation.[39] Perhaps it would be accurate to say they identified more with their new culture.

Curious to get an insider perspective, I asked a young adult named John (pseudonym) about the tensions he experienced as a second generation immigrant worshiping in a collectivistic immigrant congregation. John seemed to fit the ideal of a cultural hybrid being of Asian descent, but born and raised in Europe. He is fluent in German, English, and his parent's native language. He went to university in the U.S. for his bachelor's degree and earned his master's degree in Europe. I asked him, "If you married an Anglo-European, she probably would not speak (parents' native language). She would speak German and likely English. Where would you go to church? Would you select an English-speaking congregation or a German-speaking service?" With a serious look in his eyes, John responded, "Pastor, it would be better for me not to attend church *anywhere* (emphasis his) than to go to a different church."

Importantly, first-generation immigrants cherish worshiping together and fellowshipping with people who treasure the same cultural values.[40] So eliminating ethnic congregations would be counterproductive.

The question becomes, how can multi-congregational ICs retain their cultural hybrids in the church while continuing to reach others with the gospel?

Following in the Footsteps of Others

After examining the literature on multiethnic churches in North America, two suggestions for multi-congregational international churches arise. First, follow the example of immigrant churches in North America who have already traveled this path. Second, create new pathways following the leading of the Holy Spirit.

Regarding the first suggestion, immigrant churches in North America have often struggled to retain their youth and reach the national population with the gospel. Some have responded to the challenge by becoming bilingual. This is a difficult decision, and many older, first-generation immigrants in Latino churches have felt forced to choose between being marginalized or losing their cultural identity.[41] Still, when faced with the possibility of losing their youth, they made the change in praxis. Similarly, immigrant congregations of the ICs in Europe are faced with a choice to change or potentially lose succeeding generations who are becoming cultural hybrids. By offering a translation of their services into the host country's language, first-generation immigrants will meet the felt need of their children and grandchildren—that is, having services in a language they understand. Additionally, immigrant family communication and dynamics tend to improve when the parent's fluency increases in the host language and the children's fluency in the parents' indigenous language develops.[42] By hosting bilingual services, churches could potentially raise the fluency of both parents and children.

The added benefit of switching to a bilingual model is that hybrid youth and young adults can invite their friends to attend church. In other words, the potential for evangelism increases— which is the reason why Pentecostal ICs exist in the first place, to reach people with the gospel. A bilingual model would allow hybrids such as John to participate in services with a spouse and children who do not speak the indigenous language of the immigrant church.

Finally, research like Song's indicates that segregating youth ministries based on language is less than optimal.[43] Likewise, Ebaugh and Chafetz found that "unity is best generated by a system that does not segregate the immigrant generation along linguistic lines."[44] In Europe, where English is the *lingua franca* and second or third-generation immigrants are fluent in their host country's language, it makes sense to host bilingual services in English and the national language. Certainly, having a single youth or university ministry versus multiple ones creates less sideways energy and less competition for church resources. A few multi-congregational ICs are moving in this direction. By having one youth group or one university ministry that operates in English and the national language for the entire church, multi-congregational ICs create a safe space where cultural hybrid youth can meet and be discipled.

Creating New Pathways

Regarding my second suggestion, to create new pathways led by the Holy Spirit, I address the situation of many second and third-generation immigrants continuing to feel pressure from their collectivistic, ethnic congregations to stay within the ethnic congregation. As a result, many like John feel it is better not to attend church *anywhere* than to fight the cultural expectations of their families. Rather than justify why they choose a different church or congregation, they may feel passive resistance to not attending church at all is a better option than active resistance to defend their own choice of church. Occasionally, hybrid youth have told me that they use excuses such as work, school, or other obligations to justify their lack of attendance in the ethnic fellowships. Indeed, in one multi-congregational IC, if a cultural hybrid youth wants to change congregations, they first must seek their congregational pastor's blessing (permission) before making the change. Some hybrid youth have confessed that during these meetings, a tremendous amount of pressure is placed on them to stay in the ethnic congregation.

Accordingly, one way to retain hybrids who feel locked in ethnic fellowships is to create safe pathways for them to change congregations. This change would necessitate buy-in from the congregational pastors. They would need to learn to let people go to the congregation that best fits their needs. If Latino churches struggle with the change to become bilingual, no doubt that some immigrant congregations of ICs will initially struggle with the change. It may be that congregations that are highly collectivistic and tend towards authoritarian leadership styles may struggle the most. As Spirit-led people, however, Pentecostal IC leaders should change their church structures *kata pneuma*— according to the Holy Spirit— to best meet the needs of their culturally hybrid youth.

Conclusion

Without a doubt, the international churches of Europe are successfully reaching immigrants, refugees, and global nomads.[45] The significant presence of second and third-generation immigrants indicates that they are also reaching a substantial number of cultural hybrids in Europe's urban centers. While mono-congregational ICs seem well-positioned to reach hybrids, the multi-congregational churches could adjust their praxis to optimize their impact: first, by developing bilingual immigrant congregations that meet the language needs of their children; and second, by intentionally establishing cross-congregational ministries that minister to second and third generation immigrants in English and the national language. Finally, multi-congregational ICs should consider creating safe pathways for immigrant hybrids to move between congregations while being led by the Holy Spirit. By creating these new structures and adjustments in praxis, perhaps culturally hybrid youth like John can rediscover a home in church. Then, rather than finding excuses not to attend church, they (and their children) can be active participants in the family of God.

Notes

1 Michael Crane and Scott Carter, "Gateway to the Nations: The Strategic Value of International Churches in a Globalized Urban World," *International Journal of Urban Transformation* 4:1 (2019), 111–30; Paul Dreessen, "The International Church Experience: How English-Speaking International Churches Reach, Disciple, and Minister to Their Target Audience" (Ph.D. diss, Asbury Theological Seminary, 2020), ProQuest; Stephen D. Dye, "Mission in the Diaspora: Multicultural Churches in Urban Germany Initiated by Church Planters from the Global South" (Ph.D. diss, Biola University, 2017), ProQuest; Anthony J. Gryskiewicz, Anna K. Gryskiewicz, and Tomas Gollery, "Every Tribe and Nation: A Demographic Study of the Fellowship of European International Churches," *Missiology: An International Review* 49:4 (2021), 362–374, https://doi.org/10.1177/00918296211011713.

2   Jan Nederveen Pieterse, "Globalization as Hybridization," in *Sociology of Globalization: Cultures, Economies, and Politics*, ed. Keri E. Iyall Smith (New York: Taylor & Francis, 2013), 39.

3   Daniel Rodriguez, "Hispanic Ministry Where Language Is No Barrier: Church Growth Among U.S.-Born, English-Dominant Latinos," *Great Commission Research Journal* 1:2 (Winter 2010), 189–201; Daniel Rodriguez, *A Future for the Latino Church: Models for Multilingual, Multigenerational Hispanic Congregations* (Downers Grove, IL: InterVarsity Press Academic, 2011). Also see Nam Soon Song, "Youth Ministry That Matters: Voices of Korean Canadian Youth," *The Journal of Youth Ministry* 15:2 (2017), 97–120.

4   George Yancey, "An Examination of the Effects of Residential and Church Integration on Racial Attitudes of Whites," *Sociological Perspectives* 42:2 (1999), 279–304, https://doi.org/10.2307/1389630.

5   Rodriguez, "Hispanic Ministry Where Language Is No Barrier," 192; also Rodriguez, *A Future for the Latino Church*, 158.

6   Rodriguez, "Hispanic Ministry Where Language Is No Barrier," 198.

7   Song, "Youth Ministry That Matters," 106.

8   Yancey, "An Examination of the Effects of Residential and Church Integration," 300.

9   George Yancey, "Not White Fragility, Mutual Responsibility," *Shattering Paradigms* (blog), July 16, 2020, 19, https://www.patheos.com/blogs/shatteringparadigms/2020/07/not-white-fragility-mutual-responsibility/, accessed June 2024.

10 Gary L. McIntosh and Alan McMahan, *Being the Church in a Multi-Ethnic Community: Why it Matters and How it Works* (Indianapolis: Wesleyan Publishing House, 2012), 154.

11 Mark DeYmaz, *Building a Healthy Multi-Ethnic Church: Mandate, Commitments and Practices of a Diverse Congregation* (San Francisco: Jossey-Bass, 2007), xxvii; McIntosh and McMahan, *Being the Church*, 160.

12 McIntosh and McMahan, *Being the Church*, 160.

13 "What We Offer," Fellowship of European International Churches, https://www.feic.org/about/what-we-offer/, accessed June 2024.

14 Larry Henderson, "The Impact of International Church Ministry in Europe," AGWM Europe, 2018, https://static1.squarespace.com/static/5addfd41d274cb5da0494590/t/5bb4fe94eef1a1ffa8029417/1538588324376/Inspiring+Revitalization+Update+v1.pdf/, accessed June 2024.

15 Gryskiewicz, Gryskiewicz, and Gollery, 367.

16 Gryskiewicz, Gryskiewicz, and Gollery, 362–374; Dye, "Mission in the Diaspora," 1–286; Dreessen, "The International Church Experience," 1–173.

17 Crane and Carter, "Gateway to the Nations," 115.

18 Dreessen, "The International Church Experience," 2; Dye, "Mission in the Diaspora," 161.

19 Dye, "Mission in the Diaspora," 121.

20 Eurostat, "Foreign Language Learning Statistics," Eurostat: Statistics Explained, 2021, https://ec.europa.eu/eurostat/statistics-explained/index.php/Foreign_language_learning_statistics/, accessed June 1, 2024.

21 Dreessen, "The International Church Experience," 2.

22 Crane and Carter, "Gateway to the Nations," 112.

23 European Commission, "Free Movement–EU Nationals," Employment, Social Affairs, and Inclusion, https://ec.europa.eu/social/main.jsp?catId=457/, accessed June 17, 2019.

24 Crane and Carter, "Gateway to the Nations," 111; Gryskiewicz, Gryskiewicz, and Gollery, "Every Tribe and Nation," 367.

25 Gryskiewicz, Gryskiewicz, and Gollery, "Every Tribe and Nation," 367.

26 Gryskiewicz, Gryskiewicz, and Gollery, "Every Tribe and Nation," 369.

27 Henderson, "The Impact of International Church Ministry in Europe," 7.

28 Pieterse, "Globalization as Hybridization," 46.

29 James A. Banks, "Cultural Hybridity," in *Encyclopedia of Diversity in Education*, vol. 1 (SAGE Publications, 2012), 523.

30 Pascal-Yan Sayegh, "Cultural Hybridity and Modern Binaries: Overcoming the Opposition between Identity and Otherness?" (Liverpool, U.K.: Cultures in Transit, 2008), 1–13, https://halshs.archives-ouvertes.fr/halshs-00610753/, accessed June 2024.

31 Pieterse, "Globalization as Hybridization," 46.

32 Manuel Ortiz, *One New People: Models for Developing a Multiethnic Church* (Downers Grove: InterVarsity Press Academic, 1996).

33 Ortiz, *One New People*, 69.

34 Ortiz, *One New People*, 65.

35 Rodriguez, "Hispanic Ministry Where Language is No Barrier," 189–201; Rodriguez, *A Future for the Latino Church*.

36 Song, "Youth Ministry That Matters," 97–120.

37 Rodriguez, "Hispanic Ministry Where Language is No Barrier," 200; Song, "Youth Ministry that Matters," 98.

38 Helen Rose Ebaugh and Janet Saltzman Chafetz, "Dilemmas of Language in Immigrant Congregations: The Tie that Binds or the Tower of Babel?," *Review of Religious Research* 41:4 (2000), 447, https://doi.org/10.2307/3512314.

39 Rodriguez, "Hispanic Ministry Where Language is No Barrier," 200; Song, "Youth Ministry that Matters," 101.

40 Ebaugh and Chafetz, "Dilemmas of Language in Immigrant Congregations," 447.

41 Rodriguez, "Hispanic Ministry Where Language is No Barrier," 194.

42 Thomas Schofield et al., "Parent and Child Fluency in a Common Language: Implications for the Parent-Child Relationship and Later Academic Success in Mexican American Families," *Journal of Family Psychology* 26:6 (December 2012), 869–79, https://doi.org/10.1037/a0030423.

43 Song, "Youth Ministry that Matters," 106.

44 Ebaugh and Chafetz, "Dilemmas of Language in Immigrant Congregations," 448.

45 Crane and Carter, "Gateway to the Nations," 115; Dreessen, "The International Church Experience," 7; Dye, "Mission in the Diaspora," 144; Gryskiewicz, Gryskiewicz, and Gollery, "Every Tribe and Nation," 372.

17 Reimagining the Holy Spirit as Life-Giving Spirit for the Next Generation

Alexander Stavnichuk and Jean-Daniel Plüss

Abstract

This chapter begins with a brief review of the European contributions to this volume by J. D. Plüss, who highlights several relevant elements. Then A. Stavnichuk attempts to elaborate a pneumatological model of encounter that emphasizes creativity, resonance, and openness for the Other. These latter trends shape young Christians and are part of the reality of many churches. In connection to the Pentecostal understanding of the Holy Spirit, an ecumenically responsible pneumatological approach will be developed that draws its strength from both a deeply trinitarian understanding of God's loving nature and work through the Spirit, as well as a life-giving understanding of Spirit-baptism and a creative Spirit-inspired openness to the world. Understanding the activity of the Holy Spirit in a trinitarian person-relating and koinonia-giving mode—as love or longing for God—can provide a solid theological basis for developing a theology of Christian creativity, innovation, and openness to the world. Finally, in response to Stavnichuk's analysis, Plüss provides a short assessment of European contributions relating to the reformulation of Pentecostal theology within a twenty-first century context.

Introduction: The Next Generation of Spirit-Empowered Christians in Europe (Jean-Daniel Plüss)

While the strong growth of European Pentecostal churches in the second half of the twentieth century pushed its leaders to find ways to manage more complex congregational structures, recent developments have been marked by a drain in church attendance. The Pentecostal Assemblies of Switzerland, for instance, have not seen any significant growth within the past twenty years, despite fruitful ministry with immigrants. The situation is similar in Germany and other Western nations. If there is church growth, it is mainly due to people transferring from other churches. These congregations may be spiritually vibrant but often have little impact on society.

Furthermore, young Christians who leave their faith communities once they reach adulthood and become socially and economically independent pose a real challenge for the future of Christian presence in Europe. What cultural developments and attitudinal changes lead young adults to reassess their faith and, in some cases, abandon the church they considered their spiritual home while growing up? What are they missing in their churches? What kind of concerns are important in their lives? How are they willing to invest themselves?[1] Such questions demand serious reflection and call for responsible action.

Another significant factor in European church life is evidenced by the migration of a sizable part of the population. Never before has this continent been so multicultural. Urban churches especially, that once did well in a single language context, are now called to rethink their ministries along multilingual and multicultural lines. Here again, it is the younger generation that pushes the boundaries and calls for change. Spirit-led church leaders are called to be sensitive to the situation and meet the needs of culturally hybrid youth. One may wonder in an analogical fashion: if Pentecostal-Charismatic Christians want to be "people of the Spirit," what understanding of pneumatology are they cultivating, and are they open to insights from other church traditions?

Articles from this volume written from European contexts address some of these change issues. The piece by Anthony J. Gryskiewicz on international churches in Europe, and Caleb Nyanni's reflection on second-generation African Pentecostals in the West, address the importance of community life among Christians who have immigrated and the linguistic/multicultural challenges they face. The chapter by Ulrik Josefsson and Fredrik Wenell, and the ensuing study by Alexander Stavnichuk, explore a Pentecostal understanding of the work of the Holy Spirit that is responsive to societal shifts evident in a secular European context, where the faith of young people changes and brings unique challenges to traditional ecclesial practices and theology.

The Social Climate of Our Time (Alexander Stavnichuk)

If we ask today about current trends and dynamics of our time that are shaping the thoughts and actions of young people, and are an integral part of today's Christian church, an interesting picture emerges. In social theories of resonance, singularities, and the creative aestheticization of society, human beings desire a conscious resonant relationship with the world.² In the theory of creative dynamics of human life, an individual is oriented "towards a creative shaping of his subjectivity."³ Not only does an individual see him or herself as a creative subject, but the creation of the new stimulates the senses and has an affective effect. This effect consists of the fact that what is creatively new touches the individual through its vibrant affect and emotional involvement. Singularity, resonance, and creative aesthetic theories have in common that the role of the individual is emphasized, including their inner processes, and a person's emotional involvement in world events is perceived. Commonalities of these trends concern the inner spiritual sphere of human life and the ability to creatively encounter world reality.⁴

The aesthetic perception of reality, spiritual empathy, imaginative thinking, joyful curiosity for the new, and the ability to perceive a hidden reality and to act on it—to open oneself to new inspirations and to develop new ideas from them, to look for creative ways to encounter the other views of life—all these abilities circumscribe aesthetic and creative human behavior.⁵ This condition in the world should encourage Christians, especially in churches that see themselves as Spirit-empowered, to reflect on whether we are equipped with the necessary knowledge, attitudes, and skills to face the complexity of the creative and innovative dynamics of human society. Creating openness to world reality means painfully overcoming one's own limits. Overcoming the limits of our ego-related personhood entails the courage to give up oneself and one's way of self-centered thinking. This is a creative process of transforming our attitudes and behavioral skills. It raises the question of the motivational power of transcending one's own limits.

In Search of a Pneumatological Approach to Encountering World Reality

The search for an effective prototype for Christians' openness to the world, as well as creative and innovative action, brings pneumatology to the center of new theological reflections on an appropriate framework for innovative, active encounter with world reality. From my point of view, Pentecostalism receives a new actuality due to its theological approaches which consider the Christian life to be centered around direct encounter with the activity of the Holy Spirit as a present reality.⁶ However, the challenge is whether the traditional Pentecostal understanding of the experience of the Holy Spirit can be defined as life-giving or life-creating activity. If Pentecost is to be understood in the Christological context of Acts 1:8 ("...and you will be my witnesses..."), one has to conclude that the alive, risen Jesus Christ is at the heart of the purpose for which the Holy Spirit fills the apostles. They are to be witnesses of the fact that Jesus lives.[7] Even the Greek expression for witnesses of Christ, μάρτυρες, denotes a person who testifies from direct personal experience about events in which the person was involved.[8]

In the context of this meaning, the Holy Spirit brings about the experience of a living encounter with Jesus and his resurrection power. I wonder if it would not be the theological task to understand this encounter in terms of life-giving, aesthetic categories such as vitality, passion for life, creativity, transformation, and innovation. From this perspective, it could be assumed that Christ's resurrection power can be experienced in the human person as a flow of creative life energy of the Holy Spirit. Such renewing and life-creating is in line with the Nicene Creed that the Holy Spirit is a life-giving Spirit.[9] The concept of the Holy Spirit as the life-giving Spirit implies a thought that the action of the Holy Spirit in the life of the church has a progressive character: the action of the Holy Spirit stretches through time and is life-giving, lasting, and changing, creating new possibilities and ways through active, renewing, and dynamic activities of Christians. In a theoretical sense, in view of their exclusive relationship with the life-giving reality of the Holy Spirit, the activity of Spirit-empowered Christians must sparkle with special vital energy and with creative, life-inspiring new ideas. If Christians are to assert themselves as representing a practical worldview of resurrection faith, of new Spirit-filled life, they must show themselves to others as a movement of creative, vibrant, and inventive people. In the rediscovery or innovative shaping of the church or the mission of God-willing solutions, the church actualizes the potentialities of life, and the vital substance of the body of Christ is expressed.[10] For a non-Christian, nothing is more convincing of the vital potentiality of Christian witness as the transforming, sustainable, and creative struggle of Christians for the living actuality of their reality of faith in every situation of life.

However, what remains open for me in this thesis, and what has not yet been sufficiently elaborated by Pentecostal theologians, is an ecumenically legitimate and encouraging theological basis for establishing openness to the Holy Spirit in the daily, creative practices of Christians. For this fruitful re-imagining, Pentecostal theology needs the aid of interpretive models of the Holy Spirit from other denominations. By this I mean the Pentecostal interpretation of the meaning of Spirit-baptism should have help from pneumatological concepts and patterns of thinking from other confessional traditions. For this reason, I have attempted to place the Pentecostal model of openness to encountering the Holy Spirit into an ecumenical discourse on understanding the Holy Spirit as the life-giving Spirit.

An Ecumenical Approach to the Life-Giving Activity of the Holy Spirit

In ecumenical theological discourse, there is a broad consensus that the Holy Spirit affects the participation of Christians in *koinonia* (communion) with the triune God.[11] He is the promoter of *koinonia* (c.f. 2 Cor 13:13), that is, the one who creates *koinonia* between Christians and the Trinity. The Spirit's creative activity, therefore, has a participation-creating character. In this participation-creating activity, the Holy Spirit reveals himself as fostering two-dimensional activity, expressed not only by horizontal sharing of life within the community but also by vertical participation or sharing in God's life.[12] The Holy Spirit indeed gives humans new life by participating in the life of God. Therefore, the important question is: in what way does the Holy Spirit act as the participation-creating and life-giving Spirit of the trinitarian *koinonia*? And how can this effect be experienced?

Thinking in Christological terms, this activity is modeled first by the life of Jesus Christ. He embodies in his life and mission, as well as in the outpouring of the Holy Spirit, the life of God as the loving, passionate turning of God to the human being. This divine movement of love, or waves of God's love, expresses the life of God as he is in himself. Also, in the doctrine of the Trinity, the self-giving mutual love between the persons of the Trinity signifies the inner life of God. I refer here to the ecumenical interpretation of the relationships between the Trinity, understood as flowing love, especially in the report of the first section of the Fifth World Conference on Faith and Order in Santiago de Compostela (1993) which states that the life of the Trinity consists in giving and receiving love.[13] Each person of the Trinity is constituted in selfless giving to the other person. In mutual giving, the three persons are one. This love or mode of God's personal life is *ek-stasis* in the language of the Catholic and Orthodox trinitarian traditions, i.e. a movement of leaving oneself towards the counterpart. The life as it lives in God can therefore be experienced not only as an *ek-static* love to God but also insofar as you love others or turn to your counterpart.

If we ask about the connection between the action of the Holy Spirit and the mode of *ek-stasis*, then his trinitarian action as the life-giving Spirit of *koinonia* consists of implanting in humans this personal, *ek-static* turning that characterizes God himself.[14] This is a vertical dimension of participation in God's life. If the Holy Spirit is understood to be the bearer of the principle of God's triune life of love, then the experience of his participatory and life-giving mode is measured by the analogy to trinitarian personhood. This means his life-giving activity takes place in the experience of his moving towards the object of love. Because the Holy Spirit is God, in his longing for us he works in us the same longing or turning to God. One could say that the Holy Spirit becomes the personal turning of man to God. The Holy Spirit mingles with man and at the same time remains distinct from man. Rudolf Bohren expresses this beautiful enmeshment as, "The Spirit becomes anonymous, is hardly identifiable anymore, it mixes with the human.... It works by interfering: the creaturely, that which is."[15] In other words, man comes alive in the experience of passion for God. This is a revival by the Holy Spirit and can be experienced as passion, desire, and involvement.

For our initial question, this means that the way the Holy Spirit works is through mutual activity. He involves the human being in activity as if this activity were a passion of man. However, if the Holy Spirit is understood as a life-creating Spirit in the self-giving mode of life, the Spirit inside a person can also be experienced as an eagerness for creativity, invention, and innovation. This is because being caught up in a living, loving flow of creation can affect an experience of inventing and discovering new possibilities. It is analogous to the self-transcending or self-giving activity of the Holy Spirit, which also invents and actualizes.

A New Pentecostal Model of the Life-Giving Activity of the Holy Spirit

Now we need to relate this kind of life-giving activity of the Holy Spirit from the ecumenical perspective to a Pentecostal understanding of the Holy Spirit. To do this, I suggest the following model. The specific characteristic of a Pentecostal understanding of the Holy Spirit is that the human person encounters the Holy Spirit personally and directly in the experience of Spirit-baptism.[16] However, this need not only be for divine empowerment for mission. The implanted desire for the Holy Spirit expresses the totality of human life in relation to God. Thus the Spirit's fullness may be perceived as a subjective experience of being drawn to God, as an ongoing love or longing for God.[17]

Thereby, man is not only moved by the striving for an exclusive supernatural experience, as in Spirit-baptism, but by the affection of love for God as a counterpart. That the love of God and Spirit-baptism was thought of as one in the earlier phase of Pentecostalism has been pointed out by Geoffrey Sutton and Martin Mittelstadt:

> First, love stands as the primary motivation not only for conversion, but also Spirit baptism. Recipients of God's vast love reciprocate their love to God with vibrant enthusiasm. ... It was a baptism of love. Such abounding love! Such compassion seemed to almost kill me with its sweetness! People do not know what they are doing when they stand out against it. The devil never gave me a sweet *[sic]* thing, he was always trying to get me censuring people. This baptism fills us with divine love.[18]

Love for God is understood in this quotation as the *motivation* for Spirit-baptism and at the same time as the *result* of the baptism in the Spirit. I see in this understanding of the activity of the Holy Spirit an analogy to the *ek-static* structure of trinitarian love.[19] If one wants to understand *ek-static* love as the experience of the love-awakening efficacy of the Holy Spirit, then the circle of participation in communion with God must be extended to the personal opening of man to God in the sense of personal desire for God´s presence in the Holy Spirit.[20] To be passionately oriented towards God as counterpart, and to love God, is the same activity of the Holy Spirit towards the Father and the Son.

Moreover, in a new model, God's love is not thought of abstractly but in terms of going outside oneself into active, existential, personal moving towards God. A similar line of thought is discovered in Orthodox tradition.[21] I extend the connection between the baptism in the Spirit and love with reference to Dumitru Staniloae, by locating the reciprocal activity of the Holy Spirit in the human conscious desire to encounter the reality of the Holy Spirit.[22] In the light of the mutual trinitarian understanding of the Holy Spirit, I see the effect of the Holy Spirit in the reaching out to be filled with the Spirit because, in the process of *ek-stasis as modus vivendi*, the going out of oneself to God as a counterpart finds its expression. *Ek-static* does not only mean reaching the climax of pleasure, but also, transferred to the language of attitudes and actions, entails an energetic empathy: the ability to get outside oneself, one's ego-relatedness, one's limited knowledge, one's scheme of action felt in one's own body—and into what it means, for example, for someone else to be living in the vicious circle of poverty or in the margins.

In the same mode, namely, as the going out of oneself, the Holy Spirit works in Christians the passion and inspiration for new ways of doing mission and living as a church. He helps us break boundaries. When we discover this life-giving mode of the activity of the Holy Spirit, it makes us open and sensitive to his creative life-giving activity in us personally and in all spheres of life. In his trinitarian mode, he brings the new to life and, through their activity, brings newness into the world by inspiring us with creative and innovative ideas and enabling us to implement them. Both aspects of the life-giving action of the Holy Spirit, ecstatic and reciprocal, can be therefore experienced as electrifying—by giving new ideas, visions, motivations, fruitful imaginations, empowerment, freedom, and relentlessness for implementing our ideas. The creative and transforming effect of the Holy Spirit captures the human being as his or her own creative dynamic.

Practical Implications

The following conclusions can be drawn from the above reflections on the life-giving activity of the Holy Spirit:

Firstly, the trinitarian dimension of the Holy Spirit allows the practice of opening to the Holy Spirit from the point of view of love towards God.

The trinitarian analogy of being a person with a desire to encounter the personal presence of God frees the perception of a direct encounter with the Holy Spirit from the suspicion of excessive mystical speculation or from the danger of over-spiritualizing the Christian faith. Dealing with the reality of the Holy Spirit ceases to be a special field and moves to the center of reflection on the human condition and the Christian transformative practice of life.

Secondly, understanding the life-giving activity of the Holy Spirit makes pneumatology the starting point for applied practical theology, especially regarding Christian creativity and innovation. A good way to respond to the creative climate of the current human world is by reflecting on and unfolding Christian practice as a life-giving and creative activity of the Holy Spirit. Pneumatology is our critical theory for life. This has a significant influence on the question of "Who am I, as a person?" in view of the indwelling of the Holy Spirit. Behind this is a consideration of what I must do in my faith and life to consciously encounter the life-giving work of the Holy Spirit.

Thirdly, in the light of the trinitarian understanding of the Holy Spirit as the life-giving Spirit, such dynamic categories as inspiration, ideation, devotion, love, passion, inner involvement, enthusiasm for a vision, and creativity gain legitimate value as theological, pneumatological terms in sense of relational ontology. They can form a new framework for the development of the practical approach to life-giving pneumatology and ecclesiology.[23]

Fourth, the practicable spirituality of openness to the Holy Spirit makes Christians sensitive and attentive to their inner movement both in the spiritual, emotional, physical, and intellectual spheres. In this context, one speaks of the ethics of attentiveness. The expression "ethics of attentiveness" was developed by the Orthodox theologian Dumitru Staniloae. It involves a sensitivity to the immanence of God in the world and assumes human rationality is embedded in cosmic rationality.[24] Applying this approach to the Pentecostal openness to the Holy Spirit, the ethics of attentiveness would mean a sensitivity to the life-giving dynamism of the Holy Spirit. It expresses itself not only in forms of inner divine vision and in Christian virtues, as in the case with Staniloae, but also in the affective sphere of humans in their experience of new ideas, constructive visions, devotion, and even longing for church projects—in enthusiasm, inspiration, and motivation to design new ideas. The mode of openness to the reality of the Holy Spirit makes the theologian sensitive to discovering the themes in the Bible and in theology from the point of view of the new original, resonant, and relevant to the present issues and to express the Christian message attractively, aesthetically, and powerfully. The analogous similarity between an aesthetic effect and the effect of the Holy Spirit can help to form a theological way of thinking that connects the aesthetic way of being with the theological way of thinking. It would be the task of pastors not only to feel the impact potential of a theological thought or a biblical text but to find the creative means of expression that trigger resonance inside a person.[25]

Fifth, the trinitarian mindset of the Holy Spirit forms a spirituality for fostering creativity and innovation in every Christian, regardless of their natural gifts. By this, I do not mean glamorous, perfect, and performance-oriented creativity, but the creativity of everyday life—imperfect creativity. It will be the task for theological education to derive the practice of Christian training from the pneumatology of creativity and innovation. It will also be necessary to provide competencies for creating innovative and inspirational climates that train congregations to perceive and realize the life-giving activity of the Holy Spirit in the form of new inspirations, ideas, and motivations in themselves. When I think of the above-mentioned skills and needs for training pastors and missionaries to act innovatively, I have in mind a type of founders, the *spiritual entrepreneurs,* who, like the apostles, thought creatively and acted innovatively as pioneers of new forms of church and life in the power of the life-giving Holy Spirit.

I would like to use a practical example to show the applicability of the trinitarian approach of openness to the Holy Spirit. It is about creating a culture of encounter and openness to others in the sense of strangers, enemies, or foreigners. The dynamic that moves us towards others is the love that God pours into us. This foundation forms a spirituality of encounter with the Other. It allows a human being to experience his/her limit, being a responsive person in relation to the Other. It forms a culture of compassionate justice according to God's justice. This helps young people rediscover an inspirational pneumatological framework for such activities of the churches as creation care (a passionate turning to the sacred creation), as well as a responsibility for peace and justice.

Especially in view of Russia's war against Ukraine, the future Christian task of reconciliation means nothing else than an openness to the stranger (and enemy) as an ability to get outside oneself, an *ek-stasis*. This ecstatic love can only be brought about by the Holy Spirit. I hereby plead for the development of a theology and spirituality of encounter with Others based on the *koinonia*-mode of the Holy Spirit as love.

However, my experiences as the founder of the pastoral training program "Spiritual Entrepreneurship in Church and Mission" caused me to feel caution and restraint in churches when it comes to training innovation and openness to the world, ideas, and foreigners. An inspiring theological orientation from the point of view of encountering the life-giving activity of the Holy Spirit can encourage the next generation to open itself for new, interesting, and live-giving actions. But it also requires a new generation of theologians to rediscover effective und inspiring concepts, symbols, and narratives which move them towards creative and unconventional action, as well as provide a theological framework that aligns the practice of Christian faith with new priorities such as justice or peace.

Conclusion (Jean-Daniel Plüss)

Recently, Pentecostal theologians and authors engaging with the Charismatic renewal movement have weighed in on the future of the church.[26] This present volume is a witness to the same desire to study the current life of the churches and suggest ways forward. The contribution by Gryskiewicz looked at European international churches and the dilemmas leaders face. Is it more meaningful to operate a multi-congregational church or be part of a community that gathers different cultural and linguistic groups into one church? The answer may depend on the nature of the participants: are they part of an expat group or are they migrants? Are they mostly of the Baby Boomer generation or Gen Z? The work of Gryskiewicz is a first step in sorting the challenges.[27] One of the main points he makes resonates with the other European contributions, namely the importance of a living and relevant faith community. The contact with different ethnic groups, he suggests, will lead to less cultural prejudice. This is a point that is important to a new generation increasingly sensitive to justice issues.

Caleb Nyanni studies second-generation diaspora Pentecostals.[28] He understands that church attendance by these young adults attempts at primarily meeting their spiritual and physical needs; denominational loyalties are less important. Similarly, their understanding of Pentecostal practices is open to change. For instance, they still value Spirit-baptism but less in the sense of being empowered to address evil spirits, as their parents would have done, and more along the lines of having divine power over issues of daily life and personal conduct. Interesting is the transformation of missional zeal. The focus on evangelism and personal salvation seems to be widening to include issues of social action. These two points (widening the understanding of Spirit-baptism and evangelism) raise the question if the new generation of Pentecostals will be more ecumenically open. Furthermore, Nyanni speaks about young Christians' need to feel the empowering presence of the Holy Spirit as they worship.

This element dovetails with the Swedish contribution. The article by Ulrik Josefsson and Fredrik Wenell confronts secularization in Swedish society and its impact on their youth. Due to the Lutheran heritage in that country, there is room for privatization of faith. In other words, having faith is fine, but it no longer governs society as a whole. "[P]ersonal faith is subject to questioning," they state.[29] In my opinion, there is an opportunity among Pentecostals to reassess the role and importance of the practice of sharing testimonies publicly—both for the development of the faith of believers and as a means for sharing the living gospel in a secular and pluralist context. Fascinating is also the suggestion by Josefsson and Wenell that the notion of repentance is changing from a surrender to God experienced at a certain moment, to something that is more like a process of growing in faith. This has two implications. First, the role of the Holy Spirit in coming to faith needs to be better understood. Second, that many young Christians feel comfortable with an understanding of spiritual growth that is more common in mainline churches than traditional Pentecostal ones. This has ecumenical implications, some of which this chapter has explored.

Finally, the Swedish contribution calls the reader to reflect on the importance of community and worship. People leave a congregation, Josefsson and Wenell say, when it becomes "irrelevant and increasingly peripheral" in its beliefs and practices.[30] This is especially the case when cognitive dissonances persist. Here, the above-mentioned study by the

Barna Group is useful because it shows that cognitive dissonances appear in different areas. There are ethical dilemmas between the morality the church embraces and predominant societal views. To give an example, the attitudes of young European Christians towards gender issues are much more relaxed. But there is a dissonance between the older generations that often espouse a critical attitude towards the sciences, and the younger generations that are much more open to scientific insights. Another tension might be perceived when correlating faith and social engagement where justice and peace are concerned. Pentecostal churches need to be places where serious questions can be asked and honest answers can be given, which will hopefully also result in practical commitments.

This text by Alexander Stavnichuk, a German theologian and pastor with Ukrainian roots, takes up this issue of dissonance and introduces the social theory of resonance from a Pentecostal perspective. That is to say, that Christian faith, when it is alive, is in a resonant relationship with the world. His academic reflection focuses on the understanding of baptism in the Holy Spirit by adding to the classical Pentecostal understanding of empowerment, a dimension that is dear to the Orthodox tradition— namely, the work of the Holy Spirit in facilitating an opening to the world as sacred reality in relation to God. This opening to the world has its foundation in a trinitarian understanding of the Holy Spirit. It is, on the one hand, an introduction to fellowship (*koinonia*) with the triune God, which is based on the mutual sharing of love. On the other hand, the Spirit prompts a longing for God. This Orthodox understanding can help widen the Pentecostal view of Spirit-baptism ecumenically and facilitate a new theological articulation of the same. Stavnichuk emphasizes the transforming effect and creative dynamic of the Holy Spirit in the life of the believer. The five practical implications iterated at the end call the reader to further pursue Spirit-empowerment as an inspiring force in the life of the church; to become a community open to moving forward and interacting with the world in the name of Christ, to the glory of God. Last, but not least, Spirit-baptism opens the possibility of reconciliation of estranged people by the love of God.

Wolfgang Vondey, another Pentecostal theologian from the Old World, has similarly advocated for the renewal of the theological agenda among Pentecostals.[31] This is precisely what Stavnichuk is attempting. This task is confronted with a twofold challenge: on one hand, protecting orthodox Christian thought and praxis, while on the other hand, reaching out to the boundaries of the church's discourse. It seems to me that the European articles in this compendium are raising the right issues and making useful contributions to assessing the future of the Spirit-empowered church.

Notes

1. A number of socio-religious studies have been published by the Barna Group that look at key insights from young adults (18–35-year-olds) across the world, such as "In Review: 3 Key Insights About Young Adults Around the World," Barna Group, August 24, 2022, https://www.barna.com/research/reviewing-global-young-adults/, accessed December 14, 2022. The full study is available at "The Connected Generation–A Barna Project in Partnership with World Vision," Barna Group, 2020, https://theconnectedgeneration.com/, accessed June 1, 2024.

2. Sociologist Hartmut Rosa understands resonance as a modality of interrelation between a subject and its world. In the theory of resonance, the experiences of resonance are experiences of being touched and moved. "Singularity" means highlighting the special, a deviation from the usual. See Hartmut Rosa, *Resonanz: Eine Soziologie der Weltbeziehung* (Suhrkamp Verlag, 2016). Also Andreas Reckwitz, *Die Erfindung der Kreativität: zum Prozess gesellschaftlicher Ästhetisierung* (Berlin: Suhrkamp Verlag, 2013), 229.

3. Andreas Reckwitz, "Die Erfindung der Kreativität," in *Kulturpolitische Mitteilungen* 2:141 (2014), 23–34.

4. I would mention the recent encyclical from Pope Francis, "Fratelli Tutti," regarding openness to the world and the creation of a Christian culture of encounter with strangers. See "Encyclical Letter Fratelli Tutti of the Holy Father Francis on Fraternity and Social Friendship," §§92.88, Vatican.ca, https://www.vatican.va/content/francesco/en/encyclicals/documents/papa-francesco_20201003_enciclica-fratelli-tutti.html/, accessed January 12, 2022. A similar idea can be found in the preamble to another significant ecumenical text, "Christian Witness in a Multi-Religious World. Recommendations for Conduct," which shows a turn towards the understanding of mission as encounter and dialogue in love and respect with a genuine interest in the other person. See *Mission Respekt: Christliches Zeugnis in einer multireligiösen Welt* (Mission Respect: Christian Witness in a Multifaith World) (Hamburg/Aachen: Evangelisches Missionswerk in Deutschland/International Catholic Mission Agency mission, 2016), 5.

5 "Aesthetic behavior is the ability to perceive more in things than they are. The look, beneath that which is, turns into image." Own translation. Original: "Ästhetische Verhaltensweise ist die Fähigkeit, mehr an den Dingen wahrzunehmen als sie sind. Der Blick, unter dem, was ist, in Bild sich verwandelt," Theodor Adorno, quoted by Rudolf Bohren, *Dass Gott schön werde. Praktische Theologie als theologische Ästhetik* (München: Kaiser, 1975), 132.

6 Wonsuk Ma, "Asian Megachurch Ecclesiologies in Conversation with the Church: Towards a Common Vision," in *Towards a Global Vision of the Church: Explorations on Global Christianity and Ecclesiology*, vol. 1, Faith & Order Paper 234, eds. Cecil M. Robeck, Jr., Sotirios Boukis, Ani Ghazaryan Drisse (Geneva: WCC, 2022), 34–35.

7 This aspect was mentioned by Amos Yong, who was asked in the run-up to the Mission Conference in Arusha to work out a Pentecostal view of the transformative discipleship. The experience of the risen Christ through a direct encounter with the Holy Spirit effects the perception, mind, and feelings of Christians. See Amos Yong, "Reflection and Confessing in the Spirit," *International Review of Mission* 1:105 (November 2016), 173.

8 Herman Strathmann, μάρτυς, in *Theologisches Wörterbuch zum Neuen Testament*, Band IV, 479.

9 The third article of the Nicene Creed states, "I believe in the Holy Spirit, the Lord, the Giver of Life."

10 In the language of Nimi Wariboko, this approach of life is called the "pentecostal principle" or "passion of being". Nimi Wariboko, *The Pentecostal Principle: Ethical Methodology in New Spirit* (Grand Rapids: Eerdmans, 2012), 11–44.

11 See "The Unity of the Church as Koinonia: Gift and Calling" §4.1, in Michael Kinnamon, ed., *Signs of the Spirit. Official Report Seventh Assembly. Canberra, Australia, 7–20 February 1991* (Geneva: WCC, 1991), 174. "Guided by the Holy Spirit, we are drawn into a *koinonia* (communion) rooted in the giving and receiving life of the Holy Trinity. [...] *Koinonia* in the Holy Spirit is based on sharing in the life of the Trinitarian God …" Op. cit., 248–249. Also see *Confessing the One Faith: An Ecumenical Explanation of the Apostolic Faith as it is Confessed in the Nicene-Constantinopolitan Creed 381* (Geneva: WCC, 1991), §201, 76.

12 See *Baptism, Eucharist and Ministry 1982–1990: Report on the Process and Responses*, Faith and Order Paper 149 (Geneva: WCC, 1990), 150. Also *The Church: Towards a Common Vision*, §13.

13 See Thomas F. Best and Günther Gassmann, eds., *On the Way to Fuller Koinonia. Official Report of the Fifth World Conference on Faith and Order, Santiago de Compostela, August 1993* (Geneva: WCC, 1994), 231. Also see *Confessing the One Faith*, §§17.18.19, 20–21.

14 Here I make use of Dumitru Staniloae's formulation: "The Holy Spirit unites us in love with God and our neighbor, making himself the bearer of God's love for us and of us for God and of love among ourselves, just as the incarnate Son of God does. He moves us inwardly by the love He has from the Father, turning to us the love of the Father and the love that is between Him and the Father, thus implanting in us His love for the Father and for all men." This is my own translation from the original: *"Der Heilige Geist verbindet uns in Liebe mit Gott und unserem Nächsten, indem er sich zum Träger der Liebe Gottes zu uns und von uns zu Gott und der Liebe unter uns selbst macht, so wie dies auch der menschgewordene Sohn Gottes tut. Er bewegt uns innerlich durch seine Liebe, die er vom Vater hat, indem er uns die Liebe des Vaters und die Liebe, die zwischen ihm und dem Vater ist, zuwendet und damit seine Liebe zum Vater und zu allen Menschen in uns einpflanzt."* Dumitru Staniloae, *Orthodoxe Dogmatik* (Zürich/Einsiedeln/Köln/Benziger/Gütersloh: Gütersloher Verlag, 1984), 255. No better description of this state of affairs can be given here than that of Karl Barth: "Where he [the Holy Spirit] is rightly expected and desired to be received, this is precisely his work already begun, the unmistakable sign of his presence." This is my own translation from the original: *Wo er [der Heilige Geist] recht erwartet und zu empfangen begehrt wird, da ist das eben sein schon begonnenes Werk, das untrügliche Merkmal seiner Gegenwart."* Karl Barth, *Kirchliche Dogmatik. Die Lehre von der Versöhnung*, Band IV, Teil I (Zollikon-Zürich: Evangelischer Verlag, 1953), 723.

15 My own translation from the original: *"Der Geist wird anonym, ist kaum mehr zu identifizieren, er mischt sich mit dem Menschlichen. [...] Er wirkt, indem er sich einmischt: das Geschöpfliche, das Gemachte wird sein Vehikel."* Rudolf Bohren, *Daß Gott schön werde*, 61. This mode of the Holy Spirit's action is expressed as "a God-ordained reciprocity." Rudolf Bohren (also Rudolf Van Ruler) calls this modality "theonome reciprocity." This mode of the Holy Spirit's action has found different expressions in German theology: dialectic of counterpart and proximity (Matthias Haudel); covenant of spirit and deed (Wilhelm Dantine); a giving that gives itself (Michael Böhnke following theses on a trinitarian ontology by Klaus Hemmerle); the Spirit as communicative self-giving (Michael Böhnke); the Spirit as we in person (Heribert Mühlen); the Spirit as self-communication of Christ in the consciousness of man (Karl Barth); the Spirit as directedness of action (Johannes Fischer). See

Matthias Haudel, *Die Selbsterschliessung des dreieinigen Gottes: Grundlage eines ökumenischen Offenbarungs-, Gottes- und Kirchenverständnisses* (Göttingen: Vandenhoeck & Ruprecht, 2006), 105–106; Wilhelm Dantine, *Der heilige und unheilige Geist: Über die Erneuerung der Urteilsfähigkeit* (Stuttgart: Radius, 1973); Heribert Mühlen, *Der Heilige Geist als Person: In der Trinität, bei der Inkarnation und im Gnadenbund: Ich-Du-Wir* (Münster: Aschendorf, 1963); Michael Böhnke, *Gottes Geist im Handeln der Menschen: Praktische Pneumatologie* (Freiburg/Basel/Vienna: Herder, 2017); Karl Barth, *Das Christliche Leben: Fragment* (Zürich: EVZ-Verlag, 1967); Johannes Fischer, *Leben aus dem Geist: zur Grundlegung Christlicher Ethik* (Zürich: Theologischer Verlag, 1994).

16 "First Phase of the Dialogue between the Secretariat for Christian Unity of the Roman-Catholic Church and leading Representatives of some Pentecostal churches, §12, in Harding Meyer, et al., eds. *Dokumente wachsender Übereinstimmung: Sämtliche Berichte und Konsenstexte interkonfessioneller Gespräche auf Weltebene Vol. 1: 1931–1982* (Paderborn/Frankfurt am Main: Bonifatius, 1991), 476–486.

17 Thomas Aquinas wrote about this aspect of love: "God is the ultimate end of all human activity. Therefore, there is no measure in the love that is directed to Him as the final purpose. It is itself a measure or guideline; and the more the activity reaches this measure, the better it is." In *Die katholische Wahrheit oder die theologische Summa des Thomas von Aquin deutsch wiedergegeben durch Ceslaus Maria Schneider, 12 volumes* (translated from German), II-II, Q. 27, 6b. (Verlagsanstalt von G. J. Manz, Regensburg 1886–1892), *Universite de Fribourg*,https://bkv.unifr.ch/de/works/8/versions/811/divisions/170563/, accessed January 12, 2022.

18 Geoffrey W. Sutton and Martin W. Mittelstadt, "Loving God and Loving Others: Learning about Love from Psychological Science and Pentecostal Perspectives," *Journal of Psychology and Christianity* 31:2 (2012), 157–166, *The Free Library.com*, https://www.thefreelibrary.com/Loving+God+and+loving+others%3a+learning+about+love+from+psychological...-a0342175918/, accessed December 12, 2021. The idea of the affective experience of divine love in Spirit-baptism was later taken up in the Charismatic renewals. See Sutton and Mittelstadt refer in this context to Margaret Poloma saying, "The participant experiences divine love that in turn affects human love," in Margaret Poloma, *Main Street Mystics: The Toronto Blessing and Reviving Pentecostalism* (Walnut Creek, CA: Alta Mira Press, 2003), 19.

19 The Holy Spirit is correlated with God's love in the Bible (c.f. Rom 5:5; 1 Cor 12–14).

20 I am aware that *eros*, as man's love for God, may have a negative connotation for some Christians because of the meaning of *eros* in ancient philosophy. However, *eros* is understood in Orthodox tradition as divine eros, as an energy of the grace of God. Dumitru Staniloae refers to Dionisius of Areopagita, who saw no difference between goodness, love, and *eros*. See Staniloae, *Orthodoxe Dogmatik*, 252. Also *Des Heiligen Dionysius Areopagita angebliche Schriften über "Göttlichen Namen,"* Aus dem Griechischen übersetzt von Professor Joseph Stiglmayr S. J. Bibliothek der Kirchenväter, Zweite Reihe, Band II (München: Verlag Josef Kösel & Friedrich Pustet, 1933), 74, Universite de Fribourg, https://bkv.unifr.ch/de/works/149/versions/168/scans/b0074.jpg/, accessed January 12, 2022.

21 Dumitru Staniloae, *Orthodoxe Dogmatik*, 251–255. It is also worth mentioning that the Orthodox tradition of the Holy Fathers does not separate agape and eros. Ibid. Following Jürgen Moltmann, Dumitru Staniloae said, that affectivity constitutes the heart of the Holy Trinity. Quoted by Daniel Munteanu, "Ethik der Aufmerksamkeit. Anthropologische und umweltethische Aspekte der Theologie Dumitru Stăniloae," *International Journal of Orthodox Theology* 9:2 (2018): 32–57, fn. 24, 39.

22 C.f. fn. 14. Staniloae, *Orthodoxe Dogmatik*, 255. In fact, in the Orthodox understanding of the Eucharist, the aspect of devotional orientation towards the Holy Spirit is emphasized. That is why, in the Orthodox tradition, man is called *homo eucharisticus*, "the man who invokes the Holy Spirit." In this Eucharistic action, the original condition of human life, namely, to live in its real personal orientation (devotion) to God, is symbolically expressed. See Daniel Munteanu, "Homo eucharisticus - die anthropologische und kosmische Dimension der Eucharistie," *International Journal of Orthodox Theology* 2:3 (2011), 188–202.

23 I see this approach in Nimi Wariboko's "pentecostal principle" as capacity of social existence to begin something new. See Wariboko, *The Pentecostal Principle*.

24 See Munteanu, *Ethik der Aufmerksamkeit*, 32–57.

25 See Reckwitz, *Die Erfindung der Kreativität*, 25.

26 This has been evidenced in the four-volume-series edited by Vinson Synan, Amos Yong, et al., *Global Renewal Christianity* (Lake Mary, FL: Charisma House, 2016–2017), and publications by authors such as Wesley Granberg-Michaelson, *Future Faith: Ten Challenges Reshaping Christianity in the Twenty-first Century* (Minneapolis, MN: Fortress Press, 2018); Miroslav Volf and Matthew Croasmun, *For the Life of the Word: Theology That Makes a Difference* (Grand Rapids: Brazos Press, 2019); Miroslav Volf,

Öffentlich Glauben in einer pluralistischen Welt (Marburg an der Lahn: Francke Buchhandlung GmbH, 2015).

27 See chapter 16.

28 See chapter 11.

29 See chapter 9.

30 See chapter 9.

31 Wolfgang Vondey, *Beyond Pentecostalism: The Crisis of Global Christianity and the Renewal of the Theological Agenda* (Grand Rapids: Eerdmans, 2010), 196.

18 The Role of Pastors' Children and Young Leaders in Preserving an Awakening in Their Generation

Juan Sebastian Rodriguez

Abstract

Revivals have marked extraordinary times throughout church history. During revivals, multitudes have come to salvation, churches have been awakened, and the power of God has manifested in ways that the powers of darkness cannot oppose it, assuring the advancement of the mission of God. Nonetheless, revivals have often been short-lived. By comprehending the nature of revivals, the complexities of generational transitions, the role of education, and the importance of living in the Spirit, this paper proposes guidelines for young leaders and children of pastors who wish to preserve an awakening in their generation.

Introduction: There is Nothing New Under the Sun

Without a doubt, revival is the desire of the vast majority of ministries and churches. Pastors and young leaders are no exception. In their case, they may have seen the glory of their predecessors' ministries and are overwhelmed by the challenge of living up to such high expectations. Certainly, it is not easy to keep the fire of revival that was kindled by their fathers in a new generation.

Moreover, revivals are complex phenomena. Richard Lovelace observed that what we see in an awakening "is as confusing as a football game in which half the players are invisible."[1] Amid this confusion, historian George Marsden suggests, "Our job is to try to identify players and other forces that are visible and to offer suggestions as to which alignments of these may be most conducive to the positive work of the whole."[2] These suggestions are most welcome since, in the eagerness to experience revival, we can easily get lost. Accordingly, this chapter will suggest what the role of pastors and youth leaders should be in preserving a revival.

What is a Revival?

If pastors and youth leaders are going to play a role in a revival, they must first understand the nature of revivals. Otherwise, their actions will be erratic and, most likely, counterproductive, falling into mere mass evangelism or growth strategies. Revival is much more than an explosive growth of congregations. According to Charles I. Wallace Jr., the term revival represents a periodic need that can be found in all human cultures.[3] He describes revivals as "the most vital and yet most mysterious of all folk arts" and as "periods of cultural revitalization that begin in a general crisis of beliefs and values and extend over a period of a generation or so, during which time a profound reorientation in beliefs and values takes place."[4] Todd M. Johnson and Cindy M. Wu identify the latter crisis of beliefs and values as the starting point of revivals in the Protestant-Pentecostal conception, where the crisis is expressed as "'dead' faith that requires an awakening or revival to rekindle it."[5]

Looking back over church history, it is possible to see revivals in the early church, the Middle Ages, and modern times. Revivals have been studied and theorized, and their characteristics have been identified,[6] but many have always considered them ephemeral events that naturally tend to dissipate so that the life of the church returns to its normal course, as J. Edwin Orr describes it.[7] This is because it is uncommon to see a second generation that gives continuity to a first movement of the Spirit. When approaching this phenomenon, fears, paradigms, preconceptions, failures, oppositions, frustrations, and obstacles have all prevented a continuous flow of the Spirit into a second generation that would transform the different spheres of society such as culture, art, politics, and the economy of a nation. If this pattern is to be changed, youth ministry must assume a decisive role.

The word "revival" does not exist as such in the Bible. However, this does not mean that scripture does not record any—quite the contrary. In the Bible, it is possible to find valid precedents, for example, in the Old Testament records of Samuel (1 Sam 7:1–13:3), of Elijah on Mount Carmel (1 Kings 18:1–46), of Jonah in Nineveh (Jonah 1:1–4:11), of the reforms of kings Asa and Josiah (2 Chron 15:1–18 and 2 Kings 22:8–23:3), and of the combined post-exilic roles of Ezra and Nehemiah (Neh 8:1–11:2).[8]

However, the clearest portraits of revival in the Bible come after the outpouring of the Holy Spirit at Pentecost. The Acts of the Apostles is the most wonderful account of a movement of the Spirit with power, signs, and wonders. Roger Stronstad, in *The Charismatic Theology of St. Luke*, focuses on studying the work of the Spirit in the Gospel of Luke and the Acts of the Apostles, and sheds much light on the concept we have of revivals. According to Stronstad, the coming of the Holy Spirit meant the fulfillment of the promises of the Old Testament and the beginning of a new era.[9] Contrary to what cessationists or one branch of Latter Rain Pentecostals argue, the moving of the Spirit has been like a continuous river throughout history in which each movement of the Spirit contains the seeds for the next revival. It is imperative for every child of God to seek the waves of the Spirit, moving where the river flows since God has a fresh wind, a new wave, for each generation. These waves of the Spirit are accompanied by fresh anointing, which proves the authenticity of the movement, and, at the same time, evokes the unique and autochthonous character of the new awakening.

Based on this understanding, we could say that "revival" is the supernatural, constant, and active power of the Holy Spirit of God over a community, society, church, town, generation, and/or nation. Therefore, a true revival is an extraordinary movement of the Spirit: it is the work of God, in contrast to so-called "revivalism"—the work of men to create at all costs a scenario for a revival without supernatural substance. If revival is the work of God, it is the result of prayer, not the effort of men; although in a true movement of the Spirit, there will always be a mixture of both. Arthur Wallis thus defines "revival" as:

> [A] divine intervention in the normal course of spiritual things. It is God revealing Himself to man in awful holiness and irresistible power. It is such a manifest working of God that human personalities are overshadowed, and human programs abandoned. It is man retiring into the background because God has taken the field. It is the Lord making bare His holy arm, and working in extraordinary power on saint and sinner.[10]

The hand of God is so evident in revival that, Wallis adds, "it has the stamp of Deity upon it, which even the unregenerate and uninitiated are quick to recognise."[11]

Some additional features of revivals can be found by tracing their premodern antecedents, as Leigh Eric Schmidt does in *Holy Fairs: Scotland and the Making of American Revivalism*. Specifically, Schmidt traces the origin of Cane Ridge, one of the centers of the Second Great Awakening, to the ancient Scottish Holy Holidays, or Holy Fairs: a kind of "pious Saturnalia" or western Scottish sacramental gathering in which the holy and the festive, religion and culture, communion and community, piety and sociability were mingled.[12] In Cane Ridge, as in other revivals, we see the continuation of a long tradition as well as the renewal and awakening of not only religion, but culture, society, and art.

Generational Transfer

Having dealt with the concept of revival, now the question arises: how is it possible to maintain a revival beyond the first generation? This question must be in the heart of many young leaders and children of revival pastors. The need for a revival in church is often emphasized, but little is discussed about how one could last and whether it is possible that, once the original leaders of the movement are gone, this awakening could continue to affect the community in which it originated.

But why is it even important for a revival to continue to the second generation? Blaise Pascal hints at this by talking about the longevity of the patriarchs and the preservation of the creation and flood stories. In two of his *Pensées*, he states:

> 322. The length of the life of the patriarchs, instead of causing the histories of past things to be lost, served on the contrary to preserve them. Because what explains that sometimes we do not know the history of our ancestors well is the fact that we have seldom lived with them, and that they often died before we reached the age of reason. . . .

> 324. Trials of Moses: Why is Moses going to make the life of men so long, and so few generations? Because it is not the duration of the years, but the multitude of generations that makes things dark. Because the truth is only altered by the change of men. And yet he makes the two most memorable things ever conceived, the creation and the flood, so close together that they almost seem to be from the same time.[13]

In these thoughts, Pascal seems to be dealing with a subject completely unrelated to revivals. However, it is necessary to remember that churches, and therefore revivals, are communities of families; it is through them that the river of revival can continue to flow. Or it is in them, in the change from one generation to another, in which the fire of a spiritual awakening can be lost—just as in the change from one generation of patriarchs to another in which the memory of the flood or creation could be lost. Pascal argues that Moses speaks of generational transcendence, and so it is expected that the next generation of pastors and young leaders remember, activate, and experience the supernatural power of God in their lives. They must remember the miracles that God did in their fathers' time and see them in their own time in such clear, colorful ways that the splendor of divine glory that once dazzled their parents remains intact in their lives. And, just like their fathers, they need to walk behind the pillar of fire and make of the movement of the Spirit a constant and necessary practice in their lives so they will go where he is leading.

Stating this requires us to define "generation," which, biblically, is a group of people who remember and live a common experience. In the case of a revival, a generation would be made up of individuals who remember the supernatural power of God that initiated a spiritual awakening. Not only do they have the memory of the same supernatural events, but they continue to see and practice them in such a way that their life of faith and the life of the congregation are influenced and affected by it in a particular way. This definition supersedes age. A transgenerational revival would be a refuge where the winds of the Spirit blow to guide the church amid the confusions of current times, by affirming its roots in deep and rich Christian tradition, and leading it to grow beyond the boundaries of traditional church life.

What are the challenges to achieving this generational transcendence? As I said before, the river flows through families. Therefore, attention must be focused on the family to keep it flowing. The relationship between parents and children is key, especially among those who are leaders in the church. The relationship between pastors and their children is complicated due to the intimate knowledge that both know the faults of the other, and the rebellion or deindividuation that the latter may have against the former. From there arises the need for the offspring to placate any inner resistance and submit to the direction and vision that their parents have received from God. Likewise, they must avoid treasuring in their hearts the failures of their parents, so that the pastoral image they have of their parents does not fade. In this way, the children will attain greater authority and will be able to inherit the blessing that rests on their elders.

Moses is a valuable example in the study of the relationship between parents and children, and generational transcendence. In his case, Moses does not seem to have had problems with his sons, Gershon and Eliezer (Exod 18:4), but it is difficult to assume that they were close to their father's ministry, since in the Pentateuch they are only mentioned in two occasions. However, Joshua was close to Moses, going with him where no one else went (Exod 24:13), staying close to him and the presence of God (Exod 33:11), and staying true to the vision that Moses received from God (Num 14:6–9). The role that Moses' sons were indifferent to was treasured by Joshua, and, in this way, it was he who received the anointing that was on the father. Exodus 33:11 summarizes the devotion and closeness of Joshua to Moses: "So the Lord spoke to Moses face to face, as a man speaks to his friend. And he would return to the camp, but his servant Joshua the son of Nun, a young man, did not depart from the tabernacle."[14]

David's life puts nuances on the same problem. David had a complicated relationship with his sons, Absalom and Adonijah. The eldest sons were cut off and, in the end, Solomon inherited the throne. The causes can be found in David's relationship with his children. David was a man full of anointing because he revered God. He ignored the adulation of his men at En Gedi when he had Saul defenseless before him; instead, he respected the anointing that was on the king and refrained from raising his hand against him (1 Sam 24). David honored the anointing and so received it. Absalom, however, sought his glory and did not receive it (2 Sam 15:4–6). By contrast, Solomon did not seek those things that are glorious in the eyes of men (wealth, power, fame), but asked for wisdom (the glory of God) in 2 Kings 3:9; finally, God gave him glory, fame, wealth, and power.

In the context of revival and anointing, what breaks the relationship between parents and children? Children's criticism of their parents is one of them: children who have no qualms about criticizing their parents for their weaknesses and failures will end up imitating them. Not accepting the exhortations of parents, colleagues, or subordinates, or pretending to flee from them diminishes the authority that the children could have. Alternatively, the anointing you respect is the one you receive. Again, the Bible gives two contrasting examples through Ishmael and Isaac of one son who inherited from his father and another one who lost it: Ishmael was unable to transcend or transform his rebellion. The result was that Abraham, his father, gave him gifts and sent him away. Isaac shunned rebellion, however, which caused him to receive his father's patriarchal inheritance and blessing.

Education as an Opportunity to Transcend

Gary Dickson, in his study of revival in the Middle Ages, highlights that revivals start from an orthodoxy, from the need to renew and revitalize a tradition, and not with the motivation to destroy and build again.[15] From this perspective, revival would be about continuity rather than discontinuity, ancient beliefs and values that transcend time but take on a particular relevance at a particular moment in time. Naturally, such beliefs and values are normally transmitted through education.

Education can be understood from the Greek term *didascalia* to be the act of teaching or instructing. This is one of the tasks that Paul entrusts to Timothy: "Till I come, give attention to reading, *to exhortation, to doctrine*" (1 Tim 4:13, emphasis mine). To pastors and young leaders, the Spirit coming and bringing revival is like announcing a new "stock": a new opportunity for strength and capacity for transformation. This is why we feel the weight on our hearts of the question: "How can we maintain a revival in a second generation?" God has made an investment, and we want to steward it and grow its worth. If we are going to take on that burden and that call, pastors must take care of nurturing this new generation and imbuing it with the characteristics that the Lord has determined for the "stock" to increase its value. If the church is willing and able to train their young people, they will impact the church and all the different spheres of society with their strength. But if the stock is sold, the transformation it is meant to bring will end.

For this purpose, theological and biblical education should not be reserved for a group of professional ministers but should be extended to the entire community of believers, including the young. And it should be done with the declared aim of encouraging and mobilizing all members of the church to take part in God's mission. After all, the church is not a handful of people that make up the church leadership, it is the thousands who congregate in it. Carlos Van Engen reinforces these points when he says, "Theological research should not be research into a mysterious academic field within the reach of a privileged few. Rather, it should be the teaching of the essential foundations of biblical faith to mobilize all of God's people to live day by day the missionary implications of radical discipleship.[16]

Thus, young people's education and discipleship must include the willingness to serve. If they are in seminary, graduates must be led to foresee places where they may serve and fulfill the evangelizing task. And if young Christians are going to testify in all social spheres, it is necessary that their training equips them to face the controversies they will find there, including increasingly staunch critics of the faith. This points to the need for an education that, in addition to providing a solid theological foundation, provides a precise understanding of the world and contemporary context. Simple, easy answers to problems such as gender identity or radical feminism, to mention some of the most problematic discussions of our time, will not withstand the weight of the growing ideology and expertise that supports the positions of the contemporary world. If young Christians are to participate in these discussions, they must do so with understanding, depth, lucidity, and cunning; they must be as "wise as serpents and harmless as doves" (Matt 10:16).

Didascalia practiced in this way makes the task of the church, and specifically that of the pastor, more effective. Congregations should not be enterprises driven by the efforts of a single man or a small group of ministers who are assisted by lay servants capable of menial tasks but incapable of carrying out the mission. Instead, let us take the story of the multiplication of the loaves and fishes as a model. There, after Jesus blessed the food, multiplication occurred at the hands of the disciples. We can have this multiplying factor in our congregations if we do not limit ourselves to preaching (*kerygma*). Rather, through a transforming *didascalia*, the *diakonia* that our young people exercise can take them beyond occupying a seat, or simply giving, to become a force that turns the world upside down (Acts 17:6) and establishes the kingdom of God through mercy, justice, and love.

Life in the Spirit

Pastors and young leaders who wish to preserve a revival in a second generation would do well to heed what has been covered thus far. However, the key to revival always comes back to it being a supernatural movement that arises from the will of God and is activated by the Holy Spirit.

Consequently, everything is in vain if the Spirit is left out; if our actions are not in tune with God's desire. For this to be so we must maintain a close friendship and union with the Holy Spirit to such an extent that we dwell, or using the Greek term, live in perichoresis in his presence.

This *perichoresis* describes the life of the Trinity. The term shows us how the three persons of the Godhead live in continuous mutual giving and receiving. The most wonderful thing is that we have been invited to take part in that communion; the preamble of that perfect union has come to us with the Holy Spirit. In John 14:17, Jesus tells us about "the Spirit of truth, whom the world cannot receive because it neither sees Him nor knows Him; but you know Him, for He *dwells* with you and will be in you" (emphasis mine). The Spirit dwells, *perichoresis,* in us, so it is up to each pastor and young leader to prepare themselves for that intimacy where they can discover the blessings that God has prepared for their lives and community. Not only will they know the will of the Father, but they will be trained to do the work that has been entrusted to them.

Jesus himself was able to bear witness to the Father because he dwelt in him, as we see in John 1:18: "No one has seen God at any time. The only begotten Son, who is in the bosom of the Father, He has declared Him." The same thing happened with his disciples who walked, lived, and communed with Jesus to later preach his gospel. It was after John reclined in the Lord's bosom that he was able to say, "And the Word became flesh and dwelt among us, and we beheld His glory, the glory as of the only begotten of the Father, full of grace and truth" (John 1:14).

Conclusion

Jesus is inviting us into his abode: "Behold, I stand at the door and knock. If anyone hears My voice and opens the door, I will come in to him and dine with him, and he with Me" (Rev 3:20). He invites us because he wants to give us revival. Yet, only an intimacy with the Holy Spirit accompanied by adequate reflection on what God has done in the past makes transgenerational revival possible. The Spirit is always in constant movement; therefore, it is the obligation of each community, group, and individual to discern the direction of the Spirit by being in moving *perichoresis* with him, thus taking part in those waves of revival.

The waves and movements of the past are the seeds for new spiritual awakenings in times and places distant from their points of origin. Our role is to cry out to the Spirit so that the distance between wave and wave is reduced and that the seeds that revival plants are harvested by the children of pastors and leaders who planted them. Evidence shows that God has a fresh wind for each generation marked by a renewed understanding of the Holy Spirit, his actions, and his relationship with humankind. Everything will, therefore, depend on the passion we have and manifest for him.

Notes

1 Richard Lovelace, quoted in George M. Marsden, "Neo-Evangelicalism and Renewal since the Mid-Twentieth Century," in *Great Awakenings: Historical Perspectives for Today*, eds. David Horn and Gordon L. Isaac (Peabody: Hendrickson Publishers Marketing, 2019), 94.

2 Marsden, 94.

3 Charles I. Wallace Jr., "Wesley As Revivalist/Renewal Leader," in *The Cambridge Companion to John Wesley*, eds. Randy L. Maddox and Jason E. Vickers (Cambridge: Cambridge University Press, 2010), 82.

4 Wallace, "Wesley," 81.

5 Todd M. Johnson and Cindy M. Wu, "Awakenings and Revivals in the Context of Global Christianity," in *Great Awakenings: Historical Perspectives for Today*, eds. David Horn and Gordon L. Isaac (Peabody: Hendrickson Publishers Marketing, 2019), 210.

6 See, for example, Gary Dickson, "Revivalism as a Medieval Religious Genre," *The Journal of Ecclesiastical History* 51:3 (2000), 473–496; John L. Hammond, "The Reality of Revivals," *Sociological Analysis* 44:2 (1983), 111–115; John F. Wilson, "Perspectives on the Historiography of Religious Awakenings," *Sociological Analysis* 44:2 (1983), 117–120; Richard F. Lovelace, *Dynamics of Spiritual Life: An Evangelical Theology of Renewal* (Westmont: InterVarsity Press, 2020); Timothy L. Smith, "My Rejection of a Cyclical View of 'Great Awakenings'" *Sociological Analysis* 44:2 (1983), 97–101; and William G. McLoughlin, *Revivals, Awakening and Reform* (Chicago: University of Chicago Press, 1978).

7 J. Edwin Orr, quoted in Lovelace, *Dynamics of Spiritual Life*, 53.

8 Tom Lennie, *Land of Many Revivals: Scotland's Extraordinary Legacy of Christian Revivals Over Four Centuries* (1527–1857) (Fearn: Christian Focus Publications, 2015), 36.

9 Roger Stronstad, *The Charismatic Theology of St. Luke* (Grand Rapids: Baker Academic, 2012), 95.

10 Arthur Wallis, *In the Day of Thy Power: The Scriptural Principles of Revival* (London: Christian Literature Crusade, 1961), 20.

11 Wallis, *In the Day of Thy Power*, 23.

12 Leigh Eric Schmidt, *Holy Fairs: Scotland and the Making of American Revivalism* (Grand Rapids: Eerdmans, 2001), 4.

13 Blaise Pascal, *Pensées* (Paris: Le Livre de Poche, 2000), fr. 322, 324.

14 Unless otherwise referenced, all scripture quotations are from the New King James Version (NKJV).

15 Gary Dickson, "Revivalism as a Medieval Religious Genre," *The Journal of Ecclesiastical History* 51:3 (2000), 491.

16 Carlos Van Engen, *El Pueblo Misionero de Dios* (Grand Rapids: Libros Desafío, 2004), 167.

19 Using the Volunteer Function Inventory to Activate Aging Adults as Spirit-Empowered Disciple-Makers for the Next Generation

Kerry Loescher

Abstract

The mandate of scripture for the people of God to both retain and train the next generation is clear (Deut 6:4–9; Joel 1:3). The challenges of this task are also well documented in scripture (Judg 2:10; Ps 78:4) and endure to the modern day. However, a bright spot in the research shows that when healthy, intergenerational, faith-based relationships are present in meaningful ways, the likelihood of a young person becoming a resilient, faithful follower of Christ who enjoys a vibrant life in the Spirit grows. Aging adults in local church congregations are uniquely situated and suited to assist in this critical work. Volunteer motivation theory, especially the Volunteer Function Inventory (VFI), provides essential insight for the recruitment and retention of adult youth workers who come alongside parents, guardians, and church leaders to raise the next generation of Spirit-empowered Christ-followers. This chapter explores the VFI as a means for activating aging adults as Spirit-empowered disciple-makers for the next generation.

Introduction

Throughout my life, I have always found myself seated at the "kids table" for large family gatherings. It was not because I was banished there as an adult; instead, I found that this was where some of the most important and interesting conversations took place. At this table, there are always the best jokes, a few shenanigans that catch the attention of the adult table, and lots of laughter. There are also conversations about the challenges we face and delightful wonderment at the beauty that is possible in the world. Big questions are asked at this table that have life-shaping power. It is an honor to be invited into this conversation, and I have often wondered about the seeming disconnect between the "kids table" and the "adult table" and what that means as all generations move forward—especially regarding how the Christian faith is transmitted from one generation to another.

The idea of intergenerational relationships for the maturation of younger generations and meeting the generativity needs of older generations is not a new idea. In the Old Testament, familial relationships and communal living conditions are described. Allen, Lawton, and Seibel assert, "When God set His people Israel in order, he placed each individual within a family, each family within a tribe, and each tribe within a nation. No generation was excluded, no child left out, no older person put aside."[1] When critical moments or special events occurred within the story of the people of Israel, all the generations were present and participated together. In this way, older generations were generative in their example, and the necessary investment in younger generations for their maturation of faith and identity was instilled (Deut 6:4–9).

However, in today's modern world, life and faith look very different. With current migration trends, fewer children live near their grandparents.[2] The often economically driven reality that families of origin are not geographically close can short-circuit the natural opportunity for intergenerational relationships. While some might assert that in today's wildly changing culture and values landscape, the involvement of grandparents in the lives of grandchildren has little effect on the development of faith and maturity in young people, some research says otherwise. Bengtson, Putney, and Harris, for example, claim that much of religion and maturation in young people are rooted in the quality of intergenerational relationships.[3] Since the support and regular interaction of high-quality relationships between grandparents and grandchildren act as a strong factor for faith development and the maturation of young people, these kinds of connections must be encouraged.

The developmental needs of adolescents, young adults, and aging adults also must be addressed. Adolescence and emerging adulthood are times when young people search to discover their identity and, as Erikson and Erikson argue, establish fidelity. At the same time, aging adults typically raise questions concerning the generative nature of their lives and wonder if they have developed enough strength of integrity in who they are and how they have lived to ward off despair.[4] Interestingly, the two groups have complementary needs that offer opportunities for both to flourish when enjoying healthy relationships with each other. The Stanford Center on Longevity observes that aging adults are "uniquely suited" to assist young people in their discovery of all they are meant to be, while young people are "uniquely suited" to remind aging adults of all that they are.[5]

There is an institution strategically situated where both the young and the aging (with everyone in between) engage each other in meaningful and thriving relationships—the local church. In a time when the religious landscape exhibits volatility across cultures and increasingly more people choose to be religiously unaffiliated, the church's role in passing on a thriving faith to younger generations cannot be understated. Unfortunately, studies such as Kinnaman and Matlock's, among others, reveal a disturbing trend that many young people appear to graduate from faith when they graduate from high school—if they make it into church at all.[6] Or, as Kenda Creasy Dean states, they step into the adult world with a "do good, feel good spirituality" that has little to do with the biblical Christian faith.[7]

Thankfully, a bright spot in the research reminds us that not all hope is lost and that God continues to work in the lives of young people. Even while many young people may avoid church or step into adulthood with less than a fully developed practice of faith, Kinnaman and Matlock maintain that a meaningful number of young adults choose instead to swim against the current as fruit-bearing, discipled believers. This group reports that their relationship with Jesus is real and relevant to the point that it impacts their daily decision-making and sense of vocation.[8] Furthermore, they state that the Bible is their foundation for a life lived in Christ while living in a secular world, and that they are responsible for inviting others to become disciples by sharing the gospel.[9]

What does it take, then, to produce Jesus-followers who are resiliently faithful in the face of cultural coercion, who live vibrant lives in the Spirit?[10] One key ingredient appears to be that these young people resoundingly and overwhelmingly report that they experienced a deep sense of belonging in their local congregation in their developmental years. For many, their church included people who encouraged them in their faith, and among them were adults they counted as close personal friends.[11] Data indicates that intergenerational relationships both inspire, challenge, and teach young people how to have a meaningful relationship with God, as well as model how to live in a fulfilling community with one another. Smith and Adamczyk note that older adults may even play a crucial, relational role in circumstances where parents or guardians are unable or unwilling to spiritually nurture their young people.[12]

Intentionally cultivating a strong sense of connection and warmth within intergenerational relationships, therefore, appears to be non-negotiable for successfully transmitting a deep faith in Christ to the next generation. Studies indicate that relationships are critical in warding off the difficulties of isolation, loneliness, and general mistrust our current culture so easily creates.[13] In a hyperconnected world, Pew Research chronicles that more people of all ages report that while we are all together, we are all alone.[14] Ironically, people of all ages can fall prey to the idea that discipleship is a solo journey, while ignoring both the descriptive nature of discipleship that we see in scripture through the examples of Jesus with his closest followers—as well as the prescriptive direction the Bible lays out for Christ-followers that reminds us to love one another (John 13:34) and not abandon gathering together regularly (Heb 10:25).

Aging and the "New Old"

How, then, can we engage aging adults as relational agents in next-generation discipleship? A stream of volunteer motivation theory known as the Volunteer Function Inventory (VFI) provides structure and insight for the recruitment and retention of persistent, planned aging adult volunteer youth workers. There is a strategic opportunity for wise, seasoned adults to come alongside parents/guardians and church leaders to help raise up the next generation of Spirit-empowered Christ-followers. The rest of this chapter will explore the primary dimensions of the VFI as it relates to the motivations of aging adults. It will then make recommendations for how this tool can be used strategically to recruit and retain aging adults as Spirit-empowered disciple-makers in next-generation ministry.

While aging is a normal part of one's life course and an inherent part of the human condition, the stages of aging are typically given meaning by social, cultural, and organizational structures. Gender and chronological age are two of the key units that often describe a person's place and responsibilities in the world. However, the United States and other developed nations are experiencing what the United Nations has called a "squaring of the population pyramid."[15] This means that the age qualifier is shifting as the expected lifespan expands, creating new additions and life stage modalities. For example, Hanson describes how growing numbers of people will experience what it means to be the "frail elderly" where health is a primary factor in their life that determines what they can and cannot do. These individuals are usually over 85 years old and primarily homebound. Another group, "seniors," are between 70–84, retired, and still drive, but often not at night.[16] However, Hanson continues, a "new old" group, age 50 to approximately 70, is emerging that approaches aging differently than previous generations. This group deals with challenges such as retirement issues, grandparenting, caring for aging parents, and preparing for their own aging. Generally, this group is healthy and active and refuses to age in "typical" or traditional ways.[17] They feel there is a lot of life yet to live and intend to embrace it.

As more people live longer due to advances in health science and technology, defining what it means to be an "aging adult" becomes tricky; chronological age alone is not enough of a marker. How "young" or "old" a person feels and behaves is certainly affected by their chronological age, but physical health, mental attitude, culture, social engagement, etc., are also contributing factors. Today, people can easily and readily spend thirty to forty years as aging adults. The Stanford Center on Longevity suggests that up to half of today's 5-year-olds could become centenarians and that this once unattainable milestone may become the norm for newborns by 2050.[18]

As a result of extended lifespans, increasing numbers of aging adults plan to work longer than previously assumed. This is a necessary financial decision as most people cannot fund a 30- year retirement over a 40-year career. And, since most people are healthy enough to keep working through their sixties and well into their seventies, many do.[19] The desire to maintain physical and cognitive health by actively engaging in work provides another motivation. For others, there is a sense of pressure in their discipline as organizations scramble to fill gaps in the labor force with skilled professionals. Additionally, older workers often want and are good at jobs that make a difference or give them opportunities to mentor younger generations.[20] What then is needed to motivate aging adults in the local church to engage the younger generations as Spirit-empowered "bonus grandparents," and commit to seeing young people become life-long disciples of Jesus?

Altruism, Egoism, or Something Else?

Scholars and practitioners alike often frame the conversation of volunteer motivation against the push-pull dynamics of altruism vs. egoism, placing each on opposite ends of a continuum. Altruism is described by Kinnunen and Windmann as "other-benefiting behavior that is costly but bears no direct profit to oneself"[21] and, Angela M. Sabetes adds, is not forced.[22] Blumberg, Nardone, and Giromini describe it as simply "the desire to meet the needs of another person."[23] A clear example of altruism at work can be found in the stories of those who risked everything to hide and rescue those fleeing the nightmare of the Holocaust. Many non-Jews risked ruin or their own lives to secure the survival of Jews caught in Nazism's grip.[24]

Altruism stands opposed to the egoistic idea that, when left to their own devices, individuals will usually behave in ways that maximize their position and control over resources. The innate human desire to protect one's own welfare means that engagement with others requires some type of personal benefit, creating a very transactional relationship between people, and even between people and organizations. Reciprocity is the name of this egoistic game, with the expectation of "return in kind" or hopefully better, according to Cropanzano et al.[25] This emphasis on the importance of self-seeking goals as the ultimate and primary reason for helping behavior is the distinguishing hallmark of an egoistic motivation for involvement.

The temptation to pass judgment on the type(s) of motivating factor(s) involved in a person's decision to volunteer is strong. For example, some motives appear nobler, while others seem more selfish or practical. In truth, however, Manatchal argues that most volunteers act with a mixture of altruistic and egoistic reasons motivating them.[26] A growing body of research exploring the nuances of volunteer motivation reveals that the reasons people say "yes" to freely chosen, unpaid, formal, persistent work on behalf of another is more complicated than simply altruism or egoism.[27] The initial commitment to volunteer and the ongoing commitment to continue to volunteer is motivated by complex factors of both altruism and egoism, according to Veludo-de-Oliveira, Pallister, and Foxall.[28] Thus, scholars and practitioners see the need for integrating the areas of egoism, altruism, and social connection as motivating factors.[29] In the volunteer motivation theory research streams, the Volunteer Function Inventory (VFI) has pioneered this integration.

The Volunteer Function Inventory

The VFI approaches volunteer motivation from a functionalist perspective. Instead of trying to nail down an exhaustive or exclusive list of motives, the inventory seeks to categorize how various complex motivations function to produce desired outcomes in the life of a volunteer. Recognizing that volunteers often undertake and perform the same activities for different reasons, a functional approach allows for greater congruence between motivations and behavioral outcomes. Understanding this congruence equips leaders to determine effective strategies for recruiting and retaining satisfied volunteers.[30] The VFI sorts motivational functions into the following broad categories, as defined by Clary et al.:[31]

- Values: Volunteer service is an opportunity to "express values related to altruistic and humanitarian concern for others."
- Understanding: Volunteer service is an opportunity for "new learning experiences and the chance to exercise knowledge, skills, and abilities that might otherwise go unpracticed."
- Social: Volunteer service provides an opportunity to focus on social relationships by "being with one's friends or to engage in an activity that is viewed favorably by important others."
- Career: Volunteer service is an opportunity to do work that assists with career development by preparing new skills or "maintaining career-relevant skills."
- Protective: Volunteer service is an opportunity to protect "the ego from negative features of the self" and "may serve to reduce guilt over being more fortunate than others and to address one's own personal problems."
- Enhancement: Volunteer service is an opportunity to improve or grow one's self in meaningful ways through positive strivings and growth.

Interestingly, Chacón et al. has found that the first VFI category, the "values" function, consistently ranks the highest among volunteers regardless of gender, age, or context.[32] The values function involves what Blumberg et al. describe as "people volunteering in order to express their belief in and commitment to helping others and those individuals in need.[33] Here, the desire to engage in altruistic feelings and behaviors is expressed. The idea that most people are, or at least aspire to be, moved to care for others out of a desire to be others-focused is well supported in the literature. Expressed as prosocial behavior not limited by age, ethnicity, social standing, or other resources, the values function is the greatest factor reported as the reason for which people volunteer.[34] Chacón et al. also note that the importance of this factor only increases as people age.[35] This has relevance to the question we are pursuing as Spirit-empowered disciple-makers with multi-generational churches and young people who need discipleship.

While altruism acts as a motivating factor for people regardless of their circumstances, altruism is closely linked with religiosity. Ghose and Kassam have noted that being others-focused is often embedded within a religious ethos.[36] Moore adds that it is expected in religious practice to create a deep connection to spiritual identity.[37] According to Barna, most Christians firmly believe that being generous with one's time, talent, and resources is "a response to Christ's love" and is "driven by compassion."[38] Religious people show a higher likelihood of engaging in altruistic motivations, demonstrated by a caring for others that goes beyond the moral standard of "do no harm" or "help others," says Zollo et al.[39] The call to help others and be of service in the world often finds its roots in one's religious identity and in values tightly held, which then finds expression through volunteerism. Essentially, when there is a high degree of congruence between a person's values, an organization's purpose, and the role a volunteer fills, especially as it relates to altruism, this combination becomes the dominant influencing factor for volunteer retention.[40] As an agent of grace in the world, the local church stands primed to be a strategic place for volunteers of all ages to express the love in their hearts and care for others in meaningful ways that impact every generation.

Enhancement = Social + Understanding Functions of the VFI

The "enhancement" function is linked to "motivations centered on self-knowledge, self-development and, in general, feeling better about oneself."[41] This area also includes social engagement and a sense of belonging to the people they serve alongside, as well as the people cared for, and the work itself. These factors tend to be seen as more egoistic.

On the other hand, research by Dwyer et al. indicates that volunteers motivated by the enhancement function are more likely to be satisfied with their experience.[42] Also, volunteers who experience benefits to themselves, whether purely social or otherwise, are more likely to endure challenging or emotionally difficult volunteer work.[43] As Moreno-Jimenez and Villodres observe, doing things that enhance one's life and sense of self matters to volunteers, as do the social networks developed through persistent volunteer work.[44]

Enhancement factors become an area of particular importance as people grow older. Increased age has some protective effects from issues like volunteer burnout or exhaustion, but only when strong social ties are associated with volunteer work.[45] The need for social engagement increases with age.[46] As the time horizon shortens, emotionally meaningful engagement becomes much more salient and immediately needful.[47] These social relationships and connections prove essential as aging adults navigate challenges like geographically distant family members, transitioning to semi-retirement or retirement, or losing a spouse.

Career status changes also contribute significantly to aging adults' needs for other enhancement functions that will help them redefine their roles, their relationships, and their sense of meaningful contribution in life. Aging adults deeply desire to do things that matter and make a difference. As professional work life shifts and winds down, the change also shifts how they connect and invest in society, creating an increased need for a sense of role and place of contribution that happens outside work. Thoits explains how many develop a strong identification with their volunteer role as the place that gives them "purpose, meaning, behavior guidance, and positive self-appraisals, generating better mental and physical health."[48] Aging adults desire to maintain both meaningful roles and meaningful relationships in their life.

Some caution must be taken when considering the enhancement function of volunteer motivation. The enhancement motive contains both favorable and problematic aspects of egoism. On the positive side, making friends who are engaged in meaningful activities is healthy and productive for everyone involved. However, this "ego involvement" can be risky for the potential development of a person's sense of self.[49] Generativity might be on the line if one volunteers solely to feel better about oneself or to feel more important.[50] To safeguard against this hazard, the "sweet spot" of volunteerism incorporates strong elements of both values and enhancement.

Sweet Spot = Values + Enhancement

The sweet spot for increased volunteer satisfaction and retention occurs when the values and enhancement functions work in tandem. Motivations in combination are essential in volunteer persistence as multiple means of motivation lead to greater longevity.[51] When values and enrichment are present as initial motivators, higher degrees of sustainability and persistence among faith-based volunteers grow over time.[52] Social and enhancement factors must be partnered with values/altruism functions to increase contributions and overall satisfaction. In short, the volunteer must find more than what they came looking for initially to both persist and be productive. In particular, aging adults want to participate in activities that help others by using their skills and talents in ways that affirm and grow their sense of self as well as their legacy, all while developing strong social ties. Because of this, wise church leaders will create strategic plans to engage volunteers in ways that express the meaningful values of altruism, connect them with opportunities to be generative in their sense of self, and facilitate meaningful relationships with others—all for the glory of God.

Warning

Another word of caution: Those receiving care offered by volunteers usually evaluate why the care is really being offered. They ask themselves, "Who is all this really for?" If the volunteer activity is intended for public display instead of private care, the help is not generally associated with altruistic values. Instead, the help becomes attributed to a higher degree of egoism; this is especially true if volunteers are perceived to be of high social status.[53]

The receivers of care are not the only ones watching. Other volunteers watch as well. If the perception of the helpers by other volunteers is that someone is only helping to gain public accolades or notice, and especially if they are of perceived high social status, the likelihood of other volunteers joining them in their work or becoming connected to the cause decreases.[54] By contrast, if people notice someone helping who is not looking to become "famous" while doing it and seems to be just a "normal person," then the actions of that person are attributed to altruism by those observing. Regular people helping others out of a perceived sense of altruism is positively received and has been shown to influence potential volunteers to want to become actively involved in the care of others.[55] In a world where all kinds of things can quickly go viral on a variety of social media or news platforms, and where both individuals and organizations can be "canceled" by the crowd, volunteers and volunteer organizations would be wise to consider carefully how their acts of care are both documented and promoted. Altruistic motives, or at least the appearance of others-focused motivation, matter when recruiting potential volunteers and creating a climate of trust between an organization and those they intend to help.

Now What?

If we are to take Jesus' message seriously of going into all the world as the Great Commission commands, we must also recognize that every nation also includes every generation. A strategic part of this mission will require that the young and the old alike are not only on the same team but considered partners and siblings in Christ on a mission together. Doing this together will require several strategic steps.

First, we must frame the conversation around the role and responsibility of aging adults as one of the elders in the church. Elders are respected for their wisdom and experience, while the "elderly" are often seen as being old and feeble with little to offer.[56] The idea of contribution by elders is a concept that younger generations are willing to embrace and that the aging must engage with humility. Many of our aging adults have walked with Jesus for a long time and have deep roots in Christ. Our aging adults can be trustworthy trail guides providing needed tools and encouragement to help shelter and foster developing faith in younger generations. The church must intentionally disciple aging adults to be elders who are proactively engaged as spiritual grandparents working to reach and retain younger generations in the faith.[57]

Second, we must recognize that true intergenerational Christian formation requires more than various ages being in the same space or place. Simply gathering for a worship service or other event is insufficient for fostering the kinds of healthy intergenerational relationships needed for all to flourish. Instead, each generation must be invited into the lives of the others through shared experiences that include reciprocal dialogue, shared goals, and the creation of common memories (including inside jokes and "you had to be there" moments).[58] Each generation must belong with the others as adopted children of God. Intergenerational outreach and mission opportunities, aging adults serving as small group leaders for teenagers, and including members of multiple generations on committees/teams within the church are just a few examples of how this could happen.[59]

Third, church leaders must have an intentional strategy to win the transitions that naturally occur over the lifespan. As the different generations age, we must strengthen connectional ties so that the people of God are the family of God. The goal is for all ages to be connected so that becoming an empty nester does not mean emptying out of the church or that when one retires, they also retire from the church. Volunteering helps individuals "navigate transitions between different life stages by encouraging them to become more involved in their communities, thereby building new social connections and improving networks of social support."[60] Members of every age are needed and must be connected in meaningful ways.

Fourth, church leaders must investigate the motivational functions of aging adults in their congregations and connect the dots for how these functions can be realized and strategically invested in legacy-building volunteer opportunities. Volunteer recruitment strategies must reflect priority volunteer motivation functions. When we understand what moves someone to volunteer and then intentionally work to make that experience fulfilling, we increase volunteer engagement and retention rates. The VFI shows us that we must incorporate the critical elements of values and enhancement across all ages, as every generation strongly desires a mix of both.[61] As a result, we must clearly communicate how every volunteer opportunity facilitates explicitly the function of being others-centered and developing strong social connections while utilizing skill sets to do things that matter. Helping others is an excellent reason to get involved, but it is not the only reason. Building teams full of life-giving relationships matter. Providing opportunities for people to use their skill sets and talents in meaningful work matters. We must communicate to every generation that if you need friends, get involved. If you have friends, volunteer together. We must also communicate that the life of the church and the great needs of the world require the investment of individuals gifted in diverse ways. People who love to lead story time with toddlers, or get excited about computer spreadsheets, or know how to work with their hands, are all needed, along with so much more. Church leaders must communicate clearly how working together with friends, old and new, while utilizing our skills helps make a difference for the kingdom.

Fifth, church leaders must adopt a supportive volunteer recruitment strategy for aging adults that reflects an understanding of both the needs and the challenges of aging. While the "new old" are living longer, healthier lives, they face real pressures. What are the pressure points of the "new old" in our congregations? What resources or connections does the local church have that can help? It might mean starting a parish nurse type of program where medical professionals in the congregation volunteer some of their retired time to help sort out the often-complex medical needs of the aging. For others, it might include providing opportunities for education around financial planning through each season of life. Meeting the felt needs of aging adults through both education and resources can provide ways for all to age well. This kind of strategic care also clears the path for greater engagement within the life of the church.

Finally, we must equip spiritual grandparents as the keepers of the faith in how to practically leverage their life experiences, their encounters with the living God, and their wisdom in how to enjoy life in the Spirit to reach and retain the young. Church leaders must prepare "bonus grandparents" to both sit at the "kid's table" and learn, as well as how to invite young people to the "adult table" to contribute. Aging adults need training in how to love and lead younger generations as lifelong disciples so the latter not only know Christ but make him known.

Notes

1. Holly Catterton Allen, Christine Lawton, and Cory Seibel, *Intergenerational Christian Formation: Bringing the Whole Church Together in Ministry, Community, and Worship*, 2nd ed. (Downers Grove: InterVarsity Press, 2023), 66.

2. Rachel Duniform and Ashish Bajracharya, "The Role of Grandparents in the Lives of Youth," *National Institute of Health Public Access* 1168, https://www.ncbi.nlm.nih.gov/pmc/articles/PMC3462462/, accessed August 1, 2024.

3. Vern Bengston, Norella M. Putney, and Susan C. Harris, *Families and Faith: How Religion is Passed Down Across Generations* (New York City: Oxford University Press, 2013), xi. See also Christian Smith and Amy Adamczyk, *Handing Down the Faith: How Parents Pass Their Religion on to the Next Generation* (New York City: Oxford University Press, 2021).

4. Erik Erikson and June Erikson, *The Life Cycle Completed* (New York City: W. W. Norton, 1997), 64.

5. Stanford Center on Longevity, *Working Longer and Retirement: Applying Research to Help Manage an Aging Workforce*, April 27–28, 2017, 9, https://longevity.stanford.edu/wp-content/uploads/2018/03/Working-Longer-Post-Conference-Report-2017-final.pdf/, accessed August 1, 2024.

6. David Kinnaman and Mark Matlock, *Faith for Exiles: Five Ways for a New Generation to Follow Jesus in Digital Babylon* (Grand Rapids: Baker, 2019), 15.

7. Kenda Creasy Dean, Almost Christian (New York City: Oxford University Press, 2010), 4. The reality that many young people are "graduating from church" when they graduate from high school has been well-documented by Dean and others, including The National Study on Youth and Religion, as well as Melinda Lundquist Denton and Richard Flory, *Back-Pocket God: Religion and Spirituality in the Lives of Emerging Adults* (New York City: Oxford University Press, 2020).

8. Kinnaman and Matlock, *Faith for Exiles*, 34.

9. Kinnaman and Matlock, *Faith for Exiles*, 35.

10. This is the primary research question of the "Faith that Lasts" project conducted by the Barna Group. A review of their findings can be found in Kinnaman and Matlock, *Faith for Exiles*.

11. Kinnaman and Matlock, *Faith for Exiles*, 112.

12 Smith and Adamczyk, *Handing Down the Faith*, 180.

13 The interaction between older and younger generations provides positive outcomes for both parties. For example, there is a decreased incidence of depression for both groups reported in Sara M. Moorman and Jeffrey E. Stokes, "Solidarity in the Grandparent—Adult Grandchild Relationship and Trajectories of Depressive Symptoms," *The Gerontologist* 56:3 (May 2014), 408. Also, there is increased mental clarity and growth for both in Lewis R. Anderson, Paula Sheppard, and Christian W. S. Monden, "Grandparents' Effects on Educational Outcomes: A Systematic Review," *Sociological Science* 5:2 (February 2018), 115.

14 Patrick Van Kessel, "How Americans Feel about the Satisfactions and Stresses of Modern Life," Pew Research Center, February 5, 2020, https://www.pewresearch.org/short-reads/2020/02/05/how-americans-feel-about-the-satisfactions-and-stresses-of-modern-life/, accessed August 1, 2024.

15 The birth rate in the U.S. is expected to stay largely flat while the numbers of aging adults grow. However, in places like Africa, there is an expected significant increase in births between now and 2030 compared to the rate between 2000–2015. The world's overall population is living longer with populations of older people being more concentrated in North America and Europe. See United Nations, Department of Economic and Social Affairs, Population Division, "Population 2030: Demographic Challenges and Opportunities for Sustainable Development Planning," 2015, https://www.un.org/en/development/desa/population/publications/pdf/trends/Population2030.pdf/, accessed June 1, 2024.

16 Amy Hanson, *Baby Boomers and Beyond: Tapping the Ministry Talents and Passions of Adults over Fifty* (San Francisco: Jossey-Bass, 2010), xii.

17 Hanson, *Baby Boomers and Beyond*, xiii.

18 Stanford Center on Longevity, *Working Longer and Retirement*, 8.

19 Stanford Center on Longevity, *Working Longer and Retirement*, 10.

20 Stanford Center on Longevity, *Working Longer and Retirement*, 14.

21 Suna Pirita Kinnunen and Sabine Windmann, "Dual-Processing Altruism," *Frontiers in Psychology* 4 (April 2013), 1.

22 Angela M. Sabates, *Social Psychology in Christian Perspective: Exploring the Human Condition* (Downers Grove: InterVarsity Press Academic, 2012), 416.

23 Daniel M. Blumberg, Destiny Nardone, and Luciano Giromini, "The Motivation of Senior Volunteers in Law Enforcement," *Journal of Behavioral and Social Sciences* 7:1 (Spring 2020), 3.

24 More research into why some helped can be found in Samuel Oliner and Pearl Oliner, *The Altruistic Personality: Rescuers of Jews in Nazi Europe* (New York City: The Free Press, 1992).

25 Russell Cropanzano, Erica L. Anthony, Shanna R. Daniels, and Alison V. Hall, "Social Exchange Theory: A Critical Review with Theoretical Remedies," *Academy of Management Annals* 11:1 (January 2017), 1. It could be argued that altruism is still rooted in a flavor of egoism as the volunteer still gets the pleasure of helping or the joy of making a "right" decision in assisting another person, even when it is costly to them personally.

26 Anita Manatschal and Markus Freitag, "Reciprocity and Volunteering," *Rationality and Society* 26:2 (May 2014), 226.

27 While the reasons for volunteering may be more involved than placing them on a continuum of motives between altruism and egoism, clients often perceive unpaid helpers' motives as altruistic. This perception of altruism is critical in building trust, a strategic component of care for those people/organizations working with vulnerable populations like children or the elderly. See Niek Hoogervorst, Judith Metz, Lonneke Roza, and Evan Van Baren, "How Perceptions of Altruism and Sincerity Affect Client Trust in Volunteers Versus Paid Workers," *Non-profit and Voluntary Sector Quarterly* 45:3 (June 2016), 595.

28 Tania Veludo-De-Oliveira, John Pallister, and Gordon Foxall, "Unselfish? Understanding the Role of Altruism, Empathy, and Beliefs in Volunteer Commitment," *Journal of Nonprofit and Public Sector Marketing* 27:4 (October 2015), 290.

29 The discussion concerning driving forces of human motivation raises the question: is Jesus the only true example of a purely altruistic person? This "can of worms" question is beyond the scope of this chapter.

30 See Byeong Ju Kim, Min Han Kim, and Jaewan Lee, "Congruence Matters: Volunteer Motivation, Value Internalization, and Retention," *Journal of Organizational Psychology*, 19:5 (2019), 57.

31 Gil E. Clary, Mark Snyder, Robert D. Ridge, John Copeland, Arthur A. Stukas, Julie Haugen, and Peter Miene, "Understanding and Assessing the Motivations of Volunteers: A Functional Approach," *Journal of Personality and Social Psychology*, 74:6 (June 1998), 1517–1518. Note that the VFI does not place altruism or egoism as the ends of a continuum. Instead, they are considered as dimensions of a more complex equation.

32 Fernado Chacón, Gema Gutiérres, Verónica Sauto, María Luisa Vecina, and Alfonso Pérez, "Volunteer Functions Inventory: A Systematic Review," *Psicothema* 29:3 (July 2017), 313. Yet, there is a certain amount of utility that has remained reliable in the adaptation of the VFI to assess additional

volunteer function domains including areas like: "social justice" in Patrick Jiranek, Elizabeth Kals, Julia Sophia Humm, Isabel Theresia Strubel, and Theo Wahner, "Volunteering as a Means to an Equal End? The Impact of Social Justice Function on Intention to Volunteer," *The Journal of Social Psychology* 153:5 (2013), 520–541; "religiosity" in Lamberto Zollo, Cristiano Ciapllei, Gugliolmo Faldatta, Massimiliano Pellegrini, "Does Religiosity Influence Retention Strategies in Nonprofit Organizations?" *Voluntas* 33:2 (April 2020): 284–296; and "faith" in Bernadene Erasmus and Peter Morey, "Faith-based Volunteer Motivation: Exploring the Applicability of the Volunteer Functions Inventory to the Motivations and Satisfaction Levels of Volunteers in an Australian Faith-Based Organization," *Voluntas: International Journal of Voluntary and Nonprofit Organizations* 27:3 (June 2016), 1343–1360.

33 Blumberg et al., "The Motivation of Senior Volunteers," 3. Although, some research suggests that altruism comes in different forms, including help giving, altruistic punishment, and moral courage. See Kinnunen and Windmann, "Dual-Processing Altruism," 1. "Help giving" is the focus of the values function.

34 Eva Kahana et al., "Altruism, Helping, and Volunteering: Pathways to Well-Being in Late Life," *Journal of Aging and Health* 25:1 (February 2013), 160.

35 Chacón et al., "Volunteer Functions Inventory," 307.

36 Toorio Ghose and Meenza Kassam, "Motivations to Volunteer Among College Students in India," *Voluntas* 25:1 (February 2014), 30.

37 Erin W. Moore, Samantha Warta, and Kristen Erichsen, "College Students' Volunteering: Factors Related to Concurrent Volunteering, Volunteering Settings, and Motives for Volunteering," *College Student Journal* 38:3 (Fall 2014), 395.

38 Barna Group, *The Generosity Gap: How Christians' Perceptions and Practices of Giving are Changing and What it Means for the Church* (Ventura, CA: Barna Group, 2017), 18.

39 Lamberto Zollo et al., "Does Religiosity Influence Retention Strategies in Nonprofit Organizations?" *Voluntas* 33:2 (April 2020), 286.

40 Bill Merrilees, Dale Millera, and Raise Yakimovab, "Volunteer Retention Motives and Determinants across the Volunteer Lifecycle," *Journal of Nonprofit and Public Sector Marketing* 32:1 (2020), 38.

41 Chacón et al., "Volunteer Functions Inventory," 307.

42 Patrick Dwyer et al., "Sources of Volunteer Motivation: Transformational Leadership and Personal Motives Influence Volunteer Outcomes," *Nonprofit Management of Business* 24:2 (Winter 2013), 190.

43 Arthur Stukas et al., "Motivations to Volunteer and Their Associations with Volunteers' Well-Being," *Nonprofit and Voluntary Sector Quarterly* 45:1 (February 2016), 114.

44 M. Pilar Moreno-Jimenez and M. Carmen Hidalgo Villodres, "Prediction of Burnout in Volunteers," *Journal of Applied Psychology* 40:7 (2010), 1800.

45 Mercedes Aranda, Salvatore Zappalà, and Gabriela Topa, "Motivations for Volunteerism, Satisfaction, and Emotional Exhaustion: The Moderating Effect of Volunteers' Age," *Journal of Sustainability* 11:16 (August 2019), 6.

46 Arthur A. Stukas et al., "Motivations to Volunteer and their Associations with Volunteers' Well-Being," *Nonprofit and Voluntary Sector Quarterly* 45:1 (February 2016), 120.

47 Takashi Yamashita et al., "Older Lifelong Learners' Motivations for Participating in Formal Volunteer Activities in Urban Communities," *Adult Education Quarterly* 67:2 (May 2017), 119.

48 Peggy A. Thoits, "Role-Identity Salience, Purpose and Meaning in Life, and Well-Being Among Volunteers," *Social Psychology Quarterly* 75:4 (December 2012), 361.

49 The question of which came first, a volunteer with a strong sense of self-esteem or if volunteering created this strong sense of self, is ongoing. However, scholars can agree that a presently healthy self-esteem serves as fuel for volunteer work. See Maria Monaci, Luca Scacchi, and Monica Giolitti Monteu, "Self-Concept and Volunteering: The Mediational Role of Motivations," *Applied Psychology Bulletin* 67:285 (May 2019), 38.

50 Stefan Tomas Güntert et al., "The Quality of Volunteer's Motives: Integrating the Functional Approach and Self-Determination Theory," *The Journal of Social Psychology* 156:3 (2016), 314.

51 Moore et al., "College Students' Volunteering," 391.

52 Bernadene Erasmus and Peter Morey, "Faith-based Volunteer Motivation: Exploring the Applicability of the Volunteer Functions Inventory to the Motivations and Satisfaction Levels of Volunteers in an Australian Faith-Based Organization," *Voluntas: International Journal of Voluntary and Nonprofit Organizations* 27:3 (June 2016), 1356.

53 Birte Siem and Stefan Stürmer, "Attributions of Egoist Versus Altruistic Motives to Acts of Helping," *Social Psychology* 50:1 (2019), 53.

54 Siem and Stümer, "Attributions of Egoist," 54.

55 Siem and Stümer, "Attributions of Egoist," 58.

56 Culture has developed a dark sense of humor regarding aging adults,

including a great deal of sarcasm: Kinnaman and Matlock, *Faith for Exiles*, 120. Meaningful relationship between generations is the only way this kind of humor or negative stereotypes will be silenced. Diane E. Shallue, "Engaging the Elders Among Us," in *InterGenerate: Transforming Churches through Intergenerational Ministry*, ed. Holly Catterton Allen (Abilene, TX: Abilene Christian University Press, 2018), 195.

57 For many, this may require reframing what retirement looks like as a Christ-follower.

58 Intentionally programming "surprise and delight" moments during intergenerational interactions can help facilitate warm memories for all involved. For example, what might happen if "bonus grandparents" worked with the youth to sneakily decorate the pastor's yard for Christmas, or if the 20-somethings threw a party to celebrate couples in the church who had been married for several decades? Meaningful fun and service to others are often the keys to creating connections and memories together.

59 People who regularly volunteer in their youth also tend to volunteer as they age. The example of older people volunteering with younger people is contagious and creates a "let's do this together" legacy. See Jane Allyn Piliavin, "Volunteering Across the Life Span: Doing Well by Doing Good," in *The Psychology of Prosocial Behavior: Group Processes, Intergroup Relations and Helping*, eds. Stefan Stûmer and Mark Snyder (Hoboken, NJ: Wiley-Blackwell, 2010), 161.

60 Allison Russell et al., "Volunteering and Wellbeing Among Aging Adults: A Longitudinal Analysis," *Voluntas* 30:1 (February 2019), 115.

61 Julie E. Francis and Michael Jones, "Emergency Service Volunteers: A Comparison of Age, Motives, and Values," *University of Wollongong Research Online*, 2012, 24–25, https://ro.uow.edu.au/commpapers/2899./, accessed June 1, 2024.

20 Preparing and Sending Gen Z into Every Person's World: Encounter and Equipping through Chapel at Oral Roberts University

Allie Mendoza and Kimmie Simon

Abstract

Generation Z is hungry for a move of God in their generation and crying out for a genuine, authentic revival from the Holy Spirit that leads to a missional lifestyle for Jesus. This chapter will explore how chapel services at Oral Roberts University feed that desire by creating an environment for spiritual transformation—specifically, through providing opportunities for encounter, spiritual formation, and practical equipping. Despite the challenges facing Gen Z, chapel leaders see students' personal pursuit of Jesus, missional living, and fruit that remains. God is doing something unique in Gen Z, and it is time to increase our impartation so they can be whole leaders for the whole world.

Introduction

Tucked away in the unassuming city of Tulsa, Oklahoma, sits Oral Roberts University (ORU), a university with global reach that equips students to become Spirit-empowered leaders of tomorrow. Founded in 1963 by Oral Roberts, the vision of the school remains the words Roberts penned on a napkin when he heard the Lord say, "Raise up your students to hear My voice, to go where My light is dim, where My voice is heard small, and My healing power is not known, even to the uttermost bounds of the earth. Their work will exceed yours, and in this I am well pleased."[1] Robert's vision has led the university for fifty years, with the foundation always being the work and person of the Holy Spirit. The guiding mission statement is "to develop Holy Spirit-empowered leaders through whole-person education to impact the world."[2]

With students representing over 150 nations[3] and all fifty states, ORU is globally advancing God's kingdom through a groundbreaking Global Learning Center, a continuing legacy of international mission trips, Spirit-empowered alumni in every field, and chapel messages broadcasted worldwide. Furthermore, since 2013, the university has been under the leadership of Dr. William M. Wilson, who strongly believes Gen Z has the greatest potential to impact the world for Jesus more than any previous generation.[4]

What is happening at ORU within Gen Z is a move of God, and it is not happening by accident. As the campus has become, demographically, fully Gen Z over the last several years, there has been a resounding cry for revival from students who desire a genuine move of God. While ORU is encountering many of the same difficulties that other universities are facing with Gen Z students, including rising mental health challenges and the aftereffects of COVID-19 on academic performance, ORU students are thriving because there are spaces for authentic spiritual encounters that lead to personal transformation. With a spiritually hungry student body and spiritually alive staff and faculty, there have been three salient results: revival, missional living, and lasting fruit. Sadly, not all Christian colleges and universities are having the same experiences. The purpose of this chapter is to help Christian leaders cultivate revival and spiritual growth in their own organizations and spheres of influence by sharing what is working in ORU's chapel services to spiritually transform Gen Z students.

Who is Gen Z?

Classified by the Barna Group as being born between 1999 and 2015, Gen Zers are now the largest American generation at about 69–70 million children and teens.[5] Exquisitely unique in many of their beliefs and worldviews, Gen Z is unlike any previous generation. While some overlapping characteristics with Millennials are apparent, a Gen Z student is fundamentally different from a Millennial student in how they see themselves, their thinking habits, and their interaction with the world. According to Barna Group research, Gen Z's trajectory is formed by technology, an inclusive and individualistic worldview, fluidity of gender identity, security through financial success, and diversity. Barna documents the following startling facts:[6]

- More than half of Gen Z uses screen media for four hours or more on the average day.
- Out of 69 million individuals, just 4 percent have a biblical worldview.

- One-third of Gen Z teens say gender is how a person feels inside, not the sex they were born with.
- Many believe happiness is defined by financial success.
- Approximately 40 percent of teens interact with people who are different from them, compared to just 25 percent of Boomers.
- Half of Gen Z youth say parents are their primary role models, but only one-third say that family is core to their identity.

From statistics like these, an argument can be made that the strategies that were effective five or ten years ago in reaching students are no longer viable; the approach to reaching Gen Z needs to be as creative and innovative as the young people themselves. While much of the discussion surrounding Gen Z can trends towards cynical or critical, ORU unequivocally believes Gen Z has tremendous potential to change the world. With entrepreneurial mindsets, limitless thinking, and a global perspective, Gen Z could quite literally reach the entire globe for Jesus. However, genuine encounter and theological equipping must come first. Gen Z needs to encounter the Lord at the altar and become equipped to know, apply, and live the Word while hearing the voice of God for their generation. Here is where focusing on chapel services, which are a staple at many Christian campuses, enters the equation.

Chapel at ORU has been a pillar since the university's conception. Students, staff, and faculty attend services twice a week. However, the centrality of chapel for a campus community goes far beyond a simple service. It serves as a binding agent to the university, creating unity amongst the student body, providing space to encounter the presence of the Lord, and setting a trajectory for the future. Celebration, empowerment, and impartation stand as hallmarks surrounding the chapel experience. While the modes of worship and preaching are familiar to most believers, ORU chapel builds itself around the Holy Spirit, aiming for every moment to be touched by his marking work. Dance specials, sermon illustrations, and cultural celebrations are all created with the Spirit at the center. With the Holy Spirit welcome and present, the atmosphere aims to be a life-altering sanctuary where students can encounter God to become equipped, rooted, and motivated to go and change the world for God's glory.

Clearly, the work and movement of the Holy Spirit are indispensable to this goal. As a university built upon the Holy Spirit, the Spirit must be invited into every space and classroom to bring transformational change to students' lives. With such a sure foundation remaining constant, the modes and methods are free to grow with the times. Thus, the Holy Spirit is the common thread, the linking piece, through every graduating class. While Gen Z is invariably unique to their predecessors in most major ways, their need for the Holy Spirit is just as great as their parents and grandparents before them, which is why consistent chapel attendance is so efficacious. As a productive training ground, chapel services are marked by holy moments of worship, powerful preaching, communal living, and celebrations of joy. The challenge across most Christian campuses is crafting services for a generation that idealizes individual experiences while also creating a unified corporate setting. ORU is not immune to these challenges but has tried to embrace Gen Z's quest for honesty and authenticity on the platform.

The Purpose of Chapel

Encounter

ORU desires every student, faculty, and staff member to encounter God's transforming presence during chapel. The encounter ORU pursues is not a connection that happens by chance or occurs unintentionally, creating no significant change. Rather, ORU's targeted encounter is a life-altering moment in God's presence, which student Mel Lawrenz argues is continuous with a multitude of biblical examples: Abraham's change in location, Jacob's change in pace, Moses' change in countenance, and Saul's change in name, just to name a few.[7] Chapel services prioritize times for a tangible encounter in God's presence with subsequent transformation. Students can be marked in numerous ways throughout the entirety of service, including during worship, giving, message, and ministry.

Worship is a frequent medium of encounter for attendees. ORU offers biblical worship, or what Cheryl Taylor defines as "worth-ship" to God, ascribing him the worth and honor he deserves.[8] Students, faculty, and staff worship according to the truth of God's Word and through the power and leading of the Spirit. The worship team leads corporate psalms (melodies from God's Word), hymns (songs previously written that praise God), and spiritual songs (songs enabled and given by the Spirit).[9] They avoid watered-down Christian expressions that are vacant of God's Spirit or part of a checklist. Instead, leaders work hard to create a worship experience that is vibrant, charged, and enthusiastic. At ORU, students leave their seats and flood the altar to express their praise. Students passionately sing, dance, shout, clap, bow, and jump, offering undignified Davidic worship to the Lord.[10] ORU's animated expressions can be a hurdle for some students coming from different cultural or stylistic backgrounds. As previously stated, with the differences in denominations, culture, ages, and depths in relationship with Christ, the challenge is to bridge those gaps in the chapel experience. However, we find that exposure and openness to authentic expression of encounter impacts Gen Z, and the whole of the ORU community is changed in God's presence during worship.

Equipping

While many universities solely focus on the student's personal experience during a chapel service, ORU emphasizes collective empowerment of the student body through communal equipping—both for their current spiritual formation and their future spiritual maturity. Gen Z has a deep hunger for the things of God, but their zeal and passion need to be coupled with practical teaching; otherwise, it can lead to unsound theology or unhealthy tendencies. To synergize moments of encounter with times of equipping, there is ample student involvement in every aspect of chapel. The saliency of students being active participants, not mere spectators of what happens on stage, cannot be overstated. For students to become equipped, they must first engage and then be empowered. Empowerment comes from the administration modeling healthy practices, providing students with opportunities to walk alongside them, and then supporting them as students do it themselves, offering feedback when needed. This is demonstrated in our services in the following ways:

- The chapel worship team is composed of students who are musically talented and anointed for leading the student body into times of worship.
- Students often perform special songs, spoken words, or dances, particularly to mark special occasions or to celebrate culture.
- High-quality announcement videos are played where students inform the rest of the student body what is happening around campus that week.
- An offering is taken and prayed for, often by a student, and it is always special when an international student prays for their own country or region in their native language.

One unique equipping aspect of chapel is funding global mission projects. Although it might seem counterintuitive to ask college students, who are often struggling financially, to give regularly towards mission projects, it is part of the stitching that holds the community together. If a Christian university believes in building God's kingdom globally, then tithing is a spiritual discipline that does not start with a regular paycheck after graduation. Instead, tithing is a spiritual discipline that needs to be cultivated and intentionally woven into a person's life, even when they might just have a little to give. When one recognizes that the attitude of the heart, not the amount of money, matters most to the Lord, it becomes feasible to give cheerfully, even if it is only five or ten dollars. Whether building an orphanage in Ethiopia, supplying school supplies to children in Paraguay, providing a pastor with a motorbike in Nepal, or responding to a current global crisis, students demonstrate year after year that they want to be part of what is happening around the world through giving. Offerings remain a consistent practice at every chapel, so over a student's tenure, they get acclimated to the idea that generous giving is part of kingdom living.

A final component of equipping is preaching and teaching God's Word. ORU is thankful to have relationships with incredible men and women from around the world who come and pour into students with the power of the Holy Spirit and build sermons on God's everlasting words. We have found that interdenominational operations permit us to bring in speakers as diverse as the kingdom itself so that students can learn from men and women from different backgrounds, cultures, and movements. Speakers are encouraged to follow the prompting of the Spirit for their sermon topics but are always asked to preach the Word, for scripture remains in the hearts of listeners long after the moment of delivery. While we celebrate what God is doing through individuals, it is always God, not the preacher in the pulpit, who is given the glory.

The overall atmosphere is also important to cultivate. In our services, the Lord is free to move and speak. There is often spontaneous worship from the stage, acts of praise through dancing and jumping, and students praying over each other. Yet, with freedom, there is always a need for accountability. The following boundaries are followed in chapel services to ensure the spiritual health of the environment:

- The student worship team members maintain a certain GPA and have a staff mentor to help them stay spiritually healthy.
- Appointed student leaders called "chaplains," who have been through training and are under accountability, are called to be available to pray for the student body throughout the year.
- Every chapel speaker is carefully selected by the President's Office, ensuring they are trustworthy and full of integrity.
- Full-time staff members are always present to be a covering for the room during post-chapel worship moments and provide spiritual wisdom and discernment.

With over 3,500 people in chapel services, one great obstacle to fostering spiritual maturity is the sheer range of spiritual walks and theological worldviews represented. Such an assorted audience provides ample opportunity for either strife or spiritual erudition amongst students. Yet the administration has found that stewardship of the Spirit through encounter and equipping go together in creating an atmosphere where students can ask questions, stretch their faith, and learn from each other's point of view.

The Results
Personal Pursuit

Jesus instructed all believers in Mark 12:30–31 to "Love the Lord your God with all your heart, and with all your soul, and with all your mind, and with all your strength," and to "love your neighbor as yourself."[11] The decision to personally pursue God is the most important decision any person will make. As A. W. Tozer affirms, "What I believe about God is the most important thing about me."[12] Chapel services exist in a beautiful balance of stimulating greater hunger for God but also reflecting the hunger already stirred. Worship satisfies the soul while also making the heart cry for more of Jesus. The whole of the ORU community experiences this twice a week, which spurs personal pursuit and spiritual formation beyond the walls of chapel. We find that the pursuit of God happens during service but overflows to prayer sets, mission trips, local outreach, and personal relationships. Chapel compels every individual to know God more deeply and have an increased desire to make Christ known worldwide.

Missional Living

The concept of missional living is springing forth in churches and denominations across the globe. It is our simple way of embodying the Great Commission in Matthew 28, which connotes that living for Jesus, and like Jesus, is a conscious choice that must be cultivated daily. Erik Raymond of The Gospel Coalition states, "Living on mission means living on purpose. It looks like an embracing of a biblical identity and responding with biblical urgency."[13] In a generation filled to the brim with information, noise, conflicting opinions, and post-Christian ideas, missional living brings believers back to the centrality of the cross and the person of Jesus. Through the empowerment of the Holy Spirit, ORU students learn that the Word is more profound than the anecdotes it is often reduced to, and worship is far more than a set-list. Missional living is what every believer is called to because missional living is following Jesus in every area of life.

Augustine Mendoza, ORU's Director of Spiritual Life and Student Experience, shares that "ORU chapel is a vital aspect of the missional ethos of our university. It brings the community together, unites us in worship, focuses us on the mission of Jesus, and equips us for our part in God's missional assignment for our lives."[14] As a university whose mantra centers on going to all the world, it is only fitting that ORU has a global outlook embodied in chapel and beyond. Through the nations of the world gathering on campus, there is a glimpse of heaven in every service. Whether singing in another language, operating in the gifts of the Spirit, or growing in faith through hearing the Word, chapel is a time when students participate in the metanarrative of scripture. It provides a bridge to greater spiritual maturity, where students can deepen their identity as sons and daughters of God and embrace the lifelong journey of becoming more like Jesus.

Fruit That Remains

In John 15:16, Jesus calls us not just to bear fruit, but fruit that remains. While lasting fruit can be difficult to measure, in a recent online survey of student leaders at ORU, 100 percent reported having encountered God during chapel worship, at some point, and the majority said they had been enriched by chapel messages.[15] Some of their comments are as follows:

- "I love how every chapel is powerful and fosters the Holy Spirit."
- "Every chapel I [am] filled with overflowing joy. I've also had many visions from God [in] chapels."
- They are "beautiful encounters" (with God during the worship).
- Chapel is "a concise meeting to get a spiritual meal. Very enriching."[16]

One international student from Honduras, Annette Moradel, recalls an encounter where God showed her a vision of a public university in Honduras with numerous college students worshiping like the students at ORU. Annette heard the Lord say, "What you're seeing with your eyes right now at this chapel, you will see it at [that university]." Annette then described "feeling [a] huge burden on my heart for young people and young adults in universities back home." Her calling was clarified and solidified in that divine encounter. Annette now confidently states that she will "see the move of His Spirit in college campuses."[17]

A current staff member, Caleb Marshall, experienced the physical healing power of God when his ankle was healed in a chapel service. Caleb recalls that it was "just a normal day" in chapel when "[I] was just worshiping and all of the sudden I felt this warmth in my body... [and a] pop in my ankle... I took my boot off... I started bending and moving it around, then I started to jump... It was a very personal moment between me and the Lord."[18] In all sorts of amazing ways, the Spirit moving during chapels are impacting Gen Z and beyond; their lives are living proof.

The Marking Difference

While chapel services are not unique among Christian campuses in general, we believe some qualities mark and support our aims in particular: ORU's honor code, expectations surrounding chapel, and focus on Spirit-empowerment.

Honor Code

One component that continually sets ORU apart among Christian universities is its founding honor code, which is still in place over fifty years later. The university launched in both tumultuous and exciting times in history. The early 1960s were full of political upheavals such as the Cuban Missile Crisis and JFK's assassination, but also the salient fight for social justice in the Civil Rights Movement. With a dream that ORU would be a diverse campus in every aspect, Oral Roberts believed a unifying honor code would bind faculty, staff and students together. He also wanted ORU to be a place of consecration where students would learn to live with honor, integrity, and personal character.

The university's student handbook, therefore, states, "The Honor Code is the central criterion of conduct for all who are a part of the ORU community. It is a concept of personal honor based on the principles of integrity, common sense, reverence for God, esteem for others, and respect for social and spiritual laws."[19] While many universities have amended or retired their honor codes in recent years, ORU continues to believe that honor, integrity, and character are the backbone of personal leadership, and "whole leaders for the whole world" cannot be formed without these principles. Although the honor code seeks to encapsulate basic principles for Christian living, students sometimes struggle to embrace it because it addresses some of the hardest questions Christian culture faces today. Yet, even in the tension, students are encouraged to dialogue and seek wisdom through the lens of the Bible instead through the lens of culture. Overarchingly, the honor code has kept ORU missionally grounded through decades of shifting cultural climates.

Expectations

Chapel is a time of expectation. The administration expects students to attend, and students expect to enter an environment where they can meet with the Lord. Unvoiced expectations go unmet, so the university clearly communicates that while chapel attendance is not optional, it is an opportunity. Every full-time graduate and undergraduate student, whether residential or commuter, is asked to be present. Although this can be difficult for some, many ultimately end up viewing chapel as a built-in time to rest in the Lord and find refreshment and encouragement in the midst of their week. Additionally, staff and faculty are asked to come at least once weekly. With chapel being the binding agent of the university, it is not a token service or a wasted hour but a treasured aspect of the ORU experience.

Spirit-Empowered Structure

Another differentiator for chapel is the university's commitment to being Spirit-empowered. Having Spirit-empowered services means active submission to the Spirit in leadership, preparation, and implementation. God told Oral Roberts to establish a university built on the Holy Spirit that educated the whole person—body, mind, *and* spirit. Many institutions seek to train students in the mind, and some the body, but few place importance on the spirit. As Samuel Rodriguez aptly defines it, "Spirit-empowered" means that believers partner with the Holy Spirit by walking in freedom, power, peace, and consecration.[20] Tozer adds that when people submit to the Spirit, God's presence is unlocked.[21] Spirit-empowered ministries have a considerable impact, and ORU has seen this firsthand.[22]

Many ministries long for this same influence but ignore the most essential element—the Holy Spirit. Even in the modern American church that accepts the Spirit, a common ideology is to believe in the Holy Spirit without operating in his giftings. Wayne Grudem explains that to be "seeker-sensitive" means a desire to create a safe environment for non-believers;[23] however, our experience is that this idea dangerously prioritizes human experience oversensitivity to the Holy Spirit. To be more sensitive to the first-time seeker, rather than to God, can quench the Spirit. The seeker-focused ideal to shield newcomers from the Spirit temporarily increases attendance but consistently decreases the Spirit's moving through his gifts. ORU's chapel services are Spirit-empowered because Spirit-empowered leaders foster Spirit-empowered services.

Thus, the leadership of chapel does not shy away from the Acts 2 example in the upper room but confidently partners with the Spirit in the planning process and during services. Chapel is not a mere show, performance, or cookie-cutter church service. Rather, it is a dynamic time when students are encouraged to obey the Spirit. The emphasis on students discovering and operating in spiritual gifts can create moments of disorder, but chapel is about embracing the process of spiritual gifts, not their perfection. Creating and following a pre-set plan and being Spirit-empowered while ending on time may seem like an impossible task, yet the chapel leadership team has learned to implement this balance during the one-hour service. Because chapel is live-streamed, televised, and students have afternoon classes, there must be set time restraints. Every minute is prioritized and done through the lens of the Spirit because both the planning phase and the implementation are done in obedience to the Spirit, and each leader is given authority to accomplish God's plan.

Typical services are broken into four segments: worship, giving and transition, message, and ministry. Each segment has oversight: the Worship Director leads worship, the Spiritual Life Directors lead the giving and transition time, and the selected ministry leader (which changes per chapel) shares the message and facilitates ministry. All the leaders take ownership of their allotted time and carefully listen to the Spirit in planning and preparing. Once their plan is created, all leaders come together to compile the agenda and receive vision for the service. Working together in unity, all come under the pastoral covering and leadership of the President of the university.

Even though a clear structure is created, all leaders are empowered to obey the Spirit, even if it goes against the schedule. An understanding exists among the staff that flexibility in the Spirit is key and allows for obedience to the Spirit in pre-service planning and during the service. Moments of prophetic words and songs, Spirit-led prayers, and the operation of spiritual gifts are often the results. Kimmie Simon, ORU's Worship Director, explains this balance within chapel structure by saying, "Chapels are best described as a 'plan-flow' service because everyone plans to the best of their ability but also flows with the Spirit."[24] The plan flow often changes during worship, and the Worship Director spends time praying, planning, and practicing songs with the worship team before service in order to have the freedom to deviate when led by the Spirit. Similarly, the Spiritual Life Directors may feel led to spontaneously share a scripture or pray over a topic not previously scheduled. Although many ministries desire the impact seen at ORU in using the plan-flow example, few are truly open for the Spirit to change the plan. The leaders' organization, obedience to the Spirit, and unity under their pastoral covering create a distinctive Spirit-empowered chapel experience.

It's Your Turn

All that has been shared is meant to be an inspiration and launching pad for any campus seeking a Spirit-empowered body, especially by utilizing chapel services. The beauty of following the Holy Spirit is that while he is the same in all places, he has the freedom to look distinctive. What happens at ORU is not meant to serve as the expectation for all schools, but is one example of what God is doing in Gen Z that is working. The goal of the kingdom is not the exact replication of methods but rather the reproduction and multiplication of the movement of the Spirit, who knows precisely what each generation needs. As you consider your own organization and teams, the following reflection questions can be used to assess the shape and trajectory of the work you are doing for the kingdom:

- Can you articulate why you do what you do?
- What are you intentionally doing to strategize effective ways to reach Gen Z and future generations?
- How does your organization create moments of encounter and prioritize God's presence?
- In what ways do your events or services create spaces for a move of God?
- How do you encourage people's personal pursuit of Christ?
- In what ways are you modeling missional living, and how can you bring others along with you?
- What does the fruit of your organization look like?
- What are the expectations and standards of your organization?
- How do you practically equip and empower those under your leadership?
- How do your leadership teams obey the Holy Spirit?

Conclusion

A mighty move of God is sweeping the earth, and Gen Z is at the center of this catalytic time in history. Full of potential, Gen Z needs encounters with the living God to be rooted and equipped to change the world for Jesus. ORU's goal is to continue to impact the next generation through its chapel services, and it is our hope that your campus or institution will as well. As ORU's President ends every chapel with the same mantra, you are also charged to: "Go change your world!"

Notes

1 "Vision and Mission," Oral Roberts University, https://oru.edu/about-oru/vision-and-mission/, accessed July 19, 2024.

2 Oral Roberts University, "Vision and Mission."

3 "Reaching Every Nation," Oral Roberts University, https://oru.edu/sponsor-a-nation/index.php./, accessed July 26, 2024.

4 William M. Wilson, "Why Gen Z will be the Most Influential Generation," The Christian Post, May 18, 2022, https://www.christianpost.com/voices/

why-generation-z-will-be-the-most-influential-generation.html./, accessed July 30, 2024.

5 "Gen Z: The Culture, Beliefs and Motivations Shaping the Next Generation" (Ventura, CA: Barna Group, 2018), 10.

6 "Gen Z: The Culture, Beliefs and Motivations," 13.

7 Mel Lawrenz, *The Dynamics of Spiritual Formation* (Grand Rapids: Baker, 2000), 22. Biblical references to these can be found in Gen 12:1–4; 32:25-28; Exod 34:29–35; Acts 13:9.

8 Cheryl Taylor, *Prayer and Worship: An Independent-Study Textbook* (Springfield, MO: Global University, 2006), 153.

9 These terms can be found and defined this way in Gerhard Kittel, Gerhard Friedrich, and Geoffrey William Bromiley, *Theological Dictionary of the New Testament* (Grand Rapids: Eerdmans, 1985), 1225. For more on this subject, see Jack W. Hayford, *Worship His Majesty: How Praising the King of Kings Will Change Your Life*, ed. David Webb, rev. ed. (Ventura, CA: Regal, 2000), 171–173.

10 See, for example, 2 Sam 6:14, 22 as well as Pss 5:7; 47:1; 95:6; 98:4–6; 149:3.

11 Unless otherwise indicated, all scripture quotations are from the New Revised Standard Version (NRSV).

12 A. W. Tozer, *The Knowledge of the Holy: The Attributes of God: Their Meaning in the Christian Life* (New York: Harper One, 2009); also see Gary M. Benedict, "Foreword," in *The Life of A. W. Tozer: In Pursuit of God* (Ventura, CA: Regal, 2009), 5.

13 Erik Raymond, "Living on Mission Means Living on Purpose," The Gospel Coalition, November 27, 2018, https://www.thegospelcoalition.org/blogs/erik-raymond/living-mission-means-living-purpose/, accessed July 20, 2024.

14 Augustine Mendoza, personal interview with the author, September 1, 2023.

15 Anonymous, "ORU Chapels Survey," Oral Roberts University online survey, 2024.

16 Anonymous, "ORU Chapels Survey," Oral Roberts University online survey, 2024.

17 Annette Moradel, "ORU Chapels Survey, Oral Roberts University online survey, 2024.

18 Caleb Marshall, "ORU Chapels Survey," Oral Roberts University online survey, 2024.

19 "Oral Roberts University Student Handbook 2023–2024," Oral Roberts University, https:// www.calameo.com/read/00336977057 00336977057cdcaee60c7?view=scroll&page=1/, accessed July 19, 2024.

20 Samuel Rodriguez, "Foreword," in *A Spirit-Empowered Church: An Acts 2 Ministry Model* (Springfield, MO: Influence Resources, 2015), 13–14.

21 A. W. Tozer, *The Pursuit of God* (Camp Hill, PA: WingSpread, 2006), 60.

22 For further development and support of this concept, see Alton Garrison, *A Spirit-Empowered Church: An Acts 2 Ministry Model* (Springfield, MO: Influence Resources, 2015), 231.

23 Wayne Grudem, *Systematic Theology: An Introduction to Biblical Doctrine*, 2nd ed. (Grand Rapids: Zondervan Academic, 2020), 1523.

24 Kimmie Simon, personal interview with Director of the Worship Center at Oral Roberts University, February 14, 2023.

21 Parental Covering and Resourcing: Preserving the Future of the Church by Setting the Next Generation Up for Success

Jamie Austin

Abstract

For any organization to have a successful future, there must be an emphasis on the handoff of institutional assets and values. This is especially true when it comes to the future of the worldwide church. Today's church leaders need to commit time, energy, and resources to enable younger leaders to successfully fulfill God-birthed dreams and kingdom initiatives. Patriarchal and matriarchal leaders should lend crucial reputational and relational capital, which opens doors to ministry opportunities and vital resources that otherwise would remain out of reach. The health and success of up-and-coming leaders, called of God to shepherd and lead, ought to be a sustained priority of the modern church.

The Context

I serve as the senior pastor of Woodlake Assembly of God in Tulsa, Oklahoma. Established in 1919, Woodlake possesses a rich history and legacy of missions and ministry that spans over one hundred years in Tulsa and around the world. Since its inception, Woodlake's driving passion has been to reach the lost and impact the next generation of believers for the cause of Christ. Woodlake's overarching goals are: first, to see people come to know Jesus Christ as Lord and Savior; second, to help believers find their place in ministry; and finally, to expand the kingdom of God through the local church.

Having been born and raised in this historic church, I have the unique perspective of being a third-generation member—and now, since 2009, its pastor. Over the last decade, I have observed this congregation transition from a steep decline to a thriving multisite church through the Parent Affiliated Church (PAC) model of the Assemblies of God, and a ministry strategy that emphasizes the next generation. This distinct viewpoint has given me the chance to appreciate Woodlake's successful past and witness the harsh realities of church decline and attrition that routinely threaten today's local church.

Introduction

Managing the tension between the "what was" and "what could be" remains an ongoing but critical struggle that every church leader must face. Churches decline for various reasons ranging from depopulation, a downturn in the economy, or a lack of missional focus. Many churches suffer from antiquated missional methodologies that cease to be locally relevant or lack the necessary tools to enact creative, life-giving change. Additionally, one of the greatest contributing factors to church decline is a failure to effectively reach and disciple the next generation with the message of Jesus Christ. An unwillingness to raise up the next generation and set them up for success will only worsen the negative trends we see in many mainline denominations. Ministry to the next generation must therefore be emphasized in every congregation to preserve the future of the church.[1]

Notably, a missional strategy directed at reaching young people involves more than music and program changes. Strategies must be Spirit-led and utilize a multigenerational approach to reach the lost and make disciples, as well as meet the felt needs of local communities. Church leaders must have a solid biblical understanding of what it means to intentionally pursue young people and to see them fulfill their kingdom role. Importantly, when in pursuit of congregational health, revitalization, and multiplication, one must avoid the trap of exclusively relying on one's own skills and initiative. Knowing that his crucifixion, resurrection, and ascension were close, Jesus comforts his disciples with the promised Holy Spirit by saying, "I will not leave you as orphans" (John 14:18).[2] In the original language, the word "orphan" (ὀρφανός), speaks of one who is without comfort or fatherless.[3] Through the Holy Spirit, then, God provides a provisionary father role at the inception of the church (Acts 2:4). This fathering must be present and honored in every strategy that is planned.

Throughout scripture, God gifted and empowered individuals to serve as examples to others, especially young, up-and-coming leaders. The Apostle Paul was one such individual, a spiritual father who counseled: "Whatever you have learned or received or heard from me, or seen in me—put it into practice" (Phil 4:9). The Holy Spirit empowers certain individuals to act as spiritual mothers and fathers who provide necessary supervision and provision for those doing the work of the ministry. This chapter will examine selected biblical models of spiritual parentage and the role they played in the development of their protégés. These models, from both the Old and New Testaments, provide wisdom and guidance through spiritual parenting, covering for protection and accountability, as well as provisionary resourcing to ensure the successful accomplishment of a God-given mission. They guide us in reaching the next generation today.

Parental Covering and Resourcing in the Old Testament

The Old Testament provides a plethora of examples of spiritual patriarchs who empower and enable others to successfully proceed into their God-given calling. These patriarchs reflect the biblical concept of a father, according to Martin H. Manser, who says, "The ideal father, from a biblical perspective, is one who loves God, is obedient to him and reflects this in his daily living and in the care and upbringing of his children."[4] In keeping with this motif, this section will examine three characteristics of these types of relationships: (1) spiritual parentage: assuming a role of strategic influence that provides care, correction, and guidance; (2) covering: allowing others to ride the coattails of one's credibility, providing insight and oversight; and (3) resourcing: making provision for the success of others.

Spiritual Parentage

The theme of spiritual parentage is common throughout the entirety of Scripture. In the Old Testament, the concept of spiritual parentage appears when God chooses Abram, saying, "No longer will you be called Abram; your name will be Abraham, for I have made you a father of many nations" (Gen 17:5). The concept then appears again in the Book of Exodus, when the Lord instructs Moses by saying, "Israel is my firstborn son, and I told you, 'Let my son go, so he may worship me'" (Exod 4:22–23). By describing Israel as a "firstborn son," God conveys the unique nature of the blessings he is bestowing on the nation. As Warren Wiersbe explains, "In the ancient world, the firstborn in every family has special rights and privileges, and God would see to it that Israel, His firstborn, would be redeemed and rewarded."[5] The imagery of father and offspring is one model of spiritual parentage that is powerfully evident and appears to be intentional in the establishment of the covenant relationship between God and his people.

The story of Jethro and Moses in Exodus 18 also demonstrates the model of spiritual parentage where a concerned patriarch provides much needed guidance and correction. Moses is overwhelmed by the responsibilities of leading and caring for the people of God. During a challenging season, Moses sends his wife Zipporah and two sons to stay with his father-in-law, Jethro (Exod 18:2–3), likely because the never-ending waves of decision making, administration, and management had taken their toll.[6] Moses had neglected the care of his family and the care of himself, acting as though Israel's success relied exclusively on him. Exodus 18:13 supports this claim: "The next day Moses took his seat to serve as judge for the people, and they stood around him from morning till evening." While often celebrated, a church leader's inability to balance the tension between their vocational or ministerial calling and the prioritizing their marriage and family is a barrier to a healthy future.

Moses therefore needed an intervention from a spiritual parent—someone he respected as a trusted elder or spiritual father. Jethro immediately recognizes Moses' fatigue and lack of competence, exclaiming, "What is this you are doing for the people? Why do you alone sit as judge, while all these people stand around you from morning till evening?" (Exod 18:14). Jethro then directly challenges his son-in-law: "What you are doing is not good. You and these people who come to you will only wear yourselves out. The work is too heavy for you; you cannot handle it alone" (vv. 17–18). Jethro addresses Moses' foolishness, which only a respected father figure could do, and recognizes the inefficiency of Moses' work. Out of genuine concern, Jethro, an experienced leader himself, advises Moses on how to administrate more effectively by utilizing other gifted leaders in daily decision-making (Exod 18:19–23).

This is a perfect example of spiritual parentage. Jethro's advice marks a turning point for Israel, according to Mark A. Hassler, who notes that it "initiated a strategy for Israel to govern itself."[7] Moses needed the wisdom of a caring father figure who could recognize his weaknesses and speak to them in a way that would bring lasting change for an entire nation's governance.[8]

Covering

Next-in-line leaders often lack their predecessors' well-deserved reputation and credibility to lead effectively. Even when individuals receive their official position and title, this may not translate into immediate allegiance by followers. It takes regular and systematic success over a long period of time for leaders to gain the trust of followers.[9] It may also be necessary for the predecessor to remain in the background of the leadership structure so the new leader may leverage their time-tested influence. Access to influence not yet earned can be a priceless asset provided by a forerunner willing to lend it through covering.

Additionally, God often calls those in a position of influence to provide a covering of security and assurance that enables others to exercise courage and faith. After all, obeying the word of the Lord is often easier said than done. Spiritual parents who provide this type of covering become a physical representation of the promises of God, and function as a vital and necessary support to those called to act during tough times. This vital, relational covering is visible between Deborah and Barak when the king of Canaan oppresses God's people who were suffering the consequences of their idolatry (Judg 4:2). In Judges 4:4–5, Deborah steps into a position of leadership during a difficult time,[10] and functions as God's oracle and judiciary mechanism for the people of God. She operates as prophet and judge, deciding legal matters while holding court under the Palm of Deborah (Judg 4:5).

Despite a strong patriarchal environment, scripture indicates that the Israelites greatly respected Deborah as a leader so much so that, when she summons Barak, he responds without question (Judg 4:6–7). On behalf of the Lord, Deborah directs Barak to lead an attack against Sisera, which he agrees to with one condition: "If you go with me, I will go; but if you don't go with me, I won't go" (v. 8). According to commentary on this verse in John D. Barry et al., Barak seems to demand the presence of Deborah as a sign of assurance that the command to fight indeed came from God—that the message is reliable and authentic.[11] The commentary further hypothesizes that Deborah's reputation as God's mouthpiece superseded that of Barak's and her presence remained necessary for Barak to lead with credibility; Deborah was a known leader, but Barak was not.[12] Whatever the exact reason, Deborah's covering provides confidence and assurance for Barak, which enables him to wage war by faith. This same covering also enabled the armies of Israel to lend their allegiance to Barak, a leader who had yet to prove himself in battle. The presence of Deborah curries the favor and blessing of God, yet the Book of Hebrews lauds Barak's faith.[13]

This relationship exemplifies how rising leaders would be wise to submit to the covering of a man or woman with a proven reputation, especially those who can discern the voice of God and provide guidance while remaining fully present during difficult tasks. On the other hand, creative opportunities for young leaders can also present themselves based on their discipleship relationship with someone older. These relationships can set the stage for a favor, open doors, and positions that otherwise would not be available if not for the right interpersonal connections.

These opportunities manifest in the life of a young Moabite named Ruth and result from being the daughter-in-law of the Jewish widow Naomi (Ruth 1). After a famine and the death of her husband and sons, Ruth's willingness and desire to leave familiar life in Moab to forever link herself to Naomi, her people, and her God (1:16–17) would have profoundly diverged from the cultural norm.[14] Yet, this decision to stay committed, even after Naomi releases her from her customary responsibility, pays great dividends to both Naomi and Ruth.

With no one and no way to provide for themselves, Ruth sets out to glean the fields as a resident foreigner in need (Lev 19:9–10). After hearing of Ruth's commitment to Naomi, Boaz declares, "May the LORD repay you for what you have done. May you be richly rewarded by the LORD, the God of Israel..." (Ruth 2:12). According to Greg A. King, this foreshadowing of favor and salvation proves especially powerful since "[Ruth's] Moabite ancestry would seem to preclude her acceptance by the people of God and make her an unlikely candidate for such a work of grace."[15] Furthermore, when Boaz verbally blesses Ruth, he uses this phrase: "...under whose wings you have come to take refuge" (2:12). The verb phrase "take refuge" (ḥā·sā, חָסָה) implies that the place of refuge is one of "trust and safety."[16] But even as Ruth placed her trust in the God of the Jews, she also had to place her trust in Naomi (2:16). Ruth's commitment to Naomi fosters her belief in Yahweh, which leads to favor with Boaz.[17] Lastly, this favor with Boaz places Ruth in the larger lineage of the Messiah (Ruth 4:18–22).

Perhaps a critical key to success for upcoming leaders is the covering of their elder who is familiar with the landscape as well as its people and customs. Without Naomi, there would have been no Ruth. Naomi's nationality, and her love for Ruth—as well as Ruth's character and commitment to Naomi—opens the door to a relationship with Boaz that would have otherwise remained closed. Apprentices, unaware of what lies ahead, may require the covering of an elder who affords access and kindness that can secure their future success. Like Ruth, young leaders must willingly commit themselves to elders who will cover them with insight and oversight to open the doors of opportunity that would otherwise remain shut. Like Naomi, elders must willingly cover the younger and possibly weaker generation with assets only they possess.

Resourcing

Just as important as providing guidance as a spiritual parent, and extending covering of oversight and insight, resourcing is necessary for the healthy perpetuation of any legacy or undertaking. Ascending leaders often lack the crucial resources to initiate important change or to accomplish visionary endeavors. Men and women desiring to continue a successful legacy would do well to provide the many forms of resourcing necessary for empowering their successor.[18]

Numerous examples of critical resourcing exist in the Old Testament, such as the way David made provisions for Solomon. King David had a vision to build a magnificent temple for God and a "place of rest for the ark of the covenant of the Lord" (1 Chron 28:2). Although David harbored a deep desire to accomplish this, the responsibility ultimately fell to his son Solomon because David had shed blood in war (28:3–6). Thus, God did not reject David for disciplinary reasons but simply had a different plan.[19] The vision for a magnificent temple for the Lord and the Ark of the Covenant would be accomplished, just not through David.

Even though David could not be the one to oversee this task, he ensured its success through his son and successor, Solomon. He begins by giving the plans to Solomon, which include a detailed layout and list of building materials (1 Chron 28:11). David also makes provision out of his own resources so Solomon would have everything he needed to complete this monumental task (1 Chron 29:2–5). David also leveraged the resources of his elders to guarantee that Solomon would have more than enough support to thrive in this endeavor (v. 6).

Importantly, David went to such great lengths to ensure the success of Solomon because he recognized that his son was "inexperienced," and "this palatial structure is not for man but for the LORD God" (1 Chron 29:1). The word "inexperienced" (*rak*,רך) means not only a lack of experience but also "tender, soft, or weak."[20] David recognized that Solomon did not yet possess the fortitude necessary to initiate this massive project. The successful completion of the temple could only come from David making provision from his own personal resources, as well as extending to Solomon the weight of his own legacy of strength and achievement, which rallied his followers to a colossal cause.

Experienced church leaders today know that ministry succession is difficult even under the best of circumstances. Young leaders often lack the reputation and experience necessary to convince and mobilize followers to accomplish monumental tasks. Instead of resting on his own past successes, though, or being content with his own personal achievements, King David responded to God's plan to empower Solomon by doing everything in his power to remove as many barriers as possible for his son and successor. In return, ascending leaders like Solomon must recognize and appreciate that they can benefit greatly from the resources that only time-tested elders have acquired.

Parental Covering and Resourcing in the New Testament

Just as the concept of parental covering is evident in the Old Testament through the patriarchs and prophets leading the nation of Israel, this same model appears in the New Testament narratives describing the Early Church. The leaders of the Early Church utilized mentoring, relational backing, and provision to propel the gospel. From the earliest apostles and their apprentices, the success of one group largely depended on the involvement and investment of those who came before or were further ahead in the process. First, men and women who experienced a life-altering encounter with Christ became part of a radical countercultural movement that significantly impacted both Jewish and secular society (Acts 2:47).[21] Then Christianity expanded through Spirit-empowered men and women, young and old, willing to sacrifice their all, who were commissioned and supported by those who had gone before them.

Spiritual Parentage: Paul and Timothy

The success of the New Testament church depended on the effective handing off of the faith from the apostles and first believers to the next generation of believers and leaders. The Apostle Paul recognized this handoff in the life of young Timothy when he wrote, "I am reminded of your sincere faith, which first lived in your grandmother Lois and in your mother Eunice and, I am persuaded, now lives in you also" (2 Tim 1:5). As Paul compares himself with Timothy, the apostle recognizes that their mutual heritage of faith serves as an opportunity for Paul to insert himself as Timothy's mentor and guide.[22]

Although Paul did not have any biological children, the idea of fatherhood permeates his writings: "Even if you had ten thousand guardians in Christ, you do not have many fathers, for in Christ Jesus I became your father through the gospel. Therefore I urge you to imitate me" (1 Cor 4:15–16). The Greek word for "guardian," *paidagōgos* (παιδαγωγός), describes a "servant working as a child's guardian and tutor."[23] Paul compares his role in the life of the Corinthian church to that of a "father," *gennaō* (γεννάω), which denotes procreation or a progenitor.[24] He even asserts himself as the one responsible for the Corinthian believers. In doing this, he may have been contrasting his role of authority with those who ministered amongst the Corinthians believers but failed to correctly instruct. While a guardian holds a temporary position of guidance and limited clout, a father holds a lifelong position of authority and influence. Scripture implies that Paul took this concept seriously.

Paul applies this same notion to his young disciple Timothy, whom he deputizes to lead the church at Ephesus. The beginning of the first letter to Timothy illustrates Paul's assertion of spiritual parentage: "To Timothy my true son in the faith..." (1 Tim 1:1–2). As Gordon Fee notes, Timothy had the difficult task of "squelching unorthodox doctrine, fruitless philosophical speculation, and misleading instruction in the Mosaic law by unqualified teachers."[25] Paul provides much-needed guidance and direction for this daunting task as Timothy's spiritual father. Also, Paul shoulders the responsibility to ensure the success of the Ephesian church and its young leader, Timothy, his "son in the faith" (1:2).

Throughout Paul's first and second letters to Timothy, he gives detailed instructions concerning leadership and personal conduct: "You then, my son, be strong in the grace that is in Christ Jesus... Join with me in suffering, like a good soldier of Christ Jesus" (2 Tim 2:1–3). The Apostle Paul continues to apply familial language to Timothy by addressing him as "my son" (2 Tim 1:1). Paul repeatedly uses the Greek word for "son," *teknon* (τέκνον), which simply means "child."[26] Fee and Hubbard Jr. note the nature of Paul's unique familial relationship with Timothy: "The apostle's fatherlike affection for his protégé appears in the reflective designation of Timothy as his 'beloved' child in the faith, whose tears at their last parting Paul recalls and whom he longs to see one more time."[27] Paul genuinely viewed Timothy as a son (teknon) and would remain committed to him as any father (*gennaō*) would.

As such, Paul knew that his son in the faith was young and would encounter opposition from sources in positions difficult to refute. Thus, he instructs Timothy, saying, "Don't let anyone look down on you because you are young, but set an example for the believers in speech, in conduct, in love, in faith and in purity.... Do not neglect your gift, which was given you through prophecy when the body of elders laid their hands on you" (1 Tim 4:12–14). Barth Campbell explains why Paul specifically mentions the prophecy over Timothy: "Timothy knew God's will by means of what others said about him (the prophecies) and their confirmation of God's work in his life (the laying on the elders' hands). God's direction for believers' lives is by these means (though not exclusively so)—which are corporate as well as private."[28] When enduring hardship and opposition, Paul knew that Timothy would need to recall the public and prophetic confirmation of God's will for his life and the giftings bestowed upon him, especially when dealing with unavoidable confrontation.

Paul, therefore, protects Timothy but also challenges him in a way that only a father could. Paul uses the imagery of a soldier, athlete, and farmer as examples of how Timothy should conduct himself in 2 Timothy 2:3–6. Although familiar, Aída Besançon Spencer explains how these illustrative images are descriptive and direct and could only be used by a mentor with close relational bonds.[29] Paul furthers this challenge to remain strong and in position when dealing with false teachers in 2 Timothy 2:15–16. Spencer argues that Paul knew that young Timothy would be tempted to waste time and energy proving himself to those who sought "a road to destruction."[30] Consequently, Paul instructs him to avoid pointless and distracting interactions with anyone who opposed his message and leadership.

Like any good mentor, Paul also refused to hide the ugliness that comes with a calling: "You, however, know all about my teaching, my way of life, my purpose, faith, patience, love, endurance, persecutions, sufferings—what kinds of things happened to me in Antioch, Iconium and Lystra, the persecutions I endured" (2 Tim 3:10–11). In Antioch, Paul was driven out because of jealousy, and in Iconium, he narrowly escaped stoning; in Lystra, he was stoned and left for dead (Acts 13:50, 14:5–6, 14:19–20). For Timothy to minister successfully, he needed to understand that difficulties and persecution come as a natural part of his calling.

Paul and Timothy exemplify how ascending leaders tasked with a calling that goes beyond their current giftings and experience require the loving and watchful eye of spiritual mothers and fathers who understand firsthand the difficulties that their protégés will face. Like Timothy, potential successors need to understand that opposition and persecution accompany leadership. Paul refused to hide these realities but encouraged Timothy by saying, "Yet the Lord rescued me from all of them" (2 Tim 3:11). Spiritual mothers and fathers, having stood the test of time and experienced God's faithfulness firsthand, serve as the ideal examples of faith and conduct.

Covering: Ananias and Saul

The birth of the Early Church and the spread of the gospel required the enlistment of some unlikely individuals. These individuals needed someone to testify on their behalf as to the legitimacy of their conversion and calling, and provide oversight until the individual had earned enough credibility to be trusted. The New Testament conveys the critical nature of such strategic relationships where one individual rides the coattails of someone else to aid in their maturity and growth as well as acceptance into the community of faith until they can establish a track record of legitimacy and stability.

Saul, later known as the Apostle Paul, greatly profited from someone willing to provide relational covering. Prior to his encounter with Christ, Paul had a terrifying reputation. He was "breathing murderous threats" on his way to arrest and imprison followers of Christ when he had a radical encounter with Jesus (Acts 9:1–9). It would certainly take more than persuasive preaching or conversation to convince the leaders of the "the Way" to accept Paul as a fellow follower of Christ (Acts 9:2). It would take relational covering.

The first relational covering came from Ananias, whom God specifically calls to minister to Paul during the initial days of his transformation (Acts 9:11–12). After receiving this calling, Ananias voices his trepidation in 9:13–14, but God refuses to allow Ananias out of this assignment. Paul receives physical and spiritual sight that radically changes the course of his life and, ultimately, the New Testament church.[31] The touch of a fellow believer, the infilling of the Holy Spirit, and the healing that followed were the confirmation necessary for Paul to begin his ministry. Ananias faithfully and willingly trusted God's design to utilize Saul in a powerful way and risked his own safety and security in obedience to this plan.

Ananias even extends the title of "brother" to Saul, providing a weighty confirmation that Saul had ceased to be an enemy of Christ and the church. By addressing Saul as "brother," Horton argues that he acknowledges him as a fellow member of the Way (Acts 9:17).[32] In this passage, the Greek word for "brother," *adelphos* (ἀδελφός), can mean "fellow believer,"[33] and Horton agrees with the significance of Ananias's decision to call him this: "He undoubtedly continued living in humble obedience to the Lord and to His Word. But Saul never forgot this godly man who was the first believer to call him brother."[34] By faith and great personal risk, Ananias acknowledges Saul's calling and potential as a fellow follower of Christ. God would use Saul to propagate the cross of Christ into circles of influence inaccessible to most, but it first required a fellow brother to make this possible.

The contemporary church desperately needs those like Ananias, men and women who recognize the work of the Holy Spirit in the life of someone whom others have written off as "hard to reach," "too far gone," or "not worth the effort." Such men and women see the possibilities instead of what is visible and willingly risk personal comfort to see a calling fulfilled. There exist many "Saul's" on the verge of becoming fully devoted to Christ, but they need an Ananias to acknowledge them as "brothers."

Resourcing

Not having ample resources remains challenging for the continuation or success of any visionary endeavor. Just as Aaron aided Moses, David provided for Solomon, and King Artaxerxes supplied Nehemiah, the New Testament encourages leaders to make provision for the efforts of others. A healthy parental covering involves the supplying of resources necessary to ensure the continuation of a healthy legacy and the success of the individual or group being parented. Those in a spiritual parenting role should willingly make sacrificial investments for their sons and daughters in the faith, especially when it involves a kingdom initiative.

The Apostle Paul felt the weight of responsibility of making provision for the believers in Jerusalem. As the recipient of outside resources supplied by patrons and benefactors such as Lydia of Philippi (Acts 16) and Phoebe of Cenchrea (Rom 16:1–2), Paul understood the need for outside help.[35] Through leveraging his position, reputation, and relationships, Paul procured much-needed resources on behalf of fellow believers who could not provide for themselves (Rom 15:26).[36] Through these provisionary deeds, Paul provides a clear template for the modern church to give consistently and generously to those in need, especially fellow believers, to further the gospel (Gal 2:19, 6:10; Phil 4:18). In Jerusalem specifically, Paul takes it upon himself to rally support for them by collecting contributions from believers in Macedonia and Achaia (Rom 15:25–26).[37] He refers to these believers as "his people," using his reputation, position, and influence to ensure others shared in their burden (Acts 24:17). The apostle clearly felt a deep responsibility and took it upon himself to effectively meet their needs in a God-honoring way.

Throughout his ministry, Paul taught that generous giving and the sharing of resources should come naturally to those who claim Christ (1 Cor 16:1–2). In teaching about and gathering resources for others, he made a "widespread effort involving many of the churches"[38] and established a practice of resourcing believers. Resourcing would become not only characteristic of the New Testament church, but it unified believers. Paul celebrates the giving of the Macedonian church by challenging the Corinthians: "For I testify that they gave as much as they were able, and even beyond their ability. Entirely on their own, they urgently pleaded with us for the privilege of sharing in this service to the Lord's people" (2 Cor 8:2–4). Paul carefully explains that his goal is not to create undue hardships on others but to foster equality: "At the present time your plenty will supply what they need, so that in turn their plenty will supply what you need. The goal is equality" (2 Cor 8:13–14). John Barclay notes that Paul sought to foster equality between Jewish and non-Jewish believers as an "essential corollary of Paul's good news, as witnessed by his efforts to complete the collection for Jerusalem (Rom 15:25–27)."[39] In doing so, Paul also established the idea that generosity would be reciprocated if the need arose.

Paul's concern for the Jerusalem believers provides an example for leaders of the contemporary church. Those in a position of parental covering should leverage their influence to mobilize others with resources to share in the burden of provision. The stewardship of resources among believers involves the extending of those resources to others, especially within the community of faith (2 Cor 8:7).

Conclusion

The theme of parental covering consistently appears throughout scripture. From the patriarchs of the Old Testament to the apostolic leaders of the New Testament, God empowered men and women to serve as godly examples, willing to provide guidance and wisdom to those coming after them (Phil 4:9). These gifted and called individuals, with a track record of stability and success act as spiritual parents, provided coverings of insight and oversight. They lent relational credibility to ascending leaders in need of legitimacy. They also extended personal resources and mobilized the resources of others to safeguard their legacy and empower those they parented.

In both Old and New Testament examples of parental covering, one trait remains unmistakable: the fervent concern for the success and continuation of the work of God. This desire overrides the pursuit of personal gain and reputation building. These progenitors recognize the divine shift and embrace their supporting role in the lives of their progeny.

For the contemporary church, congregational health, revitalization, and multiplication will be championed and achieved by leaders who understand that the kingdom of God is and always will be the primary objective. They remain ready and willing to make any sacrifice and investment necessary to see this objective come to fruition. Upcoming leaders and apprentices must stay humble and take an honoring position of submission and reception as a son or daughter in the faith. As the next generation of twenty-first-century leaders emerges, aspiring ministers would do well to identify those with the mantle of parental covering, yield, and avoid the mistake of operating as if success depended solely on their own abilities and resources.

Notes

1 Much of this chapter is adapted from my doctoral project, which I completed in 2023 at Assemblies of God Theological Seminary. For more information see James Austin, *The Benefits of the Parent Affiliated Church Model for Church Revitalization and Multiplication* (Ph.D. diss., Assemblies of God Theological Seminary, Evangel University, 2023).

2 All scripture quotations, unless otherwise noted, are from the New International Version (NIV).

3 James Strong, s.v. "orphan," *Enhanced Strong's Lexicon* (Woodside Bible Fellowship, 1995), Logos.

4 Martin H. Manser, s.v. "father," *Dictionary of Bible Themes: The Accessible and Comprehensive Tool for Topical Studies* (London: Martin Manser, 2009), Logos.

5 Warren W. Wiersbe, *Be Delivered (Exodus): Finding Freedom by Following God*, Be Series Commentary (Colorado Springs, CO: Chariot Victor Publishing, 1998), 21.

6 Gordon D. Fee and Robert L. Hubbard Jr., eds., *The Eerdmans Companion to the Bible* (Grand Rapids: Eerdmans, 2011), 115.

7 Mark A. Hassler, "Jethro," in *The Lexham Bible Dictionary*, eds. John D. Barry et al. (Bellingham, WA: Lexham Press, 2016), Logos.

8 Leslie Veen, "Jethro and Moses: A Biblical Model for Supervision from Exodus 18," *Reflective Practice* 38 (August 2018), 223.

9 For more on this, refer to John Maxwell's book, *5 Levels of Leadership: Proven Steps to Maximize Your Potential* (New York: Center Street, 2013).

10 Keren Mock, "Deborah: A Rashomon of the Last Canaanite War," *Japan Mission Journal* 69:2 (Summer 2015), 109.

11 John D. Barry et al., *Faithlife Study Bible* (Bellingham, WA: Lexham Press, 2016), Judges 4:8.

12 Barry et al., *Faithlife Study Bible*, Judges 4:10.

13 Ronald W. Pierce, "Deborah: Troublesome Woman or Woman of Valor?" *Priscilla Papers* 32:2 (Spring 2018), 6, https://www.cbeinternational.org/resource/article/priscilla-papers-academic-journal/deborah-troublesome-woman-or-woman-valor/, accessed February 23, 2022.

14 Fee and Hubbard Jr., eds., *The Eerdmans Companion to the Bible*, 196.

15 Greg A. King, "Ruth 2:1-13," *Interpretation* 52:2 (April 1998), 184.

16 James Swanson, s.v. "take refuge," *Dictionary of Biblical Languages with Semantic Domains: Hebrew (Old Testament)* (Oak Harbor, WA: Logos Research Systems, Inc., 1997), Logos.

17 Timothy Paul Erdel, "The Book of Ruth and Hope in Hard Times," *Priscilla Papers* 25:1 (Winter 2011), 7, https://www.cbeinternational.org/resource/article/priscilla-papers-academic-journal/book-ruth-and-hope-hard-times/, accessed February 19, 2022.

18 "Resourcing" refers to providing the varied and necessary resources to carry out a God-ordained project or legacy continuation.

19 Charles Swindoll, *David: A Man of Passion and Destiny* (Nashville: Thomas Nelson, 2000), 267.

20 Robert L. Thomas, s.v. "inexperienced," *New American Standard Hebrew-Aramaic and Greek Dictionaries: Updated Edition* (Anaheim, CA: Foundation Publications, Inc., 1998), Logos.

21 Henry Thorne Sell, *Studies in Early Church History* (Willow Grove, PA: Woodlawn Electronic Publishing, 1998), Logos.

22 Aída Besançon Spencer, *2 Timothy and Titus*, New Covenant Commentary Series, eds. Michael F. Bird and Craig Keener (Eugene, OR: Cascade Books, 2014), 81.

23 Ceslas Spicq and James D. Ernest, *Theological Lexicon of the New Testament*, vol. 3 (Peabody, MA: Hendrickson Publishers, 1994), 1.

24 James Swanson, s.v. "father," *Dictionary of Biblical Languages with Semantic Domains: Greek (New Testament)* (Oak Harbor, WA: Logos Research Systems, Inc., 1997), Logos.

25 Fee and Hubbard Jr., eds., *The Eerdmans Companion to the Bible*, 687.

26 Rick Brannan, s.v. "son," *The Lexham Analytical Lexicon to the Greek New Testament* (Oak Harbor, WA: Logos Bible Software, 2011), Logos.

27 Fee and Hubbard Jr., eds., *The Eerdmans Companion to the Bible*, 689.

28 Barth Lynn Campbell, "Rhetorical Design in 1 Timothy 4," *Bibliotheca Sacra* 154:614 (April 1997), 204.

29 Spencer, *2 Timothy and Titus*, 99.

30 Spencer, *2 Timothy and Titus*, 106.

31 Stanley M. Horton, *Acts*, Logion Press Commentary (Springfield, MO: Logion Press, 2001), 184–185.

32 Horton, *Acts*, 184.

33 James Swanson, s.v. "brother," *Dictionary of Biblical Languages with Semantic Domains: Greek (New Testament)* (Oak Harbor, WA: Logos Research Systems, Inc., 1997), Logos.

34 Horton, *Acts*, 186.

35 Margaret Mowczko, "Wealthy Women in the First-Century Roman World and in the Church," *Priscilla Papers* 32:3 (Summer 2018), 4–5, https://www.cbeinternational.org/resource/article/priscilla-papers-academic-journal/wealthy-women-first-century-roman-world-and/, accessed 23 February 2022.

36 Warren W. Wiersbe, *The Bible Exposition Commentary*, vol. 1 (Wheaton, IL: Victor Books, 1996), 621.

37 The Book of Acts records at least two reasons as to why the believers of Jerusalem were impoverished: the large number of widows and (Acts 6) and a famine in the area (Acts 11). Either way, the Apostle Paul strongly taught that the sharing of resources should be a common practice for believers.

38 Bruce B. Barton and Grant R. Osborne, *1 & 2 Corinthians*, Life Application Bible Commentary (Wheaton, IL: Tyndale House, 1999), 243.

39 John M. G. Barclay, "Faith and Self-Detachment from Cultural Norms: A Study in Romans 14–15," *Zeitschrift Für Die Neutestamentliche Wissenschaft Und Die Kunde Der Älteren Kirche* 104:2 (2013), 208.

Postscript: The God of Hope, Across Generations

Jaime L. Riddle

What the contributors in this volume all share is a heart for the upcoming generations and their flourishing in Christ. Each author has articulated challenges that they see confronting the younger generations' Spirit-empowered future. But each has also voiced their approaches, strategies, and faith that the next generation will indeed receive the baton being passed to them and carry it forward. As we reflect on the breadth of content and contexts presented, several summary thoughts come to mind.

Pentecost as a Divine Solution for Generational Transfer

The first is that Pentecost is God's divine solution to the recurring challenges of generational transfer. To be sure, every generation since Adam and Eve has encountered the difficulties of passing on the faith. But, in Genesis 1, God's original design was for neither children nor generations to ever be lost. God created Adam and Eve to be fruitful, multiply, and spread his dominion over the earth (1:26–28) while never being separated from his voice, his presence, or one another. With no sin or death intervening, generational transfer would have been unproblematic. The original extended family from Eden would have become like one holy generation that filled the world with the knowledge of God—and actualized Loescher's perfect intergenerational ministry of old and young seated at the same table "as partners and siblings...on mission together."[1] No generation gaps, no rejection of the truth, no one lost.

The Fall, however, made generational transfer challenging by destroying communion with God and one another. Bunn outlines the struggle in the Old Testament to disciple the next generation to hear, obey, and obtain God's better promises[2]—only to fail many times except for instances where, as Austin chronicles, leaders were peculiarly intentional.[3] God became "a God of generations," Luce says, incarnating his eternal plans progressively, but obstructed by separation and rebellion.[4] Doubt, rejection of God and elders, and subsistence faith were common for the same reasons they still are. To that end, when Jesus himself came and faced the end of his own life and ministry, he looked at his next-generation team and told them to wait (Luke 24:49; Acts 1:4). They were saved, willing disciples, and he was ready to pass the baton. But he knew they needed something before they could go further. They needed to be empowered and filled with the same breath of life that he had, and that recalled God's breath into Adam where it had all started (Gen 2:7; 1 Cor 15:45).

Thus, Jesus atoned for "the gift" and "the promise" (Acts 2:38–39). God dispatched the Holy Spirit from heaven to overcome the obstacles inherent to generational transfer and enable the intergenerational walk with God that he originally envisioned. Bunn describes this as the Spirit uniting "the one people of God across time and space" and helping them enter the theological "today," which "extends far off into the future, as well as back to the beginning when the LORD first spoke to humans in the garden."[5] Spirit-baptism gives God's people their identity and bearings by being the transcendent experience that unites them to the past, the future, and each other. The Spirit also empowers followers for Christlike love and action in every context across the world they can find themselves in. This is why Rodriguez is wise to exhort that "Everything is in vain if the Spirit is left out."[6] After salvation, Pentecost becomes the method given by God and employed by Jesus for subsequent generations to navigate the next phase of the mission, stay fervent, and overcome the cruelty, confusion, impurity, impoverishment, and brokenness that lost cultures exude.

Herein lies the importance of the current Spirit-empowered movement and the bold opening remark by Ma, Onyinah, and Saylor that the Holy Spirit would have "the centrality in reshaping the world."[7] *Centrality* goes past the Spirit as intellectual shibboleth and even the importance of his filling and presence. It goes further by presenting a vision for Spirit-empowerment that recalls creation and enables recreation by urging us to imitate how Jesus made the Spirit's leading the center of his life and ministry transfer. Thus, Stavnichuk and Plüss declare at the outset: "Pneumatology is our critical theory for life" and the "starting point" for all theological or ministerial conversations.[8] Clark similarly contends that in any discussion of youth or the next generation, "we should never stop talking about the baptism of the Holy Spirit."[9] But it is so easy to! In a church where I worked with young adults for years, Spirit-baptism was often seen as "messy," complicated, or something to do somewhere else, privately. I am therefore personally thankful to be challenged by these chapters to rethink twenty-first century global youth ministry with Spirit-centrality. To meet the level of challenge presented, prioritizing Christ's own method of empowerment and transformation seems like exactly the wisdom we need.

The Challenges are Real

Acknowledging the power and priority of the Holy Spirit is not meant to diminish the difficulties that Millennials, Gen Z, and the newer generations face. Globally, no one has been exempt from the impact of the pandemic, international conflicts, modernity, and cultural deterioration. Harris warns that everyone is now expected to deal with a "fast-moving world where people have little time to process before other adverse things occur," and that "the good, bad, holy, profane, and propaganda all flood the digital audience at the click of a button."[10] Change appears to be the new norm while the "unparalleled cultural milieu" described by Saylor and Savage is "drowning out the voices" of family and the church.[11] Life feels fast and unstable, and the church seems largely incapable of rescuing society from the downward spiral of secularism. Within the West especially, Stavnichuk and Plüss lament how the lack of warmth and *koinonia* in mainstream theology has branded Christianity as sterile, and sidelined it as an option for the average citizen.[12] Thus the medicine which would heal many has been taken off the market.

While the more mature generations have undoubtedly had trouble adapting to these changes, Josefsson and Wenell maintain that the younger generations bear the primary burden of "negotiating" the transformation of life brought on by modernity and global secularism.[13] The difficulty of doing so bears out Saylor and Savage's data, for example, that youth across the globe are struggling with gender identity, same-sex attraction, depression, anxiety, and suicidal thoughts.[14] Tjihenuna observes it in Namibian youth, saying anxiety, eating disorders, substance abuse, and gender confusion "are nothing new to the Born-Free generation."[15] Khai and Khai report depression and suicidal ideation within the Burmese American immigrant community.[16] And the Oginos' ministry to lost and spiritually distressed young adults in Japan reveals deep contemporary angst.[17] Exacerbating the global crisis in mental health is that a world of unprecedented media and technology is causing Gen Z to be what Harris calls, "anxiously digital." Overall, the authors in this volume collectively report significant concern about the raw data that describes the one-fourth of the global population which is currently youth and young adults.

Christian youth need even more support in figuring out redemptive ways to handle modern life. Saylor and Savage report that 40 percent of self-identified Christian teens say they have never read the Bible. A substantial number disclose ignorance of basic truths and disciplines, despite a professed desire to know them. Between 40 to 50 percent admit struggling with pornography and sexual activity prior to marriage.[18] Harris explains that, especially in the realm of sexual and ethical beliefs, Christian youth are "participating in secularization" even while "rejecting secularism."[19] This type of cognitive dissonance is noted in Josefsson and Wenell, who point to cultural pressure on Swedish youth who want to follow Christ but believe Christian morals are at odds with contemporary ones. They further describe the result of overwhelming secularization as "an ideological trial" that puts each Christian youth in the role of "constantly fend[ing] off and negotiat[ing] with other ways of understanding life based on the beliefs that they themselves need to be the guarantor of."[20] This is a heavy load to bear.

Lastly, the numerical loss of Christians throughout the world is concerning and addressed by multiple authors. Luce, who compares the trajectory of Christian growth to Islam's, concludes that "At the present rate, Christianity will not continue being the dominant belief system of the world."[21] In part, this is due to the rise of the "nones" who report no religious affiliation. Relatedly, Loescher expresses concern over young adults who "graduate from church" when they graduate high school.[22] The ensuing aging-up problem of churches is passionately addressed by Pastors Lia and How,[23] with "antiquated methodologies" being addressed by almost every contributor in this book.[24] These are the types of realities confronting the twenty-first-century global church and why Spirit-empowerment is such a crucial variable in the fight for youth and their future.

The Holy Spirit is the Difference-Maker

In view of this, Harris prophetically asserts, "This is no small task, yet we have hope!"[25] The Holy Spirit, who resurrected Jesus' body from the grave (Rom 8:11), is adequate in every century for the task of reviving, rejuvenating, restoring, and redeeming. The modern age has not specially handicapped Gen Z and the younger generations from receiving everything God wants to give them; but they do need support and guidance to turn the current challenges into opportunities for the Spirit to show himself strong. Saylor and Savage frame the data in an exemplary way for Spirit-empowered readers: that such reports, even when the numbers are disappointing, "give voice to the issues that young people globally are facing, in order to more strategically confront the narratives of culture with *the better story of God and his kingdom."*[26]

Praise God for his "better story!" This begins with the gospel and a "sacred reality in relation to God" that the Holy Spirit reveals to the world.[27] The Spirit witnesses that humanity is not alone and that there is hope, power, and divine enablement. This greater, "sacred reality" is what Mendoza and Simon endeavor to bring into ORU chapel services as they craft moments of encounter for students.[28] It is what Michio and Chaa Chaa Ogino bring into the rural countryside of Japan when they demonstrate the compassion of Jesus to suffering young adults. Both sets of these practitioners are talented, yet they articulate permitting *Jesus* "to be fully in charge"[29] so that the Spirit may transform identities, systems, and spiritual atmosphere.

Welcoming Change

Importantly, all the authors in this volume emphasize permitting the Spirit to change, modernize, and move with the times. Stavnichuk describes the Spirit as operating not from a static transcendental mindset but rather in a "resonant" relationship with the world: hearing, moving, and being moved in response to problems and circumstances.[30] Rodriguez concurs, saying, "The Spirit is always in constant movement; therefore it is the obligation of each community, group, and individual to discern the direction of the Spirit by...moving...with him."[31] Gryskiewicz agrees, exhorting Pentecostal church leaders to change and create structures *kata pneuma* [according to the Spirit].[32] These exhortations confront our inner concerns about how things are changing and if we should change with people—or should people change with us. Fortunately, the New Testament describes both. The apostles had to move with the Spirit to reach new cities, solve new problems, and construct applications in line with Jesus' original teachings. It was challenging—but apparently not contradictory—to be both moved by the Spirit to change the entire world, while staying grounded in the Spirit regarding what Jesus and scriptural faith said.

Mendoza and Simon reaffirm this tension as being both "rooted *and* equipped to change the world for Jesus."[33] Rodriguez, similarly, construes the Spirit-empowered church as "affirming its roots in the deep and rich Christian tradition, *and* leading it to grow beyond the boundaries of traditional church life."[34] Onyinah, in his reformation of the Church of Pentecost, has been leading his denomination through this tension in order to figure out what a twenty-first century holiness identity looks like—and doesn't look like.[35] Prempeh describes Onyinah's efforts as protecting the sanctity of the CoP's doctrine and establishment while pruning unfruitful branches and some of its harsher elements. His wisdom that "while the words of the covenant remain canonized, the world of the covenant changes" implies why a Spirit-empowered community must be brave enough to welcome change and not see it as opposed to honoring foundations. Not only do the meanings of older traditions change as the world around them changes, but there are new things to do that need attending to.

Nyanni describes a similar deliberation process in diaspora communities, with Millennial Afro-Western churches moving away from heavy cosmological dualism and towards a view of the Spirit leading people to make better choices. He promotes modern worship, social media, and service times, yet lauds aspects of traditional African theology and Pentecostal services that he hopes churches will retain.[36] Tjihenuna, likewise, appreciates her Namibian church roots but urges Spirit-empowered denominations to repent of any unfruitful alliances from the past, historically passive roles, or "tainted narratives" that were morally irresponsible. In her view, it is time to have better conversations about "progressive Pentecostalism" and social action.[37] Her quoting of Veli-Matti Kärkkäinen—that the church should be "cooperating with God in the work of evangelism and social action in the anticipation of the new creation"—is apropos for acknowledging rootedness, modernization, and a resonant relationship with the Spirit all at once. The topic of what "new creation social action is" is timely for Spirit-empowered generations to explore. As is discussion of how the Holy

Spirit might change deeper levels of society as an extension of revival—not in place of it, but because of it.

Other authors explore the dynamism of the Spirit. Luce asserts that the church needs "new wineskins."[38] Harris says "revisioning," especially when it comes to Gen Z's passion for justice, peace, technology, and the arts. His statement that "Podcasts and YouTube are the new pulpits" is another area the Spirit-empowered community could explore further.[39] On the mission field, Jane Kim testifies that online technology has radically changed the success of children's Sunday schools across the Global South.[40] This provokes more of the needed discussion about how technology could bring the world to deeper faith. We may conclude that, on the one hand, Bunn is right to emphasize that the Spirit has been building continuously through the ages so that "in order to grasp what the Spirit is now doing, the new generation must become acquainted with what the Spirit has been doing."[41] This prevents us from having an arrogant, deconstructionist stance that tears down rather than builds up. And yet, this rootedness probably works best when combined with what Harris calls "reimagining faith," so that "'better' is not a return to some previous generation's way" but is "a search for a way forward that includes the digital age with guidance and temperance."[42]

Promoting Experimentation

When it comes to Luce's "new wineskins," some authors have offered new models of church altogether, with new atmospheres attached to them. For example, Gryskiewicz describes European international churches (ICs) experimenting with different kinds of mono-cultural and multi-cultural models to reach diaspora youth, immigrants, refugees, and cultural hybrids. ICs are a new phenomenon, and more research will help discover what works best for different kinds of communities. But the Spirit is likely leading if 61 percent of churches report that refugees are responding to the gospel![43]

Spirit-empowered churches are also experimenting with ways to bridge multigenerational ethnic congregations. Khai and Khai, for example, hold both ethnic and hybrid services, lead worship in Zomi and English, and teach language classes for fluency in both native and English tongues.[44] Spirit-led bridging is also described in Nyanni, where he reports that churches with a fusion of Anglican, Evangelical, Charismatic, and

Pentecostal influences experience greater evangelistic success.[45] There is no template for what these authors relay, but the Spirit seems to be leading God's people to experiment with new expressions and service flows in response to what is right for a certain time, place, and people. Interestingly, Nyanni describes "play" in the Spirit as a feature of African Pentecostal services where the goal is to discern where the Spirit is or what he is doing in that particular meeting.[46] Perhaps on a more macrocosmic level, the Spirit is permitting "play" for leaders to discover what he is doing as they create, invent, and do more of what bears fruit.

Experimentation can also be seen in Josefsson and Wenell's discussion over what kind of place church should be in the twenty-first century. Should the church continue its trajectory away from being a place where content is transmitted and people are led towards a moment of repentance and conversion? Should it instead gravitate towards providing "space" for each individual to work out the slower process of "life negotiation" that they need to own their own faith?[47] This question is one that will take time to answer. Along with it are subsidiary questions Josefsson and Wenell consider about whether worship songs might convey theology better than the sermon, or at least foster deeper internalization of truth.[48] Much of this goes against the traditional model of church in Western Europe, but Mendoza and Simon wisely warn that "the goal of the Kingdom is not the exact replication of methods but rather the reproduction and multiplication of the movement of the Spirit that knows precisely what that generation needs."[49] So, the question about altering the atmosphere or function of churches remains one of experimentation, to see if spiritual fruit actually multiplies.

Lastly, the church becoming an intergenerational space is explored by Austin, Loescher, Lia and How. To figure out how to bond generations so that young and old alike are on the same team is a challenging goal. But this is Loescher's aim. She suggests that the church intentionally network "spiritual grandparents" with young adults because they are "uniquely suited" to impart what the other needs.[50] Lia and How, with similar assumptions, advocate "veterans" and young ones being partnered and affirmed until they see each other as "reinforcements."[51] Austin recommends that any authoritarianism that has characterized older generation ministries be exchanged for a style of openness, resourcing, and parenting.[52] All of these church-shifting dynamics require significant experimentation led by the Spirit. It may be that the Spirit is taking the next step with intergenerational church and changing baton-passing to be more like baton-sharing, in order to face the world's challenges.

Embracing the Supra-Rational

The Holy Spirit may also modernize the church through prophetically innovative ideas that I will term "supra-rational," because—like Spirit-baptism and the tongues of fire that came from heaven—they appear foolish or laughable to onlookers when they are actually the wisdom of God. Khai and Khai, for example, were laughed at as they prayed for the Zomi people to be brought to Tulsa—until Tulsa became the home of the Zomi people in the U.S.! They crossed a culture gap and a generation gap with their strategy to sing and preach in Burmese and English at the World Cup USA, reaching over 160,000 people. Then their soccer ministry was used to bring the first open-air crusade to Myanmar, where it is illegal to preach the gospel! Their motto, "For the Game, For the Gospel," which could have appeared foolish to some, was wisdom to God.[53]

Petersen, likewise, laughed at himself when he thought of starting a ministry to children. But ultimately he obeyed the Spirit's prompting about "the upside-down kingdom" and "Jesus' rules remain[ing] a complete reversal of the order of things."[54] Now he, Kim, and Loescher argue that the universality of the Pentecostal message needs to expand to include the young generations as equal to adult generations in the Great Commission.[55] Put a different way, "Children need to take their place in the life of our churches—and not just as little kids we chase around," insists Kim.[56] Their ministries must not be inferior or secondary in importance.

Like Pentecost sounded to the onlookers, some Spirit-empowered convictions like these can sound foolish because they are ahead of their time; they are only explicable later, as part of overcoming an entrenched difficulty. Luce says, for example, that the church growth movement is only just catching on that "investing in youth is the key intervention in church decline."[57] So the argument for prioritizing children can either sound strange or poignantly prophetic. We know that through abortion, trafficking, and countless forms of corruption, children are under significant attack. Perhaps there is something the Spirit is unlocking in this call to generational universality that is timely for Gen Z and those who will meet the enemy's onslaught against children in this age. Petersen's and Kim's related exhortation that children's ministry must come first in church could even end up changing the trajectory of Christian growth that everyone is concerned about for the next century. It may not make sense that driving seven hours up a mountain to clothe a child could have an impact[58]—or that old, discarded materials on Facebook could empower an entire demographic[59]—but evidence suggests that both are true. Children that ChildHope helped years ago are now returning as young adults to minister to more children, and the under-resourced children whom FSST serves in the Global South are demographically the future of the Spirit-empowered movement.

Then there are those taking an axe to the iconic youth group, like Luce, who claims, "The construct of youth ministry as it has evolved over the past fifty years is dead; it is ineffective and threatens the future of the church."[60] The language is provocative, but churches like Heart of God Church and Planetshakers are reconstructing their entire communities and seeing fruit. HOGC has made a church "for youth, run by youth" and is now a global voice in the potential of children to lead.[61] Planetshakers has been volunteering its youth ministry, Planetboom, to be on the streets of Melbourne as agents of racial and ethnic reconciliation in areas where adults have failed. They first practiced it within their own walls by interceding, inviting, and discipling troubled groups; raising up diverse leadership; and refusing to believe that a demographic in their city was unreachable.[62] To Luce's point, this type of serious faith is not fostered by the typical youth group. He, along with Saylor and Savage, and Coombs, Harrison, and Harrison all warn that the gospel bar should be higher, to create more committed youth.[63] Meanwhile, the discipleship program Planetboom uses has enabled ongoing revival in their youth for two decades.[64] This indicates that the Holy Spirit is desiring young people to wed deep encounter with becoming a source of healing, justice, and peace—exactly where Harris says Gen Z's heart is.[65]

When all is said and done, the supernatural existence of the Spirit, with ideas that are the deep things of God's (1 Cor 2:10) rather than our own, must be acknowledged. As Ma, Onyinah, and Saylor humbly state at the outset of this book: "The organizers and editors have been careful not to pretend that the present generation can shape the next one—the agent will ultimately have to be the Holy Spirit."[66] This is foolishness to the non-

Spirit-empowered mind. And yet, some new, foolish things will continue to shame the wise (1 Cor 1:27). This is not because God is irrational or reactionary, but because he is supra-rational and mysteriously wise. As scholars and practitioners, we observe what is going on and speak about what we see to capture it, explain it, and guide it more intentionally. But ultimately the Spirit's work goes on through us as a current of God that operates whether people take note of it or not, like it or not, or conceptualize it rightly or not. It is a fearful but wonderful thing to recognize. May he have that centrality. And may we be postured rightly, so we can discern it and participate as much as we can.

Being the People of Hope

Finally, it must be said that one of our biggest assets as Spirit-empowered people is hope. Admittedly, it can be hard in the modern age to hope, especially given the disasters and the pressures of a digitally connected world. As a young adult pastor myself, I have observed a corporate depression at times in Millennials and Gen Z—it has been hard for them to have hope in themselves in or in the world they are inheriting.

However, as many contributors in this volume bravely remind us, it is our job to have hope for them—and in them, alongside of them—until they hope. We sit at "the kids table," as Loescher puts it, and enjoy encouraging them and tutoring them into mature Spirit-empowerment.[67] This ministry is "always warranted," maintains Clark, because it comes around.[68] Like many others, I would not be in the position I am had a spiritual family not adopted me, believed in me, and invested in me as a young adult. Eventually, I became a young adult leader, and now I have four young adult children with whom I am walking alongside. So I have been walking the journey of prophetically hoping in the future for some time—but first, someone extended that grace to me. The future depends on this continual, hopeful outreach.

Furthermore, hope works! Who would have thought, just a few decades ago, that it was possible that young people would abandon secularism? After the church's tenacity in the face of an enormous campaign to abandon faith in the twentieth century, Saylor and Savage report that two-thirds of current teens globally say that their spiritual journey is important to their identity. Additionally, most would go to church if invited. And 71 percent say that the Christians they know are kind and caring![69] What a reversal from the picture of the church that the world painted to scare everyone away from Christian community. Luce insists that the track record of more than two decades of focusing on the young generations "is reason for *hope* for Christian leaders around the world."[70] Confirming his point, Saylor and Savage report that the majority of religious teens still see their churches, scriptures, and parents as the guiding moral influence in their lives.[71] Social media and peers are certainly competitive influences, but evidence shows that teens are not, in large part, rebelling from their parents or the faith of the older generations. In fact, Harris reports the biggest youth rebellion currently exists in areas of intense secularism, where teens are searching for God again.[72] These are huge victories that the Holy Spirit has wrought in the last generation or two as a hopeful church has believed, interceded, and walked alongside their natural and spiritual children.

Another victory lies in the area of racial, ethnic, and generational reconciliation. Since Azusa planted a seed, Pentecostal-Charismatic churches have spent the last century working towards loving each other and bonding through Christ. Tjihenuna's chapter reminds us how rocky that path has been at times.[73] But today, especially in culturally hybrid churches, people from different nations, races, and languages are working hard to unite while having honest conversations about social action and Western overreach.[74] Bridging of all different kinds has made it amazing to see—literally, on television, YouTube, social media—the nations worshipping Jesus in Spirit and in truth (John 4:23). Lia and How testify that the Yoido Full Gospel Church anniversary service looked to them like the multitudes of Revelation 7:9.[75] The work of prior, current, and newer generations is coming together before our very eyes so that we can now celebrate something the Spirit has been doing—and God has been seeing—in the works for many years. In this context, Mendoza and Simon express hope that "Gen Z could quite literally reach the entire globe for Jesus."[76] Harris concurs with the younger generations' "potential to lead a revolution of faith."[77] The technology, tools, support, and innovation that are now present make what our nineteenth and twentieth-century forebears only dreamed was possible.

There remains, of course, major hurdles to jump, revivals to kindle, and works of reconciliation to expand. But Romans 8:24–25 exhorts us,

"For who hopes for what he can already see? But if we hope for what we do not yet see, through perseverance we wait eagerly for it."[78] We are therefore a hope people. God still has good things he wants to bring out of the treasure of his good heart (Luke 6:45; 1 Cor 2:9). Bunn reminds us that the Spirit has been building continually from the beginning, and has put in place good things that the newer generations can build upon.[79] God also has a good poetics of remembrance, and a non-critical spirit that counters the cynical, deconstructionist spirit of our age.

So let us celebrate the Spirit's successes that we see in the family, the marketplace, the nations, and the generations. Let us reinvigorate the Pentecostal value of testimony being practiced in places like Planetboom's Instagram channel,[80] which celebrates the stories of the Spirit's power and goodness right in our midst.[81] Let us hope in Saylor and Savage's "better story of God"[82] and the good works he has prepared in advance for the newer generations to do (Eph 2:10). All the authors in this volume urge a twenty-first century pneumatological orthopraxy that is mature, winsome, and powerful. Let us pray that this emerges, and for more generations to be joined to one another through the baptism and leading of the Holy Spirit.

Notes

1 Loescher, chapter 19.
2 Bunn, chapter 2.
3 Austin, chapter 21.
4 Luce, chapter 4.
5 Bunn, chapter 2.
6 Rodriguez, chapter 18.
7 Ma, Onyinah, and Saylor, Introduction.
8 Stavnichuk and Pluss, chapter 17.
9 Clark, chapter 1.
10 Harris, chapter 10.
11 Saylor and Savage, chapter 3.
12 Stavnichuk and Pluss, chapter 17.
13 Josefsson and Wenell, chapter 9.

14 Saylor and Savage, chapter 3.
15 Tjihenuna, chapter 6.
16 Khai and Khai, chapter 7.
17 Ogino and Ogino, chapter 13.
18 Saylor and Savage, chapter 3.
19 Harris, chapter 10.
20 Josefsson and Wenell, chapter 9.
21 Luce, chapter 4.
22 Loescher, chapter 19.
23 How and Chan, chapter 14.
24 used in Austin, chapter 21.
25 Harris, chapter 10.
26 Emphasis mine, Saylor and Savage, chapter 3.
27 Stavnichuk and Pluss, chapter 17.
28 Mendoza and Simon, chapter 20.
29 Ogino and Ogino, chapter 13.
30 Stavnichuk and Pluss, chapter 17.
31 Rodriguez, chapter 18.
32 Gryskiewicz, chapter 16.
33 Mendoza and Simon, chapter 20.
34 Rodriguez, chapter 18.
35 Described through various anecdotes in Prempeh, chapter 12.
36 Nyanni, chapter 11.
37 Tjihenuna, chapter 6.
38 Luce, chapter 4.
39 Harris, chapter 10.
40 Kim, chapter 8.
41 Bunn, chapter 2.
42 Harris, chapter 10.
43 Gryskiewicz, chapter 16.
44 Khai and Khai, chapter 7.

45 Nyanni, chapter 11.
46 Nyanni, chapter 11.
47 Josefsson and Wenell, chapter 9.
48 Josefsson and Wenell, chapter 9.
49 Mendoza and Simon, chapter 20.
50 Loescher, chapter 19.
51 How and Chan, chapter 14.
52 Austin, chapter 21.
53 Khai and Khai, chapter 7.
54 Petersen, chapter 5.
55 See chapters 5, 8, 19.
56 Kim, chapter 8.
57 Luce, chapter 4.
58 Petersen, chapter 5.
59 Kim, chapter 8.
60 Luce, chapter 4.
61 How and Chan, chapter 14.
62 Coombs, Harrison, and Harrison, chapter 15.
63 See chapters 3, 4, 15.
64 Coombs, Harrison, and Harrison, chapter 15.
65 Harris, chapter 10.
66 Ma, Onyinah, and Saylor, Introduction.
67 Loescher, chapter 19.
68 Clark, chapter 1.
69 Saylor and Savage, chapter 3.
70 Luce, emphasis in original, chapter 4.
71 Saylor and Savage, chapter 3.
72 Harris, chapter 10.
73 Tjihenuna, chapter 6.
74 Gryskiewicz, Nyanni, Prempeh, Tjihenuna contain examples of these conversations; chapters 6, 11, 12, 16.

75 How and Chan, chapter 14.
76 Mendoza and Simon, chapter 20.
77 Harris, chapter 10.
78 NASB
79 Bunn, chapter 2.
80 Coombs, Harrison, and Harrison, chapter 15.
81 The importance of this also emphasized in Rodriguez, chapter 18.
82 Saylor and Savage, chapter 3.

Contributors

Jamie Austin graduated from Southwestern Assemblies of God University and spent the better part of ten years leading a thriving youth ministry in Lawton, Oklahoma that reached hundreds of students each week. In 2009, he accepted the call to return to his home church, Woodlake, as the Lead Pastor. Since then, he has seen Woodlake expand to multiple locations and reach many people in the Tulsa area.

Daniel D. Bunn, Jr. is Associate Professor of Old Testament in the Undergraduate Theology Department at Oral Roberts University in Tulsa, Oklahoma.

Cecilia Chan (Pastor Lia) is the visionary and leading voice of GenerationS internationally, having dedicated over 25 years to discipling young leaders in Heart of God Church in Singapore. She is highly valued as a speaker and trainer of pastors around the world. She and her husband, Tan Seow How, co-authored the book *GenerationS: How to Grow Your Church Younger and Stronger.*

Randy Clark is a revivalist, international speaker, and founder and president of Global Awakening. With more than 30 years of pastoral experience and 44 years of ministry, Randy demonstrates the Lord's power to heal, transform, and revive with great tenacity. Since his life-changing night on January 20, 1994, Randy has traveled to over 50 countries and continues to travel extensively to see God's mandate be fulfilled.

Clayton Coombs is the Academic Dean of Planetshakers College and an ordained minister of Planetshakers Church, a large multi-campus Pentecostal church based in Melbourne, Australia. In addition to a Fortress Press monograph, Clayton has published articles in Pentecostal theology and Greek philology.

Anthony J. Gryskiewicz is a missionary with Assemblies of God World Missions. His research interests include intercultural youth ministry, faith and development of teen ethnic racial identity, and international churches.

Antipas L. Harris has spent thirty years in ministry. He is the founder of Harris Institute and President of the Urban Renewal Center (URC).

He is the former founding President and Dean of Jakes Divinity School, and served on the pastoral staff at The Potter's House in Dallas, Texas. Additionally, Harris is an ordained minister, theological educator, and musician who has ministered in churches across the world.

Andrew Harrison radically encountered God in 2002 at a Planetshakers Conference and attended Planetshakers College in 2006. Later, while serving in Planetboom youth ministry, Andy met and married Susannah, where they pastored faithfully and fruitfully for eight years. Andy is also an accomplished drummer and songwriter who writes many of the songs for Planetshakers Band. He travels the world extensively and is the author of *Jesus Over Everything: Notes for the Next Generation of Planetshakers*.

Susannah Harrison is a pastor, leader, and speaker at Planetshakers Church. She has earned great influence in the community by partnering with different groups, including the police force, to achieve the best outcomes for vulnerable youth. She and her husband Andy pastored Planetshakers East Campus for a year in 2022, and now serve as staff at Planetshakers City Campus.

Tan Seow How (Pastor How) and his wife Cecilia Chan are founding Senior Pastors of Heart of God Church in Singapore – a church operated by youths, for youths, to reach youths. Together with his wife, Pastor Lia, he designed the annual GenerationS pastors conference with the goal of discipling generations of pastors to build strong churches, not just big churches.

Ulrik Josefsson is President and senior lecturer at ALT School of Leadership and Theology, and Director of The Institute of Pentecostal Studies in Uppsala. He has written numerous articles including "Practitioners and Pentecostalism: An Epistemological Investigation into Learning as Doing, Experience, and Reflection" (*Pneuma*, 2022). Ulrik is also Vice-Chair for the World Alliance for Pentecostal Theological Education (WAPTE).

Kham Khai is the founding Senior Pastor of Myanmar Christian Church in Tulsa, Oklahoma. He serves as the President of Myanmar Christian Churches of Fellowship of America. Currently, he also serves as an advisory board member of the Graduate School of Theology and Ministry at Oral Roberts University.

Samuel Khai is the son of Kham Khai and is a graduate from Oral Roberts University in psychology and worship arts. He is pursuing further education to become a counselor. He is currently the music director and a youth leader where he assists his father closely.

Jane C. Kim is the founder and director of FSST (For Sunday School Teachers), a non-profit Christian organization that supports approximately 18,000 Sunday school teachers from over fifty countries through its online platform. Jane has pioneered children's ministries in Mongolia and the Philippines and has been serving as a missionary in the Philippines since 2004. She attended Asia Pacific Theological Seminary.

Kerry Loescher is an award-winning professor at Oral Roberts University and pursuing further education at Trinity Evangelical Divinity School where her research is focused on intergenerational Christian formation. With more than thirty years of youth ministry experience, Kerry is a sought-after national speaker and author who specializes in helping children and families connect with the gospel and each other.

Ron Luce founded and led Teen Mania, reaching three million youth in conferences and taking 80,000 overseas. He has worked with 100,000 churches, raised approximately 330 million dollars, and authored thirty books. Ron has guest-lectured at Harvard Business School and Oral Roberts University, where he served on the Board of Trustees. He is currently focused on empowering church leaders to impact this generation for Christ by leveraging global best-practices to help youth effectively influence the world.

Wonsuk Ma, a Korean Pentecostal, is a Distinguished Professor of Global Christianity and serves as the Executive Director of the Center for Spirit-Empowered Research at Oral Roberts University in Tulsa, Oklahoma. He previously served as Dean of the College of Theology and Ministry at the latter, as well as Executive Director of the Oxford Centre for Mission Studies at Oxford, U.K. He currently serves as Co-Chair of the Global Network of Spirit-Empowered Scholars (GNSES), part of Empowered21.

Allie Mendoza is the Associate Director of Spiritual Life at Oral Roberts University and helps students find their identity in Christ through strategic short-term missions, leadership development, and personal discipleship. Allie also serves as an adjunct professor and serves the global Spirit-empowered movement as one of the Co-Vice Chairs of Empowered21 NextGen.

Caleb Nyanni is the Academic Dean at Birmingham Christian Centre. He is also a Senior Fellow of the High Education Academy (SFHEA) and a Fellow at the Institute of Pentecostal Theology. Additionally, Nyanni serves as the Senior Pastor at Elim Church in Sparkbrook, Birmingham in the U.K.

Chaa Chaa Ogino is Burmese and a Myanmar-ordained minister of the Japan Assemblies of God as well as a graduate of Asia Pacific Theological Seminary. She currently serves as Assistant Pastor of Galilee Maruko Christ Church with her husband Michio. She also works as a counselor and teacher at Samurai Gakuen, which helps *hikikomori* re-establish relationships and reintegrate back into society. She is the CEO of the company Quietude, L.L.C., which is a translation agency and consultancy.

Michio Ogino is native Japanese, and a Japanese-ordained minister of the Japan Assemblies of God. He currently serves as Senior Pastor of Galilee Maruko Christ Church. He also serves as the Dean of Students and teacher of Greek Language and Systematic Theology at Central Bible College.

Opoku Onyinah serves as Co-Chair of the Global Network of Spirit-Empowered Scholars of Empowered21. He is the immediate past President of Ghana Pentecostal and Charismatic Council and the immediate past Chairman of the Church of Pentecost, Ghana, with branches in 135 countries. He was also the first International Missions Director of the Church of Pentecost, and the founding rector of Pentecost University. Currently, he lectures at Pentecostal University, Accra, Ghana, and is President of the Bible Society of Ghana.

Douglas Petersen is the Co-Director of Graduate Studies at Vanguard University. Together with his wife, Myrna, he founded Latin America's ChildHope to help educate the poor. In four decades, they built 300 schools in 20 countries across Central America and the Caribbean, providing education to more than 2 million children in poverty.

Jean-Daniel Plüss chairs the European Pentecostal Charismatic Research Association and is a member of the Christian Unity Commission of Pentecostal World Fellowship. He has been involved in various international ecumenical dialogues involving Pentecostals and older church traditions. He has written numerous articles on Pentecostalism and a book on the history of Swiss Pentecostalism.

Charles Prempeh is a Research Fellow at the Centre for Cultural and African Studies, Kwame Nkrumah University of Science and Technology, Ghana. After studying in Ghana, he pursued graduate studies in Cambridge, U.K. He is a Fellow of the IFE Institute of Advance Studies and a former Fellow of the Social Science Research Council (SSRC–2016). His recent book is entitled *Nima-Maamobi in Ghana's Postcolonial Development: Migration, Islam, and Social Transformation*.

Jaime L. Riddle serves as the administrative assistant to the Director of the Center of Spirit-Empowered Research at Oral Roberts University. She is managing editor of this title and has spent twenty years in lay ministry, focused on young adults and biblical education.

Juan Sebastian Rodriguez is Co-Pastor at one of the largest churches in the world, Centro Mundial de Avivamiento, in Bogotá, Colombia. Working with passion for revival in Colombia and the world, he seeks to integrate theological, ministerial, and contextual reflection in his work.

Patricia Savage serves as the Design Lead for OneHope, collaborating with Research and Development to support the creation of scripture engagement programs for the next generation. Since 1987, OneHope has reached more than 2 billion young people with God's Word and has a vision to reach every child with the hope of the gospel.

Barry L. Saylor is Senior Researcher at OneHope, a ministry dedicated to reaching children and youth worldwide with God's Word. Saylor also serves as the Executive Director for the World Alliance for Pentecostal Theological Education (WAPTE) and as a faculty member at the Hoskins School of Mission at Southeastern University in Lakeland, FL.

Kimmie Simon is the Director of the Worship Center at Oral Roberts University, where she raises up Spirit-empowered worshippers and oversees all teams, programs, and album projects. Kimmie leads worship nationally and internationally for ministries like Empowered21 and Pentecostal World Fellowship.

Alexander Stavnichuk, born in Ukraine, currently lives and works in Germany as a pastor of the Protestant Church of Baden. He was formerly a Pentecostal pastor, and taught systematic theology, ethics, and comparative theology at Sankt-Petersburg Christian University (Russia) and at the Theological Seminary Adelshofen (Germany). He currently guest lectures in systematic theology at the International Seminary of Theology and Leadership in Switzerland.

Caroline Polly Tjihenuna serves as the Fellow of the Dean of Theology and Ministry at Oral Roberts University. She recently led a mission trip to Paraguay and staffed a School of Revival and Reformation in Sao Paulo, Brazil. A mission trip to South Korea is underway and soon after she will be at the World Council of Churches Youth Ecumenical Conference in Karlsruhe, Germany.

Fredrik Wenell is an Associate Professor in systematic theology at the ALT School of Theology, Sweden. His most recently published article in English is "Baptist Identity in a Christian Welfare State," and "Swedish Christian Schools as a Case Study of How New Practices Relate to Theological Issues" (ORCID 0000-0002-1274-8775).

Select Bibliography

Allen, Holly Catterton, Christine Lawton, and Cory Seibel. *Intergenerational Christian Formation: Bringing the Whole Church Together in Ministry, Community, and Worship,* 2nd edition. Downers Grove, IL: InterVarsity Press, 2023.

Annor-Antwi, Gibson. *Myth or Mystery: The "Bio-autobiography" of Apostle Professor Opoku Onyinah.* U.K.: Inved, 2016.

Barna Group, *Gen Z: The Culture, Beliefs and Motivations Shaping the Next Generation.* Barna Group and Impact 360 Institute, 2018.

Becker, Heike. "A Country on Fire: Protests in Namibia." *A Review of African Political Economy,* November 3, 2020. https://roape.net/2020/11/03/a-country-on-fire-protests-in-namibia/.

Bredwa-Mensah, Yaw. "The Church of Pentecost in Retrospect, 1937–1960." In *James McKeown Memorial Lectures: 50 Years of the Church of Pentecost,* edited by Opoku Onyinah. Accra: Church of Pentecost, 2004.

Brueggemann, Walter. *Deuteronomy.* Abingdon Old Testament Commentaries. Nashville: Abingdon Press, 2001.

Burg, Ryan P. *The Nones: Where They Came From, Who They Are, and Where They Are Going.* Minneapolis: Fortress Press, 2021.

"Burmese Refugee Health Profile." United States Centers for Disease Control and Prevention (CDC), March 12, 2022. http://www.cdc.gov/immigrantrefugeehealth/profiles/burmese/index.html.

Buys, G. L. and S. V. V. Nambala. *History of the Church in Namibia: An Introduction.* Windhoek, Namibia: Gamsberg Macmillan Publishers, 2003.

Carson, D. A. "Matthew." *The Expositor's Bible Commentary,* vol. 8. Edited by Frank E. Gaebelein. Grand Rapids: Zondervan, 1984.

Casanova, José. "Rethinking Secularization." *Hedgehog Review* 8, nos. 1–2 (Spring/Summer 2006): 7–22. https://hedgehogreview.com/issues/after-secularization-special-double-issue/articles/rethinking-secularization.

Coombs, Clayton and Scott Lim. "Planetshakers." In *Brill's Encyclopedia of Global Pentecostalism Online,* edited by Michael Wilkinson, Connie Au, Jörg Haustein, and Todd M. Johnson. Brill, online edition 2019. http://dx.doi.org/10.1163/2589-3807_EGPO_COM_044872.

Crane, Michael and Scott Carter. "Gateway to the Nations: The Strategic Value of International Churches in a Globalized Urban World." *International Journal of Urban Transformation* 4, no. 1 (2019): 111–30.

Drake, Nick. *A Deeper Note: The "Informal" Theology of Contemporary Sung Worship.* Cambridge: Grove Books, 2015.

Evans, Craig A. *Matthew.* New Cambridge Bible Commentary. Edited by Ben Witherington III. New York: Cambridge University, 2012.

"The Future of World Religions 2010–2050." Pew Research Center, http://www.pewforum.org/2015/04/02/muslims.

Garrison, Alton. *A Spirit-Empowered Church: An Acts 2 Ministry Model.* Springfield: Influence Resources, 2015.

Gijsbert van den Brink, Eveline van Staalduine-Sulman, and Maarten Wisse, eds. *The Spirit Is Moving: New Pathways in Pneumatology.* Leiden: Brill, 2019.

"Global Teens Share Their Perceptions of Jesus, the Bible and Justice." Barna Group, October 5, 2022. https://www.barna.com/research/open-generation-perceptions/.

Global Youth Culture: Global Report. Pompano Beach, FL: OneHope, 2020. www.globalyouthculture.net/.

Gryskiewicz, Anthony J., Anna K. Gryskiewicz, and Tomas Gollery. "Every Tribe and Nation: A Demographic Study of the Fellowship of European International Churches." *Missiology: An International Review* 49, no. 4 (2021): 362–74. https://doi.org/10.1177/00918296211011713.

Habermas, Jürgen, et al. *An Awareness of What is Missing: Faith and Reason in a Post-Secular Age.* Translated by Ciaran Cronin. Cambridge, U.K.: Polity Press, 2010.

Hartmut Rosa. *Resonance: A Sociology of Our Relationship to the World.* Cambridge U.K.: Polity Press 2019.

Heinlein, Michael R. "The Selfless Leadership of St. Barnabas: Paul's Companion Provides an Excellent Model for Ministry." *The Priest* 75, no. 6 (June 2019): 42–46.

Hilborn, David. "Anglicans, Pentecostals and Ecumenical Theology." In The Many Voices of Global Pentecostalism, edited by Harold D. Hunter and Neil Ormerod. Cleveland: CPT, 2013.

Horn, Nico. "Crossing Racial Borders in Southern Africa: A Lesson from History." *Cyber Journal for Pentecostal-Charismatic Research* (June 1991). http://www.pctii.org/cyberj/cyberj3/nico.html#N_10_.

Johnson, Todd M., and Cindy M. Wu. "Awakenings and Revivals in the Context of Global Christianity." In *Great Awakenings: Historical Perspectives for Today*, edited by David Horn and Gordon L. Isaac. Peabody, MA: Hendrickson, 2019.

Josefsson, Ulrik, *Liv och över nog. Den tidiga pingströrelsens spiritualitet*. Skellefteå: Artos, 2005.

Josefsson, Ulrik and Fredrik Wenell, eds. *Kristen tro på glid? Tron hos unga vuxna i svensk frikyrklighet*. Stockholm: IPS-forskningsrapporter, 2022.

Kay, William K. and Anne E: Dyer, eds. *European Pentecostalism*. Leiden: Brill, 2011.

"Keeping the Faith." *Insight*. SBS on demand, 2022. https://www.sbs.com.au/ondemand/watch/2074704963548.

Kimble, David. *A Political History of Ghana: The Rise of Gold Coast Nationalism*, 1850-1928. Oxford: Clarendon Press, 1963.

Kinnaman, David and Mark Matlock. *Faith for Exiles: Five Ways for a New Generation to Follow Jesus in Digital Babylon*. Grand Rapids: Baker, 2019.

Lebrija, Lorenzo. *How to Try: Design Thinking and Church Innovation*. New York: NY Church Publishing, 2021.

Leonard, Christine. *A Giant in Ghana: 3,000 churches in 50 years: The Story of James McKeown and the Church of Pentecost*. Chichester: New Wine Press, 1989.

Lian, Don Ngaih. *Ka Piantit Pai Sese* [My France Odyssey]. Kalay Myo, Myanmar: U Nang Sawm Piang, Zomi Christian Literature Society, 2018.

Lovelace, Richard F. *Dynamics of Spiritual Life: An Evangelical Theology of Renewal*. Westmont, IL: InterVarsity Press, 2020.

Luce, Ron. *Faith at the Speed of Light*. Tustin: Trilogy Publishing, 2019.

Ma, Wonsuk. "Asian Pentecostalism in Context." In *The Cambridge Companion to Pentecostalism*, edited by Cecil M. Robeck, Jr. and Amos Yong. Cambridge: Cambridge University Press, 2014.

Maciariello, Joseph. "Lessons in Leadership and Management from Nehemiah." *Theology Today* 60, no. 3 (October 2003): 397–407.

Malphurs, Aubrey. "The State of the American Church: Plateaued or Declining." *The Malphurs Group*, 2014. http://malphursgroup.com/state-of-the-american-church-plateaued-declining.

Marsden, George M. "Neo-Evangelicalism and Renewal Since the Mid-Twentieth Century." In *Great Awakenings: Historical Perspectives for Today,* edited by David Horn and Gordon L. Isaac. Peabody, MA: Hendrickson, 2019.

Matsumoto, Masashi. 「ひきこもり」支援論の再検討—新たな支援への視点 ["Reexamination of Discussion about 'Hikikomori' Support: The New Aspect for Support"]. 日本社会分析学会 [*Japan Sociological Association for Social Analysis*] 35 (2008): 79-100.

McConville, J. Gordon. *Deuteronomy.* Apollos Old Testament Commentary, vol. 5. Downers Grove: InterVarsity Press, 2002.

McLoughlin, William G. *Revivals, Awakening and Reform.* Chicago: University of Chicago Press, 1978.

Miner, M. and Dowson, M., eds. *Creativity and Spirituality: A Multidisciplinary Perspective.* Charlotte, NC: Information Age Publishing, 2017.

Myanmar Christian Church. "Myanmar Christian Church's Facebook Page." Facebook, November 14, 2022. https://www.facebook.com/mcctulsa.

Neller, Kenneth V. "A Model for Those Who Seek to Win Souls: 1 Corinthians 9:19–23." *Restoration Quarterly* 29, no. 3 (1987): 129–142.

Noll, Mark A. *The New Shape of World Christianity: How American Experience Reflects Global Faith.* Downers Grove: InterVarsity Press Academic, 2009.

Nyanni, Caleb. *Second Generation African Pentecostals in the West.* Eugene, OR: Wipf & Stock, 2021.

Onyinah, Opoku. "African Christianity in the Twenty-first Century." *Word & World* 27, no. 3 (2007): 305–314.

Ott, Craig. *Teaching and Learning Across Cultures: A Guide to Theory and Practice.* Grand Rapids: Baker Academic, 2021.

"Over Half of Gen Z Teens Feel Motivated to Learn More about Jesus." Barna Group, February 1, 2023. https://www.barna.com/research/teens-and-jesus/.

Philipps, Joschka. "A Global Generation? Youth Studies in a Postcolonial World." *Societies* 8, no. 1 (2018). https://doi.org/10.3390/soc8010014.

Pieterse, Jan Nederveen. "Globalization as Hybridization." In *Sociology of Globalization: Cultures, Economies, and Politics,* edited by Keri E. Iyall Smith. London: Routledge, 2013.

Powell, Kara, Jake Mulder, and Brad Griffin. *Growing Young: Six Essential Strategies to Help Young People Discover and Love Your Church.* Grand Rapids: Baker Books, 2016.

Prinsloo, Louis F. "The Early History of the AFM Church in Namibia." Boet Prinsloo Ministries. http://www.boetprinslooministries.com/early-history-of-the-afm-church/.

Rodriguez, Daniel. "Hispanic Ministry Where Language Is No Barrier: Church Growth Among U.S.-Born, English-Dominant Latinos." *Great Commission Research Journal* 1, no. 2 (Winter 2010): 189–201.

Rogers, Carl R. *On Becoming a Person: A Therapist View of Psychotherapy.* Boston: Houghton Mifflin Company, 1961.

Root, Andrew. *Faith Formation in a Secular Age: Responding to the Church's Obsession with Youthfulness.* Grand Rapids: Baker Academic, 2017.

Saitō, Tamaki. *Social Withdrawal: Adolescence without End.* Translated by Jeffrey Angles. Minneapolis: University of Minnesota Press, 2012.

Shallue, Diane E. "Engaging the Elders Among Us." In *InterGenerate: Transforming Churches through Intergenerational Ministry*, edited by Holly Catterton Allen. Abilene, TX: Abilene Christian University Press. 2018.

Smith, Christian and Amy Adamczyk. *Handing Down the Faith: How Parents Pass Their Religion on to the Next Generation.* New York: Oxford University Press, 2021.

Song, Nam Soon. "Youth Ministry That Matters: Voices of Korean Canadian Youth." *The Journal of Youth Ministry* 15, no. 2 (2017): 97–120.

Sorge, Bob. *Exploring Worship: A Practical Guide to Praise and Worship*, 3rd edition. Grandview, MO: Oasis House, 2018.

Stroh, K. Linda. *The Basic Principles of Effective Consulting.* New York: Taylor and Francis, Kindle Edition, 2019.

Stuart, Douglas. "Hosea–Jonah." World Biblical Commentary, vol. 31. Edited by David A. Hubbard and Glenn W. Barker. Waco, Texas: Word Books, 1987.

Taylor, Charles. *A Secular Age.* Cambridge, MA: Belknap Press, 2007.

Theological Education Fund (TEF) Staff. *Ministry in Context: The Third Mandate Programme of the Theological Education Fund (1970-77).* Bromley, U.K.: Theological Education Fund, 1972.

Topf, Daniel. "Ten Characteristics of Pentecostal Theological Education in the Twenty-First Century." *Pentecostal Education: A Journal of WAPTE* 5, nos. 1–2 (2020): 45–57, https://wapte.org/wp-content/uploads/2020/10/pentecostal-edu-vol-5.pdf.

Tuan, C. Thang Za. *Zomite Pusuahcilna, Khanlawhna leh Khantohna.* Tedim, Myanmar: Tedim *BEHS NO. 1 Golden Jubilee Commemorative Magazine 1948-1998* (1999): 173.

The U.N. Refugee Agency, USA. "Figures at a Glance in Malaysia." UNHCR, 2022. https://www.unhcr.org/en-us/figures-at-a-glance-in-malaysia.

Veen, Leslie. "Jethro and Moses: A Biblical Model for Supervision from Exodus 18." *Reflective Practice* 38 (August 2018): 220–228.

"Victoria Police and Planetshakers at Moomba 2019!" Facebook Live Stream, 2019. https://www.facebook.com/victoriapolice/videos/victoria-police-at-moomba-2019/556072128240238/.

Vondey, Wolfgang. *Beyond Pentecostalism: The Crisis of Global Christianity and the Renewal of the Theological Agenda.* Grand Rapids: Eerdmans, 2021.

Wallace, Charles I., Jr. "Wesley as Revivalist/Renewal Leader." In *The Cambridge Companion to John Wesley,* edited by Randy L. Maddox and Jason E. Vickers. Cambridge, U.K.: Cambridge University Press, 2010.

Warrington, Keith. *Pentecostal Theology: A Theology of Encounter.* London: T & T Clark, 2008.

Wenell, Fredrik, *Omvändelsens skillna: En diasporateologisk granskning av frikyrklig ungdomskultur i folkkyrka och folkhem.* Uppsala: Uppsala universitet, 2015.

Willard, Dallas. *Hearing God.* Grand Rapids: InterVarsity Press, 2012.

Woods, Edward J. *Deuteronomy.* Tyndale Old Testament Commentaries. Nottingham, U.K.: InterVarsity Press, 2011.

Wright, Walter C. *Relational Leadership: A Biblical Model for Influence and Service.* Downers Grove: InterVarsity Press, 2009.

Name and Subject Index

A
Abraham-Isaac-Jacob ministry, 65
Accra, Ghana, 206
Adegbite, Tunji, 173
ADHD, 230
admonition to the new generation, 26–37
Adogame, Afeosemime, 193
Africa, 44, 60, 331n15. *See also specific locations*
African Pentecostals
  encountering the Spirit and, 193–195
  fresh approach to mission by, 191–192
  generations of, 186–187
  Generation Z as, 187
  introduction to, 185–186
  Millennials as, 187
  next generation of, 187–190
  Pentecostal practices and the next generation of, 187–190
  societal impacts on, 195
Afro-Western Millennials, 186–187, 192, 195, 196, 197, 376. *See also* Millennials
Afro-Western Pentecostals, 192
AGILE metric, 71–72
aging adults
  as bonus grandparents, 321, 329, 378
  intergenerational relationships with, 318–319
  mission regarding, 327
Ahlu Sunna Wal'Jamah, 206
Ahn, Che, 18
Akan culture, 205, 207
Akyeampong, Emmanuel, 205
Albrecht brothers, 88
alcohol usage, 49, 93–94, 113
altruism, 322–323, 324, 332n27

Alvarado, J. E., 194
"Amazing Grace" (Newton), 153
Anderson, Allan, 187, 188, 212
anxiety, 46, 48–49, 53, 175
Apostolic Faith Mission (AFM), 89–93
Apuskeleke, 204
Argolo, Felipe, 114
Arnan, Daniel Kwabena, 208
Artificial Intelligence (AI), 2
Asamoah-Gyadu, J. Kwabena, 95, 172, 212
Asbury Revival, 178, 179
Asia, 44, 60. *See also specific locations*
Asia Football Federation, 116
Assemblies of God, 188
Attitudes and Behaviors of Youth (ABY) study, 42
Australia, 220, 236, 262–263. *See also* Planetboom; Planetshakers Church
Azusa Street Revival, 188, 256

B
Baker, Heidi and Rolland, 17, 20, 21
Bakish, Bob, 70
Banks, James A., 274
Barak, 357–358
Barclay, John, 366
Barry, John D., 357
Becker, Heike, 94, 95
Bethel Church (Redding, California), 18
Björkander, Martina, 144, 145, 146, 147
Black Lives Matter, 94
Boaz, 358
Bob-Milliar, George M., 206
Bohren, Rudolf, 290
Bolivia, 20
Bomana prison, 259

Bonney, Blessed, 215
Boomers, 164. *See also* aging adults
Born-Free generation (Namibia), 87–88, 93–96, 97–98
Bradford Apostolic Church, 202
Bradshaw, Brother, 16
Britain, 188, 190
"Broken Vessels" (Houston), 153
Bronner, Bishop, 248
Bruce, F. F., 125
Bucharest, Romania, 276
Bueno, John, 77
Burge, Ryan P., 163
Burmese Americans (Myanmar people), 104–114
    Myanmar Christian Church of, 107–108
    soccer and, 114–118
    spiritual issues of, 109–110
    spiritual revival and, 113

C

Cambodia, 15
Campbell, Barth, 362
Campus Crusade for Christ, 96
Canada, 106, 271
Cane Ridge, 308
Carmichael, Matt, 168
Carson, D. A., 123–124
Casanova, José, 166
Castellano, Cesar, 18–19
Casual Loop Diagram (CLD), 62–64
Catholic Church, 206
celebration model, of international churches, 276
Certificate for Students Achieving the Proficiency Level of Upper Secondary School Graduates, 227–228
Chafetz, Janet Saltzman, 278, 279–280
Chan, Simon, 194
changes, in the world, 163–164, 373–374

ChatGPT, 2
Chigor, Chike, 195
ChildHope, 380
children
    attack on, 379
    bonus grandparents to, 321, 329, 378
    as coming to Jesus, 82–83
    gospel of Mark's call to, 78–83
    as greatest in the kingdom, 81–82
    parent relationship with, 310
    positive reinforcement of, 112
    psychosocial development theory and, 112
    receiving the call to, 77–78
children's ministry
    adult ministry as priority over, 122
    financial barriers in, 130–131
    foundation of, from missional-Pentecostal perspective, 122–125
    Great Commission and, 122–124
    hesitancy regarding, 133–134
    importance of, 121, 134, 379–380
    online resourcing for teachers in, 125–135
    outpouring of the Holy Spirit and, 124–125
    statistics regarding, 121
China, 220
Chinese Americans, 270
Ching, Ava, 255
Chin United FC, 116
chosenness, by God, 202–203
Christian Fellowship, 206
Christianity
    in Asia, 60
    in Australia, 236
    cynicism regarding, 163
    decline of, 59, 374
    departures from, 61
    extinction possibilities of, 235–237
    growth of, 60
    in Indonesia, 236

in Namibia, 88
pilgrim principle and, 187–188
in South Korea, 235–236
statistics regarding, 60–61
in Sweden, 141
Christians
Committed, 44–46, 48
Cultural, 68
demographics of, 41
Generation Z as, 44–46
median age of, 60–61
Mental, 68
Nominal, 45–46, 48, 52, 54
Social, 68
church. *See also* international churches (ICs)
adaptability in, 178
aging-up problem of, 374
attendance of, by Committed Christian teenagers, 45–46
attendance statistics regarding, 59
believe-become-belong sequence in, 246
belonging in, 319
building of, 21
Casual Loop Diagram (CLD) regarding, 62–64
challenges of, 354, 373
as cooperating with God, 376
decline of involvement in, 92
decline reasons of, 354
denominational uprootedness from, 172–173
didascalia in, 312
discipleship in, 63–64, 67
disengagement in, 63
ethical issues in, 147, 297
"the exchange zone" in, 66
experimentation in, 377–379
exponentially growing, 67, 72
generation gap in, 240
for Generation Z, 45–46, 53, 56, 177–178, 381–382
geographical redistribution of, 41
giving in, 62–63
gospel presentation in, 68–70
as growing younger, 242
as home for youth, 245–246
immigrant, 270–272, 279
infighting of, 177–178
as integrative, 178
intergenerational relationships in, 327–328, 378–379
morality in, 297
as multicultural, 270
as multiethnic, 270
multiplying factor in, 312
new wineskins of, 377
opportunity for, 61–72
Pathway to Leadership program in, 65
as place of belonging, 53
positivity in, 177–178
process-oriented *versus* event-oriented, 62–64
propinquity effect in, 271
reasons for leaving, 147
reconciliation, 271–272
replacement threat in, 245
secularism and, 167
simplicity in, 178
social factors of, 147
as Spirit-empowered, 376
spiritual assessments in, 67
and state, 167
success of, 71–72
training in, 64–65
veterans in, 245
Church of Jesus Christ of Latter-Day Saints, 203
Church of Pentecost (CoP) (Ghana)
in Accra, 206
background of, 201–206
branches of, 212
English Assembly concept and, 208

God's covenant with, 201–206, 215
growth of, 70, 201, 211, 214
headscarves and, 204, 205, 213
holiness theology and, 201–206
incorporation of young generations in, 213
modernization and, 210
Pentecostal International Worship Centers (PIWC) and, 208, 209–210, 212
Pentecost Students and Associates (PENSA) and, 210
reforms of, 204, 209, 214
religious rejuvenation of, 207–213, 214–215
Royal Conference of, 212
segregation in, 205–206
theomacracy and, 207–208, 209
Women's Movement of, 204, 214
Colombia, 19, 20
colonialism, 88
Committed Christian teenagers, 44–46, 48, 49, 52, 54. *See also* Generation Z
communication, listening and understanding in, 222
community, in revival movements, 154
contact hypothesis, 271–272
Coulter, Dale M., 163, 170
COVID-19 pandemic, 126–128, 244–245
Cox, Daniel A., 166
Creek, Josh, 255
cultural hybridity, 273–274, 277–281, 382
cultural nationalism, 205
culture of encounter, 294
culture shock, 103, 109
Cyril of Alexandria, 68–69

D

Daugherty, Billy Joe, 107, 108
Daugherty, Paul, 108
Daugherty, Sharon, 107, 108
David (king), 12, 37, 70, 260, 310, 359–360, 365
Davis, Jim, 117
Dean, Kenda Creasy, 319
Deborah, 37, 357–358
demons/demonic presence, 19, 79–80, 81
denominational uprootedness, 172–173
depression, 46, 48–49, 53, 167–168, 224
Deuteronomy
  chapter 5 of, 27–29, 36
  chapter 6 of, 34
  chapter 8 of, 29–32, 36
  chapter 30, 32–36
  chapter 30 of, 34, 36–37
  today concept in, 26, 28
diaspora pneumatology, 197
Dickson, Gary, 311
didascalia, 312
digital revolution, 1–2
Dimock, Michael, 162, 163–164
disciple, 92–93, 372
discipleship
  of aging adults, 327
  of Burmese Americans (Myanmar people), 111–113
  in the church, 63–64, 67
  of Generation Z, 48, 50, 55–56
  Great Commission and, 122–124
  in intergenerational relationships, 320
  at Planetboom, 380
  resilient disciple in, 92–93
  of youth, 63–64
Diversity Visa (DV) program, 107–108
Dopmul, Thangminlian Khai, 116
Dorsland Trekkers, 90
Dressen, Paul, 272
drug usage, 53, 93–94, 113
Dutch Reformed Church, 89
Dye, Stephen D., 272

E

Ebaugh, Helen Rose, 278, 279–280
ecumenical theological discourse, 289
education. *See also* children's ministry
  equality in, 135–136
  financial barriers in, 130–131
  importance of, 121–122
  language barriers in, 129, 130
  online resourcing for teachers in, 125–135
  revivals and, 311–312
  as shaper of culture, 174
egoism, 322–323, 325–326
ek-stasis, 290, 291, 292, 295
Elijah Mohammed's Nation of Islam, 206
Elim Pentecostal Church, 188, 211
Ellis, Malisa, 168
Emmanuel Church Windhoek (Namibia), 92
Empower (Planetshakers Church), 260
Empowered21, 3–7
encountering, at ORU chapel, 340–341
English language, 269, 272–273, 280. *See also* language
Erikson, Erik, 112
Escuro, Sophia, 255
Ethiopia, 42
Eunice, 361
Europe, 285–287. *See also specific locations*
European International Churches, 274–277
Evangelical Free Church, 144
evangelism/evangelization, 259, 272, 376
Evans, Aimee, 265
Evans, Craig, 123
Evans, Russell, 255, 256, 257–258, 260
Evans, Sam, 256
Eve, 35, 371
evil spirits, 196
"the exchange zone," 66

F

faith
  attributes for decline of, 163
  in Christian community, 146–147
  content changing of, 148–149
  emotional aspects of, 149
  ethical and ontological boundaries in, 207
  factors in participation of, 172
  generational transfer of, 371–373
  in Ghana, 172
  growing into, 154
  Holy Spirit's role in, 296
  personal pursuit of, 343
  positions of, 149–150
  privatization of, 296
  reimagining, 377
  social relationships and, 154
  of teenagers, 381–382
  understanding, 154
  worship as key to, 153
Fakhrsadeh, Mohammed, 259–260
Family Church Syndrome, 240–241
Fellowship of European International Churches (FEIC), 269–270, 272–273
femicide, 94
Fifth World Conference on Faith and Order, 289–290
Finney, Charles, 17
Floyd, George, 94
For Sunday School Teachers (FSST), 125–135, 138n22
France, 220
Free Church identity, 143, 146–148, 153
Free Church revival, 145–146, 148–149
"Fresh Expressions" (FX) initiative, 191–192
Full Gospel Church (Namibia), 89, 90

G

G12 movement, 19
Gakuen, Samurai, 220
Galilee Maruko Christ Church (GMCC), 219
Garden of Eden, 36
Garland, David E., 221
Garrett, Duane A., 124–125
gender-based violence, 94
gender identity confusion, 46, 51–53
generational thinking, 164
generational transfer, Pentecost as divine solution for, 371–373
generations. *See also specific titles*
  defined, 242, 308
  gap of, in the church, 240
  God of, 371
  going back down for, 241–242
  reconciliation of, 382
  transfer of revivals in, 308–311
GenerationS, 237–248
GenerationS Pastors Conference, 250
Generation Z
  adaptability and, 178
  African, 186–187
  alcohol and drug usage in, 49
  anxiety of, 48–49, 53, 175
  as anxiously digital, 170–171, 374
  behavior trends of, 164
  belonging of, 53
  categorizing precautions regarding, 162
  challenges of, 93–94
  changing world and, 163–164
  characteristics of, 338–339
  church and, 45–46, 53, 56, 177–178, 381–382
  as Committed Christians, 44–46, 48
  correlating factors in, 49
  creativity regarding, 55–56, 176–177
  decline in traditional systems and values and, 166–167
  defined, 41, 161, 338
  denominational uprootedness and, 172–173
  depression and, 46, 48–49, 53, 167–168
  discipleship of, 48, 50, 55–56
  faith participation factors of, 164–169
  family trust by, 53–54
  female struggles in, 49, 51
  friends as guiding voice for, 54
  gender identity and relationships of, 51–53
  hope regarding, 178–179, 380
  hunger in, 175–177
  as iGen, 168
  image insecurity and, 168
  implications regarding, 47–48
  influences and guiding voices for, 53–54
  integration and, 176–177, 178
  internet as guiding voice for, 54
  journey with, 55
  leadership capacity of, 64, 174
  loneliness of, 48–49, 167–168, 175
  mental health of, 48–49
  Millennials as compared to, 338
  as Nominal Christians, 45–46, 48
  as Non-Christians, 45
  as "nones," 173, 179
  and non-faith-based spiritual search, 176–177
  non-religious spirituality and, 165–166
  open-mindedness of, 47–48
  opportunities regarding, 174–175
  overview of, 338–340
  passions of, 377
  personal struggles of, 46, 48–51
  perspective of, 42
  pornography and, 50, 51, 53
  positivity and, 177–178
  potential of, 338

precautions regarding, 162
recreational drug usage of, 53
religious affiliation of, 164, 165–166
religious attitudes and behaviors of, 43–51
religious identification of, 44
religious scripture reading by, 43
same-sex attraction and, 52–53
self-injury and, 168
sexuality and, 48, 49–50
social isolationism and, 167–169
social media and, 54, 168, 171
spiritual identity of, 46–47
spiritual inclinations of, 161
statistics regarding, 381–382
suicidal thoughts/attempts and, 46, 48–49, 52–53, 168
technology and, 167–169, 173
training of, 64–65
George V (king), 104, 118
gerontocratic culture, 213
Ghana, 172–173, 179, 204, 206, 211, 213
Ghana Fellowship of Evangelical Students, 206
globalization, 57n16, 87–88
global *mélange*, 270, 274
Global Youth Culture (GYC) study (One Hope).
  background of, 42–43
  gender identity and relationships topic of, 51–53
  influences and guiding voices topic of, 53–54
  personal experience and struggles topic of, 48–51
  religious attitudes and behaviors in, 43–48
Goldman, Russell, 106
Graham, Billy, 14–15, 16
grandparents, 318. *See also* aging adults
Great Britain, 59
Great Commission, 122–124, 344

Great Evangelical Revival, 13
Great Welsh Revivals, 14
Grudem, Wayne, 347
Gyimah, J. S., 203

H

Haddad, Fadi, 168
Hagar, 35
Ham, Mordecai, 16
Hart, Will, 20
Hassler, Mark A., 356
Hayford, J. E. A. Casely, 205
headscarves, 204, 205, 213
healing, 13, 15, 17, 78–79, 264–265
Heart of God Church (HOGC) (Singapore)
  age gap of, 235
  COVID-19 pandemic and, 244–245
  empowering youth in, 244–245
  GenerationS Pastors Conference of, 250
  as home for youth, 245–246
  inviting, including, and involving youth in, 242–244
  kingmaking in, 247–248
  leadership of, 247
  overview of, 237–238, 380
  reaching, retaining, and releasing lessons of, 240–248
  Reinforcements Weekend of, 244
  vision of, 238–239
Hessmallach, Thomas, 90
Hezekiah, 37
hikikomori ministry, 220–230
Hilborn, David, 191, 194
Hillsong, 153–154
history maker, characteristics of, 11
holiness theology, 201–206, 207–208
Holmgaard, Henrik, 144, 145–146, 148, 151, 152
Holy Fairs, 308
Holy Spirit

active presence of, 197
African Pentecostals and, 186–187
baptism in, 11, 17, 20, 21, 291, 297, 372
centrality of, 372
in coming to faith, 296
continuity of, 38
creative activity of, 289, 294, 297
diaspora pneumatology and, 197
as difference-maker, 374–381
dwelling of, 313
ecumenical approach to life-giving activity of, 289–290
ek-stasis and, 290, 291, 292, 295
embracing the supra-rational and, 379–381
empowerment from, 189–190, 297, 346–347, 354–355, 372
expressions regarding, 194–195
function of, 372
gifts of, 13, 193
koinonia and, 289, 290
as life-giving, 288–289, 292–295
life in, 312–313
living encounter with Jesus and, 288
longing for God and, 297
meaning and purpose from, 162
in modern landscape, 2
motivation regarding, 291
mutual activity of, 290
openness to, 289, 294
outpouring of, 124–125, 255–256, 306–307
as patient teacher, 231
at Pentecost, 306–307
in Pentecostalism, 188–189
Pentecostal model of life-giving activity of, 291–292
Pentecostal pneumatology and, 193–195, 288
at Planetboom Conference 2023, 255–256

"play" in, 378
pneumatology and, 293
power to witness and, 191
practical implications regarding, 292–295
promise of, 354
purpose of, 354
reciprocal activity of, 292
revivals and, 307, 312–313, 314
as river, 307
role of, in Pentecostalism, 96
seeker-sensitive ideal *versus*, 347
seeking, 17
success of, 383
theology of encounter and, 193, 196
transformation through, 297
trinitarian dimension of, 292–293
understanding of, 195–196
unity in, 372
in university education, 339–340
waves of, 307
welcoming change regarding, 375–377
homosexuality, 147–148
Hong Kong, 142, 220
honor code, of Oral Roberts University (ORU), 345–346
hope, 381–383
Hordon, Joe, 15–17
Horeb, 27
Howe, Neil, 186
hybridization, 274

I

identity, spirituality as, 46–47
identity vs. confusion stage, 112–113
image insecurity, 168
immigrant churches, 270–272, 279. *See also* church; international churches (ICs)
immigration, 273
India, 220

Indonesia, 60, 236
industry vs. inferiority stage, 112, 113
Information Age, 2
institutionalization, 1
Inter-College Camp, 206
intergenerational relationships
   benefits of, 319, 320
   in the Bible, 318
   connection in, 320, 328
   discipleship in, 320
   migration trends and, 318
   overview of, 378–379
   in the same space, 327–328
   shared experiences in, 328
   surprise and delight moments in, 335n58
international churches (ICs)
   benefits of, 273
   bilingual model of, 279
   celebration model of, 276
   characteristics of, 269
   creating new pathways in, 280–281
   cultural hybridity in, 273–274, 277–281, 382
   evangelism of, 272
   experimentation in, 377
   language in, 276, 278, 279, 377–378
   model and praxis of, 274–277
   mono-congregational model of, 274–275, 277–278, 281
   multi-congregational model of, 274–275, 276–277, 279–280, 281
   nationality representation in, 273
   reconciliation in, 271
   statistics regarding, 273
   tensions in, 278
   unity in, 279–280
International Fellowship (IF), 278
International Theological Institute of Yoido Full Gospel Church, 3–7
internet, 1–2, 54, 128, 192–193
Iran, 220

Islam, 60–61, 164
Israel
   Babylonian captivity of, 37
   circumcision of, 33
   as corporate personality, 28
   covering of, 357
   crisis moment of, 35–36
   deliverance of, 25–26
   in Deuteronomy 5, 27–29, 36
   in Deuteronomy 6, 34
   in Deuteronomy 8, 29–32, 36
   in Deuteronomy 30, 32–37
   disobedience of, 30
   exhortation to, 27
   exile of, 37
   failures of, 37
   God's covenant with, 27, 29
   God's expectations for, 35
   God's favor to, 32–33
   grace to, 33
   identity of, 32
   implications regarding, 36–38
   lack of sustenance of, 30, 31
   as light to the nations, 26
   love of God by, 33–34
   obedience of, 33, 34
   path of life and, 34–35
   repentance of, 33
   restoration of, 32
   testing of, 29–30
   theological identity of, 29
   theological unity of, 36
   today concept and, 26, 28, 31, 36
   way of death and, 34–35
   in the wilderness, 30
Italy, 220

J

Jakwot, Emmanuel (EJ), 264
Japan, 142, 219, 220
Japanese young adults, 219–220
Jeganathan, Max, 175

Jehovah's Witnesses, 203
Jesus Movement, 16
JesusZentrum (JZ), 278
Johnson, Bill, 17–18
Johnson, Todd M., 306
joint consultation, 3–7
Josephus, 12
Joyful Way, 206
Judaism, 202–203

K

Kärkkäinen, Veli-Matti, 95, 376
Karlsson, Maria, 144, 152
Khai, Hau Suan, 118
Khai, Jonathan, 110
Khai, Mary, 107–108, 110
Kham, Chin Do, 107
Kham, Hau Lian, 107
Khup, Do Khan, 116
Kimble, David, 205
King, Greg A., 358
kingdom of God, 82–83, 378
kingmaking, 247–248
Kinnaman, David, 92–93
Knill, Richard, 13–14, 16
Kock, Andries de, 91, 96
Kock, Wynand J. de, 89
Koduah, Alfred, 214
Koh, Pearlyn, 173, 174
koinonia, 289
Korean immigrant churches, 270
Korean War, 235
Kuala Lumpur, 105, 106
Kuhlman, Kathryn, 20
Kuku, Joanna, 255
Kyi, Aung San Suu, 106

L

Lake, John G., 90
language, 129, 130, 270–271, 276, 278, 279, 377–378
Latin American teenagers, 53–54

Latino immigrant churches, 270
Latter Rain, 202, 307
Lawrenz, Mel, 340
leadership, 11, 357–359, 363
Lehman, Jacob, 90
Licciardi, Sebastian, 255–256
London Missionary Society, 88
loneliness, 48–49, 167–168, 175
Lovelace, Richard, 305
Lozano, Jason, 67
Lutheranism, 87, 95, 141, 150, 152, 296
Lwin, Thuzar Wint, 117

M

Macau, 142
Macedonian church, 365–366
Madava, Henry, 18
Makhuwa tribe, 17
Malaysia, 105, 106
Manalang, Aprilfaye T., 170
Mandang, Dr. Ronnie, 60
Mang, Thang Sian, 116
Manser, Martin H., 355
Marsden, George, 305
Marseille, France, 104
Marshall, Caleb, 345
Martinson, Mattias, 150
Matsumoto, Takashi, 220
Matsuyoshi, Rieko, 219
Mauger, Sophie, 255
McGee, Gary B., 191
McIntosh, Gary L., 271–272
McKeown, James, 201–202, 204, 205, 208
McMahan, Alan, 271–272
McMillan, Randy, 18, 19–20
Mental Christians, 68
mental health, 48–49, 110–111, 373
migration, 286
Millard, Craig, 170–171
Millennials
African, 186–187

Afro-Western, 186–187
   church attendance of, 236
   defined, 163
   evil spirits and, 196
   faith erosion of, 170
   Generation Z as compared to, 338
   hunger in, 176
   religious disaffiliation and, 163
   in the United States, 170
Miller, Donald E., 96
Misono, Minami, 220
mission, Pentecostal approach to, 191–193
missional living, 344
missionaries, 88
Missionary Day (Church of Pentecost), 204
Mittelstadt, Martin, 291
Mulla, Rode, 42
Molutsi, Patrick, 96
mono-congregational model, of international churches, 274–275, 277–278, 281
Moody, Dwight L., 17
Moomba Festival (Australia), 262
Moradel, Annette, 345
Moses, 25, 27, 29, 30–36, 308, 310, 340, 355, 356, 365
Mozambique, 17
MTV, 70
multi-congregational model, of international churches, 275, 276–277, 279–280, 281
multicultural church literature, 270–272
multicultural society, 151
Munyika, Veikko, 88
music, 149, 153, 340–341
Muslims, 43, 52, 60–61
Myanmar, 104, 105–106
Myanmar American Soccer Association, 116

Myanmar Christian Church, 107–108, 114–118
Myanmar World Cup USA soccer tournament, 103–104, 116–118, 379

N

Nagano, Japan, 219
Nambindi, Paulus, 91
Namibia
   Apostolic Faith Mission (AFM) in, 89–93
   Born-Free generation in, 87–88, 93–95, 97–98
   colonialism in, 88
   drug and alcohol usage in, 93–94
   globalization in, 87–88
   liberation movement in, 89
   Lutheranism in, 95
   missionaries in, 88
   parachurch ministries in, 96
   Pentecostalism in, 87–88, 89–93, 95–98
   protesting in, 94
   religions in, 87
   Roman Catholicism in, 95
   six waves in, 90–91
   social matters in, 94
   socio-political dimension of, 95
Netherlands, 169–170
Neville, Lisa, 263
new generation, 1, 2. *See also* young adults
"new old" adults, 320–321. *See also* aging adults
Ng, Deborah, 174, 175
Nimoh, David Osei, 215
Noll, Mark, 41, 55
Nominal Christian teenagers, 45–46, 48, 52, 54
Non-Christian teenagers, 45–46
nones, 59, 173, 179
non-religious spirituality, 165–166

nova effect, 143
Ntumy, Michael, 207, 211

O

Old Dominion University, 175–176
Olofinjana, Israel, 195
Omaboe, Grace, 204
Oman, 220
OneHope, 42–43. *See also* Global Youth Culture (GYC) study (OneHope)
Oral Roberts University (ORU)
   chapel at, 339, 340–349
   expectations at, 346
   global mission projects of, 342
   honor code of, 345–346
   missional living at, 344
   origin of, 345–346
   personal pursuit at, 343
   spirit-empowered structure at, 346–347
Örebro Mission, 149
Orr, J. Edwin, 306
Orthodox tradition, 292, 297
Osborne, Grant R., 122
Otabil, Mensa, 172
Ott, Craig, 55

P

Pacific Islanders, 261–262
Papua New Guinea, 259–260
Paradise Community Church (Australia), 256
Parent Affiliated Church (PAC), 353
parental covering
   covering in, 357–359, 363–365
   in the New Testament, 360–366
   in the Old Testament, 355–360
   overview of, 355, 366–367
   resourcing and, 359–360, 365–366
   spiritual parentage and, 355–356, 361–363
Pascal, Blaise, 308

Pathway to Leadership program, 65
Paul, 12, 151, 221, 311, 354, 361–366
Pazmino, Robert, 123
Pentecost, 306–307, 371–373
Pentecostal Assemblies of Switzerland, 285
Pentecostal-Charismatic Christian spirituality, 178–179
Pentecostal International Churches, 272
Pentecostal International Worship Centers (PIWC), 208, 209–210, 212
Pentecostalism
   actuality of, 287–288
   approach to mission in, 191–193
   Born-Free generation and, 87–88, 95–96, 97–98
   in Britain, 188, 190
   characteristics of, 185
   complexities of, 188–189
   defined, 188
   defining factors of, 95
   denominations and, 190
   expressions in, 194–195
   "Fresh Expressions" (FX) initiative and, 191–192
   in Ghana, 172
   growth of, 60, 185
   identity of, 124
   indigenous, 189
   mission of, 91
   in Namibia, 87–88, 89–93, 95–98
   new chapter of, 190
   origins of, 188
   outpouring of the Holy Spirit and, 124–125
   power in, 189–190
   progressive, 96
   role of Holy Spirit in, 96
   in South Africa, 89–90
   worship in, 194
Pentecostal pneumatology, 193–195

Pentecostal Protestant Church (Namibia), 90
Pentecostal World Conference, 3–7, 121
Pentecostal World Fellowship, 3–7
Pentecost Students and Associates (PENSA), 210
people of hope, 381–383
persecution, 15
pervasive developmental disorder, 228
Pi, Cingh, 116
Pieterse, Jan Nederveen, 270, 274
Pietism, 143
pilgrim principle, 187–188
Planetboom, 253–265
Planetshakers Church, 253–264
Planetshakers College, 259–260
pneumatological approach, to encountering world reality, 287–289
pneumatology, 293
pornography, 50, 51, 53
Prinsloo, Louis F., 90
progressive Pentecostalism, 96. *See also* Pentecostalism
propinquity effect, 271
psychosocial development theory, 112

Q
Quietude, 225–226

R
racial discrimination, 89
Rainer, Thom, 177–178
Raymond, Erik, 344
reconciliation churches, 271–272, 382. *See also* church
recreational drug usage, 49, 53
Reformist Islam, 206
Regent Divinity School, 11
Regents College, 211
religion, 47, 52, 166, 167. *See also specific religions/denominations*
religious affiliation, 163, 164

religious movements, 202–203
religious rejuvenation, 207–213, 214–215
repentance, 33, 69–70, 145–146, 148, 150
replacement, in the church, 245
resilient disciple, 92–93
resourcing, 355–366
revivals
  anointing and, 310
  in the Bible, 306
  characteristics of, 305
  complexities of, 305
  education and, 311–312
  features of, 307–308
  generational transfer of, 308–311
  Holy Spirit's role in, 307, 312–313, 314
  introduction to, 305
  Jesus' invitation to, 313
  life in the Spirit and, 312–313
  newness in, 311
  as nothing new under the sun, 305
  origin of, 311
  our role in, 314
  overview of, 306–308
  stewardship of, 311
  transgenerational, 308
Roberts, Evan, 14
Roberts, Oral, 337, 346, 347
Rodriguez, Daniel, 270–271
Rodriguez, Samuel, 347
Rogers, Carl, 222
Roman Catholicism, 95
Royal Conference, of Church of Pentecost (CoP) (Ghana), 212
Ruibal, Julio Cesar, 20

S
Saad, Samantha, 164
Sabetes, Angela M., 322
Safo, Fred Stephen Kwasi Mensah, 208

Saitō, Tamaki, 220
salvation, 145–146, 148, 153
same-sex attraction, in Generation Z, 46, 52–53
Samurai Gakuen, 224, 226, 227, 229
San community (Namibia), 91–92
Sanders, E. P., 231
Sarbah, J. Mensah, 205
Saul, 310, 340, 363–365
Sayegh, Pascal-Yan, 274
Schepers, Peer, 169
schizophrenia, 223
Schmidt, Leigh Eric, 307–308
Schnabel, Eckhard J., 124, 125
Scottish Holy Holidays, 308
Scripture Union, 96, 206
Second Great Awakening, 308
secular, defined, 56n4
secular humanism, 165, 166
secularism/secularization, 1, 142–143, 150, 165–166, 167, 169, 173, 296, 373, 374
seeker-sensitive ideal, 347
segregation, 89, 205–206
Seventh-Day Adventists, 203
sexuality, 48, 49–50
Shi'a, 206
Silvoso, Ed, 14
Singapore, 173–175, 179. *See also* Heart of God Church (HOGC) (Singapore)
Sisera, 357
Smith, Samuel, 59
social action, 296, 376
Social Christians, 68
social climate, of Europe, 286–287
social engagement, 324
social isolationism, 167–169
social media, 1–2, 54, 168, 171, 192–193, 213, 382
social relationships, in volunteer service, 323

socio-political transformation, 1
Song, Nam Soon, 271, 278
South Africa, 89–90
Southern Baptist Theological Seminary, 14
South Korea, 60, 142, 220, 235–236
South West Africa People's Organization (SWAPO), 88
Spain, 220
Spencer, Aída Besançon, 362–363
Spirit-empowered movement, 38
spiritual casualty, 111
spiritual entrepreneurs, 294
spirituality, 46–47, 161–162, 165–166
spiritual parentage, 355–356, 361–363
spiritual powers, 151
Spurgeon, Charles Haddon, 13–14, 16
Staniloae, Dumitru, 292, 293
Stanley, Brian, 205
stewardship, 246–247
Strauss, William, 186
Stroh, Linda K., 61
Strong Church Model, 250
Stronstad, Roger, 307
Stuart, Douglas, 124
Sudanese youth, 261
suicidal thoughts/attempts, 46, 48–49, 52–53, 168
Sunday schools, 125–135. *See also* children's ministry
Sutton, Geoffrey, 291
Svensson, Jakob, 144
Sweden
  Christianity in, 150
  culture of, 150, 152
  Free Church identity in, 143, 146–148
  Free Church revival in, 145–146, 148–149
  implications and synthesis regarding, 149–150
  Lutheranism in, 150, 152, 296

secularization in, 142, 143, 296
societal changes in, 141
theological challenges in, 150–151
understanding faith in, 154
worship as language school in, 153–154
young adults in, 141–142, 144–148, 149–150
Swedish Alliance Mission, 144

T

Taithul, Thawng Khan, 110
Taiwan, 220
Tandiokusuma-Fakhrsadeh, Audrey, 258–260
Tan Seow How, 66
Taylor, Charles, 142–143, 150
Taylor, Cheryl, 340
Taylor, Jack, 16
technology, 136, 167–169, 173, 192–193, 377
teenagers. *See* Generation Z
Te Grotenhuis, Manfred, 169
Thailand, 105, 106, 220
theology of encounter, 193, 196
theomacracy, 207–208, 209
Third Mandate Program of the Theological Education Fund, 130
Tobgui, Lilly, 255
Tombing, Pum Za Thang, 107
Topf, Daniel, 134
Tozer, A. W., 343, 347
Tresch, W. Kyle, 117
Trinity, 289–290, 292–293, 313
Trump, Donald, 108
Tukuafu, Lavei, 256
Tulsa, Oklahoma, 107–108, 109, 118, 379
Twenge, Jean M., 167–168, 171

U

Ukraine, 18, 220, 295

Ung, SoPhal, 15
United Nations High Commissioner for Refugees (UNHCR), 103
United States
  birth rate of, 331n15
  churches as multiethnic in, 270
  cultural commonalities in, 270
  faith erosion in, 170
  Generation Z in, 170–172
  immigrant churches in, 270–271
  Myanmar people's immigration to, 105–106
University of Birmingham, 212

V

van der Walt, B. J., 165
Van der Walt, P. J., 89–90, 91
Van Engen, Carlos, 311–312
Vatican II, 206
Venter, A. J., 90
Victoria Police, 261, 262, 263
Victory Church, 107, 108
Vienna Christian Center (VCC), 276, 278
Volunteer Function Inventory (VFI), 317–328
volunteerism
  altruism and, 322
  benefits of, 328
  communication regarding, 329
  egoism and, 322
  motivations in, 326, 328
  recruitment strategies for, 328
  warning regarding, 326–327
Vondey, Wolfgang, 188, 297–298

W

Wagner Leadership Institute, 18
Walker, Noah, 264, 265
Wallace, Charles I., Jr., 306
Wallis, Arthur, 307
Walls, Andrew, 187–188

Walter, N., 123
Warrington, Keith, 191, 193, 196, 209
Weber, Max, 1
Welker, Michael, 231
Wesley, John, 13
Western world, 1
Wettey, Matthew L., 208
"What a Beautiful Name" (Hillsong), 153
White, Anneli, 179
Whitefield, George, 13
White Night (Australia), 262
Wiersbe, Warren, 355
Wilkins, Michael J., 123
will, giving Jesus access to, 69
Willard, Dallas, 69
William, Michelet, 97
Williams, Demetrius K., 125
Wilson, William M., 108, 338
Winter, Ralph, 274
Wood, Ekow Badu, 215
Woodlake Assembly of God (Oklahoma), 353–354
World Alliance for Pentecostal Theological Education (WAPTE), 3–7
World War I, 205
worship, 133, 153–154, 194, 340–341
Wu, Cindy M., 306

X

Xavier, Francisco, 219

Y

Yamomori, Tetsunao, 96
Yancey, George, 271
Yeboah, Martinson Kwadwo, 201, 203, 208–210
Yoido Full Gospel Church, 235, 382
young adults. *See also specific persons*
  biblical examples of, in ministry, 12
  bonus grandparents to, 321, 329, 378
  call of, 21
  church attendance of, 295–296
  in Church of Pentecost (CoP) (Ghana), 210
  contemporary examples of, in ministry, 14–15
  development needs of, 318
  disengagement with the church and, 151–152
  ethical dilemmas of, 152
  Free Church identity and, 146–148
  historical examples of, in ministry, 13–14
  intergenerational relationships with, 318–319
  mission regarding, 327
  multicultural society to, 151
  negative view of religion in, 150
  negotiating life by, 151
  Pentecostal viewpoint of, 296
  surprise and delight moments for, 335n58
  in Sweden, 141–142, 144–148, 149–150
  worship importance to, 153–154
youth. *See also* Generation Z;
  bonus grandparents to, 321, 329, 378
  as casualties, 236–237
  challenges to, 285–286
  church as home for, 245–246
  church attendance of, 236
  cognitive dissonance regarding, 374
  defined, 93
  development needs of, 318
  discipleship of, 63–64, 67
  embracing the gospel by, 66
  empowering, 244–245
  as evolving, 239, 242
  hybrid, 273–274, 280–281, 382
  impressing, 242–244
  intergenerational relationships with, 318–319
  leadership capacity of, 64, 248

legacy in, 248
mental health challenges of, 373
mission regarding, 327, 354
as needing to be invited, included, involved, 242–244
rebellion of, 382
relevance to, 248–249
secularization and, 374
social climate of, 286–287
spiritual assessments for, 67
statistics regarding, 374
success regarding, 71–72
support for, 374
surprise and delight moments for, 335n58
training of, 64–65
willingness to serve by, 312
Youth Crime Summit (Australia), 262
Youth for Christ, 96
youth leaders, role of, in revival, 306–308
youth ministry, evolution of, 65–66, 380
YouTube, 176, 377

Z
Zeiffert, Roald, 144, 145, 147–148, 153
Zomi France Labour Corps, 104, 118
Zomi Innkua Oklahoma (ZIOK), 118
Zylstra, Sarah Eekhoff, 168, 170–171

www.ingramcontent.com/pod-product-compliance
Lightning Source LLC
Chambersburg PA
CBHW070044080526
44586CB00013B/901